India Before Europe

India is a land of enormous diversity. Cross-cultural influences are everywhere in evidence, in the food people eat, the clothes they wear, and in the places they worship. This was ever the case, and at no time more so than in the India that existed from 1200 to 1750, before the European intervention. In this absorbing and richly illustrated book, the authors take the reader on a journey across the political, economic, religious, and cultural landscapes of medieval India from the Ghurid conquests and the Delhi Sultanate, through the rise and fall of the southern kingdom of Vijayanagara, to the peripheries of empire and, finally, to the great court of the Mughals. This was a time of conquest and consolidation, when Muslims and Hindus came together to create a culture, an architecture, and a tradition which was uniquely their own and which still resonates in today's India. As the first survey of its kind in over a decade, the book is a *tour de force*. It is fluently composed, with a cast of characters which will educate and entertain students and general readers alike.

CATHERINE B. ASHER is Associate Professor in the Department of Art History at the University of Minnesota. Her previous publications include *Architecture of Mughal India* (1992) and, as editor with Thomas R. Metcalf, *Perceptions of South Asia's Visual Past* (1994).

CYNTHIA TALBOT is Associate Professor of History and Asian Studies at the University of Texas at Austin. She has published *Precolonial India in Practice: Society, Region, and Identity in Medieval Andhra* (2001).

India Before Europe

Catherine B. Asher
University of Minnesota

and

Cynthia Talbot
University of Texas at Austin

CAMBRIDGE
UNIVERSITY PRESS

CAMBRIDGE UNIVERSITY PRESS
Cambridge, New York, Melbourne, Madrid, Cape Town, Singapore, São Paulo

Cambridge University Press
The Edinburgh Building, Cambridge CB2 2RU, UK

Published in the United States of America by Cambridge University Press, New York

www.cambridge.org
Information on this title: www.cambridge.org/9780521005935

© Cambridge University Press 2006

First published 2006
Reprinted with corrections 2007

Printed in the United Kingdom at the University Press, Cambridge

A catalogue record for this publication is available from the British Library

Library of Congress cataloguing in publication data
Asher, Catherine Ella Blanshard.
India Before Europe / Catherine B. Asher and Cynthia Talbot.
    p.   cm.
Includes bibliographical references and index.
ISBN 0-521-80904-5 (hardback) – ISBN 0-521-00539-6 (pbk.)
1. India – History – 1000–1765.   2. South Asia – History.   3. India – Civilization –
1200–1765.   4. South Asia – Civilization.   I. Talbot, Cynthia.   II. Title.
DS452.A84   2005
954′.02 – dc22   2005024164

ISBN-13 978-0-521-80904-7 hardback

ISBN-13 978-0-521-00593-5 paperback

Contents

List of illustrations   *page* vi
List of maps   xi
Preface   xiii
Glossary   xvi
Place names: alternative spellings   xxii

1   Introduction: situating India   1

2   The expansion of Turkic power, 1180–1350   25

3   Southern India in the age of Vijayanagara, 1350–1550   53

4   North India between empires: history, society, and
    culture, 1350–1550   84

5   Sixteenth-century north India: empire reformulated   115

6   Expanding political and economic spheres, 1550–1650   152

7   Elite cultures in seventeenth-century South Asia   186

8   Challenging central authority, 1650–1750   225

9   Changing socio-economic formations, 1650–1750   256

    Epilogue   287

    Biographical notes   292
    Bibliography   295
    Index   308

Illustrations

Unless otherwise acknowledged all photographs are by Frederick M. Asher and Catherine B. Asher

1.1	Rajarajeshvara temple, Tanjavur	*page* 15
1.2	Kandariya Mahadeva temple, Khajuraho	16
1.3	Great Mosque of Isfahan, Iran	23
2.1	Delhi's original Jami mosque, entrance to the prayer chamber dated 1198	29
2.2	Qutb Minar commenced 1199, Delhi's original Jami mosque	31
2.3	Alai Darwaza, dated 1311, Delhi's original Jami mosque. Courtesy of Ebba Koch	38
2.4	Stone monolith dating to third century BCE, Firuzabad (Kotla Firuz Shah), Delhi	44
3.1	Plan of Vijayanagara. Courtesy of the Vijayanagara Research Project	61
3.2	Mahanavami Dibba, Vijayanagara	62
3.3	Gopura, Virupaksha temple, Vijayanagara. Courtesy of John Gollings	66
3.4	Detail of carvings on the exterior enclosure wall, Ramachandra temple, Vijayanagara	68
3.5	Krishnadeva Raya and queens, Shri Venkateshvara temple, Tirupati. Courtesy Archaeological Survey of India	69
3.6	Royal building known as the Elephant Stables, Vijayanagara	71
3.7	Mosque/*dharmasale*, 1439, Vijayanagara	72
3.8	Painting showing court dress of Vijayanagara period, Virabhadra temple, Lepakshi. Courtesy Archaeological Survey of India	73
4.1	Relief carving of hanging lamp in the mihrab (prayer niche), Adina mosque, Pandua	87

4.2   Tomb of Shaikh Ahmad Khattu, at the dargah of Shaikh
      Ahmad Khattu, Sarkhej, Ahmedabad   93
4.3   Kalaka and the Shahi King in Conversation, *Kalpa Sutra*
      (Book of Sacred Precepts) and Kalakacharya Katha (Story
      of the Teacher Kalaka). Manuscript (99v), 1442,
      Satyapur, Gujarat, India. Los Angeles County Museum
      of Art, from the Nasli and Alice Heeramaneck
      Collection, Museum Associates Purchase, M.72.53.18.
      Photograph © 2005 Museum Associates/LACMA   95
4.4   Preparation of Sherbat, *Nimatnama*. By permission of
      the British Library, Ms Pers 149 f. 46r.   98
4.5   Tower of Victory, Chittor   101
4.6   Krishna and the Gopis, leaf from a *Bhagavata Purana*
      series *c.* 1525–40. Delhi-Agra Region, Uttar Pradesh,
      Opaque watercolor on paper sheet: $6\frac{7}{8} \times 9\frac{1}{8}$ in (17.5 ×
      23.2 cm) image: $5\frac{3}{8} \times 8\frac{7}{8}$ in (13.7 × 22.5 cm). Brooklyn
      Museum of Art, gift of Mr. and Mrs. H. Peter Findlay,
      80.41   112
4.7   The Princess Seduced by her Tutor, *Chaurapanchashika*.
      Courtesy Bharat Kala Bhavan, Varanasi   113
5.1   Kabuli Bagh mosque, Panipat   120
5.2   Qila-i Kuhna mosque, Purana Qila (Din Panah), Delhi   122
5.3   Tomb of Sher Shah, Sasaram   123
5.4   Tomb of Shaikh Salim Chishti, Fatehpur Sikri   133
5.5   Interior pillar, Diwan-i Khass, Fatehpur Sikri   135
5.6   Tale XLIV; Kojasta, the Wife, Tries to Convince the
      Parrot to Give Her Permission to Meet Her Lover,
      Tutinama (Tales of a Parrot). India, Mughal school, reign
      of Akbar, Color and gold on paper, 20.3 × 14 cm. © The
      Cleveland Museum of Art, 1997, gift of Mrs. A. Dean
      Perry, 1962.279.282.b   137
5.7   Virgin Mary. Courtesy Bharat Kala Bhavan, Varanasi   139
5.8   Krishna Holding Up Mount Govardhan, *Hari Vamsha*.
      Mughal period (1526–1858), date *c.* 1590–95, ink,
      colors and gold on paper $11\frac{3}{4} \times 7\frac{7}{8}$ in (28.9 × 20 cm).
      The Metropolitan Museum of Art, Purchase, Edward C.
      Moore Jr., Gift, 1928 (28.63.1). Photograph, all rights
      reserved, The Metropolitan Museum of Art   141
5.9   Akbar Riding a Mad Elephant, *Akbarnama*. V&A Picture
      Library, IS. 2:21–1896   143
5.10 Akbar Walking to Ajmer, *Akbarnama*. V&A Picture
      Library, IS.2:77–1896   145

5.11 Rama Stalks a Demon Who Has Assumed the Form of a
      Golden Deer, *Ramayana*. Freer Museum of Art,
      Smithsonian Institution, Washington, DC: Gift of
      Charles Lang Freer, F1907.271.128b   147
5.12 Interior, Govinda Deva temple. Vrindavan   150
6.1   Allegorical Representation of Emperor Jahangir and
      Shah Abbas of Persia, *The St. Petersberg Album*. Freer
      Museum of Art, Smithsonian Institution, Washington,
      DC: Purchase, F1945.9   157
6.2   Gujarati cotton resist dyed cloth for the Southeast Asian
      market, fourteenth-century detail showing hand painted
      floral forms. Courtesy Tapi Collection   160
6.3   Ludolf Bakhuizen, *View of Surat from Sea*, seventeenth
      century. © National Maritime Museum, London   162
6.4   Char Minar, Hyderabad   165
6.5   Sufi Receiving a Visitor, Bijapur. Ms. Douce Or b.2 folio 1
      recto. The Bodleian Library, University of Oxford   167
6.6   Portrait of Ibrahim Adil Shah II, Bijapur. © The Trustees
      of The British Museum   171
6.7   Procession of Muhammad Quli Qutb Shah and
      Bhagmati, Golkonda. Courtesy Sir Howard Hodgkin
      Collection   172
6.8   Tent cloth, seventeenth century, Golkonda. V&A Picture
      Library, IS. 19–1989   174
6.9   A loving couple. Ivory, seventeenth century, Shrirangam
      temple. Photo Courtesy: French Institute of
      Pondicherry / Ecole Française d'Extrême-Orient   179
6.10 South Indian textile showing Vijayanagara influence,
      cloth, 1 of 7 pieces, *c.* 1610–1620. India. Cotton, drawn
      and painted resist and mordants, dyed $109\frac{1}{4} \times 38\frac{1}{4}$ in
      (277.5 × 97.2 cm). Brooklyn Museum. 14.719.7.
      Museum Expedition 1913–1914, Museum Collection
      Fund 14.719.7   184
7.1   Allegorical portrait of Jahangir and Muin al-Din Chishti.
      © The Trustees of the Chester Beatty Library, Dublin   188
7.2   Darbar of Jahangir, *Jahangirnama*, attributed to
      Manohar. Indian, Mughal period, about 1620. Object
      Place: Northern India, Opaque watercolor and gold on
      paper 35 × 20 cm ($13\frac{3}{4} \times 7\frac{7}{8}$ in). Museum of Fine Arts,
      Boston. Francis Bartlett Donation of 1912 and Picture
      Fund, 14.654. Photograph © 2006 Museum of Fine
      Arts, Boston   189

7.3   Shah Jahan Standing on a Globe. Freer Gallery of Art,
      Smithsonian Institution, Washington, DC: Purchase,
      F1939.49   190
7.4   Jahangir Receives Prince Khurram on His Return from
      the Deccan, *Padshahnama*. The Royal Collection. © HM
      Queen Elizabeth II, MS 1367, folios 48B, 49A   192
7.5   The Illumined Tomb (Taj Mahal), Agra. Courtesy
      American Institute of Indian Studies, Center for Art and
      Archaeology   195
7.6   Jami mosque, Shahjahanabad, Delhi   199
7.7   Shah Jahan's jharoka, Public Audience Hall,
      Shahjahanabad Palace, Delhi   201
7.8   Tomb of Nur Jahan's parents known as the tomb of
      Itimad al-Daula, Agra   205
7.9   Jagdish temple, Udaipur   209
7.10 Ravana Prepares for Battle, *Ramayana* of Jagat Singh
      Sisodiya. By permission of the British Library, add.
      15297 (1) f. 138r   210
7.11 Map of Amber, 1711, detail showing the palace and the
      temple built by Raja Man Singh for his heir. Courtesy
      National Museum, New Delhi   212
7.12 Amar Singh Sisodiya sati memorial, Ahar, Udaipur.
      Courtesy Jennifer Joffee   215
7.13 Shyam Ray temple, 1643, Vishnupur, West Bengal.
      Courtesy Pika Ghosh   218
7.14 Tomb of Muin al-Din Chishti, Ajmer   220
7.15 Minakshi temple, Madurai. Photo courtesy French
      Institute of Pondicherry / Ecole Française
      d'Extrême-Orient   223
8.1   Jahanara's tomb, Nizam al-Din Auliya dargah, Delhi   229
8.2   Posthumous portrait of Shivaji. Courtesy Guimet,
      Paris   241
8.3   Shiva temple, 1674, Raigad. Courtesy George Michell   243
8.4   Fortification wall, Pratapgad   244
8.5   Fakhr al-Masajid, 1728–29, Shahjahanabad, Delhi   246
8.6   Jami mosque known as the Katra mosque, Murshidabad   251
8.7   Street showing the Natani family mansion, Jaipur   253
9.1   Chintz palampore, Coromandel Coast. Courtesy Tapi
      Collection   258
9.2   Hendrik van Schuylenberg, *Headquarters of the Dutch
      Trading Company at Hugli*. Courtesy Rijksmuseum
      Foundation, Amsterdam   262

9.3   Half rupee issued with names of King William and
      Queen Mary, 1692, Silver. © The Trustees of The
      British Museum   263
9.4   Palace, Dig, Badan Singh (1722–56) and enlarged
      1756–63 under Suraj Mal   266
9.5   Imaginary Meeting Between Guru Nanak, Mardana
      Sahib, and Other Sikh Gurus, c. 1780. India, Andhra
      Pradesh, Hyderabad. Los Angeles County Museum of
      Art, Purchased with funds provided by Dorothy and
      Richard Sherwood, M.74.88.3. Photography © 2005
      Museum Associates/LACMA   268
9.6   Daud Khan serai, Daudnagar, Bihar c. 1659–64   274
9.7   Portrait of an Officer of the East India Company,
      probably William Fullerton of Rosemount,
      Murshidabad. V&A Picture Library, IM.33–1912   285

Maps

1.1 South Asia today   *page* 6
1.2 Physical geography of South Asia   10
2.1 South Asia and Afghanistan, *c.* 1200   26
2.2 Ala al-Din Khalji's campaigns   36
3.1 South India in the fifteenth century   55
4.1 North India in the fifteenth century   90
5.1 Mughal empire under Babur, Akbar, and Aurangzeb   117
6.1 South India, *c.* 1550   164
7.1 Seven cities of Delhi   198
8.1 Maratha expansion through the eighteenth century   234
9.1 South Asia, *c.* 1750   261

Preface

India Before Europe is the product of collaboration between two scholars from different disciplines, who have joined together to write a volume on Indian history and culture from 1200 to 1750. Catherine Asher is an art historian who has worked on north India's Indic, Islamic, and Islamicate cultural traditions. Cynthia Talbot is a historian who has worked largely on the social history of pre-Mughal south India and also is aware of larger trends in world history. When first approached by Marigold Acland of Cambridge University Press to write a history of the five hundred plus years immediately prior to the rise of British colonial power in India, neither of us felt competent to tackle this challenging task alone. Only by pooling our quite distinct spheres of training and knowledge, we thought, could we possibly do justice to the complexity and richness of this very important era. Little did we realize then how much more we had to learn, not only from each other but also from a wide range of individuals upon whose scholarship we relied. The end result is one that neither of us could have achieved on our own.

The book was written jointly in Austin and Minneapolis when the two authors could meet, but more often it evolved in cyberspace, where attachments were constantly zinging across the country or, at times, even across countries, for the other person's perusal. Although first drafts of specific sections or chapters were composed individually, in the end every word was evaluated and edited by both of us. We hope the outcome is a text that reads as if it were authored by a single writer, not two.

An important motivation for both of us was the desire to provide a text that would be useful to specialists and non-specialists alike, something that would bridge the vast gap in the secondary literature between the introductory work on South Asia, on the one hand, and the many scholarly monographs and articles, on the other. The need for an up-to-date survey is particularly acute for the period with which we are concerned here, the years from 1200 to 1750, since the roots of many controversial issues that divide the peoples of South Asia along national, regional, religious, and ethnic lines today are thought to lie in that era.

We have attempted to offer a balanced, interdisciplinary perspective, one that encompasses artistic culture as well as political achievement, and also recognizes the role played by different communities from a variety of regions. By this means, we hope to express our appreciation of the diverse cultures and societies of South Asia that we have had the privilege to study for many years.

A small note on the text is in order. We have italicized foreign words and terms only the first time they are introduced. If a word is used more than once with a gloss, then it is included in the glossary. There is an appendix with short biographies of the most important personalities discussed in the work. We have used many of the older terms for Indian cities, since these are often closer to the names that were used during the period under consideration than are today's more modern ones. While we have made an attempt to use a consistent transliteration system, in a number of cases we have used commonly accepted spellings, especially for temple names.

Since we are not able to mention, in the body of the text, all the scholars whose works we consulted in the writing of this book, we present an extensive bibliography instead. The help and cooperation of many other individuals and institutions were needed to complete this project, however. To provide a complete list would not be possible, but some indeed must be acknowledged. Three institutions should be thanked for their generous financial assistance: the American Institute of Indian Studies, the University of Minnesota, and the University of Texas at Austin.

Others we must thank include current and former students whose work has benefited ours in so many ways, especially Deborah Hutton, Jennifer Joffee, and Riyaz Latif, upon whose expertise we frequently relied. Colleagues at institutions here and abroad to whom we are indebted include Steven Cohen, Rosemary Crill, Carl Ernst, John Fritz, Henry Ginsberg, Pika Ghosh, Catherine Glynn, Donald Clay Johnson, Janice Leoshko, Stephen Markel, George Michell, Carla Petievich, Dede Ruggles and Susan Stronge. We are grateful to Susan Deans-Smith, Julie Hardwick, and Martha Newman for their thoughtful comments on the introductory chapter, and also to Phillip Wagoner for carefully reading the entire text during a very busy time and providing useful suggestions. Barbara Metcalf, Thomas Metcalf, Sandria Frietag, and David Gilmartin have provided much-needed support throughout the project. In India, Dr. Pradeep Mehendiratta and Purnima Mehta have opened doors when we thought nothing could be done. M. A. Dhaky, U. S. Moorti, and Jagdish Yadav have also provided tremendous assistance over the years. Alisa Eimen worked tirelessly on procuring plates from museums and institutions. Virginia Larson and Rebecca Moss spent hours scanning the illustrations. Julianna Budding deserves our deep appreciation for the speed with which she produced the elegant maps included here, with the exception of Map 1.2 which Maria Lane provided. We thank our families – Eric Schenk, Rick Asher, Alice Asher, Tom Asher, and Dana Bilsky – for the help and support they have given throughout this project. We are especially grateful to Eric Schenk for his meticulous reading of our final draft. To all of you, including those who helped but go unmentioned, many thanks.

Glossary

Adi Granth the most sacred scripture in the Sikh religion

Afaqi foreign-born nobility in the Deccan Sultanates, most of whom came from Iran and Central Asia

amir a noble in a Muslim court

Avadhi an important literary language of early modern north India; a vernacular form of Hindi from the Lucknow region

bangla a roof with a curved cornice

baraka a Sufi saint's spiritual power, thought to emanate from the tomb even after death

Bengali a regional language of eastern India, spoken today in India's West Bengal state and in Bangladesh

bhakti a type of Hindu religious worship characterized by an intense personal devotion to a deity often expressed in poem-songs

Brahmi a writing system dating back to at least the third century BCE, from which all subsequent Indian scripts were derived except the few based on Perso-Arabic

Brahmin the highest category in the Hindu *varna* or class system whose traditional occupation was that of priest or religious teacher, but who often served as poets, ministers, or accountants to kings and lords because of their literacy and education

char bagh a four part garden generally believed to have been introduced into India by the Mughals; the Mughal version has its origins in the traditions of the Timurids

chintz a printed and/or hand painted cotton fabric

Chishti the most popular Sufi order in India; the major Chishti saints included here are Muin al-Din Chishti, Nizam al-Din Auliya, and

Shaikh Salim Chishti; the Mughals were especially devoted to the Chishti order

Dakani a form of Hindavi developed in the Deccan between the fourteenth and seventeenth centuries as a literary language; also referred to as Old Urdu

dargah the tomb of a Sufi saint that becomes a shrine

darshan(a) seeing or beholding a Hindu or Jain deity or a king

Deccani local nobility in the Deccan Sultanates as opposed to the foreign-born Afaqi

deshmukh headman of 20–100 villages in the Maratha country; a type of rural gentry

dharma broadly connotes righteousness, religious truth, or moral duty in Indic thought, but also often refers to one's social obligations to family or community

dhoti an unsewn garment for a male that is wrapped around the waist

Din-i Ilahi a discipleship relation between Akbar and his closest nobles

Diwan-i Amm Public Audience Hall in the Mughal and related courts

Diwan-i Khass Private Audience Hall in the Mughal and related courts

doab literally, two rivers; the alluvial land lying between two rivers that eventually merge into each other

gopura a gateway into the compound of a south Indian temple; tall, elaborate *gopuras* are common from the fourteenth century onward

haram literally, forbidden; the female quarters of a household or court; the female members of the court

Hindavi an Indo-Islamic term for the indigenous languages of India that were the predecessors of modern Hindi and Urdu, sometimes referred to simply as "Hindi"

hookah a water pipe used for smoking tobacco

iqta in Muslim states of the pre-Mughal era, a territory assigned to a political subordinate who had administrative authority over it and used some its revenue to maintain troops

jagir lands whose revenues were assigned to a Mughal *mansabdar* in lieu of salary *jagirdar* the holder of a *jagir*

Jain a follower of the enlightened beings known as Jinas and the religion today called Jainism; Jains strive to lead an ascetic lifestyle and are often bankers and merchants

jharoka the term for a throne used by the Mughal rulers

jharoka-i darshan the Mughal emperor's public viewing window where he appeared each morning so the public could behold his image

jizya a tax on non-Muslims that in turn gave them protection under Muslim law

Kannada a regional language of southern India, spoken today in Karnataka state

khanazad literally, son; a noble who served the Mughal emperor loyally as if he was a family member

khanqah residential compound of a Sufi teacher

Krishna an incarnation of the god Vishnu whose exploits as a child and a young man are particularly popular among worshippers

kshatriya the second highest category in the Hindu *varna* or class system whose traditional occupation was that of king or warrior

madrasa school for Islamic religious instruction

Mahabharata one of India's two great epics transmitted both in Sanskrit and in regional languages, focusing on a struggle for succession between cousins and featuring the god Krishna

mandapa a porch or porches that are before the inner sanctum of a Hindu or Jain temple

mansabdar a noble who held a mansab rank in the Mughal administrative system, which entitled him to either a salary or lands (*jagir*) whose yields would equal a salary, in return for supplying a specified number of troops and horses

Marathi a regional language of the Deccan, spoken today in Maharashtra state

mihrab niche in the *qibla* wall of a mosque

Natha a Hindu ascetic order that sought immortality through the practice of yoga *naubat* official orchestra that would play when the emperor was in court; sometimes called a *naqqar*

nayaka a warrior lord of south India; later the name of several dynasties who succeeded the Vijayanagara state

nayamkara a territory assigned to a political subordinate of the Vijayanagara empire who used some of its revenue to maintain troops

patola a luxury fabric where the threads of both the warp and woof are tie-dyed prior to weaving, creating a reversible design

Persian the court language of Muslims in Iran, Central Asia, and India, especially under the Mughals

peshwa Brahmin prime minister of the Maratha court who became the *de facto* ruler

prasad(a) food offered to Hindu deities and thus sanctified; often distributed or sold later to devotees for their consumption

purdah seclusion of women

qawwali ecstatic songs in honor of Sufis by *qawwal* singer-musicians

qibla direction of Mecca toward which all Muslims pray

raja a non-Muslim king or lord; the Sisodiyas of Mewar used the title *rana* instead

Ram(a) an incarnation of the Hindu god Vishnu who was an exemplary king

Ramayana one of India's two great epics transmitted both in Sanskrit and in regional languages, focusing on the life of the god-king Rama

rasa a term used in Indian aesthetics to denote specific moods or emotions; also connoisseurship, flavor

rupee the monetary unit used in north India since the sixteenth century; a silver coin

sama listening to music, often with an ecstatic character, at Chishti *dargah*s, with the goal of finding union with god

Sanskrit classical language of India that continued to be used for literary production at many non-Muslim courts and religious centers

Sant a saint-poet of fifteenth- and sixteenth-century north India who sought direct experience of god; often they were of low caste and envisioned god or the divine as lacking form and attributes

serai an inn for a traveler

sharia laws concerning all aspects of a Muslim's life

Shia the smaller of the two main groups of Muslims, who reject the authority of the caliphs, and instead believe that members of the Prophet Muhammad's family were his rightful successors

shikhara the spired superstructure of a Hindu or Jain temple

Shiva a major Hindu god, celebrated for his ascetic ways and his dance of destruction that brings about the end of time; he is the husband of Parvati and father of Ganesha and Skanda

shudra the lowest category in the Hindu *varna* or class system whose traditional occupation was service, but who engaged in many activities including agriculture

Sikh member of a religious faith first established by Guru Nanak *c.* 1500 that developed largely in the Punjab

Sufi Muslim mystics, often organized in various orders, whose spiritual leaders guide novices through meditation, prayer, and at times specific practices, in order to find oneness with god

sulh-i kul peace to all; universal toleration promoted by the Mughal state under Akbar and Abu al-Fazl

sultan title initially used by Muslim rulers of Turkic extraction to indicate their possession of political power, but later employed by many Muslim kings; a state ruled by a sultan is known as a sultanate

Sunni the majority of Muslims who accept the historical development of Islam after the Prophet Muhammad's death

Tamil a regional language of southern India with a long literary history, spoken today in Tamil Nadu state

Telugu a regional language of southern India, spoken today in Andhra Pradesh state

ulama Muslim scholars versed in religious and legal texts

Urdu identified with north Indian Muslim culture since the eighteenth century, this language blends vernacular Hindi grammar with Perso-Arabic vocabulary

urs literally, marriage; the date a Muslim saint or a member of royalty died; anniversary commemoration at the tomb of a deceased saint, ruler, or member of a royal family

Vaishnava individuals or groups devoted to the worship of Vishnu in his various forms; their beliefs and practices are collectively designated as Vaishnavism in English

varna one of the four classes in the classical Indian conception of society; sometimes used in reference to the entire system of four classes

Vishnu a major Hindu god whose ten incarnations include Rama and Krishna; he is the husband of Lakshmi and often regarded as the preserver of the universe

watan jagir ancestral lands of Mughal nobles who were princes in their own right

zamindar a person who had the hereditary right to collect revenues from a village or group of villages, often designated as a tax-collector by the Mughal state

zikr recollection of god's ninety-nine names, in Islam

zimmi a Muslim term for people of the Book, Jews and Christians, whose histories are included in the Quran as having a shared religious tradition with Islam

Place names: alternative spellings

Older spellings	Contemporary spellings
Benares	Varanasi
Bombay	Mumbai
Calcutta	Kolkata
Dacca	Dhaka
Madras	Chennai

1   Introduction: situating India

Today in Mumbai, Kolkata, Delhi – in any big city in India – people, old, young and in-between, are everywhere chatting on cell phones or mobiles. The ring tones that chime constantly from every conceivable nook and cranny are ubiquitous, adding to the general cacophony of a modern South Asian street scene. The sound of portable phones is the most recent addition to the hodgepodge of noises one might hear, intermingling with loudspeakers playing music from the latest Bollywood hits, car and bus horns blaring, vendors of food and other items shouting out their wares, temple bells being struck, and the calling of Muslims to prayer. The new telecommunication technologies allow a person in Bangalore or Hyderabad to answer the questions of a customer of a multinational corporation calling from North America, while TV networks based in the West such as MTV, BBC, and CNN are now broadcast throughout the Indian subcontinent. Meanwhile, the Western pop culture transmitted to other parts of the globe is more and more permeated with influences from South Asia: Nora Jones, the daughter of world famous sitarist Ravi Shankar, is among the best selling artists of the early 2000s; the voice of the late Nusrat Ali Khan serves as a backdrop to the hit film *Dead Man Walking*; and the grocer Apu figures on the long-running animated TV show, *The Simpsons*. Cultural influences across national and regional boundaries are much more conspicuous today than ever before, but people have exchanged ideas, technologies, and goods with different societies since the beginning of human history.

The food served at any good Indian restaurant offers a useful illustration of just how much the culture of each region of the world is indebted to others. Kabobs, keema, and korma are all derived from the cuisines of the Middle East and Central Asia; these areas also contributed the rich, creamy sauces that are so prominent in Indian restaurant fare abroad. Many items long considered staples of the Indian diet such as chili peppers, potatoes, and tomatoes were introduced from the New World beginning in the sixteenth century, as were fruits like pineapple and papaya. Other popular Indian foods like cauliflower and cabbage, of European origin, were not grown in the subcontinent until after 1850. South Asia, in its turn, contributed the cucumber, black pepper, cinnamon, and possibly also the sweet orange and eggplant to the world; it also transmitted rice, sugarcane, citrus fruits, tea, and cotton to the lands lying to its west.

Although cross-cultural interaction has always been a factor in the history of South Asia, as in the history of every region of Eurasia, it was particularly significant during the period covered in this book, the years from 1200 to 1750. Beginning in 1200, much of north India came under the control of warriors whose family origins lay in Afghanistan or Central Asia. They were not large in number, but their political importance encouraged an influx of educated immigrants from the Islamic world and closer ties between South Asia and the regions to its west. The Central Asian ethnic heritage, Persian cultural orientation, and Islamic religious affiliation of this ruling class introduced many novel elements into the subcontinent, including different forms of art and architecture, political ideologies and practices, and techniques of warfare. Muslim scholars, mystics, and institutions also received much patronage from this new political elite, leading eventually to the presence of a sizeable Muslim population in the subcontinent. The already pluralistic human landscape of South Asia was enriched as a consequence and, over time, a composite culture developed that drew on both the Indic and Perso-Islamic traditions. This is especially visible in the material culture of South Asia today, where forms of dress like the *salwar-kamiz* (tunics worn over long, loose pants) worn by many urban women, textile designs like paisley, or the enameled and filigreed patterns on metal objects owe their inspiration largely to contact with the Islamic world.

In the centuries after 1200, the society and culture of South Asia became more diverse not only because of influences from Central Asia and the Middle East but also because the multiple regions within the subcontinent increasingly followed different paths. The modern regional societies of the subcontinent – as distinct from each other as those of France, England, and Italy in Europe – vary in their traditional dress, diet, ritual observances, social groupings, and most notably in their languages. Although their evolution was a long and complex historical process, several of the regional societies of the modern day had begun to take shape by 1200. This is most true of south India, where the four major language cultures had found political expression in separate states. Regions farther to the north were less distinctly articulated in political terms, but also gradually developed separate literary cultures in a process similar to the vernacularization of European literature, which took place roughly in the same time period. Regional differences were also increasingly apparent in numerous ways ranging from architectural styles (which we will discuss later in this chapter), the prevalence of certain religions or religious sects, and involvement in overseas trade. At the same time, however, the diverse regional societies of South Asia came into ever closer contact with each other from 1200 onward as their political histories intersected and internal trade expanded.

A multiregional perspective on historical developments and an interest in the interaction between Indic and Islamic cultures and peoples are the hallmarks of this book, two ways in which it departs most significantly from its predecessors. By this means, we aim to provide a better understanding of the antecedents of modern South Asia, an intricate montage assembled from assorted materials that were incorporated at different points of time. Although we cannot do justice to all the multiple cultures and societies of South Asia in a book of this size, some consideration of the differing historical trajectories of its various regions is essential in order to appreciate its rich and complex heritage. Rather than focusing almost exclusively on the Gangetic north as many earlier scholars have, therefore, we adopt a wider view that also covers events and processes taking place in south India and elsewhere. Secondly, we acknowledge that the encounter between Indic and Islamic peoples and cultures led to short-term conflicts, as historians in the past have often described. Frequently overlooked in standard accounts, however, is the extent to which cultural productions and practices inspired by Perso-Islamic traditions became integral to the subcontinent as a whole over the long run. South Asia's art and architecture, its political rituals, its administrative and military technologies, and even aspects of its popular religions were deeply inflected by the new forms introduced, beginning in 1200, as we have attempted to demonstrate.

Another distinguishing feature of this book is its coverage of political culture, particularly as manifested in elite cultural productions such as paintings and monuments. This is not to say that we omit other dimensions of South Asia's history from 1200 to 1750; an overview of the most important developments in the society, economy, and religious sphere is provided, as well as an account of the significant political events. The overall survey is supplemented, however, by a more extensive treatment of art, architecture, and royal courts than is typical of general books on the period. Partly because of our own interests and expertise, we have chosen to emphasize culture more than political economy, maritime trade, the agrarian system, or administrative structures. We also wished to provide an alternative to the numerous works on the latter topics that already exist. Having stated that our emphasis is on culture, it is necessary to make clear that we are referring to the culture of South Asia's political elites. Only the most powerful members of the population had the means to commission texts, monuments, and other objects that have lasted to the current day. Over the centuries, as India became more prosperous, certain features of elite culture were transmitted downward to more modest social levels such as that of the rural gentry or urban banking community. But not until we arrive at almost the end of our period can we say much about the lives of those below the upper class.

The time span surveyed in this book, the years from 1200 to 1750, was previously known as either the medieval or Muslim period of India's history, with everything preceding it lumped together in a single ancient era. Over the past several decades, the way historians have divided up India's past has changed and been brought more in line with the periodization of European history. Medieval now refers to the centuries from either 500 or 700 CE up to approximately 1500, while the 300 years from 1500 and 1800 are called early modern, just as in the case of Europe. Although the new scheme of periodization is easier to grasp due to its similarity to the way Europe's history is conceptualized, this is not the primary reason it was adopted. There are good justifications internal to Indian history why the 1,000 years between 500 and 1500 should be considered as a single unit of the past. Shortly after 500, the last of the ancient Indian empires disappeared and for the next millennium India's states were typically smaller and more decentralized. Between approximately 1500 and 1800, as we argue in chapter 6, larger and more efficient states once again emerge in India, along with a host of other phenomena, such as commercialization, that are characteristic of the early modern period throughout much of the world. Since the central concerns of many historians are political structures and the economic systems that underpin them, the new periodization of Indian history with a dividing point at 1500 is more appropriate.

From the perspective of political culture, on the other hand, the 1200–1750 period is a more coherent and thus better unit of time to study. The twin processes of growing Perso-Islamic influence and increasing regionalization have started gaining momentum by 1200 and continue to flourish with vigor up to our ending point in 1750. Soon thereafter, the course of Indian history becomes more and more entangled with that of Britain, and its political culture undergoes substantial transformation, ushering in a different age. In terms of our specific concerns, therefore, it makes sense to set the parameters of the era surveyed at 1200 to 1750. However, we do not endorse the label "Muslim" that was applied to this period in histories of South Asia written during the late nineteenth and early twentieth centuries, in contrast to the preceding "Hindu" and subsequent "British" periods. The use of a religious affiliation to characterize the first two sets of rulers, Hindu and Muslim, is highly objectionable, especially when the colonial rulers are described rather by their British nationality. This is a striking illustration of the Orientalist belief that religion was the most important force in traditional Indian society and thus, by extension, that the actions of its political elites were primarily motivated by their religious faith. Worst of all, the Hindu–Muslim binary sets up these two alleged social groups in opposition to each other as natural competitors or even foes, ignoring the many ways in which Indic and Indo-Muslim elites interacted and created a joint political and artistic culture.

Instead, we view the era from 1200 to 1750 as the foundation for the highly pluralistic human landscape of modern South Asia, with its composite culture that draws on both Indic and Islamic high traditions in many regional variants. In order to better understand South Asia's pluralism, we turn next to a consideration of India's physical and cultural geography, both in relation to the world setting and internally.

India as a world region

The word "subcontinent" used to describe the South Asian landmass highlights the fact that it is a natural physical region separate from the rest of Eurasia. To the north, the series of mountain ranges collectively known as the Himalayas form a belt about 2,500 kilometers in length and between 200 and 400 kilometers in width, beyond which lies the arid and high Tibetan plateau. The combination of inhospitable plateau and formidable mountain barrier has largely sealed off access to the subcontinent from the north. The Arabian Sea in the west and the Bay of Bengal in the east, bodies of water that comprise part of the larger Indian Ocean, surround much of South Asia and provide it with a coastline of approximately 8,500 kilometers. Hills run between the mountains and the ocean at both ends of the subcontinent, to its west and to its east, serving to further demarcate the subcontinent's boundaries and impede entry into it. South Asia – that is, the modern nations of Pakistan, India, Nepal, Bhutan, and Bangladesh on the subcontinent, along with the large island nation of Sri Lanka – is set apart from the rest of the world by these various natural geographical features, and its identity as a discrete world region appears logical to us.

If we look back in history, however, it is clear that there was constant movement into and out of the subcontinent. The geographic features that clearly define South Asia as a physical region by no means sealed it off from the rest of the world. A lively sea traffic connected the coasts of India with the Persian Gulf and Red Sea during the height of the Roman empire, while maritime contact with mainland Southeast Asia was established by

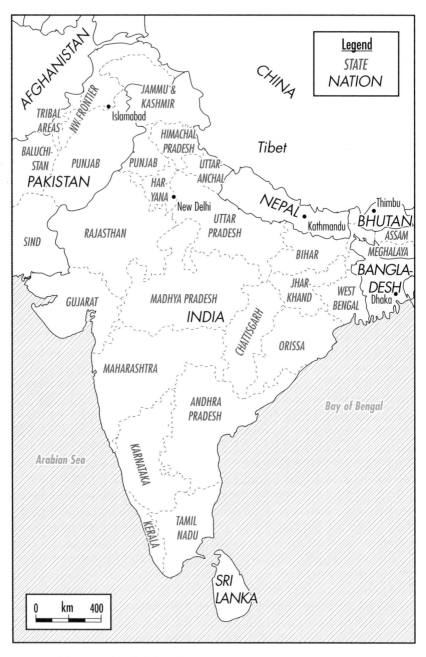

Map 1.1   South Asia today

at least the fourth century CE. Overland routes into the subcontinent from the northwest were accessible enough that Alexander the Great could lead a large army into the Punjab during the fourth century BCE. To be sure, there was less overland traffic over the Himalayas, although Buddhism and other aspects of Indian culture did diffuse into the Tibetan plateau during the medieval period. Likewise, the eastern land corridor seems to have been little used: the eastern extremities of the subcontinent were sparsely inhabited (as was the adjoining territory in modern Myanmar) and lay outside the cultural and political perimeters of Indian civilization until 500 or less years ago.

From a historical perspective, the western and eastern boundaries of South Asia as a cultural and political region appear quite different from the current national borders that separate Pakistan from Afghanistan and Iran to the west, on the one hand, and India and Bangladesh from Myanmar to the east, on the other. Not until well into the period we are covering in this book did Bangladesh become incorporated into the South Asian sphere. The situation in the west is even more ambiguous. The area of Afghanistan and even parts of Central Asia were several times in the distant past included in a polity based in South Asia. The cultural impact of Indian civilization was similarly felt far outside South Asia's current limits during much of the first millennium CE: Buddhism flourished throughout Afghanistan and Central Asia, while the North Indian Brahmi script was adapted to several Central Asian languages such as Khotanese and Tocharian. For these reasons alone, one could make a strong case that Afghanistan is (or at least once was) an integral part of South Asia, rather than the Middle East, in cultural and political terms.

We have gone into this point at some length because history books today routinely characterize any people whose origins lie to the west of Pakistan as "foreign" to South Asia and their large-scale movements toward the southeast as "invasions" of the subcontinent. The Khyber Pass in northern Pakistan and the Bolan Pass in southern Pakistan are typically described as the weak points in South Asia's defenses which have repeatedly been penetrated by foreign invaders. This mindset ignores the many interconnections over the millennia across the terrain that is now divided up between the countries of Afghanistan, Pakistan, and India. Instead, it projects backward into the past a geo-political reality that took shape only at the very end of the nineteenth century, after the British proved incapable of extending their control westward to a line that ran on a north–south diagonal through the Afghan cities of Kabul, Ghazni, and Qandahar (see Maps 2.1 and 5.1). Historically, there was far more contact and communication between the people living around Delhi and Kabul, separated by only 1,000 kilometers, than between the major cities of north and south India, separated by 2,000 kilometers or more; even Mumbai is 1,400 kilometers distant from Delhi.

In other words, the coherence of South Asia as a world region in our current perception is largely a legacy of British colonialism. The British were the first and only political power to ever extend their sway over all of South Asia and the limits of their dominion now define the boundaries of the region. The large size of the subcontinent, the varied nature of its physical environments, and the great diversity of its human population – in language, ethnicity, and mode of subsistence – made it impossible for any precolonial polity to conquer much less govern. The diversity of South Asia's physical and human geography makes it most comparable to (western and central) Europe among world regions, in the view of Martin W. Lewis and Karen E. Wigen. In *The Myth of Continents: A Critique of Metageography*, they argue that defining Europe as a continent overstates its size, importance, and uniqueness, and so they prefer to classify it as one of several Eurasian subcontinents. Furthermore, in terms of territorial extent, historic levels of population, multiplicity of regional languages and cultures, and reliance on shared literary languages, they believe Europe is more analogous to South Asia than to any other part of the world.

Regarding South Asia as similar to Europe is instructive in a number of ways. While the term Europe certainly refers to a particular location on the globe, the exact perimeters of Europe are difficult to pin down and have shifted over time. As Robert Bartlett has said in reference to the high middle ages, "Europe is both a region and an idea."[1] That is, Europe is not defined simply by its physical geography but also by cultural and political criteria. We should recognize that the current national boundaries of South Asia are similarly not intrinsic or natural to the region but have been constructed through human action. All world regions have had porous and ill-defined border zones through which an assortment of peoples and their cultures have migrated back and forth. Instead of acknowledging that movement, migration, and change are the most fundamental of historical experiences, scholars of South Asia have tended to depict any influences or peoples from the outside as intrusive violations of the subcontinent's integrity or true essence. At the same time, South Asia has been characterized as a place that was exceptionally susceptible to invasion beginning with the migrations of Indo-Aryan speakers into the subcontinent sometime around the early second millennium BCE. This stands in marked contrast to China, which is typically said

---

[1] *The Making of Europe: Conquest, Colonization and Cultural Change, 950–1350* (Princeton: Princeton University Press, 1993), p. 1.

to have assimilated its numerous nomadic invaders and thus triumphed over them, or Europe, despite its history of invasion and colonization by Rome, the Huns, Vikings, Magyars, and Arabs.

If we think of South Asia as akin to Europe, our perspective on its political fragmentation also changes. Rather than expecting that the sub-continent's vast territory should have been politically unified as was the case in China, we can view the presence of numerous kingdoms in 1000 CE as a normal course of affairs in such a large and diverse area. The proliferation of polities then becomes a sign of dynamism and not a civilizational defect that facilitated the conquest of South Asia by out-siders. It testifies to the expansion of agrarian settlement throughout the subcontinent, to the growth of locality-based societies, and to the evolution of regional cultures. Like Europe, South Asia had a common elite "civilization" that served to unify it culturally in a general sense prior to 1200, although there were many different local practices and beliefs. From 1200 onward, the pan-Indic civilization was increasingly eclipsed in importance by regional cultures that had evolved their own distinctive variations on the Indic theme. Just as in Europe, regionaliza-tion occurred at the expense of a cosmopolitan language and culture, in South Asia's case, Sanskrit, and was a sign of the growing relevance of more localized concerns and identities among the elite populations. These regional cultures also interacted with or were affected by aspects of the cosmopolitan culture of Persia and the Middle East in differing ways in the centuries after 1200. It is thus to a discussion of the unity and diversity of South Asia's internal physical and cultural landscapes that we now turn.

India's physical and human landscapes

The greatest divide in South Asia's physical and human geography is between north and south. The environment of the north has been shaped by the Himalayas, a geologically young set of mountains with extraordi-narily high crests such as Mt. Everest (in Nepal), the highest mountain in the world at 8,850 meters (29,028 feet), and Kanchenjunga (in India) at 8,586 meters. The weight of this massive mountain system caused the land lying to its south to sink and form a vast low plain. The melting snows of the Himalayas feed numerous streams that have contributed a fertile overlay of soil to this plain, named the Indo-Gangetic after the two major river systems. The Indus river and its four tributaries lie at the western end of the plain; the Ganges with its many tributaries such as the Yamuna, which joins the Ganges river at the city of Allahabad, form the central portion. At the eastern end, the Ganges is approached by the

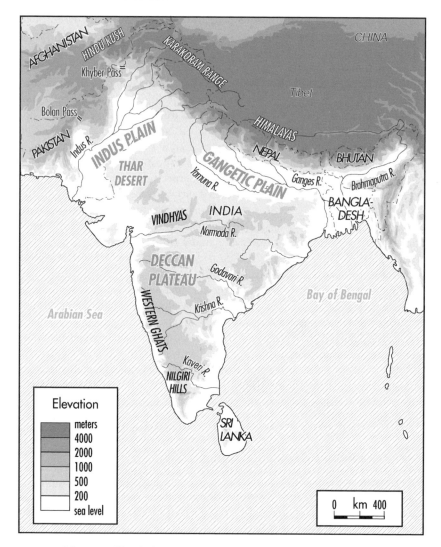

Map 1.2   Physical geography of South Asia

Brahmaputra river originating in Tibet. Large sections of these perennial rivers of north India are navigable and were major routes of transport in the past.

The Vindhya range and the adjacent Narmada river are the traditional boundaries between north India and peninsular or south India. Most of the peninsula is a slightly elevated plateau that inclines gently toward the east. Close to the ocean along the west coast run the Western Ghats, a range of hills that starts out low in the north but culminates in the Nilgiri Hills in the south, at an altitude of 2,300 to 2,600 meters. Several major peninsular rivers, including the Godavari, Krishna, and Kaveri, have their headwaters in the Western Ghats; unlike the northern rivers, these have steep gradients which limit flooding but also make them difficult to navigate. Many other streams in the peninsula dry up for part of the year because they are fed only by the rains and not by glaciers, as in the north. South of the Narmada, all rivers drain into the Bay of Bengal on the peninsula's east coast, where small plains of fertile alluvial soil have been formed. Much of the soil elsewhere in the peninsula is of poorer quality, and the landscape is uneven and rocky. Although the entire peninsula is sometimes known as the Deccan (derived from the word for south), in this book we divide the peninsula into the far south (roughly the modern states of Tamil Nadu, Kerala, and southern Karnataka) and the Deccan to its north.

North and south are also differentiated by language, although this cultural contour does not correspond exactly with the geographic divide of the Vindhya range and Narmada river. Linguistically, modern Maharashtra in the western Deccan is part of the northern zone, reflecting its historic character as an area of transition between the two. South of Maharashtra the languages belong to the Dravidian family found only in India, whereas Maharashtra's Marathi language and all the major languages to its north belong to the Indo-Aryan family, a subset of the larger Indo-European group. While totally different in their origins, the Dravidian and Indo-Aryan languages have developed some common features through long interaction, including a large body of joint vocabulary.

Most parts of both north and south India share a climate dominated by the seasonal monsoon winds. In the middle of the year, the prevailing southwest winds carry moisture from the Indian Ocean and drench most of South Asia with heavy rains. The winds reverse direction in the winter and blow out of the dry, cold interior of inner Asia. This system of alternating monsoon winds produces three main seasons: the rainy period of the southwest monsoon (mid June to early October) when the weather is hot and wet; the cool, dry weather from early October to February corresponding to winter; and the hot dry season, or summer, from about March to mid June.

The coming of the rains, which almost instantly transforms the parched brown landscape into a lush expanse of green, is critical to Indian agriculture. Both the quantity and timing of the southwest monsoon can vary considerably from year to year, leading to large differences in crop yields and occasional flooding. The southwest monsoon is of such vital importance that rain has long been the symbol of fertility in Indian art and poetry. In the premodern era, the monsoon rains also made roads and rivers impassable, bringing a halt to long-distance travel – military campaigns were typically suspended and wandering holy men had to settle down for the duration of the rainy season.

While the monsoon rains cover most of the subcontinent, rainfall amounts vary considerably from place to place and so create another set of differences between regions. On the whole, the eastern portion of South Asia receives notably more precipitation than does the western half. The west coast of peninsular India is an exception to the general pattern, since the southwest monsoon winds drop their moisture on the narrow strip of land along the coast as they approach the Western Ghats. Disparities in rainfall levels are particularly great in the northern half of the subcontinent and lead us to differentiate two more regions: the dry territory of the west (central and southern Pakistan, along with the Indian states of Rajasthan and Gujarat) and the wet lands in the east (from India's West Bengal state to Myanmar). Camels were widely used for transport in the arid zone of Rajasthan, while small boats were common along the numerous waterways and swampy marshes of Bengal. Animal herding was once the primary occupation of much of west India's population, while the hunting and gathering lifestyle persisted for a long time in east India along with fishing. (Here, as elsewhere in this book, we use the term India in its older sense as a synonym for the entire subcontinent rather than specifically for the modern nation.)

The heartland of South Asia has long been the western and central portion of the Gangetic plain, where the bulk of the Hindi-speaking population resides today. When we refer to north India, this is the area we most often have in mind. Travel and communication is easy in the Gangetic plain, with its large, open expanse of land, as well as many navigable rivers. Perennial sources of water, adequate rainfall, and good soils were a boon to settled agriculture, the economic mainstay of the region. The greatest empires of ancient India were based in the Gangetic plain which, along with the Indus plain, boasted the earliest urban centers of the subcontinent. In south India, in contrast, settled agriculture was confined to relatively small pockets, although it had a longer history there than in western or eastern India. Because of its more difficult terrain, dispersed agrarian zones, and localized social circles, the peninsula's kingdoms were typically smaller than those of the Gangetic north prior to 1000 CE. The only states that had ever extended their power across the Vindhyas were those based in the north. Eastern and western Indian states were even later to develop than those in the south and were similarly restricted in size, for the most part.

Regional cultures of India, 1000–1200

For much of India's ancient history, the earlier development, greater wealth, and larger population of the Gangetic north gave it political and cultural dominance. This explains why it was the Sanskrit language once spoken in the north that eventually developed into the pan-Indic literary medium. For a period of approximately a thousand years beginning in 300 CE, the prestige of classical Sanskrit was so great that it eclipsed all other languages and literatures. It created what Sheldon Pollock has called a Sanskrit cosmopolis, a far-flung realm of shared aesthetics, political discourse, and religious knowledge. The Sanskrit cosmopolis was chiefly embodied in the person of the learned Brahmin, who occupied the preeminent position in the four-fold *varna* or caste system of social classification. Traditionally priests and religious scholars, Brahmins had for centuries also served as court poets, ministers of state, scribes, and record-keepers. Brahmins were crucial propagators of the ideologies and rituals of kingship and so were heavily patronized throughout the subcontinent, and even in parts of Southeast Asia, by kings and warriors who belonged to the class known as *kshatriya*.

Although the religious beliefs and practices of India were never systematized by a central institution or spiritual authority, the circulation of Sanskrit and Brahmins throughout the subcontinent did produce some semblance of a unified religious culture at the elite level by 1000 CE. Over the previous millennium, numerous local gods and goddesses had been appropriated and subsumed into the three main deities of classical Hinduism: Shiva, Vishnu, and the Goddess (Devi). Shiva, often worshipped in the form of the cylindrical *linga*, is an ascetic lord dwelling in the Himalayas whose dance of destruction brings about the periodic end of all life so that the universe might be renewed. Shiva is also depicted in sculpture in multiple forms, including as a happily married husband and father. Vishnu is even more complex, for his personality includes those of his ten incarnations among which are the well-known gods, Krishna and Rama, to whom we will refer a number of times in this text. In general, Vishnu is a rather more benevolent god than Shiva; medieval Indian kings particularly liked him in his Boar incarnation, when he rescued the earth from the depths of the ocean where she had been dragged by a fierce demon. The Goddess is worshipped by many names and in many forms, both benevolent and wrathful, sometimes in association with a male god, but often alone.

By 1000 CE, stone temples for the elite worship of the major Hindu deities had been built in many localities of the subcontinent. The rituals of worship followed the same fundamental format regardless of location:

the enshrined image of the god or goddess was bathed, dressed, decorated with ornaments, and fed at least twice a day. The layout of temple complexes also bore a rough resemblance to each other, enough so that they would have been immediately recognizable as temples to visitors from a different region. The most important deity dwelt in the inner sanctum, over which a high superstructure known as a *shikhara* reached toward the heavens. One or more pillared porches (*mandapa*) were adjoined to the front of the main building that contained the inner sanctum. Devotees could enter the porches and even the main building but not the inner sanctum itself, for that was the domain of the deity and the Brahmin priests who served the gods and goddesses.

Within this basic template found all over India, there were significant regional divergences in style. Just as the numerous scripts for the regional languages of India prior to 1200 were all derived from the same ancient Brahmi script, so too regional idioms in temple architecture increasingly deviated from classical prototypes. Variation in temple styles is a manifestation of the growing regionalization of Indian culture, a phenomenon that we have already stated becomes more important after approximately 1200. As each regional society developed, its political leaders who sponsored the creation of monuments and its artisans who constructed them chose somewhat different ways of making their vision of an abode for the gods into a physical reality. Architecture is only a single aspect of culture, of course, and one that may not have affected the lives of many people. However, temple styles are the most readily recognizable marker of regional identity in the medieval era. A good way to illustrate the cultural diversity that existed in the subcontinent within the larger overall unity is by looking at two temples dating to around 1000 CE, one from south India and the other from the north.

The largest temple in eleventh-century India was located in Tanjavur, the capital of the mighty Chola dynasty of the far south (see Map 2.2 for location of Tanjavur). Consecrated in 1010, the temple housed a form of Shiva named Rajarajeshvara after the Chola ruler Rajaraja, who was its main patron. As was standard in the south Indian or Dravidian style of architecture, the temple was demarcated as a sacred space by a walled enclosure. Entry into the enclosure was through a large towered gate known as a *gopura*, which in the temple architecture of later centuries would grow so large as to dwarf the temple itself. At this eleventh-century site, however, the temple was still the dominant feature in the complex. Made of carved granite, the exterior of the temple hosts a variety of complex figural images and inscriptions intended to praise both the god Shiva and the king who so ostentatiously made his piety known to the world. An unusually large mandapa (porch) fronts the temple's inner

Figure 1.1 The Rajarajeshvara temple, Tanjavur, dated 1010, is topped
by a pyramidal spire typical of south Indian temples.

sanctum which in turn is topped by a shikhara (pyramidal superstructure)
that soars to a height of 65 meters. Its tightly stepped pyramidal spire
adorned with a smooth circular cap is typical of superstructures on south
Indian temples and provides an imposing profile (Figure 1.1).

While the far south of India was thriving under the Chola dynasty,
political power in the northern half of the subcontinent continued to
devolve to an increasing number of small states. Despite their more lim-
ited resources, north Indian kings were also vigorous patrons of temples
and the artistic creativity of the region remained high. A good example
is the Kandariya Mahadeva temple at the site of Khajuraho (Figure 1.2),
on the southern edge of the Gangetic plain, in the modern state of
Madhya Pradesh. It is dedicated to Shiva but stands among a group
of more than twenty extant structures, constructed over three centuries,
which house Jain deities as well as other Hindu ones. (Jains, like Hindus,
believe in continuous rebirth until the soul achieves perfection and
are staunch adherents of non-violence, but they reject the authority of
Brahmins.) We have no information on who built this largest and most
elaborate monument at Khajuraho, but given its size and scale it is generally assumed to have been the reigning king of the Chandela dynasty that
ruled this area during the ninth through early twelfth centuries. Built at
about the same time as Tanjavur's Rajarajeshvara temple, the Kandariya

Figure 1.2   The Kandariya Mahadeva temple, Khajuraho, dating to the early eleventh century, has a superstructure composed of clustered spires typical of north Indian temples.

Mahadeva is the most acclaimed temple to survive from the eleventh-century north and provides a striking contrast to the southern style of architecture. Once again, as we noted previously in relation to terrain and language, north and south India can be sharply differentiated.

The Kandariya Mahadeva, richly covered with carved gods and goddesses, sits on a high plinth and the inner sanctum is approached by three porches, each increasingly larger than the previous one. The porches are surmounted by elaborate corbelled roofs; what might be an otherwise dark interior is illuminated by open balconies. Its superstructure, one of the most beautiful examples of the north Indian style, is radically different from the south Indian type exemplified at Tanjavur. The Kandariya Mahadeva's superstructure is composed not of a series of separate stories that gradually recede as they ascend, as in the case with the Rajarajeshvara temple, but rather of reduplicated clusters of small spires that line a central core. This gives the temple's roof line a jagged outline not unlike a great mountain range. Since it can be considered a replica of Mt. Kailasa, the Himalayan abode of the god Shiva, the temple's visual reference to mountains is highly appropriate. While the Kandariya Mahadeva is only about half the height of the Rajarajeshvara temple, the progressively rising spires of the roof emphasize the vertical dimension and give the temple a sense of considerable height. The temple's height is also emphasized by the extremely steep stairs that lead from the ground level to the elevated entrance and climbing them gives the devotee the sense of scaling Mt. Kailasa, an intended reference to Shiva's home.

Eastern and western India also had their own distinctive types of temple architecture by 1000 CE, within the broader northern style. The four regions of India – south, north, east, and west – thus each had their own separate interpretation of temple architecture within a common template that consisted of one or more porches in front of an inner sanctum surmounted by a tall spire. The exterior of the temple was generally the most heavily decorated portion, usually embellished with images of gods and demi-gods that could be contemplated and worshipped as the devotee circumambulated the exterior, before and after paying homage to the interior deity. To see the deity's image was considered an especially auspicious act known as *darshana* or *darshan*, that might be loosely translated as beholding.

The Indian focus on a religious structure's exterior stands in contrast to Muslim practice in the larger Islamic world, where it is not until the thirteenth and fourteenth centuries that magnificent exteriors become the norm. While Muslim prayer can be performed anywhere as long as the believer faces in the direction of Mecca, it is often done in the interior of a mosque – in the prayer chamber itself or in the mosque's interior courtyard, which serves as an overflow area. Ritual at Indian temples and Indian mosques would always remain specific to each religion, but over time the different building styles of temples and mosques merged to create structures that were Islamic in appearance but not in function. In addition, by around 1600 the Indian practice of beholding a deity was extended to royalty, both Hindu and Muslim.

By the year 1000, as we have seen, the different regions of the subcontinent had begun to exhibit distinctive elite cultures. Another notable trend was the rise of south India, whose historical development had long lagged behind that of the north. The soaring height of the superstructure of Tanjavur's Rajarajeshvara temple reflected the stature of the dynasty that sponsored its construction, for under Rajaraja (r. 985–1014) and his son Rajendra (r. 1014–1044), the Chola kingdom became the greatest Indian state of its era. This was not due to any advance in political or military organization, since the eleventh- and twelfth-century kingdoms of South Asia were all roughly comparable in their decentralized political structures and small standing armies supplemented with troops supplied by subordinate lords. However, the Cholas had the advantage of being based in the richest agrarian zone of the peninsula, the Kaveri river delta area, at a time when south India's economic development had finally caught up with and even surpassed the level of the north. This gave them the resources to extract tribute from the entire far south and even send an army all the way to the Ganges in the north Indian heartland.

The Cholas also had the advantage of proximity to the most active sector of long-distance trade within the Indian Ocean in this period, the eastern stretch extending from southeastern India through Southeast Asia and into south China. Rajaraja most likely desired more control over international trade when he annexed the northern half of the neighboring island of Sri Lanka, on the sea route between India and regions to its east. His successor Rajendra completed the conquest of Sri Lanka and went on to dispatch a naval expedition against Shrivijaya, a maritime trading kingdom based on the Indonesian island of Sumatra. The victory of the Chola fleet led to fifty years of Indian dominance over the Strait of Malacca, the vital sea passage between the Malayan peninsula and Indonesia through which all trade to and from China was funneled. This was the apex of Indian influence in Southeast Asia, which had assimilated many elements of Indian civilization over the past six or more centuries, including the Sanskrit language, south Indian scripts, and the religions of Hinduism and Buddhism.

Mahmud of Ghazni and the Islamic world, c. 1000

At the same time that King Rajaraja I of the Chola dynasty was making plans to build his enormous temple at Tanjavur, another great king had emerged in far-off Afghanistan. Known to posterity simply as Mahmud of Ghazni (r. 998–1030) after the Afghan city that was his capital (see Map 2.1), he is usually regarded as the first Muslim king to have a major impact on the subcontinent. Muslim rule had in fact been introduced centuries earlier, when Arab forces seized control of the Sind region of the southern Indus plain (now in Pakistan) in 711. Muslims continued to rule over Sind for centuries but the presence of the great Thar desert to their east made further penetration into the subcontinent difficult. Developments in Sind had little effect on the rest of South Asia, and Muslim influence was confined primarily to this backwater region. Even Indo-Muslim chronicles of a later time ignore the Arabs of Sind and begin their narrative of Muslim rule in India with Mahmud of Ghazni.

Mahmud lived about 350 years after the inception of Islam, at a time when many in the Islamic world feared that their centuries of political supremacy might be at an end. In the years immediately after the death of the Prophet Muhammad (d. 632), Muslims had given their allegiance to a single caliph or head of state. Under the Umayyad dynasty of caliphs (661–750) based in Damascus and then the Abbasids of Baghdad, much of the Islamic world had been politically unified, at least in theory. This unity had fragmented by the tenth century, with three different rulers – one in Umayyad Spain, another in Abbasid Baghdad, and yet another in Fatimid Cairo – each claiming to be the sole caliph. While all Muslims would never again be brought together in one state, the tenth-century fear that Muslim dominance was on an irreversible decline proved to be wrong. Instead, the influx of a new group of people, the Turks, would politically reinvigorate much territory ruled under the banner of Islam. From the ninth century onward, Muslim rulers had increasingly relied on personal troops composed of enslaved Turks from the Central Asian steppes. These military slaves or *mamluks* were considered more loyal than other soldiers because they were taken captive at a young age and owed loyalty only to their master. Many mamluks went on to become prominent generals and leaders in the Islamic world in this era; at the same time, various tribes of Turks were gradually migrating into Muslim lands and becoming Islamicized. Due to their nomadic background, the Turkic peoples were skilled at cavalry warfare.

Mahmud of Ghazni's ascendance occurred in this context of rising Turkic military and political power. His grandfather, Alptigin, was a Turk who began as a military slave and ended his career as governor of Ghazni, a city in the center of what is now Afghanistan. Sebuktigin, Mahmud's father, was also a slave at one time, before he married Alptigin's daughter and succeeded to Alptigin's position as governor. He eventually declared his independence and annexed much of modern Afghanistan, becoming the first in the Ghaznavid line of Turkic rulers. After Mahmud, the Ghaznavids lost their base in Afghanistan to the Seljuq Turks, a group of nomadic tribes who went on to conquer a huge swath of territory encompassing modern Turkey, Iraq, Iran, and much of Central Asia. The Ghaznavids and Seljuqs were conscious of their status as newcomers to Islam and so never sought symbolic leadership over the entire Islamic world. Instead of claiming the ultimate authority as caliphs, Mahmud and other Turkic rulers were called *sultans*, a title for Muslim kings that spread widely in later centuries. After several centuries during which the Islamic frontiers had hardly advanced, the Turkic sultans of the eleventh century initiated major expansions of the Islamic realm, the Ghaznavids toward the east and the Seljuqs toward the west.

Mahmud of Ghazni started making frequent campaigns into the Indian subcontinent in 1001. Keen on building up his prestige within the international Muslim community, Mahmud portrayed his entry into the subcontinent as an instance of *jihad,* in this case a war against infidels. Making this claim also allowed him to legitimately take booty, which Mahmud did in great quantities. Mahmud commenced by taking territory around the Indus river in what is today Pakistan and eventually made his way as far east as the Gangetic valley. After each of his seventeen expeditions within South Asia, he would return to Ghazni before the summer rains, laden with booty including slaves, gold, elephants and jewels. Mahmud's last campaign in 1025–26 is the one for which he is most famous. At that time he sacked the Somanatha temple, built about fifty years earlier by the western Indian king of Gujarat (see Map 2.1). This coastal area was a prosperous and wealthy one, thanks to vigorous maritime trading activities. According to a later tradition, 50,000 devotees lost their lives in trying to stop Mahmud from not only taking the temple's considerable wealth, but also destroying the form of the Hindu god Shiva housed within it. Subsequent kings of the Gujarat region constructed a much grander and elaborate temple in place of the one that Mahmud had destroyed; this rebuilt temple was to be attacked in the thirteenth century by Muslims attempting to reenact Mahmud's legacy. The Somanatha temple thus became a primary site for regional contestation and a marker for political control over western India.

To this day a lively debate continues over Mahmud's motives in invading India and taking booty, for his incursions involved hostilities not only to Hindu sites, but also Buddhist ones; he even attacked Shia Muslims residing in India, whom he intensely disliked. Some people believe Mahmud was driven mainly by religious zeal while others argue his reasons for attacking Somanatha and other temples were purely economic. It is likely that he was motivated by a combination of incentives – a desire for additional territory and glory for both himself and Islam. What is most significant, however, is that from Mahmud's time onward we see an increasing amount of rhetoric in literary texts produced by both Muslims and Hindus. India becomes the bastion of idol worshippers in Muslim eyes, whereas Muslims are depicted as evil iconoclasts in Hindu sources; each is cast as the other's enemy. As we will see, there was in fact much peaceful and fruitful interaction between Muslims and Hindus in the centuries after Mahmud of Ghazni. But a polemical tradition is initiated by Mahmud's incursions that has been repeatedly claimed in the past century as typical of precolonial Hindu–Muslim relations.

Unlike Indians who had little conscious sense of unity in the year 1000, Muslims felt they were members of a single world-wide Islamic community known as the *ummah*. This was in spite of the differences between Sunnis and Shias, who make up the two main branches of Islam. Sunnis, who are the overwhelmingly dominant group, accept the historical development of Islam through a succession of caliphs including the Umayyad and Abbasid dynasties, whereas Shias believe the position of caliph should have passed on to the descendants of the Prophet Muhammad. Although this meant that Shias rejected the authority of the Abbasid caliph, he was in any case a mere figurehead by the eleventh century. Because the large majority of Muslims are Sunni, the sense of an ummah was almost readymade. Also significant in creating unity among Muslims was the existence of a common language, Arabic, for religious purposes, as well as common cultural practices and constructs.

Islam requires that Muslims adhere to a certain set of beliefs and practices. Among these are the five messages of the Quran, the divinely revealed Muslim holy book. These include the beliefs in god's mono-theistic nature, his creation of the entire world, the need for all people to be good and generous, the coming of a Day of Judgment, and the fact that Muhammad was the final prophet. In addition, there are a set of practices that all Muslims should engage in: the profession of faith in a single god, paying of a tithe, fasting during the month of Ramadan, a pilgrimage to Mecca if at all possible, and prayer five times a day. It is the act of praying that most immediately binds the ummah. While praying can be done indi-vidually, the Friday noon prayer should be done as a congregation. For this reason, each town has a mosque or in some cases multiple mosques, where Muslims can gather together in a visible reminder that they form part of a single community of faith. The brotherhood of all Muslims is further affirmed by the lack of a religious hierarchy in comparison to Hin-duism. Islam has a class of religious scholars called *ulama* whose status is based solely on their knowledge of religious texts and practice. They give informed advice and are held in great esteem but do not hold any formal religious institutional office.

Upon hearing the call to prayer from a tall minaret on Fridays around noon, the devout Muslims of Mahmud of Ghazni's realm would have flocked to the mosque for congregational prayer. Leaving their shoes at the mosque's austere brick exterior, the devout would enter into the court-yard. In its middle would be an ablution tank where ritual cleansing was performed. The courtyard's interior perimeters were lined with arched galleries used for multiple purposes, including teaching. The gallery on the side of the compound that faced the direction of Mecca, known as the *qibla*, was deeper than the other galleries, for here was the prayer cham-ber. Pointed arched entrances led into the prayer chamber's interior while arched niches called *mihrabs*, symbolic reminders of the Prophet Muham-mad's role in teaching the messages of Islam, would mark the qibla wall. Although mihrabs might be inscribed with verses from the Quran or abstract floral or geometric forms, they would never bear human or ani-mal imagery as you would find in a Hindu temple, for such figural rep-resentation is very strongly discouraged in the Muslim religious context. The prayer chamber would be surmounted by domes and/or vaults.

Very little intact architecture from the Ghaznavid period survives, but we do have existing examples from their Seljuq successors that are quite similar to the Ghaznavid style. The most notable example of a

Seljuq monument is the Great Mosque of Isfahan in Iran, which adheres closely to the hypothetical model described in the previous paragraph (Figure 1.3). Adapting earlier pre-Islamic Iranian techniques, Muslim architecture in Iran and Afghanistan was arcuated – that is, employing arches, vaults, and domes – regardless of whether the building was a tomb, palace, fort, or mosque. Due to a lack of stone quarries, almost all of this building was done in brick. While this figure shows the mosque's original brick façade, much of it was later covered with elaborate blue tile. This use of brick contrasts to the largely stone-built architecture found in India which is trabeated, based on the principle of stacking or corbelling where height is achieved by piling one stone on top of another. Another difference is that the only surviving building type in India from this era is the temple. Secular buildings must have been largely built in wood, and tombs were not required, since Indian religions prescribe cremation of the dead rather than the Islamic practice of burial. The merger of the eastern Islamic and indigenous Indic building techniques and traditions would create highly original and creative forms after 1200.

Although Mahmud could claim to belong to a worldwide Muslim community, the Ghaznavid Turks had adopted an ideology and style of kingship that originated in just one part of the Islamic world, its eastern segment. This mode of kingship drew heavily on the pre-Islamic traditions of Persia and cast the king as an all-powerful autocrat deemed superior to other mortals. The elevated position of a ruler in later Perso-Islamic society was a far cry from the egalitarian ethos of the early days of Islam, when the ruler was simply an esteemed man who was elected from a body of equals just as an Arab chief had been chosen from the elders of the tribe. The Perso-Islamic king had great responsibilities, including the execution of justice and the maintenance of Islam. Rulers such as Mahmud of Ghazni were considered shadows of god on earth and, as such, merited great respect and awe.

The fact that Mahmud of Ghazni used Persian as a court language also differentiated him and other contemporary rulers in Iran and Central Asia from their counterparts in Spain, Egypt, and Baghdad who spoke Arabic. Persian increasingly came into its own during the eleventh century. One example is provided by the famous *Shahnama* (Book of Kings) written by the poet Ferdowsi and dedicated to Mahmud of Ghazni. This lengthy epic, composed of some 60,000 verses, is not only written in Persian but also deals with a subject, the rise and fall of pre-Islamic Iranian kings, that would only have interested those who felt they were heirs to a long-standing Persian culture. In spite of the increasing importance of Persian, Arabic remained an important language, especially for scholars and religious specialists. Al-Biruni, the famous scientist and scholar who lived

Figure 1.3 The Great Mosque of Isfahan, mostly dating to the eleventh century, features arches, vaults, and domes, representative of Islamic architecture.

for some time in Ghazni and served at Mahmud's court, wrote much of his voluminous scholarship in Arabic, including his *Kitab al-Hind* (Book of India) which was then translated into Persian. This work was based on research he did in India when he accompanied Mahmud there in the 1020s, and was considered one of the most important books on India even into the sixteenth century.

These intertwined traditions of Turkic military prowess, Islamic religion, and Persian culture were introduced into the Indian subcontinent by Mahmud of Ghazni and his successors. Mahmud's son had to yield most of the Ghaznavid realm to the much larger and more powerful Seljuq Turks, but the dynasty managed to retain a small stronghold around Lahore, today in Pakistan. There the Ghaznavids survived for almost two hundred years, until they were dislodged by another upstart dynasty from Afghanistan, the Ghurids, who further spread Perso-Islamic culture in South Asia. Although Arab sailors and merchants, as well as the early Muslim Arabs who conquered Sind, were no strangers to South Asia, the Muslims who became politically dominant in the subcontinent would typically be Turco-Mongol in ethnic background, horse-riding warriors in occupation, and Persian in cultural heritage.

In the year 1000, two kings at the extremities of the greater South Asian world region had been poised for expansion. There was Rajaraja Chola of Tanjavur, on the one hand, who envisioned an extension of power into Southeast Asia that would be realized by his son Rajendra. At the same time, Mahmud of Ghazni, situated in the borderland between the Middle East, Central Asia, and South Asia, was setting his sights on the area of northwestern India. By 1200, however, the Chola dynasty had withered away along with Indian influence in Southeast Asia, whereas a second wave of Turkic warriors following in Mahmud of Ghazni's footsteps was overrunning much of north India. The Cholas flourished toward the end of one long phase, a period of roughly a thousand years when Indian culture had spread far beyond the confines of the modern region not only into Southeast Asia but also into central and eastern Asia. Mahmud of Ghazni, on the other hand, stood at the inception of a second phase, during which Islamic religion and culture were transmitted as far east as the southern Philippine islands. What happened subsequently in India was not so much a clash of civilizations as a revitalization of its politics and an enrichment of its already diverse culture. That is the story to which we now turn our attention.

The year 1206 is a watershed in the history of the Indian subcontinent. In that year Qutb al-Din Aibak, a slave of Turkic origin, seized control of the armies from Afghanistan that were occupying numerous forts in the heartland of north India. Qutb al-Din Aibak's act was but the first in a series of struggles for dominance among the leading members of the Turkic forces in India. This event easily could have been relegated to the status of a footnote in history had the occupying Turkic armies eventually retreated back to their area of origin, as had Mahmud of Ghazni two hundred years earlier, or had the fledgling Islamic state torn itself apart in internal conflict. Instead, Qutb al-Din's political successors were able to entrench themselves in India for centuries thereafter and, in doing so, ushered in momentous changes not only in the political makeup of the subcontinent but also in its culture. The importance of the date 1206, when the first of a series of dynasties collectively known as the Delhi Sultanate was founded, is thus clear as we look backwards in time.

Establishment of the Delhi Sultanate

The Ghurid conquest

The origins of the Delhi Sultanate can be traced to the career of Muhammad Ghuri, so-called after the mountainous region in Afghanistan where his family was based. His full name was Shihab al-Din Muhammad bin Sam, but he is also known in the historical sources as Muizz al-Din. Muhammad Ghuri was based in Ghazni, the former capital of the renowned Mahmud, and from there he turned his attention eastward toward India beginning in 1175. Like Mahmud, Muhammad Ghuri spent years campaigning in the Indian subcontinent and won victory after victory. Unlike Mahmud, however, Muhammad's goal was to annex territory and not merely to carry out profitable raids. Muhammad's first conquest in South Asia was the region of Punjab, held by the Muslim descendants of Mahmud of Ghazni. For two decades from 1186, the main city in the

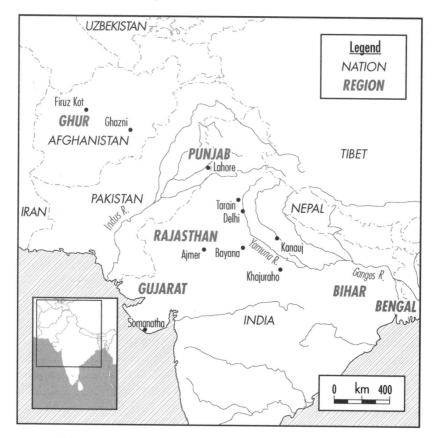

Map 2.1 South Asia and Afghanistan, *c.* 1200

Punjab, Lahore, served as the primary Ghurid base in South Asia for a series of successful attacks on north India proper (Map 2.1).

Muhammad's two chief targets in north India were the powerful Hindu kings Prithviraj Chauhan of Ajmer and Jayachandra Gahadavala of Kanauj. After their victory in 1192 against Prithviraj Chauhan at the battlefield of Tarain, about 120 kilometers northwest of modern Delhi, the Ghurid armies immediately set off toward Prithviraj's capital at Ajmer, seizing forts along the way. In the following year, Ghurid forces under Qutb al-Din Aibak set up a permanent garrison in Delhi, which would become the future center of Muslim power in north India but was then a town of minor military and political significance. The Ghurid forces next moved into the Gangetic valley and defeated King Jayachandra by 1194. While Muhammad Ghuri directed these major battles himself, most of the other campaigns in the heartland of north India were directed by his Turkic slave-general, Qutb al-Din Aibak. Bengal and Bihar in the east, on the other hand, were acquired by a military adventurer, Muhammad bin Bakhtiyar Khalji.

Muhammad Ghuri, Qutb al-Din Aibak, and Muhammad bin Bakhtiyar Khalji amply illustrate the ethnic diversity found among the warriors in the victorious Ghurid armies. Muhammad Ghuri was an aristocrat from a people who were culturally and linguistically Persian; he was a member of the urbane, civilized world. Other elite men from Ghur served as commanders for Muhammad Ghuri in his early years of expansion, but they were replaced almost entirely by military slaves of Turkic origin like Qutb al-Din Aibak after the Battle of Tarain in 1192. Military slaves were more reliable in their loyalties than aristocratic warriors because they had no family allegiances. They were typically non-Muslims enslaved as young boys and converted to Islam. Muhammad bin Bakhtiyar Khalji, on the other hand, was a member of a nomadic people who lived to the east of the Ghur region of Afghanistan and were considered of humble social status by others. Turks who were not slaves also fought for Muhammad Ghuri and his successors in India, as did a number of mounted warriors from Khurasan, a Persian-speaking region encompassing modern eastern Iran, western Afghanistan, and Uzbekistan. The men fighting under Muhammad Ghuri's banner in India were a highly eclectic group: they came from a variety of ethnic communities, spoke several different languages, were sometimes but not always of nomadic background, and could be either enslaved or free. The multiplicity of their origins reflects the turbulent recent history of the lands to the west of the subcontinent, which served as a crossroads for peoples converging from all over Asia and the Middle East.

The sophisticated military system of their native Afghanistan was the principal reason for the success of the Ghurid armies in India. The ease of the Ghurid conquest has puzzled historians in the past, given the far greater agrarian wealth and population of the conquered Indian kingdoms that should have provided them with ample resources for military defense. Hence, early twentieth-century scholars often pointed to the lack of unity among Indians as the chief explanation for their defeat. Since the concept of India as a nation was still centuries away, Prithviraj Chauhan and Jayachandra Gahadavala – Muhammad Ghuri's opponents – had no incentive to forge a united front and indeed are depicted as mortal enemies in a later ballad that champions Prithviraj. Similarly, there was no sense of a common religious identity among Indian warriors at the time, for the notion of a unified Hinduism is a modern one. In the premodern period a variety of distinct sects, many of them focusing on a single deity rather than multiple ones, comprised what we group together today under the rubric of Hinduism. Recent historical scholarship instead attributes the victory of the Ghurid armies to a number of concrete advantages that gave them a distinct military edge.

The Ghurids were in a better position than Indian rulers in this age of cavalry warfare both in terms of the supply of horses and of trained manpower. Coming from Afghanistan, the Ghurids had easy access to the high-quality horses of Central Asia, Persia, and the Arabian Peninsula. The Indian subcontinent was, in contrast, ill suited for the breeding of horses. Since indigenous horses were inferior, Indian rulers had long imported horses from the regions to its west by various overland and maritime routes. Imported horses soon deteriorated in quality, however, because most of the subcontinent lacked good fodder and pasture lands. The Ghurids (and the later sultans of Delhi) were highly skilled in deploying horses in warfare. Employing a classic nomadic tactic of the Central Asian steppes, their light cavalry could fan out and flank the enemy from all sides, but still retreat quickly out of range of the enemy's heavy cavalry charge. The damage inflicted by the mounted archers of the Ghurid light cavalry was considerable, whereas Indian armies had few men accomplished enough to wield a bow while riding, according to the recent work of André Wink. Indian armies instead generally engaged in mass frontal attacks and employed rows of war-elephants to break enemy lines. Slow and cumbersome, the elephant, if panicked, might also inflict serious damage on its own troops.

Other factors also worked to the benefit of the Ghurid forces. Foremost among these was the highly centralized organization of their armies, for the Ghurids had a permanent core of professional soldiers who were accustomed to fighting together. Indian armies, on the other hand, were coalitions composed of the separate fighting forces under individual lords who were called for duty when required. As a consequence, they often failed to coordinate on the battlefield. All of these elements in conjunction resulted in a superior military system or complex that enabled the Ghurid armies to extend the political and cultural frontiers of the crossroads zone of Afghanistan, eastern Iran, and Uzbekistan well beyond the Punjab, where it had remained stationary for nearly two centuries.

Their intention to stay permanently in South Asia is indicated by the building of numerous monuments. Islamic texts on statecraft that would have been well known to the Ghurids required that kings establish large fortified palaces to display their power and wealth to the populace. In addition, mosques are essential for congregational prayer during which all Muslim men gather together around noon on Friday, the Muslim holy day. For a new ruler to achieve legitimate status, he needed to have his

Figure 2.1 This pseudo-arched newly carved façade was added as an entrance to the prayer chamber of Delhi's first congregational mosque in 1198.

name proclaimed during the Friday prayer as well as on coins. Inscriptional and textual evidence indicates that Aibak constructed many structures on behalf of his Ghurid lord including fine palace complexes, but the two most important surviving structures are the Jami (congregational) mosques in Delhi and Ajmer. The names by which these mosques are known today are not their original ones. The popular name of the Delhi Jami mosque, the one on which we focus our discussion since it was built first, is the Quwwat al-Islam, meaning the Might of Islam (Figure 2.1). If this name is accepted as its original one then there is an implicit suggestion that the mosque was intended as a victory statement over indigenous Indian religious traditions. However, as Sunil Kumar indicates, Quwwat al-Islam is simply a corruption of Qubbat al-Islam (Sanctuary of Islam), the title given to Delhi later in the thirteenth century and then subsequently applied to the Jami mosque and a nearby *dargah* (tomb-shrine) of an important Muslim saint.

The first phase of both the Delhi and Ajmer mosques used recycled materials, predominantly temple pillars, following building patterns used elsewhere in the Muslim world when Islam was initially introduced in a new region. These mosques had to be quickly built for practical and political reasons, especially in order to promote new dynastic authority. The most expedient method was to use precut materials taken from local temples. But all the same, a mosque that appeared as a rearranged temple must have seemed like an affront to those who had previously worshipped in those buildings. And perhaps a mosque built from pre-existing religious structures caused discomfiture to the mosque's patrons. This may be why a large five-arched free-standing screen was placed before the prayer chamber of the Delhi mosque in 1198, just a few years after its initial construction. Not using any spolia, that is, recycled material, this exquisitely carved work employing indigenous vegetal motifs combined with passages in Arabic from the Quran was clearly intended to evoke the arched appearance of the prayer chambers of contemporary mosques in the Ghurid homeland. Figure 1.3 of chapter 1 gives an idea of the façade that the Ghurids were attempting to emulate.

The second addition to the Delhi congregational mosque was commenced in 1199 (Figure 2.2). Known today as the Qutb Minar, it is modeled on and intended to surpass freestanding Iranian and Afghan minarets, in particular one built by the brother of Muhammad bin Sam in the Ghurid capital of Firuz Kot (today Jam) shortly before the construction of the Delhi minaret. By the time of its completion in the thirteenth century, the Qutb Minar was about 83 meters high, making it the tallest minaret in the world, and it served multiple purposes. Too tall for the call to prayer, its practical function was as a watch tower from whose top any approaching army could be seen for miles. Second, it may have been intended as a warning to those who did not convert to Islam, for the Arabic inscriptional bands that embellish its façade tell of the doom that awaits disbelievers on the day of judgment. But the fact that the script was alien in a land where only Brahmins were literate suggests its message went largely unnoticed.

The remaining inscriptions in Persian which proclaim the Ghurid overlord as the king of the Arabs and Persians, coupled with its vast scale, suggest that this minaret was less a religious symbol than one of political import. It was intended not only to legitimize Ghurid rule locally but also in the larger Islamic world. Through the establishment of religious sites, the alien territory of India was gradually assimilated into the far-flung Islamic civilization, and the diverse Muslim warriors of the Ghurid armies were provided a sacred space in common. This marked a radical break with the practice of Mahmud of Ghazni, who had no desire to absorb into his empire the localities of western and northern India that he repeatedly plundered for their wealth. And as home to numerous warriors from Afghanistan and its vicinity, India's course of historical development was now inextricably interwoven with that of its western neighbors.

Figure 2.2 This towering minaret, known as the Qutb Minar, is part of Delhi's first mosque complex, and was commenced in 1199.

The seemingly strident tone expressed in this state-sponsored mosque was not the only voice of Islam in the subcontinent. Sufis, Muslim mystics dedicated to seeking an immediate and personal relationship with god, had arrived in India even prior to the Ghurids. Sufis often served as a bridge between the new Muslim overlords and the large Indic population. The most important of these mystics, Muin al-Din Chishti (d. 1236), still generally regarded as India's supreme Sufi, came from Chisht in Afghanistan around the time of Prithviraj Chauhan's defeat by the Ghurids, and settled in the Chauhan capital, Ajmer. Hagiographies claim Muin al-Din, who achieved the status of a saint, attracted scores of followers charmed by his message of remembering and experiencing god through intense love. Because there are no contemporary sources or writings surviving from the time of Muin al-Din, early Chishti practice is unknown. During the thirteenth and fourteenth centuries, the Chishtis perfected an approach to spiritual union with god through a combination of *zikr* (recollection of god's ninety-nine names) and *sama* (music and song). Their extensive use of music in a religious context must have been appealing in the Indian setting, where poem-songs were often part of religious ceremony.

Carl Ernst and Bruce Lawrence have pointed out that, contrary to much popular belief, Sufism is not at odds with orthodox Islam but is rather part of it. The early Chishti mystics had to negotiate a difficult course of following orthodox Islamic practice, such as marrying and praying five times a day, while maintaining a vow of poverty and practicing an ecstatic form of Islam. Over the course of the thirteenth and fourteenth centuries, the Chishti order became a uniquely South Asian one, producing four significant spiritual heirs to Muin al-Din, among whom only Nizam al-Din Auliya (d. 1325) has earned the title Beloved of God. The early Chishtis, in particular Nizam al-Din, made a conscious effort to avoid the patronage of rulers; therefore, this mystic order can be seen as an alternative voice to the state, but not necessarily to orthodoxy. Prominent Sufis were buried in their humble abodes, which were then transformed into dargahs, that is, shrines replete with teaching facilities and kitchens for feeding the poor. Thus, the power of these saintly mystics to transform the lives of ordinary people endured even after death.

Early sultans of Delhi

Muhammad Ghuri's sudden death in 1206 precipitated an intense contest for power among the leading Turkic military slaves upon whom Muhammad had so heavily relied. Because the Indian portion of the Ghurid empire was severed from the home territory in Afghanistan in this power struggle, historians generally view 1206 as the beginning point of the Delhi Sultanate, a solely South Asian kingdom. The true architect of the Delhi Sultanate was Aibak's son-in-law and successor, Shams al-Din Iltutmish (r. 1210–36). Iltutmish consolidated Muhammad Ghuri's conquests, turning a motley collection of recently occupied towns into the most powerful state in north India. In order to do so, Iltutmish had to confront several problems that were to plague the Delhi Sultanate throughout its existence: the unclear nature of succession to the throne which led to constant disputes within the ruling elite, the continuing active resistance by Indian kings and chiefs, and the military threat from the west. Through his vigorous leadership, Iltutmish managed to strengthen the new kingdom sufficiently to ensure its survival for decades afterward.

While the extent of Delhi's territory under Iltutmish approximated the area conquered by Ghurid armies except in the northwest, conventional maps are misleading since they depict solid blocs of land throughout which the state's authority presumably held sway uniformly. In fact, Delhi's power was concentrated in a series of garrisoned towns and was diffused weakly from each of these centers out into the surrounding countryside – not unlike a string of colored lights in which certain bulbs (or towns) are dimmer and/or flicker off intermittently. A case in point is a mosque in nearby Bayana, only 187 kilometers southwest of Delhi, built by a rival of Iltutmish who proclaimed himself sultan and emperor (*padshah*) in the building's inscription; this underscores just how fragile the situation was.

Iltutmish continued with vigor the building campaign initiated by Aibak, for a dynamic construction program was a sign of a strong ruler. Near the Delhi mosque complex he added tanks to ensure the inhabitants had water, his civic duty. Tripling the size of the mosque there, he also completed the Qutb Minar. His own tomb was added to the rear of the complex. All of these additions were newly carved; stone-carved spolia was not used. By now a new type of sculptural form became the norm. Unlike the earlier organic, naturalistic carving seen on Aibak's screen, it consisted of only high and low relief, representing very abstracted floral and geometric patterns. This design type adhered closely to the aesthetic favored in the larger Islamic world, not surprising for a ruler who also used titles claiming he was master of the kings of the Arabs and Persians. But at the same time, as F. Flood has recently argued, Iltutmish, by erecting an iron pillar in the mosque's courtyard that predated the advent of Islam by several centuries, followed a traditional method used by Indian kings for proclaiming military victory. In this case, we see a continuity rather than a rupture with Indic tradition.

As elsewhere in the Islamic world, Iltutmish wished to provide his dynasty with a cosmopolitan urban setting, of which the mosque complex is all that survives today. Paralleling his desire for visual prominence, he also wished to make Delhi a center of learning and culture. He invited the elite, poets, scholars and others, from Central Asia to come to Delhi, where he rewarded them with land and patronage. Many were eager to do so, despite the Delhi Sultanate's frontier status, once the Mongols began their devastating attacks on regions that formed part of Islamic civilization, starting with Transoxiana (modern Uzbekistan) in 1219. The Mongols, descended from the feared warriors Genghis Khan and Khubilai Khan, twice entered South Asia during Iltutmish's reign but remained outside the Delhi Sultanate's territory. As a result, Delhi quickly became a safety net in a time of turmoil. To ensure the sophistication of Delhi's elite, Iltutmish had classic Arabic texts, religious and others, translated into Persian, the court language of the Delhi Sultanate. Chronicles and poetry were encouraged as well. The Mongol invasions of Iltutmish's reign thus only had an indirect impact on India. They contributed to the formation of a cosmopolitan elite in Delhi, which allowed the Sultanate to maintain a largely Muslim ruling class. At the same time, Mongol expansionism isolated the new state in India from its Islamic counterparts to the west, thereby ensuring that it would continue on an independent path.

The last strong ruler of the early Delhi Sultanate was Balban, who wielded effective power from 1249 until his death in 1287. During his long career, Balban managed to restore some measure of authority to the position of sultan, dealing harshly with any communities or localities that defied his commands. Despite Balban's efforts, however, Sultanate rule was constantly challenged both by rebellious Muslim officials and by the resurgent local kings and chiefs. The greatest threat faced by Balban was the incursions of the Mongols, who by the late 1250s had reached the Punjab. Fortunately for Delhi, internal tensions within the Mongol empire split it into several competing groups around 1260, and the Mongol armies were never again as large. The Mongols were the most reviled enemies of the Delhi Sultanate, described in far more vitriolic terms than ever were any Hindus. In spite of a similarity of language and style of warfare shared by the Turks and Mongols, the Turks had migrated to the Persian cultural sphere much earlier and were now Muslims, whereas the Mongols were still true nomads and followed a shamanistic religion. Eventually the Mongols who migrated to southern Russia, Iran, and greater Afghanistan converted to Islam and assimilated into the Turkic populations of those areas. But in the thirteenth century, the

Mongols epitomized the pagan barbarian in the minds of Delhi's ruling elite. The Mongols compounded their offense when they sacked Baghdad in 1258 and killed the Abbasid caliph, symbolically the ruler of all Sunni Muslims.

The Delhi Sultanate's expansionist phase

Reign of Ala al-Din Khalji

The Delhi Sultanate reached its peak during the reign of Ala al-Din Khalji (r. 1296–1316). He was the strongest of all Delhi sultans, centralizing power and ruthlessly suppressing all threats to his authority. The greatest military triumphs of the Sultanate were achieved under the direction of Ala al-Din, who called himself a second Alexander the Great, that is, a world conqueror. Due to Ala al-Din Khalji's military adventurism, the Delhi Sultanate became a force to be reckoned with over the entire subcontinent, in the south as well as in the north.

The advantages to be gained from raiding distant kingdoms were evident to Ala al-Din Khalji from the outset of his career. In 1296, while serving under the current sultan, Ala al-Din embarked on an unauthorized expedition against Devagiri, the capital of the south Indian Yadava kingdom in the western Deccan. Once victory was achieved, Ala al-Din, armed with tremendous wealth seized in the campaign, had the sultan assassinated. Although this act was condemned by later chroniclers, the gold and other treasure from Devagiri that Ala al-Din distributed liberally eliminated most of the opposition to his seizure of the throne.

After becoming sultan, Ala al-Din first targeted Gujarat in western India, a prosperous area both because of its agricultural fertility and its maritime trade. In 1299 his army raided the Somanatha temple on the Gujarat coast, well known in the Islamic world since Mahmud of Ghazni's raid on it in the early eleventh century. Next Ala al-Din besieged the formidable fortress at Ranthambhor in northern Rajasthan, which was ruled by a descendant of Prithviraj Chauhan. As the home of Rajasthan's most powerful kingdom, Ranthambhor was a logical starting point for Ala al-Din's bid to subjugate this region strategically situated between Delhi and the route to Gujarat as well as to the Deccan. After capturing Ranthambhor in 1301, Ala al-Din quickly seized the other celebrated fort of Rajasthan, Chittor, in 1303 and in 1305 Mandu, the capital of the neighboring Malwa kingdom in central India.

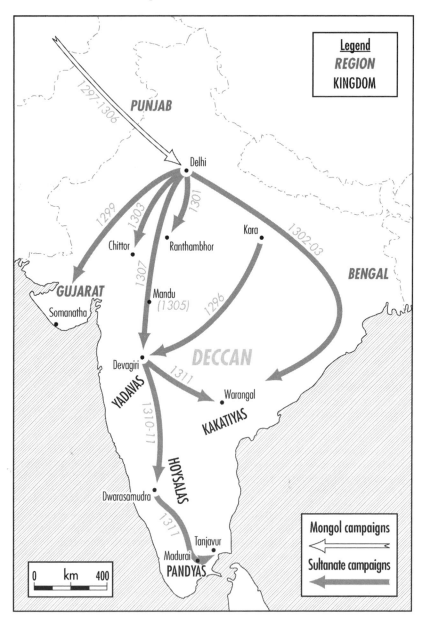

Map 2.2 Ala al-Din Khalji's compaigns (based on Keay, *India: A History*, p. 253)

Because Ala al-Din was preoccupied with the area south of Delhi, he neglected the long-standing threat to his realm from the west. The Mongols were becoming increasingly powerful and mounted massive attacks in the vicinity of Delhi in 1300 and again in the winter of 1302–03, while the bulk of the Sultanate forces were away from the capital on campaign. The fourteenth-century chronicler, Zia al-Din Barani, depicts the reaction of the Delhi population to the approaching Mongols in these words:

> The people of the adjoining districts all flocked into the fortress of Delhi, and the old fortifications had not yet been built up, so that such consternation among men has never been witnessed, nor even heard of; for all the inhabitants of the city both great and small were completely overpowered with terror.[1]

Luckily for Delhi's residents, the Mongols soon withdrew, perhaps because of power struggles back in Central Asia.

Galvanized into action by these Mongol attacks, Ala al-Din Khalji turned his attention to the improvement of his defenses. He provided a citadel on the plain known as Siri, north of the original city of Delhi, repaired the walls of the old city, and perhaps most significantly:

> issued orders that forts on the line of march of the Mughals [Mongols], which had gone to ruin, should be erected wherever they were required, and distinguished and able governors appointed to all these strongholds . . . He further commanded that they should make up numerous warlike engines, enlist expert marksmen, establish magazines for arms of all kinds and accumulate stores of grain and fodder . . . that numerous . . . troops should be . . . kept ready for service.[2]

For Ala al-Din, this Mongol invasion highlighted the importance of fortifying the frontier, since Delhi, despite its walls, would have been unable to withstand a concerted onslaught. Ala al-Din's new fortified walled city, Siri, was built on the plain where earlier he had defeated Mongol forces (see Map 7.1). Its foundation, along with a mosque and new palace on the site of victory, probably was intended to glorify his successful campaigns and himself.

Ala al-Din also commenced an ambitious enlargement of the first Delhi mosque built by Aibak that was intended to increase its size again by four times. Adjacent to this mosque is the shell of a second minaret which, if completed, would have dwarfed the Qutb Minar. Of the mosque's additions, only the south gate known as the Alai Darwaza, dated 1311, was ever completed. Introducing a new aesthetic of red and white stone, this

---

[1] Zia al-Din Barani, *The Reign of Alauddin Khilji, translated from Zia-ud-din Barani's Tarikh-i-Firuz Shahi*, trans. A. R. Fuller and A. Khallaque (Calcutta: Pilgrim Publishers, 1967), pp. 28–29.
[2] *Ibid.*, pp. 99–100.

Figure 2.3 Ala al-Din Khalji added this red and white stone entrance known as the Alai Darwaza to Delhi's first mosque complex in 1311.

gate would serve as an important visual source for Delhi's sixteenth-century cities (Figure 2.3). Unlike the earlier inscriptions on the mosque proper (excluding the minaret) which are almost completely religious in nature, Ala al-Din's entrance is peppered with epigraphs proclaiming his greatness and likening him to the victorious Darius the Great, Alexander, and even King Solomon. Ala al-Din built this gate after he improved Delhi's fortifications and as part of a campaign to restore the citizens' morale after their near defeat by the Mongols. The mosque, its sheer size a statement of the sultan's and Delhi's military strength, essentially underscored the message sent by the restoration of the city's walls and the construction of a new palace.

Despite Ala al-Din's restoration to Delhi's premier mosque, this ruler fares unfavorably in popular literature concerning his relations with the city's leading living Sufi, Nizam al-Din Auliya. The Sufi voice can be seen as a counter to that of the official state, but to cast the Sufi and state voice in terms of a polarity is overstating the situation. Nizam al-Din clearly was a charismatic religious thinker who wished to reduce human misery and suffering and to do so on his own terms without state support. While Nizam al-Din shunned direct contact with any sultan, he lived and worked in Delhi for about a half century as the head of the Chishti Sufi order. As a consequence of his physical proximity to the center of political power, several of the court's leading nobles, including the celebrated poet Amir Khusrau, became his ardent followers. This suggests that the rift between state and Sufi was not a great as might be believed. Other disciples of Nizam al-Din Auliya followed in the steps of Delhi Sultanate armies, as for instance to the western Deccan region that Ala al-Din Khalji later conquered, helping to disseminate Chishti teachings and thus ultimately leading to the order's pan-Indian popularity.

The critique by contemporaries that Ala al-Din lacked sufficient interest in religion may be accurate, for the sultan's main concerns were pragmatic. In order to maintain an effective large standing army, he introduced a number of economic and administrative reforms. Many of the new measures sought to increase the amount received by the state in taxes, while others attempted to control the cost of living so that the wages paid to soldiers could be kept low. So, for instance, Ala al-Din greatly enlarged the area directly taxed by the sultan's own treasury and raised the land tax to the high rate of half the estimated yield. He also enforced strict price controls in the Delhi area on vital items such as grains, cloth, sugar, oil, horses, and cattle.

While Ala al-Din's economic policies were implemented primarily so that he could support a larger military force, they had the supplemental effect of enhancing his power at the expense of others. Since the inception of the Delhi Sultanate, its nobles and officers had been recompensed for their service by means of the *iqta*, an assignment of revenues from a given area. Within the territory of his iqta, a Sultanate officer acted as the paramount political authority in charge of fiscal, administrative, and military affairs. He would retain a portion of the revenues he collected in lieu of a salary but was obligated to send the remainder on to Delhi. Ala al-Din not only increased the proportion of crown land in relation to that held in iqta, he also took steps to ensure that Delhi received its stipulated share of iqta revenues. Thus, Sultanate officers as well as merchants were now coming under heavier supervision by Delhi and undoubtedly experienced a loss of income.

With his enhanced military force, Ala al-Din resumed his strategy of plundering kingdoms to the south as the danger from the Mongols lessened. He no longer led the expeditions himself but sent in his place the notorious Malik Kafur, a former slave from Gujarat. The most ambitious of Kafur's campaigns occurred in 1310–11 when he attacked Dwarasamudra, the capital of the Hoysala kingdom in modern Karnataka state, and then marched to the Pandya territory in the far south, in modern Tamil Nadu. Kafur had less success against the Pandyas, who abandoned Madurai and other cities rather than face the enemy, than he did against the three other dynasties of the peninsula: the Yadavas, the Kakatiyas, and the Hoysalas. The siege of Warangal, the Kakatiya capital, is discussed at length by Amir Khusrau in his *Khazain al-Futuh* or Treasury of Victories, a eulogistic account of Ala al-Din's reign. Two formidable sets of fortifications protected Warangal for as long as four months. Malik Kafur had to erect high fences to protect his men from the stones hurled from within Warangal fort and build tall wooden structures as a means of scaling the walls. This suggests that dramatic advances had occurred in siege technology and fortifications since the time of the Ghurid conquests, when victories were won principally through battlefield engagements.

It is evident from Amir Khusrau's account that Ala al-Din's major objective was to acquire booty. Khusrau makes much of the gold, gems, and other precious items offered in tribute by the conquered kings of the Indian peninsula. The elephants and horses obtained from each place were recorded with particular detail, perhaps because they were essential war supplies as well as being valuable in their own right. So, for example, Khusrau tells us that 20,000 horses and 100 elephants were given up by the Kakatiya king, along with the famous diamond later known as the Koh-i Nur, meaning Mountain of Light. After each expedition, the best of the spoils brought back by Kafur was presented to the sultan in a public ceremony attended by the court elite. Less prized goods would already have been divided up among the soldiers. The campaigns to the peninsula hence benefited the military as a whole – providing them with practical battle experience and augmenting their salaries – in addition to serving as a source of additional income for the sultan. The defeated kings were reinstated on their thrones, but had to publicly acknowledge the overlordship of the Delhi sultan and send tribute on a regular basis. Failure to do so led to further military action on the part of the Delhi Sultanate, which sent several expeditions into the peninsula during Ala al-Din's reign. With the exception of the Yadava kingdom in modern Maharashtra, however, no attempt was made to annex these territories.

Ala al-Din Khalji's many conquests were long remembered, especially in Rajasthan and western India. Best known is the story of Ala al-Din's desire for the queen of Chittor, although it has little basis in historical fact. The earliest surviving version appears in Malik Muhammad Jayasi's *Padmavat*, written in 1540 in Avadhi, a medieval Hindi literary language. According to Jayasi, Ala al-Din attacked Chittor fort because of his longing for Padmavati, a queen whose beauty was legendary. Refusing to surrender her, Padmavati's husband is eventually captured and taken to Delhi, but manages to escape and return to Chittor. He dies soon thereafter, allowing Ala al-Din to capture Chittor fort, but the victory is an empty one, for Padmavati has already killed herself. Ala al-Din's love for a Yadava princess is the theme of another narrative, while an entire cycle of tales centers on his conflict with the king of Ranthambhor. Such stories cast the fierce military struggles of Ala al-Din's era in an overly romanticized light and should not be taken as historical truth; at the same time, they inform us that later generations of north Indians viewed Ala al-Din as a mighty conqueror whose actions were to change the history of many kingdoms.

Muhammad and Firuz Shah Tughluq: a rise and fall of fortunes

Although the repeated incursions of Delhi armies had weakened the states of the peninsula, only the Yadava kingdom had been taken over during the reign of the Khalji sultans. Under the Tughluqs (1320–1412), the next dynasty of the Delhi Sultanate, the political and cultural landscape of peninsular India was irrevocably altered. Decisive military actions were carried out by Muhammad Tughluq while he was still a subordinate of his father, Sultan Ghiyas al-Din Tughluq (r. 1320–24). Ghiyas al-Din came to prominence as a fighter against the Mongols and seized the throne after court intrigue led to the death of the last Khalji sultan. He further fortified Delhi by building an immense fortress, Tughluqabad, to the east of the original city of Delhi and Ala al-Din's city of Siri (see Map 7.1). Nineteenth-century British engineers who usually scorned Indian military fortifications had nothing but praise for Ghiyas al-Din's Tughluqabad.

As part of his military enterprise Ghiyas al-Din dispatched his son Muhammad to south India. In campaigns fought between 1321 and 1323, Muhammad captured the Kakatiya capital, Warangal, and the Pandya capital of Madurai. He also subdued the Hoysalas, thus bringing all the regional kingdoms of the peninsula under Delhi's control. Meanwhile, Ghiyas al-Din Tughluq had been consolidating Sultanate control in Bengal. A victory pavilion erected to commemorate his triumphant return in 1324 collapsed and killed him – whether this happened by accident or by Muhammad's design has been a matter of debate ever since.

The first of Muhammad Tughluq's many controversial acts as sultan (r. 1324–51) was the decision to make the western Deccan city of Devagiri the second capital of the realm, under the new name Daulatabad. Devagiri had proved invaluable as a forward base for campaigns further into the peninsula and Muhammad's decision was strategically sound. In his desire to make his second capital flourish, however, he forced many high-ranking Delhi Muslims to relocate to Daulatabad in 1327 and 1328. Although they could have numbered no more than a few thousand people, chroniclers claimed that Delhi was depopulated thereafter, meaning that everyone of significance to them had departed. The extent of suffering caused by the compulsory relocation to Daulatabad has no doubt been exaggerated, but it did earn Muhammad Tughluq the unanimous censure of later Indo-Islamic writers.

In a clear indication that he intended to retain Delhi as his primary seat of power, Muhammad Tughluq began a number of construction projects in Delhi which included fortifying the then unwalled areas between the original city of Delhi, Siri, and Tughluqabad. Naming this portion of Delhi Jahan Panah, that is, the Refuge of Religion, he constructed an elaborate palace complex attached to a huge mosque within its walls (see Map 7.1). In fact, the sultan needed these fortified walled areas within Delhi as a vast garrison because, not long after making Daulatabad his second capital, he started to raise an army that was huge, even by Indian standards, to send to the lands west of India. His intention was most probably to take the offensive against the Mongols who had twice raided north India during his reign, but a shortage of funds forced the abandonment of this project.

The innovative and bold nature of Muhammad Tughluq's thinking is also revealed in his introduction of a new kind of money. Beginning in about 1330, the Sultanate issued new brass and copper coins that were assigned a higher, arbitrary value rather than the actual value of their metallic content. The idea of a token currency was taken from the Chinese who were already using paper bills as money. The fact that there was a worldwide shortage of silver may also have inspired this scheme, which was soon undermined by widespread forgery of the new coins. As with other schemes that Muhammad devised, the idea of a token currency was imaginative but ultimately impractical. Muhammad's ambition to directly rule peninsular India and his various visionary projects were a considerable drain on the treasury. In response, Muhammad raised the land tax to an even higher level than had Ala al-Din Khalji, and he added several new taxes. The burden of this increased demand for revenue led the peasantry to rise up in revolt in 1332 and 1333.

The unsettled conditions in the Sultanate's north Indian heartland may have encouraged people elsewhere to break away from Delhi's control, for a series of rebellions occurred in the distant provinces from 1334 onward. In a little more than a decade after he became sultan, all the regions that Muhammad Tughluq and his father had added to the empire – Bengal and the former territories of the Kakatiyas, Pandyas, and Hoysalas – became autonomous once again. Muhammad Tughluq faced more setbacks in the last few years of his reign. Local military commanders in Gujarat and the Deccan, upset over Delhi's oppressive supervision of them, rose up in arms in 1345. After the leading Deccan rebel gained enough support to crown himself as an independent king in 1347 under the name Ala al-Din Bahman Shah, Muhammad gave up his attempts to regain Daulatabad and its vicinity. Instead, he concentrated on Gujarat in western India until his death three years later. Although the Tughluq sultans exercised direct control over the peninsula for a mere three decades, the consequences of their intervention were to last far longer. By shattering the existing political networks, they facilitated the rise of new political elites, both Hindu and Muslim. The Tughluqs had also successfully transplanted Indo-Islamic culture and religion to the western Deccan, where it continued to thrive under a series of regional sultanates. In this way, the cultural histories of north and south India were brought into closer proximity.

By the time Muhammad Tughluq died, the Delhi Sultanate was considerably smaller in size than it had been at the outset of his reign. His successor, Firuz Shah (r. 1351–88), largely refrained from military activity and the area under Sultanate control remained unchanged. Firuz Shah was also an indifferent administrator and allowed his nobles and officers to acquire more privileges and power than had his Khalji and Tughluq predecessors. Yet, Ala al-Din and Muhammad had left a sufficiently strong legacy of centralization that the Delhi Sultanate remained the paramount power of north India throughout Firuz Shah's lifetime and the turbulent succession of six other Tughluq sultans that followed.

In spite of Firuz Shah's weakness as an administrator, he was a prolific builder and provided yet another city, Firuzabad or Kotla Firuz Shah, to the north of Delhi's walled cities (see Map 7.1). Firuz Shah used architectural patronage as a means to give a visual boost to what was otherwise a relatively inept regime. Among his most interesting projects noted by several contemporary historians were the transport of two enormous stone monoliths dating to the third century BCE. Firuz Shah marked the two ends of his city not with walls, but with public references to India's ancient

Figure 2.4 The fourteenth-century Muslim ruler, Firuz Shah Tughluq, added this ancient stone monolith to his palace pavilion in Delhi, as a way of showing his Indic as well as Islamic origins.

past (Figure 2.4). While Firuz Shah did not know the actual dates or historical events associated with these two pillars, he was aware that they were of considerable antiquity – so old that the script written on them, which we today call Brahmi, could be deciphered by no living person. In time, these pillars from the reign of the Mauryan emperor Ashoka became associated with Alexander the Great, a hero in the Islamic tradition, thereby giving Firuz Shah a dual-edged legitimacy he needed to cover for his lack of an expansionist policy.

In a period of 200 years, Delhi was transformed from an insignificant garrison town to what Ibn Battuta, the Moroccan judge who stayed there in the 1330s, declared was the "largest of the cities of India, and even of all the cities of Islam in the East."[3] Following well-established Islamic precedent, Delhi's sultans each wished to establish separate cities in their own name in part to glorify themselves and in part to bolster the economy and thus the welfare of their subjects. All that survives of the projects of the earliest sultans are city walls and religious complexes which, as we noted, often had political agendas. For over a century, kingly patronage centered

[3] Ibn Battuta, *The Rehla of Ibn Battuta (India, Maldive Islands and Ceylon)*, trans. Mahdi Husain (Baroda: Oriental Institute, 1953), p. 24.

on Delhi's Jami mosque, adjacent to the Qutb Minar, as at least three ruling sultans enhanced its size, adding layers to its message of political legitimacy. It is only by the fourteenth century that we have a sense of a functioning city. Ibn Battuta describes the mosques, *madrasa*s (schools for religious instruction), palaces, elite mansions and water tanks, no longer extant, that so impressed him. Firuz Shah Tughluq added to the flourishing city his most important contribution. These were canals he had excavated, bringing much needed water from areas to the north of the city, thus encouraging agriculture essential to a healthy economy.

The Delhi Sultanate's military establishment was allowed to gradually decline from Firuz Shah's reign onward. Its weakness was fatally exposed in 1398, when the great Central Asian warlord Timur invaded India. The Sultanate could muster no more than a force of 10,000 cavalry in defense of the capital, which was easily seized and sacked by Timur's army for days. After centuries of struggle, Delhi had finally been defeated by the Mongols, for Timur, or Tamerlane as he is known in English literature, was a member of a minor Mongol tribe that had long been settled and undergone Turkic influence. A Tughluq sultan survived Timur's invasion and lived until 1412, and two subsequent dynasties – the Sayyids (1414–51) and the Lodis (1451–1526) – continued to rule from Delhi. The glory of the Delhi Sultanate had passed, however, and after 1398 it was no more than one among numerous states contending for power in north India.

Impact of the Delhi Sultanate

Delhi Sultanate as a conquest state

The Delhi Sultanate is usually described as an Islamic conquest state. That is, it is represented in standard accounts of Indian history as zealously Islamic in orientation, with a ruling elite that was alien to the subcontinent and oppressive in its treatment of indigenous peoples. The ideology of the Sultanate, as publicly expressed in its monuments and in its literary products, promotes this interpretation of it as militantly Islamic and fundamentally foreign. Let us again consider one famous example: the Qutb Minar and its accompanying mosque, the earliest monuments constructed at the seat of Sultanate power. As the tallest structure in India at the time, the Qutb Minar can be interpreted as a sign of the ascendance of foreign Muslims over non-Muslim Indians. But recall that the Qutb Minar was also the tallest minaret in the Islamic world. Thus, the height of the minaret testified to Islamic civilization as a whole, the greatness of this new polity established on the margins of *dar al-Islam* (the world of Islam) by Turks and other relative newcomers to the faith. While it is nowadays generally assumed that Sultanate monuments and texts were meant to convey certain messages to the Indians whom they had subjugated, the intended audience – at least during the first century of Sultanate rule – included fellow Muslims living both within and outside India.

Among the most important of the Muslims whom the Qutb Minar and other Sultanate cultural productions were trying to impress were the core supporters of the sultans, their military and administrative personnel. Without a shared language or region of origin, it was only Islam that could act as a focal point for the loyalties of these men from all over the wide expanse of Afghanistan, eastern Persia, and Central Asia. Moreover, because the authority of the Delhi sultans was often internally contested, it was in a ruler's best interests to promote himself as pious and therefore legitimate. Hence, military campaigns were described in chronicles not as expeditions for the purpose of amassing plunder but as attempts to spread the religion of Islam. Because of the many political advantages of adopting a militantly Islamic discourse, we must be careful not to take such statements at face value.

It is difficult, however, to get beyond the rhetoric – both of the Sultanate sources that cast its actors as warriors for the cause of Islam and of Indian language sources that portray indigenous leaders as defenders of *dharma* (righteousness) – and assess the actual impact of Sultanate rule on the people of north India. The group that suffered the greatest loss was undoubtedly those who had occupied the uppermost layer of political authority: the indigenous kings, along with their families and chief followers. These individuals were ousted from political control and their place was taken by Turk, Persian, and Afghan military leaders. Few Indians were permitted to attain high rank in the Delhi Sultanate until the fourteenth century and even then they were almost exclusively Muslims, albeit sometimes recently converted. The Sultanate commanders were few in number; they stayed mainly in the garrisoned cities while the countryside was left largely in the hands of local chiefs and lords. Since the Sultanate consisted of a thin veneer of personnel overlaid on the pre-existing rural power structure, its disruptive effects were experienced mainly by the most elite Indians. For less powerful Indians, life must have continued much as it had prior to the establishment of the Delhi Sultanate. Suggesting this are, for example, graffiti carved by indigenous masons in obscure places on Delhi's Jami mosque that give the sultan good wishes or thank the Hindu deity Vishvakarma (Divine Architect) for its fine workmanship.

A second group that was most probably adversely affected by the imposition of Sultanate rule were religious specialists like Brahmins, Hindu temple priests, Jain monks, and sectarian leaders. Though not actively persecuted, they were dependent on the patronage of kings, chiefs, and other local magnates and the amount of financial support available to them declined notably with the elimination of the indigenous ruling elite. Learned Brahmins and Jains had also often served as ministers and counselors in the courts of indigenous kings, an opportunity that similarly diminished during the thirteenth and fourteenth centuries. However, the influence of some Hindu and Jain groups apparently reemerged as they began to serve as money lenders and bankers to royal houses, both Muslim and non-Muslim.

The bulk of the non-Muslim population of India was largely left to pursue its religions in peace. Though technically infidels, Indians had been classified as *zimmis* by the first Islamic rulers in the subcontinent, the eighth-century Arabs of Sind, and this practice was followed by subsequent Muslim kings. Because it was originally a category reserved for Christians and Jews who, as "people of the book," had a shared religious tradition with Muslims, those defined as zimmi were allowed to practice their own religions without interference. Since theoretically they did not perform military service on behalf of the state, unlike male Muslims, in theory they were expected to pay the *jizya* tax. Perhaps due to the fact that the vast majority of the rural populace were non-Muslim, the Delhi sultans do not appear to have levied a separate jizya tax on the Indian peasantry. Moreover, the size of these armies suggests that a considerable percentage must have been non-Muslims. And the only firm evidence that non-Muslim urban residents had to pay the jizya comes from the late fourteenth-century reign of Firuz Shah Tughluq (r. 1351–88), although it is possible that they had to do so previously in the major Sultanate cities.

Despite the supposedly protected status of zimmi religions, Hindu and Jain temples in India were sacked, damaged, and even destroyed on occasion. The most serious accusation made in modern times against the Delhi sultans, as well as subsequent Muslim rulers in India, is that they deliberately engaged in a policy of plundering Hindu temples and destroying images of the gods. It is well known that Islam prohibits the worship of idols and that the destruction of religious images by Muslims has been an intermittent feature of Islamic history. But it is virtually impossible to estimate the exact extent of such iconoclastic activity in India. For one thing, authors of Indo-Islamic texts typically inflated the extent of damage inflicted on "idol-houses" in order to glorify the image of the sultan whom they were praising. Secondly, there are a series of different acts that are subsumed under the category of temple desecration, ranging from the looting of temple treasuries to the defacing of an image and the complete destruction of temple buildings. Richard M. Eaton has recently argued that there are no more than eighty confirmed instances of temple desecration from the 500 plus years between 1192 and 1729. While his is a conservative estimate, it is likely to be far closer to the truth than the figure of thousands of destroyed temples that is sometimes claimed, without evidence, by today's Hindu nationalists.

Temple desecration was not a random act but typically occurred in the context of a moving frontier of military conflict. That is, temples that were damaged or destroyed by Muslim rulers were almost always situated within an enemy's (or rebel's) territory, had a strong connection with the enemy, and were attacked in the course of warfare. This was a practice known in the Indian subcontinent well before Islam became a political force, although it was never common. Desecrating a god and an institution associated with an enemy king was a serious blow to his claim to kingship and could also be very attractive for financial reasons – the motives for temple desecration were by no means restricted to Islamic hostility to idol worship. Once an area had been incorporated into Sultanate territory or had come to terms with it, its temples were rarely desecrated. Most of the Delhi sultans allowed new temples to be constructed and old ones to be renovated, although this was not permissible according to a strict interpretation of Islamic law. Aside from the loss of a certain amount of royal patronage, therefore, Indian religions do not appear to have suffered greatly from the rise to dominance of Muslim kings.

The Delhi Sultanate was, in a formal sense, Islamic. The sultans did not allow open violations of Islamic religious law and they appointed Muslim scholars to profitable offices. All the same, state policy was based not on Islamic law or the desire to extend Islam, but on the pragmatic realities of maintaining the rule of a minority over a large subject population. Indeed, both Ala al-Din Khalji and Muhammad Tughluq were criticized by Ziya al-Din Barani, a well-known literary figure of the fourteenth century, for their lack of concern for Islamic law. For the mass of Indian people, the negative repercussions of the rule of sultans like Ala al-Din Khalji and Muhammad Tughluq resulted not from their Islamic affiliation but from the fact that they were strong rulers who attempted to increase their own power by extracting higher tax revenues. During the reign of Muhammad Tughluq, peasants near the capital rebelled as a result of the severity of the state's revenue demands. In other parts of north India, the life of the average Indian peasant appears little affected by the rule of the distant Delhi overlords.

A consequence of Sultanate rule that may have had the worst repercussions on the life of the Indian masses was an increase in the scale of slavery.

This cannot be attributed to the Islamic affiliation of the new kings, for slavery had been practiced in the Middle East prior to the advent of Islam. The acquisition of slaves was a major objective in South Asian campaigns of the Mongols who at that point had not yet converted to Islam. Nor was slavery unknown previously in India. But both the volume and character of slavery changed during the thirteenth and fourteenth centuries. In earlier times, people in India became slaves mainly because they were in debt and also sometimes out of religious devotion to a god or goddess. Slavery as a result of being captured in warfare seems to have been rare until the Sultanate period. Because Islam condoned the enslavement of non-Muslim captives at times of war (although not of Muslim captives), people in areas that were hostile to the Sultanate militarily or which refused to pay taxes were enslaved in considerable numbers. Rather than remaining within their localities, as had been the case with those enthralled in debt bondage in the past, slaves in Sultanate territory might be sold in the flourishing slave market of Delhi and sent to destinations as far off as Central Asia. But the majority probably remained in India, where only a few achieved the elite status of a military slave, while the rest worked in domestic settings. By the fifteenth century, slavery was once again on the wane in India, evidently due to the availability of cheap skilled labor.

On a more positive note, historians of the Delhi Sultanate have often pointed to the growth of cities and an increased use of money as two notable trends of thirteenth- and fourteenth-century north India, particularly within the region between the Sutlej river and the upper Ganges. One cause of greater urbanization in this Lahore–Delhi–Agra corridor, the heartland of both the Delhi Sultanate and the later Mughal empire, was the fact that the Sultanate's ruling class resided largely in cities, where they spent the agrarian revenues extracted from the countryside. New manufacturing technologies – in the building trades, in paper-making, and in spinning – also contributed to the flourishing of urban economies, as did the escalating trade along the overland routes, in the aftermath of the Mongol conquests throughout much of Eurasia. The high quality of Delhi Sultanate coins, in contrast to the debased coinage that had circulated in northern India during the previous few centuries, is testimony both to a high level of international trade and the military might of the sultans. Through the conquest of Bengal, for instance, the Delhi Sultanate acquired a steady source of silver metal. Similarly, tribute from the successful campaigns against the regional kingdoms of western and southern India was another way large sums of metal money were injected into the north Indian economy. There is little firm evidence from this era, unfortunately, and it is therefore difficult to say whether the economic growth of north India in the Sultanate era was truly as dramatic as some scholars would suggest.

India in a growing world system

What happened in India beginning in the late twelfth century was part of a larger trend occurring throughout much of Eurasia, in which nomadic peoples migrated from the steppes of Inner Asia and became politically dominant over sedentary agrarian societies. Rather than characterizing the establishment of the Delhi Sultanate as the "invasion" or "conquest" of India by a foreign group, it is more useful to understand that the entire settled world of West and South Asia was being transformed in this era through the influx of people of nomadic background and their military technologies.

This was not the first time in Indian history that peoples of nomadic origin had moved into South Asia. India's susceptibility to recurrent waves of migration from the northwest is explained by its geography: although there are large pockets of fertile land suited to intensive agriculture, the subcontinent also has a broad semi-arid expanse extending from the Indus valley, through Rajasthan, and into central India and the Deccan. This so-called arid zone, with its pasturelands, had long served as a corridor for the movement of pastoral-nomadic peoples and their herds. From the twelfth century onward, the arid zone became a more decisive factor in Indian history due to improvements in livestock, advances in horse-riding technology, and the greater political influence of arid zone peoples. Many of the most innovative changes of this period took place on the frontier between the arid zone and settled society. Like the Indian seacoast, which comprised a frontier between the maritime zone of the Indian Ocean and the Indian hinterland, the inner frontier along the arid zone was a place of social dynamism and fluidity.

The last, and greatest, wave of nomadic migration occurred in the thirteenth century, when the Mongol tribes were united by Genghis Khan and rapidly expanded out of Mongolia and Inner Asia. This time the course of history was altered not only in West and South Asia but also equally in China, Russia, and Eastern Europe. Although internal dissensions among Mongols are the primary reason that India was spared greater devastation, the Sultanate's ability to mobilize large numbers of fighting men with some expertise in the cavalry tactics of Central Asia, used to maximum effect by the Mongols, must have been a contributing factor. Had the Ghurid armies not successfully established themselves in the subcontinent by the late twelfth century, it is possible that at least the

northwestern sections of South Asia would have come under the dominion of a Mongol or other Central Asian power.

The most important result of the establishment of the Delhi Sultanate
was the incorporation of South Asia into the growing geographic sphere
of Islam. Ties between north India and the eastern Persian world were
reinforced due to the presence in the subcontinent of many fighting men
whose family origins lay in Central Asia, Afghanistan, or Khurasan. The
initial Mongol incursions into Iran led to an even greater cultural link
between north India and the lands to the west, as scholars and administrators fled to Sultanate territory for refuge. With the conversion of most
Mongol groups to Islam over time, the world of Islam became even larger:
it covered a huge band of territory from the borders of China in the east
to eastern Europe in the west. While overland travel in Eurasia may have
reached its peak during the late thirteenth and early fourteenth centuries
due to the ease of travel through a succession of Mongol territories, maritime routes across the Indian Ocean continued to be vigorously utilized.
From East Africa in the west to South China in the east, ships converged
on the coasts of the Indian peninsula. Islam was transmitted by maritime
routes as well and gradually spread into Southeast Asia by the fourteenth
century.

Through its integration into this expansive realm, within which a common religion and culture circulated widely, India itself became a considerably more cosmopolitan place. The best way to illustrate this may be
through following the career of Abu Abd Allah ibn Battuta, the famous
Muslim traveler who spent several years in India during the reign of
Muhammad Tughluq. Ibn Battuta came from Morocco, in the far western reach of the Islamic world, and had traveled across north Africa to the
Arabian peninsula and toured Asia Minor, Palestine, Syria, Iraq, Persia,
and Central Asia, as well as the east coast of Africa and part of eastern
Europe prior to arriving in South Asia in 1333. After almost eight years
in Sultanate territory, Ibn Battuta was assigned to a diplomatic mission
to China. He traveled by ship down the coast of southwestern India,
but his mission came to grief when a storm sank his ship along with the
gifts to be taken to China. Afraid to face the Delhi sultan's wrath, Ibn
Battuta spent over two years working for local rulers in southern India,
Sri Lanka, and even the Maldive Islands, a group of small islands lying
more than 600 kilometers off the southwest coast of the subcontinent. He
then went to south China on his own before slowly wending his way back
to north Africa. In the course of his life, Ibn Battuta traversed 120,000
kilometers, far more than Marco Polo had fifty years earlier. What is most
remarkable about his travels is that virtually all of them occurred within
the *dar al-Islam*, "the abode of Islam," whether to Mali or Sumatra or the

Volga river. Even when he had left the region where Islam prevailed, as in southern China or south India, Ibn Battuta resided with local Muslims and enjoyed their hospitality. On his initial trip down the coast of south-western India, Ibn Battuta noted that "in all the resting-places along this road there are houses of the Muslims with whom the Muslim travelers lodge; from them they buy everything which they need."[4]

Like many people from his native Morocco, Ibn Battuta was most probably not an Arab by ethnicity. But he was culturally an Arab and a member of the ulama or educated class. His "Arab" identity stood him in good stead when he arrived in India, for Muhammad Tughluq was actively recruiting officials of foreign – that is, non-Indian – birth and especially favored Arabs. Ibn Battuta was granted the position of *qazi* or judge in Delhi and assigned two Persian-speaking deputies. Arabic was not unknown in India but Persian was the primary literary language – a situation that is nicely illustrated in Ibn Battuta's first audience with Muhammad Tughluq when he addressed the sultan in Arabic but the sultan responded in Persian. Ibn Battuta picked up some Persian during his sojourn in north India. With knowledge of just the two languages of Arabic and Persian, a gentleman-traveler could make himself understood throughout much of the civilized world of the fourteenth century.

Ibn Battuta was an exceptional man, of course, and not representative of the typical official of the Delhi Sultanate. But the fact that he was able to travel with relative ease over so large an area of the globe demonstrates the wide-ranging social and economic networks in existence during his day. The founding of the Delhi Sultanate drew India firmly into these international networks and into the multicultural and pluralistic society that had been created by adherents of Islam. The thirteenth and fourteenth centuries were an exciting if turbulent age, during which a man's fortunes could rapidly rise or equally rapidly decline. It was an era of escalating circulation – of goods, of peoples, of technologies, and of ideas. The passing of political power to Turkic Muslims, in the form of the Delhi Sultanate, may initially have been disruptive and even devastating for Indian elites. In the long term, however, the cultural and social enrichment that resulted from participation in the world's most cosmopolitan civilization of the middle ages was to become an inextricable part of India's greatness.

[4] *Rehla of Ibn Battuta*, p. 182.

3 / Southern India in the age of Vijayanagara, 1350–1550

question 1. (11-18-13 worksheet)

The rise of the Delhi Sultanate, although it brought many changes to north India, had little direct impact on the lands south of the Narmada river. Only from around 1300, when the Delhi Sultanate began sending armies down into the peninsula, did the histories of these two parts of the subcontinent start to converge. The military successes of the Delhi Sultanate gave a north Indian state control over portions of south India for the first time in many centuries. Although the Delhi Sultanate did not retain this control for long, its intervention into the affairs of the peninsula was to have long-lasting repercussions. Because a separate state headed by Central Asian Muslim warriors known as the Bahmanis was founded in the Deccan in 1347, the Islamic religion and culture that had taken root in the Deccan under the Tughluq sultans of Delhi continued to flourish in subsequent times. Another significant result of Delhi's military expeditions was the destruction of the existing regional kingdoms of the south. This paved the way for the emergence of Vijayanagara, a new state ruled by indigenous warriors that shaped the society and culture of south India for centuries thereafter. The empire of Vijayanagara is often credited with preserving a distinctly Hindu way of life in south India that had been lost in the north, a misconception that overlooks both the creativity and cosmopolitan nature of the Vijayanagara elite. By 1550, south India was a considerably more diverse and complex place than it had been in 1300.

Rise and decline of the Vijayanagara kingdom

Political history of the Deccan

The origins of the Vijayanagara kingdom have been a subject of intense debate. We know that its first rulers were two brothers belonging to the Sangama family, but opinions on where they came from and what they did prior to becoming independent lords differ greatly. For much of the twentieth century, it was thought that the Sangama brothers were warriors of a local king defeated by the Delhi sultan whose service they then

entered, converting to Islam in the process. Only after they had been
sent from Delhi to the Karnataka region of south India as the sultan's
representatives did the Sangamas return to the Hindu fold and set up
their own independent kingdom, with the help of a Hindu sage, according to this line of thinking. Implicit in this narrative is the conception of
Vijayanagara as an overtly Hindu state, originating from a rejection of
the Islamic religion and a Muslim overlord. Scholars also disagreed on
whether the Sangamas were warriors initially from the Karnataka region
or from the Andhra region to its east, since both regions wished to claim
them as sons of the soil.

More recent scholarship, particularly by Hermann Kulke and Phillip
Wagoner, has presented a radically different interpretation of the events
leading to the founding of Vijayanagara. While the Sangama brothers were
probably local warriors from Karnataka who first served in the army of
the Hoysala king, they neither converted to Islam nor were they affiliated
with a Hindu sage. Instead, they appear to have voluntarily given political
allegiance to Muhammad Tughluq during the years when he was based at
Daulatabad. Once Tughluq power waned in the Deccan, the Sangamas
sought to establish their own state and held a major ceremony in 1346
to celebrate their conquests up to that time; this probably marks the
true commencement of their kingdom, rather than the traditional date of
1336. Because the Sangamas were but the first of four ruling dynasties,
we call the kingdom not after the kings but after the new name coined
for the capital, Vijayanagara or "City of Victory." Today the site is known
both as Vijayanagara and also as Hampi, a variation on the name of the
goddess, Pampa Devi, long associated with the region.

Although the Vijayanagara kingdom was to eventually become the
largest state ever created in south India, its expansion occurred quite
slowly. In its first decades, the various members of the extended Sangama
family ruled in a semi-autonomous fashion the different provinces of the
small kingdom, extending only from central and southern Karnataka into
the interior portion of southern Andhra. In the first half of the fifteenth
century, the state finally began to grow after power was consolidated
within one lineage of the Sangamas. Under Devaraya II (r. 1432–46),
generally considered to be the greatest of the Sangama dynasty of rulers,
Vijayanagara controlled both the eastern and western coasts of the
Deccan and was the pre-eminent state of the peninsula.

Vijayanagara's chief rival during its first century of existence was the
Bahmani Sultanate, established as an independent state in 1347 after a
revolt among the officers of the Delhi Sultanate stationed in the Deccan.
The Bahmani capital was soon moved from Daulatabad to the more
centrally located Gulbarga and then during the 1420s to Bidar. The

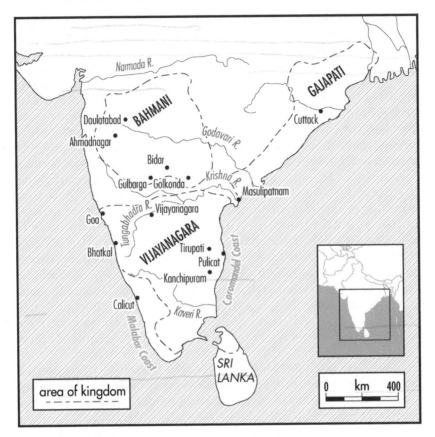

Map 3.1 South India in the fifteenth century

Bahmanis held sway in the western Deccan north of the Krishna river, while Vijayanagara was dominant in the western Deccan south of the Tungabhadra river. The alluvial zone in between those rivers, known as the Raichur *doab*, was hotly contested by the two states; both also tried to extend their influence into the fertile Krishna-Godavari river delta of the Andhra region to the east. A third area of conflict between the two states was the western coast, which would confer direct access to the maritime routes of Indian Ocean trade and thus to the most important military supplies of the time: war horses imported from Arabia, Persia, and Central Asia.

Initially, Vijayanagara troops could not prevail over the smaller army of the Bahmani sultan. The sultan's advantage was in cavalry and so he was known as the Ashvapati or Lord of Horses, in contrast to the

Vijayanagara king who was called the Lord of Men or Infantry (Nara-pati). Only after the borrowing of both military personnel and technologies from the Bahmani Sultanate was the Vijayanagara kingdom able to expand its sphere of influence. Devaraya II (r. 1432–46) was largely responsible for narrowing the military gap, welcoming Muslims, highly respected for their martial skills, to the state. Significantly, Muslims were defined not in religious terms but by ethnic labels such as Turk. Devaraya II reputedly enlisted 200 Muslims at the officer rank, as well as many more at lower levels – up to 10,000, according to a probably exaggerated claim. As early as 1439, one of these officers had a mosque constructed in the section of the capital city that became a Muslim quarter (see Figure 3.7). A number of Muslim tombs dot the surrounding area, indicating an elite Muslim presence. The adoption of advanced military techniques and the importation of war-horses contributed considerably to the success of Devaraya II's military ambitions.

A second major competitor for power from Devaraya II's reign onward was the Hindu dynasty of the Gajapatis, who had usurped the throne of northeastern Andhra and southern Orissa in the 1430s. Ruling a humid and forested region where elephants were still plentiful, the title "Lord of the Elephants" or Gajapati was given to these Orissa kings by their contemporaries, in admiration of their supply of war-elephants. After Devaraya II's death in 1446, his less capable successors could not contain Gajapati power and the Gajapatis began to overrun Vijayanagara's eastern lands, eventually reaching as far south as the Kaveri delta in the central Tamil country. They also wrested portions of northern Andhra away from Bahmani control. By the 1480s, the Vijayanagara kingdom had lost so much territory to the Gajapatis and the Bahmanis, who had overrun much of the west coast, that it was scarcely larger than it had been at its inception. This led Saluva Narasimha, the most active general in the struggle against Vijayanagara's enemies, to usurp the throne in 1485. The short-lived Saluva dynasty was ousted in turn in 1505 when another general, this time from the Tuluva family, seized power. Under the Tuluvas, the third royal dynasty of Vijayanagara, the kingdom not only regained its strength but went on to achieve its greatest glory.

Krishnadeva Raya (r. 1509–29), the second of Vijayanagara's Tuluva rulers, is largely responsible for making Vijayanagara the paramount polity in the peninsula. Ascending the throne while in his twenties, Krishnadeva Raya pursued a vigorous policy of consolidating Vijayanagara power from the outset. He is best known for the aggressive campaign against the Gajapatis initiated in 1513 which led to the recovery within two years of important sites situated to the south of the Krishna river. Vijayanagara forces kept pressing northward until they reached Cuttack,

question 3

the Gajapati capital in southern Orissa, in 1517. The Gajapati king eventually surrendered and offered his daughter in marriage to Krishnadeva, who in turn gave all the coastal territory north of the Krishna river back to the Gajapatis. Krishnadeva Raya's Orissa campaign has been called "one of the most brilliant military episodes in the history of sixteenth-century India."[1]

Partly because of his many military successes, Krishnadeva Raya was the most celebrated Vijayanagara king among later generations of south Indians. Even Domingo Paes, a foreign visitor to Vijayanagara city during the period when Krishnadeva Raya was king, praises him as "a great ruler and a man of much justice." In physical appearance, however, Krishnadeva Raya was not impressive, for Paes describes him as "of medium height, and of fair complexion and good figure, rather fat than thin, he has on his face signs of small-pox."[2] Krishnadeva Raya was reputedly quite hospitable to foreigners who came to his capital seeking trade, although Paes, as a minor member of a Portuguese delegation from Goa, had little direct contact with him. Nonetheless, Paes witnessed much of the city's public life and left behind a travel account that is valuable both for its many details and because it is the only foreign testimony contemporary to Krishnadeva's reign.

Vijayanagara was able to become dominant in the early sixteenth century not only because of the military abilities of kings like Krishnadeva Raya but also because its second important rival, the Bahmani Sultanate, had begun to disintegrate into smaller segments. The Bahmanis could not contain the long-term factionalism between the Deccanis, who were mainly descendants of settlers from north India and saw themselves as the old nobility, and new immigrants known as Afaqis, from Iran and Central Asia. The provincial governors of Bijapur and Ahmadnagar were independent by 1500 for all practical purposes, while the separate states of Golkonda, Berar, and Bidar emerged over the next few decades from what was left of the Bahmani Sultanate. Krishnadeva Raya had little trouble establishing Vijayanagara supremacy over the armies of the Bahmanis and their now virtually autonomous governors in 1509. He also brought the southern territories more firmly under control. With growing numbers of Vijayanagara *nayaka*s or warrior lords settled in the various localities of the Tamil country, the mantle of Vijayanagara rule came to rest more heavily on the far south.

---

[1] K. Nilakantha Sastri, *A History of South India from Prehistoric Times to the Fall of Vijayanagar*, 3rd edn (Madras: Oxford University Press, 1966), p. 281.
[2] "Narrative of Domingo Paes," in *A Forgotten Empire (Vijayanagara)*, trans. Robert Sewell (Delhi: Asian Educational Services, 1982 [1900]), pp. 246–47.

During Krishnadeva Raya's reign, the Vijayanagara kingdom attained its largest size and its greatest degree of centralization, although small tributary states under the rule of their own kings lingered on in portions of southern Karnataka, southern Tamil Nadu, and along the western seaboard. Command over the outlying territories was entrusted to elite Vijayanagara warriors, often men with the title nayaka who carried out both military and civilian duties. With increasing frequency from the late fifteenth century on, members of the ruling class were rewarded with the assignment of *nayamkara* territories – villages, districts, or even entire provinces over which they had the right to retain certain revenues. Taxes on agricultural produce and the selling or transport of goods as well as the fee on grazing animals, that would otherwise be owed to the king, were instead given to the man who held the nayamkara assignment. The expectation was that the assigned revenues would be used to maintain troops in readiness for the overlord's military needs. The king had the right to revoke a nayamkara assignment or switch the land included in a nayamkara, so that no subordinate could build up his own local power base and pose a challenge to the king.

Some of the duties and privileges of Vijayanagara's nayaka lords are described by Paes, in the following passage:

These captains whom he [the king] has over these troops of his are the nobles of his kingdom; they are lords, and they hold the city, and the towns and villages of the kingdom; there are captains amongst them who have a revenue of a million and a million & half of *pardaos*, others a hundred thousand *pardaos*, others two hundred, three hundred or five hundred thousand *pardaos*, and as each one has revenue so the king fixes for him the number of troops he must maintain, in foot, horse, and elephants . . . Besides maintaining these troops, each captain has to make his annual payments to the king . . . Whenever a son happens to be born to this king, or a daughter, all the nobles of the kingdom offer him great presents of money and jewels of price, and so they do to him every year on the day of his birth.[3]

The Vijayanagara lords were, in other words, required to maintain a stipulated number of troops and to make annual revenue payments to the king, depending on the size of the nayamkara territory they were assigned. In addition, they were expected to give the king gifts on special occasions. Other evidence indicates that lords who did not fulfill their obligations had their nayamkara assignments taken away.

Two Tuluva rulers followed Krishnadeva Raya on the Vijayanagara throne, but internal struggles at court and the increasing independence of the major lords led to a weakening of the king's position. From the

[3] Ibid., pp. 280–81.

1540s on, Rama Raya of the powerful Aravidu family acted in the name
of the king and wielded the actual power. For more than twenty years,
Rama Raya ruthlessly repressed all opposition at court and in the southern territories. He also kept the Deccan states that had emerged from
the Bahmani Sultanate's demise at bay through skillfully playing one off
against another. His brilliant, if deceitful, strategy eventually backfired –
their distrust of Vijayanagara grew so strong over the years that the rulers
of Ahmadnagar, Bijapur, and Golkonda overcame their own mutual hostility and banded together to attack Vijayanagara forces. At the fateful
battle of Talikota in 1565, Rama Raya was killed and the city of Vijayanagara left defenseless. Rama Raya's brother Tirumala soon abandoned the
capital and retrenched in southern Andhra, where he became the first
member of the Vijayanagara's final royal dynasty, the Aravidus. Although
the Vijayanagara kingdom, now based in Andhra and much smaller in
size, remained in existence for another century, its days of greatness were
gone after 1565.

Vijayanagara's militarism

Vijayanagara is widely acknowledged to be the most militarized of the
non-Muslim states of south India. Much of this militaristic orientation
was a result of its origins as a polity created by an upwardly mobile warrior lineage in the Deccan. The semi-arid environment of the peninsular
interior had long hosted peoples engaged in slash-and-burn agriculture,
herding, and trade. The upland economy was precarious, encouraging
the development of martial skills and the emergence of warlords. Since
the late twelfth century, warriors from the semi-arid zone had become
politically dominant throughout the peninsula. Facilitating their dominance were improvements in horse-riding equipment that had disseminated from the northwest into the Deccan during the century or two prior
to the establishment of the Vijayanagara state. The innovations included
the foot-stirrup providing greater support for the rider, better harnesses
allowing more control over the horse, high saddles with pommels, and
nailed horseshoes. These changes in horse-riding technology enhanced
the destructive capabilities of cavalry and made it the decisive factor in
an army's success in battle. The availability of quality horses, which had
also contributed to the Ghurid and Delhi Sultanate's military successes,
was another factor leading to greater militancy in the peninsula in the
period immediately before the founding of Vijayanagara.

The early fourteenth-century incursions of the Khalji and Tughluq
armies, by dislodging indigenous warrior lineages from their positions of
power, further promoted the growth of militarism in the peninsula. In

the power vacuum that resulted from the disruption of earlier political networks, there was plenty of scope for military adventurism for those with sufficient martial skills and motivation. The Sangama founders of Vijayanagara came out of this turbulent and competitive milieu and were successful in carving out a territory at the expense of numerous others who similarly aspired to kingship. The Bahmani Sultanate, with its more sophisticated cavalry techniques, was a persistent opponent to Vijayanagara's expansionist ambitions and this forced Vijayanagara to commit more resources to building up its army.

But Vijayanagara's militaristic character cannot be attributed to the presence of Muslim states in its vicinity, for this was an era when the scale and lethal capacity of armed force was escalating not only throughout the subcontinent but also throughout most of the Eurasian landmass. Armies were increasing in size, new weapons were being introduced, and more massive fortifications were being erected to defend the centers of political power. Gunpowder was introduced into thirteenth-century India by the Mongols, who learned about it from the Chinese. Gunpowder was first used to create burning projectiles or exploding devices that were used primarily during siege warfare. By the second half of the fifteenth century, gunpowder also came to be used in cannons, to propel a ball through the metal tube. According to one text, as many as 2,300 cannon and many smaller guns were deployed by the Vijayanagara army at the battle of Talikota in 1565.

The Vijayanagara capital was a massive site, the largest surviving in South Asia today, the defensive walls of which were intended to fend off invaders physically and at the same time overwhelm viewers by their awesome scale. Abd al-Razzaq, an emissary who arrived in the city in 1443 from Herat, was clearly impressed by the surrounding walls, for he notes that there were seven concentric walls, although in reality there are fewer. Huge earth-packed and stone-faced walls surrounded the suburbs and nearby villages. These walls were commenced with the city's founding and as the state became increasingly militaristic in nature, the importance of having massive walls grew. Recent work indicates that some 650 square kilometers were encircled by these huge walls, manned by soldiers who monitored from ramparts, watch posts, and bastions the broad roads that ran in and out of the city. The walls also served daily needs, for catchment basins and reservoirs were part of the protective walls. The ground between the various walled areas of the greater Vijayanagara metropolitan area was often filled with large boulders known as horse-stones that would guarantee an invading foot soldier or cavalry unit difficulty in traversing the terrain. The inner city, consisting of roughly two parts divided along an east–west axis, which today are referred to as the sacred and royal

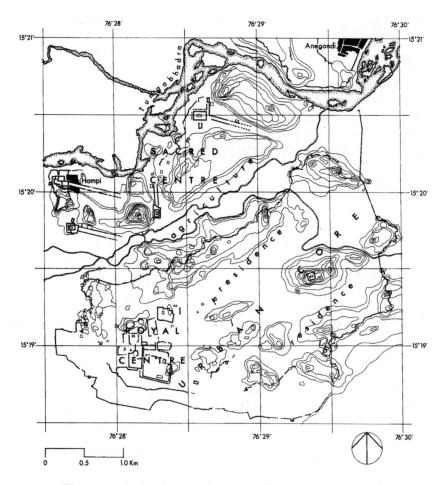

Figure 3.1 As this site plan shows, the Vijayanagara capital city and its suburbs covered a vast area. The core area was divided into sacred and royal zones.

centers, was also walled (Figure 3.1). Within the city's perimeter were more walled compounds, but their walls often were designed to ensure privacy rather than for defensive purposes.

Public rituals in the capital city highlighted the state's military prowess. A case in point is the nine-day Mahanavami festival associated with veneration of the goddess Durga. All the great nayaka lords and their armies were required to attend the festival, after which a general muster of the troops was held outside the city proper. Witnessing the vastness

Figure 3.2 This tiered platform known as the Mahanavami Dibba was
used for the many royal ceremonies held at the Vijayanagara capital.

of the assembled forces about 1522, the Portuguese traveler Domingo
Paes was so overwhelmed that he reported "it seemed as if what I saw
was a vision."[4] During the festival itself, the goddess was worshipped by
the king both privately and publicly; the two sometimes also shared the
Mahanavami Dibba, the large platform upon which the king displayed
himself to his lords and in turn was paid homage by them.

The great platform as it stands today was built in four successive stages,
the last one by Krishnadeva Raya in celebration of his victorious campaign in Orissa (Figure 3.2). While Paes observed the Mahanavami festival, carvings on the platform showing courtly figures throwing water
indicate that the spring festival, also a nine-day event, was celebrated
there as well. Given the prominence of this tiered structure in the heart
of the royal center next to ritual baths and the important Ramachandra
temple, it must have been the focal point for multiple royal ceremonies.
All these festivals, while essentially religious, were in fact a celebration
of the regime's success in the economic and political realms. This multi-
tiered platform dominates the skyline of the royal center. That aspect

[4] "Narrative of Domingo Paes," p. 279.

of it is visible from a considerable distance; however, it is only on close scrutiny that the sculpted carvings on every tier are noted. Here we see no religious themes whatsoever, but only those depicting the ruler, the military, and the endless processions essential to these royal celebrations, thus providing an important insight into the concept of kingship under the Vijayanagara rulers.

The royal center at Vijayanagara remained in use until the capital was abandoned in 1565, even when new complexes were built outside the city limits. So, for example, we know from the testimony of foreign travelers that Krishnadeva Raya continued to conduct the public ceremonial of the state in the royal center, although he actually dwelt in a fortified sub-urb built supposedly for the benefit of his beloved queen, Chinnadevi, a former courtesan who had been his mistress before he became king. This stands in sharp contrast to the practice in Delhi, where kings often had entirely new walled complexes, encompassing both residential and cer-emonial functions, constructed at some distance from previous centers. Another difference is that the built environment of the Vijayanagara cap-ital has undergone few changes since 1565, due to the dispersal of its population following the city's fall from power. Delhi, on the other hand, was not only an urban locality comprised of a whole series of royal com-plexes but also one that continued to serve as a capital or major center for over 700 years, during which time its urban fabrics were constantly being rebuilt and expanded. The modern visitor to Vijayanagara's exten-sive remains built over a 200 year period and to those of Delhi today, a city occupied by kings since about 1200, might therefore believe that Vijayanagara was the larger and more urban setting. This impression would be erroneous, for travelers such as Ibn Battuta had declared Delhi to be the greatest city of the Persian-speaking world, and its position as a major crossroads of trade and communications should not be underesti-mated. For peninsular India, however, Vijayanagara city was undoubt-edly both the largest and most important of all urban centers in the precolonial era.

Cultural orientations in peninsular India

Vijayanagara kings as exemplary Hindu rulers

Since the early twentieth century, Vijayanagara has often been described as a state established in order to halt the advance of Muslim power in the peninsula. According to this view, the kingdom was born out of a desire to protect Hindu religion and culture, and so its militarism was a direct response to the threat posed by the Muslim presence, that is, the

Bahmani Sultanate and its successor states. Vijayanagara allegedly stood as a bulwark against the burgeoning tide of Muslim conquest and thus became the savior of the south Indian people. This interpretation, which sees the Vijayanagara kingdom as inspired by and imbued with a deep sense of Hindu nationalism, is clearly anachronistic – a case of projecting a present-day situation back into the past.

A hundred years later, the flaws in the earlier depiction of Vijayanagara as a nation whose mission was the defense of Hinduism against Islam are readily apparent. For one thing, the concept of a unified Hindu religion did not exist in the fourteenth century, nor did that of a nation composed of all the peoples within a state's borders. Vijayanagara's militarism was largely a result of indigenous developments, although it was intensified by competition with more technologically advanced states in an age of escalating warfare worldwide. And the Vijayanagara state's greatest rival for power was not the Bahmani Sultanate but the Gajapati kingdom of Orissa, a state headed by rulers who were Hindu. Continuing research on the material culture of Vijayanagara has, moreover, uncovered increasing evidence that it was strongly influenced by the states of the Deccan and the wider civilization of Islam.

The Vijayanagara kings did not see themselves as engaged in mortal combat for the survival of Hinduism and south Indian society. However, the rulers of Vijayanagara did attempt to act as righteous kings behaving according to dharma, that is, who lived up to traditional Indic expectations of rulers. An important aspect of kingly duties in classical Indian thought was the protection of the social order and most particularly the upholding of Brahmin privilege. Hence, the Vijayanagara kings sought to portray themselves as champions of the ideal hierarchical society envisioned in Brahmin law books by claiming the title "upholders of *varnashrama dharma*" (the moral duties of class and stage of life). The early Vijayanagara rulers also sponsored Brahmin scholarship, including a series of commentaries on Vedic literature. Throughout the Vijayanagara era, Brahmins continued to be employed by the court in considerable numbers, and Brahmin lands received preferential tax treatment, not unlike the manner in which the sultanates favored Muslim theologians and institutions. Increasingly from the early medieval period onward, however, notions of royal legitimacy came to rest on linkages with temple deities rather than with Brahmins. It was in the combined role of servant and patron of the gods that the Vijayanagara kings excelled.

Almost simultaneously with their decision to settle in Hampi, the site of the capital city, the Sangamas adopted as their family deity the god Virupaksha, a form of Shiva, who was the most celebrated deity in that locality. In deference to the greatness of the deity they had chosen to be the protector of their family, capital, and kingdom, the Sangamas typically signed the name of Virupaksha to royal decrees rather than their own, suggesting that he was the true lord of the realm. Later Vijayanagara kings continued to engrave Virupaksha's name on the copper-plate records of their religious grants, well after the capital had been abandoned in 1565. Another acknowledgment of Virupaksha's pre-eminent status was the practice of announcing all religious endowments made throughout the kingdom in his temple. Virupaksha was thus informed of the meritorious behavior of the donors of religious gifts and, as a witness to their intentions, could safeguard the endowments they had made.

The Vijayanagara rulers honored Virupaksha in more concrete terms as well. Numerous grants of land and villages were made by the kings, their relatives, and their high officials in order to supply the material goods and labor required for the daily worship services dedicated to Virupaksha in his Hampi temple. This temple commenced as a small shrine, essentially a pilgrimage site, prior to the rulers taking over the locality. Extensive construction and renovation of the buildings in the temple complex had begun by the late fourteenth century. One of the most generous benefactors of the temple was Krishnadeva Raya. On the occasion of his coronation in 1509–10, he had a large pillared hall built, along with an enormous towered gateway (gopura) (Figure 3.3). Increasingly, since the fifteenth century, temples in territory ruled by Vijayanagara diverged from the local style common to the Telugu and Kannada-speaking areas. Temples in the local style, such as the earliest temples found at Vijayanagara city, are small with no sense of height or grandeur. Later kings and lords of Vijayanagara chose to build temples that evoked the monumental style of the imperial Cholas, who ruled much of south India until the twelfth century. Thus, the large pillared hall provided by Krishnadeva Raya at the Virupaksha temple, as well as the towering entrances added to this temple and others, were intended to visually rank the Vijayanagara rulers on par with the legendary Cholas, whose temples reflected a sense of the rulers' extraordinary military feats and their support of dharma.

Virupaksha was not the only god favored by the Vijayanagara kings. A temple to Rama, an incarnation of the god Vishnu, was constructed in the early fifteenth century, most probably by King Devaraya I (r. 1406–22). It was situated in the middle of the city's royal zone, at some distance from the Virupaksha and other earlier temples. Because Vishnu was thought to have repeatedly rescued the earth and its people from evil demons, he and his various incarnations had long been popular with Indian kings who sought to cast themselves similarly as saviors of their kingdoms. The

Figure 3.3 The enormous gateway into the Virupaksha temple at Vijayanagara was added by Krishnadeva Raya in the early sixteenth century.

association of Rama with this site dates back as far as the eleventh century, and the whole region is often identified with Kishkindha, the realm of the monkeys whose help the god-king Rama enlisted in the search for his abducted wife, Sita. Malyavanta Hill is where Rama is said to have spent a rainy season while monkey scouts scoured the peninsula for signs of Sita. Earlier Matanga Hill, the highest spot in the locality, had been the refuge of Rama's monkey allies, Hanuman and Sugriva, when they were hiding from the wrath of a deposed monkey king.

The importance of Rama to the Vijayanagara kings is evident from the centrality given to the Ramachandra temple in the overall plan of the capital city as it evolved in the first half of the fifteenth century. The temple is both literally and figuratively at the heart of the buildings and public spaces utilized by the court, and it divides this royal zone into two sections. To the west of the temple is the area where the royal family resided; to the temple's east is the area including the great Mahanavami platform where the public activities of the court were conducted. Further accentuating the centrality of the Ramachandra temple were a series of roads that radiated out from the enclosure in front of the temple toward the north, northeast, and other directions. A different set of roads that circle the metropolitan area have the royal zone, and its Ramachandra temple, at their center.

The link between Rama's life-story and the city is emphasized by the placement of the Ramachandra temple in relation to the hills associated with Rama's monkey helpers. The temple's inner shrine is aligned directly south of Matanga Hill, and both Matanga and Malyavanta Hills can be seen from within the temple complex. Sculptures narrating the *Ramayana* epic are located both on the exterior walls of the principal shrine and on the inner face of the walls enclosing the temple complex, visibly reminding the visitor of the god's significance. On the outer face of the enclosure walls, in contrast, there are numerous scenes of court life at the capital, including depictions of elephants and war-horses, military parades, and female dancers. A complementarity, perhaps even a correspondence, between the king of the city and the god Rama is suggested by this distribution of sculptures, with Rama's sphere internal to the temple and the king's sphere external to it (Figure 3.4).

Patronage of Virupaksha's temple, the major pilgrimage site in their locality, and the construction of new temples like that of Ramachandra in their urban center were important means by which the Vijayanagara kings sought to show themselves as exemplary Indic rulers. But it was not enough to act as a patron of temples within the capital, the locus of royal power, for the king's righteousness had to be evident throughout the kingdom. Outside of their capitals or home bases, medieval south

Figure 3.4 These carvings on the exterior wall of the Ramachandra temple compound at Vijayanagara's capital, Hampi, show royal processions so central to Vijayanagara ceremonial.

Indian kings were most likely to endow temples in areas that had recently come under their control. By commissioning buildings or making lavish presents to temples in outlying or frontier territories, kings not only displayed their piety but also visibly demonstrated their ability to allocate resources in that locality.

Krishnadeva Raya, the greatest of all Vijayanagara kings, was a master at this type of symbolic statement made through the medium of religious patronage. At various stages in his long campaign against the Gajapati kings of Orissa, Krishnadeva gave lavish donations to major temple complexes in the territories that had just been conquered. After the successful siege of Udayagiri, a well-fortified stronghold in southern Andhra, for instance, the king and his queens made a triumphant visit to the Shri Venkateshvara temple at Tirupati, then as now the pre-eminent Vishnu temple of the Andhra region, donating jewels and life-size copper images of himself flanked by his two queens, Tirumaladevi and Chinnadevi (Figure 3.5). (Tirumaladevi was the daughter of one of Vijayanagara's tributary kings and thus became the chief queen, but Chinnadevi, a former courtesan, was elevated to the status of queen only because of the king's great love for her.) The images of the king and his wives were installed so that they would permanently be paying homage to the deity.

Figure 3.5 These life-size bronze images of Krishnadeva Raya and two of his queens were installed at the Shri Venkateshvara temple, Tirupati, as a symbol of Vijayanagara's military victory over this territory.

When the second major fort in Andhra, Kondavidu, was captured in 1515, the king, again accompanied by his two queens, made a pilgrimage to the renowned Shiva temples at Amaravati and Shrisailam in the general vicinity of Kondavidu. Once the war was finally won, Krishnadeva Raya embarked on a victory tour of his southern territories. He stopped at the premier temple complexes along the way – at Tirupati and Kalahasti in southernmost Andhra, at Kanchipuram in northern Tamil Nadu, and at Tiruvannamalai and Chidambaram in the central Tamil country – and at each place he gave valuables to the deities, commissioned temple buildings and monumental gateways, or ordered other improvements to the facilities. Following each military victory, the king thus expressed his gratitude to a major god of the newly subjugated area, but at the same time publicized the power he possessed and the good favor shown to him by the gods.

Islamicate influence at Vijayanagara

Although the Vijayanagara kings were personally devoted to certain Hindu gods and dedicated substantial resources to the support of Hindu temples, this does not mean that they or their people were hostile to other religions and cultures. Indeed, Vijayanagara's ability to flourish for over 200 years owes much to the kingdom's willingness to adopt new technologies of control that were introduced into the peninsula by the Deccan Sultanates. This is most true in the military sphere, where Turkic cavalry and archery techniques were quickly assimilated. Skilled personnel who were Muslims were also hired into the Vijayanagara army, something the Hoysala rulers had also done in the early fourteenth century. The awarding of nayamkara assignments in return for military service may also have been modeled on the medieval Islamic practice of giving iqtas, which was introduced to India by the Delhi Sultanate. Earlier Indian warrior chiefs had acquired land through inheritance or conquest and thus were lords in their own right, whereas nayamkara, like iqta, was granted to an elite warrior by his overlord and could be revoked at the overlord's pleasure. The many Perso-Arabic words relating to revenue collection and other administrative procedures that were absorbed into the regional languages of the Deccan – Marathi, Kannada, and Telugu – beginning in the mid fifteenth century suggest that there was considerable borrowing in this realm as well.

It is easy to see the practical value of adopting new military techniques and administrative systems, but less utilitarian aspects of Islamic culture in India were also embraced by the Vijayanagara ruling class. The most visible manifestation of Islamic influence is in the secular architecture of

Figure 3.6 The Islamicate style used for courtly buildings at the Vijayanagara capital, Hampi, is apparent in the so-called Elephant Stables, which was probably a royal viewing pavilion.

the Vijayanagara capital. While the function of much of Vijayanagara's secular architecture is not altogether certain, pavilions used for administrative purposes, such as private audience halls and council chambers, or to enclose water, feature arches, domes, vaulting, and delicate stucco ornamentation similar to that seen on the architecture of the Bahmani Sultanate. These structures at the capital city, for example, the Lotus Mahal, the Elephant Stables, and the Queen's Bath (all modern names), use architectural and decorative components of Islamic architecture, but they are combined in a highly creative manner unique to the Vijayanagara kingdom (Figure 3.6).

In contrast to secular architecture, traditional Indic architectural forms were retained for all religious structures, whether they were temples of any denomination (Jain, Shaiva or Vaishnava) or even mosques. A case in point is the mosque which a Muslim noble built in 1439 that, like Vijayanagara's temples, uses only traditional Indic, that is, post and lintel construction (Figure 3.7). Likewise, the inscription on the mosque refers to the structure not as a mosque but as a *dharmasale* (hall of dharma or religion), employing Indic terminology. And, as in Indic traditions, the mosque / dharmasale was built to provide merit for the ruler. As Phillip

Figure 3.7 This mosque at Vijayanagara, dated 1439, is built in an Indic
style and also has an Indic name, *dharmasale*, hall of religion.

Wagoner has argued, the patron was perfectly adept at code switching
from an Indic to an Islamic idiom in any given situation. Wagoner has
also pointed out that Vijayanagara rulers and courtiers made a similar
distinction between Indic and Islamic styles when it came to clothing:
they wore traditional south Indian garb when engaged in a Hindu religious
activity or in a domestic setting, but opted for an Islamic style of dress
for formal public audiences (Figure 3.8). The court was a place where
the Vijayanagara elite might frequently meet and interact with Muslim
visitors or guests, and so Islamic norms which stressed the covering of
the body were observed. By wearing tunics, tall caps, and other articles
of Islamic dress, the Vijayanagara ruling class was conforming to the
fashions not only of the Muslim-ruled polities to their north but also of
the larger Islamic civilizational sphere. The adoption of Islamic clothing in
certain contexts and the choice of Islamic buildings for secular ceremony
was a sign of the sophistication of the Vijayanagara court and its desire
to participate in a cosmopolitan culture that extended far beyond the
confines of south India.

Some scholars prefer the term "Islamicate" rather than "Islamic" to
describe this cultural complex because it was created and carried by people who followed Islam but was not intrinsically related to the religion *per
se*. Stitched clothing, true arches, and paper were all aspects of material

Figure 3.8 The court dress of the Vijayanagara elite was, like their courtly buildings, Islamicate in style as shown in this painting from the Virabhadra temple at Lepakshi.

culture that were introduced into India by Muslims but had nothing to do with the Islamic faith. The Vijayanagara kings incorporated many facets of Islamicate culture and practice in a dynamic synthesis that heralded a major break with the earlier cultural patterns of south India. The Vijayanagara kingdom may largely have been Hindu, but, contrary to what is often said, it was by no means the last gasp of the *ancien régime* or a mere continuation under heavy odds of the traditional ways of south India.

Creation of a pan-south Indian culture

The Vijayanagara kingdom is important for the ways in which it creatively assimilated Islamicate material culture, technologies, and terminologies and transformed them into something new. Its longest lasting legacy, however, was the formation of an elite culture that spanned the southern Deccan and the Tamil country. In the first millennium CE, both Karnataka and Tamil Nadu had contained major political and cultural centers from which waves of influence had radiated outward into other areas. The situation became more fragmented during the twelfth and thirteenth centuries, when the regional kingdoms of the Yadavas (in Maharashtra), Kakatiyas (in Andhra Pradesh), Hoysalas (in Karnataka), and Pandyas (in Tamil Nadu) each fostered the development of a different literary language and temple architectural style. What happened during the Vijayanagara period was unprecedented in that parts of Karnataka, Andhra Pradesh, and Tamil Nadu came to share a common culture at the elite level – this melding of Deccan and far southern ways and people lingered on well into the colonial era.

The Vijayanagara kings were responsible in part for the emergence of this pan-south Indian cultural complex. While the rulers of later successor states transmitted certain elements such as the innovations in palace architecture or the Mahanavami festival, some of the commonality was a result of conscious policy by the Vijayanagara monarchs. The clearest example comes, once again, from the realm of architecture. We have already seen how, from the fifteenth century on, the Vijayanagara rulers purposefully chose to emulate in their temple architecture that of the imperial Cholas with all its attendant meanings.

Royal patronage was also directed to the support of literature in several languages: Sanskrit (the pan-Indic literary language), Kannada (the language of the Vijayanagara home base in Karnataka), and Telugu (the language of Andhra). Works in all three languages were produced by poets assembled at the courts of the Vijayanagara kings, while Krishnadeva Raya was himself an accomplished writer in both Sanskrit and

Telugu. His most famous work is the *Amuktamalyada*, a Telugu poem dealing with religious devotion to Vishnu. The multi-linguistic character of Krishnadeva Raya's far-flung territories explains why his inscriptions often repeated the same text in three or four languages. The Telugu language became particularly prominent in ruling circles by the early sixteenth century, because of the large number of warrior lords who were either from Andhra or had served the kingdom there.

Much of the growing cosmopolitanism of south India occurred because people increasingly moved around within the large area where Vijayanagara power held sway. Military and political needs dictated the movement of some people from one place to another, while others were drawn by the growing demand for artisanal production or the rise in long-distance trade. One example is Ettapa Nayaka, originally from the southernmost district of Andhra, who became a migrant not as the result of imperial intervention but simply as an entrepreneur venturing into a new locality on his own. Disturbances in his home locale caused Ettapa Nayaka to move southward to the Tamil country in the 1420s at the head of a group of almost 1,400 people, most of whom were his soldiers and retainers. In such a manner, a substantial Telugu-speaking presence was established in the Tamil-speaking zone.

The Bahmani court

The Bahmani state, founded in 1347 as a successor to Tughluq authority in the Deccan, resembled the Vijayanagara state in several significant ways. A notable similarity was their desire for territorial expansion, explaining the continual wars not only with each other but with their neighboring state to the east, that of the Gajapatis of Orissa. Due to its location in the northern Deccan, the Bahmani Sultanate was also in frequent conflict with the Sultanates of Malwa and Gujarat. This near-incessant warfare was rarely truly decisive, allowing the Bahmani state to first expand on its eastern and western borders and then survive until 1538. Soon after 1500, however, the governors of its provinces had become the independent rulers of their own sultanates, the most important of which were the Bijapur state led by the Adil Shahs and the Golkonda state ruled by the Qutb Shahs.

The Bahmani kingdom was also like Vijayanagara in having a multi-ethnic and multi-lingual elite, but this diversity proved to be a greater problem for the Bahmanis. What undermined the state in the long run was not so much external threats as the tensions between two factions who dominated the military and administrative system. The Indian-born nobles known as Deccanis felt threatened by the Afaqis, the foreign-born nobility, most of whom came from Iran or Central Asia. Although wise kings and counselors tried to mitigate these problems by, for example, maintaining an equal balance between the two groups when appointing governors, the problems were never adequately resolved. The differences between these groups were exacerbated by the fact that many of the Afaqis were Shia Muslims and the Deccanis were Sunnis, thus adding fuel to the fire. Hindus too were included in the administrative and military system, but generally they did not hold ranks as high as the Afaqis or Deccanis.

Mahmud Gawan, an Afaqi newcomer from Iran, was prime minister to several Bahmani rulers from 1463 to 1482 and it is thanks to his administrative reforms that the Bahmani state reached its height during his time in office. He was able to curb the increasing power of the nobility by diminishing much of their authority and giving it to the center. Mahmud Gawan also instituted a systematic measurement of land to determine accurate revenue assessment. In the end, however, his success was his downfall, for the nobility resented having to answer to the center. Some of the Deccani nobles forged a document which convinced the king to have Mahmud Gawan executed on the charge of treason.

The Bahmani capital was first established in Gulbarga, where the city's architecture was built in the weighty austere style of their former Tughluq overlords. By the reign of Firuz Shah Bahmani (r. 1397–1422), buildings had become more refined, with walls articulated by a series of recessed niches. This is seen not only in Firuz Shah's own tomb, but also in the more important one built at Gulbarga for the Chishti Sufi, Gesu Daraz. The Bahmani sultans had long associated themselves with Sufi saints, in particular, the shrine of Burhan al-Din Chishti at Khuldabad, just outside of Daulatabad. Unlike the north Indian Chishtis, those in the Deccan had close contact with the court, accepting cash and donations from them. These Chishtis in turn had an impact on the Bahmani state and its policies.

In the 1420s the successor of Firuz Shah shifted the capital north to Bidar. As contact with Iran and Central Asia increased, especially during the period of Mahmud Gawan's prime ministership, the entire city took on a Persian appearance, with buildings and even the urban layout modeled on those in Iran and Central Asia. The most compelling example is the madrasa (school for religious instruction) provided by Mahmud Gawan to promote Shia Islam. Its plan, not found elsewhere in the Indian subcontinent, adheres to that of contemporary madrasas built in the kingdoms of Timur's successors. Even more notable is its lavish tile work, similar in design, color, and technique to those on buildings in the Timurid capital of Samarqand, and again unique in India. Since during this period the descendants of Timur were considered among the most powerful and cultured of Muslim kings, Mahmud Gawan was drawing a parallel between Bahmani authority and that of the Timurids.

Over time, the Bahmanis thus shifted from a reliance on Tughluq prototypes to an architecture which was more akin to that found in contemporary Iran and Central Asia, in part as a response to the growing links with those regions caused by the migration of foreign nobles. Although the distinct Bahmani style had a considerable impact on the secular architecture of Vijayanagara, the same cannot be said in reverse. It was not in architecture but rather in the realm of language and literature that the northern Deccan developed its most composite culture. By about 1500, Sufis and others began to use a new language called Dakani. Based on many aspects of the grammar and syntax of north Indian vernaculars, this Dakani language contained numerous Indic words, in addition to the many words derived from Persian and Arabic. The successors to the Bahmanis not only made frequent use of Dakani, but they also patronized the local regional languages, particularly from the late sixteenth century onward. Linguistic pluralism was hence just as much a feature of the northern Deccan culture as it was farther in the south.

Trade and commerce in the Vijayanagara period

Maritime trade

The Vijayanagara kings called themselves "Lords of the Eastern and Western Oceans," a title that asserted hegemony over the Bay of Bengal to the east and the Arabian Sea to the west of the Indian peninsula. Domination over the coastal territories was one of Vijayanagara's primary geo-political objectives and a frequent cause of conflict with other kingdoms. Krishnadeva Raya tells us why coasts were so important:

A king should improve the harbours of his country and so encourage its commerce that horses, elephants, precious gems, sandalwood, pearls and other articles are freely imported . . . Make the merchants of distant foreign countries who import elephants and good horses attached to yourself by providing them with villages and decent dwellings in the city, by affording them daily audience, presents and allowing decent profits. Then those articles will never go to your enemies.[5]

Access to ports meant access to a range of coveted goods, including the essential war-horse. Other items like sandalwood, musk, and camphor were deeply embedded in the rituals and gift exchanges that pervaded court life and helped constitute the charisma of kings.

[5] A. Rangasvami Sarasvati, "Political Maxims of the Emperor Poet, Krishnadeva Raya," *Journal of Indian History* 6 (1925): 69 and 72.

Despite the claim implicit in their title, the Vijayanagara kings seldom exercised direct control over the western seaboard, a narrow strip of land that was separated from the peninsular interior by the Western Ghats. The western littoral had for centuries been ruled by a multitude of small chiefs who might enter into tributary relations with the more powerful overlords of the interior but were nonetheless lords in their own right. One such lineage was the Jain chiefs of Bhatkal port, on the Kanara coast (of modern Karnataka state) to the southwest of the Vijayanagara capital. Shipments of war-horses came to Bhatkal from the Arabian peninsula and Iran and were sent overland to the Vijayanagara capital. Copper and gold were also imported to Bhatkal from the Middle East while pepper, sugar, and textiles were among the items exported. As these goods were moving into or out of Vijayanagara territory, they would be subject to various taxes, but the revenues from the commercial transactions that took place at international ports like Bhatkal went to local chiefs rather than to the Vijayanagara state.

The lords of Bhatkal and other western ports took active measures to encourage foreign merchants to come to their towns since revenues from maritime trade were virtually their only income. Consequently, Arab traders from all over the Middle East did business on the southwestern coast and communities of indigenous Muslims also emerged in places, as a result of conversion and/or intermarriage with local residents. The largest concentration of Muslim population was found around Calicut in northern Kerala, on what is known as the Malabar coast. Calicut became the greatest entrepôt or free port of the western seaboard during the fourteenth and fifteenth centuries partly because of the policies of its rulers, the Zamorins. Unlike other lords on the western littoral, the Zamorins did not plunder ships seeking refuge from storms, nor did they claim shipwrecks as treasure; rather they provided security. So many Arab merchants were attracted to Calicut that Ma Huan, a Chinese visitor of the early fifteenth century, believed its entire population to be Muslim.

A community of indigenous Muslims known as Mappilas also flourished in the Calicut region. The Mappilas spoke the local language, Malayalam, and observed many local customs but were actively engaged in maritime commerce, unlike other local communities. While the Arab merchants dominated the overseas trade from the Malabar coast to the west, the Mappilas were mostly involved in commercial activities along India's coast and also on the routes to Southeast Asia. According to an estimate by an early sixteenth-century Portuguese traveler, Mappilas comprised a fifth of the people within the Zamorins' domain.

The Malabar coast, on which Calicut is situated, has a long history of international maritime trade going back to the era of the Roman empire. Its chief export to the western world was black pepper; other items produced in Malabar were ginger, cardamom, teak (a hard wood used in ship building), and the aromatic sandalwood. Because indigenous social groups were almost entirely preoccupied with local agrarian matters, maritime trade along the Malabar coast had always been in the hands of immigrant trading communities. Two of the immigrant communities were the Syrian Christians and the Jews, who had been resident in Kerala probably hundreds of years before their presence is definitively attested in copper-plate grants, from the ninth and late tenth centuries, respectively. Similarly, although the earliest proof of Muslim presence dates back only to the ninth century, Arab sailors must have come to the Malabar coast long before the advent of Islam. Hindu mercantile groups from other areas of India had joined the cosmopolitan society of the Malabar coast by the fifteenth century, among whom were Chettis from the southeastern coast and Baniyas from Gujarat in western India.

Calicut was such a bustling emporium that it was visited even by Chinese ships – Ibn Battuta witnessed thirteen of them upon his arrival in Calicut during the 1340s. The Chinese came to "the great country of the Western Ocean," as Ma Huan described Calicut a century later, in order to acquire items like frankincense and myrrh from the Middle East as well as pepper, diamonds, pearls, and cotton cloth from India. In exchange, they sold Chinese silks and ceramics which were in high demand in both India and areas to its west. Establishing diplomatic relations with the Zamorin, which involved the exchange of trade items, was the main objective behind the first state-sponsored naval expedition to Calicut. Led by Admiral Cheng Ho (who was accompanied on later expeditions by Ma Huan, acting as translator), it included 317 ships and over 27,000 men. Calicut continued to be a major stop on Cheng Ho's subsequent voyages, but he gradually journeyed farther west: to Hormuz, Aden, and eventually Mogadishu on the east coast of Africa.

Cheng Ho's ships were exceptional in traversing the entire Indian Ocean from one end to the other; instead, most ships just sailed one segment of that expanse: from south China to Java or Malacca, from Malacca to Sri Lanka or India, and from the subcontinent to the Persian Gulf or the Red Sea, and then to destinations westward. The great appeal of the Malabar coast was the availability of goods from China, Southeast Asia, the Middle East, and other areas of India, which were brought there for trans-shipment because of its geographical location as a midway point. When Vasco da Gama, sailing on behalf of the Portuguese crown, became the first European to find a direct sea route to Asia in 1498, it was to Calicut that he headed in search of pepper and fine spices.

Portuguese hostility toward the Muslim ships and traders who frequented the Malabar coast soon led to open conflict and introduced a new phenomenon to the Indian Ocean: the use of violence as a means of furthering commercial objectives. The artillery mounted on Portuguese ships, which were heavier than the indigenous vessels, gave them a decisive advantage and enabled them to rapidly seize a series of coastal sites including the Sri Lankan port of Colombo in 1505, the Malay port of Malacca in 1511, and the Persian Gulf port of Hormuz in 1515. With possession of this string of strategically located harbor cities, the Portuguese tried to control all sea trade in spices from Asia to Europe. They also profited from the maritime trade within Indian Ocean waters, through the requirement that local ships pay custom duties to them or face bombardment. The center of the maritime empire the Portuguese established was Goa, a port seized in 1510 which was further north on India's west coast than the Malabar region. Portuguese Goa was in direct competition with Calicut, which declined in importance over the long run. The introduction of Roman Catholicism and the emergence of a mixed population through intermarriage between the Portuguese and local women were two of the most important consequences of the Portuguese arrival, adding even more to the cultural diversity of India's west coast.

On India's southeastern or Coromandel coast, Pulicat was the major port in the fifteenth and early sixteenth centuries. Situated on the border between modern Andhra Pradesh and Tamil Nadu, Pulicat was part of Vijayanagara territory and was linked to the capital by a road. Textiles were the principal export from Pulicat to Southeast Asia, sent by Muslim and Hindu merchants from Coromandel and a diasporic community of Armenian traders. The imports included Indonesian spices (nutmeg, cloves, and mace) and non-precious metals. Pulicat also had an on-going coastal trade with Bengal, which supplied many foodstuffs to the Coromandel coast and Sri Lanka and possibly some of its better textiles. Bengal was renowned for the quality of its textiles, for Ma Huan names six different kinds of fine Bengal cloth, both cotton and silken.[6] Bengal too had maritime links with Southeast Asia. Although ships and sailors from other parts of the world appear to have dominated the international trade, Indians had a greater role in the shipping within the waters of India and Sri Lanka and, to a lesser extent, to Southeast Asia.

Domestic economy

Little of what was being bought and sold in the ports of Calicut, Pulicat, Cambay in Gujarat, or Chittagong in Bangladesh was produced in their

---

[6] Ma Huan, *Ying-yai Sheng-lan, "The Overall Survey of the Ocean's Shores" (1433)*, trans. and ed. J. V. G. Mills (Cambridge: Hakluyt Society, 1970), p. 160.

immediate vicinities. Most commodities were brought to these major emporia by boats engaged in coastal trading or overland by pack bullock. Since the thirteenth century, the volume of domestic trade in peninsular India had increased for reasons that had little to do with the international maritime trade. South India's thriving networks of internal trade and production of marketable commodities certainly contributed to the success of India's international port cities and, in turn, received an additional boost from international demand. Despite the greater attention paid by historians to the international commerce of this era, the domestic sector was much larger in scale and value.

Even before the Vijayanagara period, the peninsula's agrarian economy had been growing due to construction of new irrigational facilities, large reservoirs that captured rainfall and the seasonal flows of small streams. The agricultural productivity of the semi-arid uplands was considerably enhanced by better water supplies and, as a result, the agrarian frontier was gradually pushed back into more marginal areas. Commercial agriculture – that is, the cultivation of crops for sale – increased, and different localities specialized in different products including cotton, indigo, and sugarcane. These commercial crops had to be hauled long distances, for sale in market towns, periodic fairs, and distribution points along the coasts. Long-distance trade during the Vijayanagara era was facilitated by the development of excellent roads linking the main urban centers and by the creation of roadside facilities for travelers.

At least eighty major trade centers are mentioned within Vijayanagara territory, a clear indication that urbanization was on the rise. The greatest of all was the Vijayanagara capital, with an estimated population of 300,000 to 400,000. It sprawled out over a huge area – the central city was an estimated 25 square kilometers in size, while the greater metropolitan area, encompassing the outermost fortifications as well as the city's waterworks, covered as much as 650 square kilometers. The city's people must have consumed massive quantities of food, while the demand for luxury goods from the kingdom's ruling elite, who were congregated at the capital, was no doubt considerable. The extent to which trade networks were centered on the capital is clear from the rapid decline of Bhatkal and Pulicat ports after the city was abandoned. The much smaller kingdom that was left after the disastrous defeat at the Battle of Talikota in 1565 shifted its base to southern Andhra and thus away from the old supply routes. The activities of the Portuguese, who had arrived in India in 1498, were also a contributing factor, but the primary cause for the decay of Bhatkal and Pulicat was the loss of the Vijayanagara market, with its enormous consumer demand and purchasing power. Pulicat was supplanted by Masulipatnam, the chief entrepôt of the growing Golkonda kingdom, once again demonstrating the impact of political centers on the geographic patterning of trade.

Large temple complexes were also major consumers of goods and served as a stimulus to trade. Temples accumulated large quantities of land, livestock, and valuables like gems, precious metals, and coins from the donations of pious pilgrims. Much of this wealth was used to support daily rituals in worship of temple deities as well as for periodic festivals, both of which increased in number and in scale over the Vijayanagara period. Oils and incense were lighted for the gods' pleasure, perfumes and flowers adorned their images, and offerings of foods were made several times a day. In addition to administrators, priests, cooks, gardeners, and guards, large temples also had musicians and dancers to entertain and honor the gods. Sculptors, metalworkers, and other artisans found employment in the towns that sprang up around large temples, as did merchants catering to the pilgrim trade.

The hundreds of inscriptions at the Shri Venkateshvara temple in Tirupati record the great expansion in ritual activities that occurred during the Vijayanagara period. According to Burton Stein, the temple received grants of over a hundred villages as well as large sums of cash from more than 300 donors. Most of the endowments, whether in the form of land or money, were meant to support ritual services, both on a daily basis and on special festive occasions. At Tirupati, as at other temples belonging to the Shri Vaishnava sect, food offerings were of particular centrality. While food given to the deity at Shiva temples was consumed only by priests, at Shri Vaishnava temples the food was redistributed to donors and pilgrims as a sacred substance (*prasada*). The volume of food provided to the god, and later to his devotees, reached a surprisingly high level; by one calculation, the Shri Venkateshvara temple had sufficient resources in 1504 to feed over 1,400 pilgrims on an ordinary day and about 3,800 on a festival day.

Tirupati was not a typical situation, for it was one of the largest centers of the Shri Vaishnava sect, whose influence had been gradually spreading northward from the Tamil country since the days of the famous theologian, Ramanuja, *c.* 1100. Ramanuja integrated the orthodox philosophy of the Sanskrit Vedanta, which emphasized a transcendent and universal absolute essence (*brahman*), with the emotional devotion to a personal god (*bhakti*) that had been characteristic of the Tamil region for centuries. The Shri Vaishnava movement developed around temple complexes that were favored by Vijayanagara kings and high officials, more than those of any other persuasion, from the late fifteenth century onward. Each of the forms of Vishnu enshrined in a Shri Vaishnava temple has a distinct life history and a different appeal, as is the case with all south Indian deities. Lord Venkateshvara of Tirupati, for instance, takes the shape of an unusually large image that supposedly manifested itself in an ant-hill. It is commonly believed that he is especially receptive to devotees who vow to shave their heads in return for a boon.

Records of donations to temples like Tirupati show that merchants and skilled artisans benefited from the growing prosperity of Vijayanagara India. So, for example, professional organizations of traders would agree to make voluntary contributions to a specific temple, usually assessed as a percentage of goods sold. Individual merchants might make donations of land or cash, as did some wealthy weavers and workers in precious metals. While merchant-traders had been occasional patrons of temples even earlier, it was only in the Vijayanagara period that skilled artisans became prosperous enough to do so. As their economic standing rose, weavers and other artisan communities began to demand more social recognition and sought prominent roles in temple ceremonies. Many artisans appear to have favored the Tengalai branch of the Shri Vaishnava sect, which used the vernacular Tamil language in its liturgy rather than Sanskrit and was thus more accessible to the non-Brahmin and non-elite elements of society. The Tamil community of weavers known as the Kaikkola are one example. They successfully attained positions of responsibility at the two major Tengalai temples, Shrirangam and Tirupati. At the latter, they were in charge of the important task of distributing consecrated food offerings to the worshippers.

The growing trade and urbanization of Vijayanagara India parallel trends that had occurred earlier in north India at the height of the Delhi Sultanate. During the fifteenth and early sixteenth centuries, south India became the most dynamic area of the subcontinent both economically and culturally. This was an age of physical mobility, social diversity, and cross-cultural borrowing all over the Indian peninsula. The reality that some ruling elites were Muslim while others were Hindu made a considerable difference in what institutions and individuals received the bulk of that state's religious patronage. It also determined to a considerable degree what artistic styles and literary traditions would be prominent at a court. In countless other respects, however, ranging from revenue systems to military technologies to palace architecture, the large kingdoms of the peninsula were strikingly alike.

End Essay #3

4 North India between empires: history, society, and culture, 1350–1550

During the fifteenth century a series of regional states developed across north India, some ruled by Muslims and some by Hindus, but in all of them considerable tolerance was shown toward other religions, a fact that most histories overlook. In these independent states what it meant to be culturally sophisticated was increasingly defined not only by parties who subscribed to pan-Indian trends but also by those who promoted distinctly regional vocabularies. The new cultural styles are in part reflected in the production of progressively more substantial architectural projects, both secular and religious, and of illustrated manuscripts and music. The products of the regional kingdoms were more composite in nature, incorporating local cultures with larger Indic and Islamicate ones. In addition, literature in the regional languages began to flourish as never before. Religion too took on new forms in both the Muslim and Hindu traditions, with some movements seeking ways to bypass the traditional ulama in the case of Islam or Brahman priests in the case of Hinduism. Thus, saints and devotees, intense in their emotion for the divine, infused society with an impassioned discourse that was transmitted in literature and religious practice. Although the fifteenth and early sixteenth centuries were a time of political fragmentation and weakness in north India, it was simultaneously an era of considerable cultural innovation.

Regional sultanates

Beginning in the late fourteenth century the now weakened Tughluq dynasty, once spanning much of the Indian subcontinent, began breaking into a series of small regional successor states. In the Deccan the Bahmanis, discussed in chapter 3, declared independence from the Tughluqs in 1347. In north India too a series of regional states arose in former Tughluq territory, of which the most notable are Bengal in the east, Jaunpur in the mid Gangetic region between Delhi and Bengal, Gujarat in the west, and Malwa in central India to the east of Gujarat. In general, these new regional states initially emulated Delhi in terms of governance and culture while later developing their own individual characteristics that reflected local models. The emergence of composite Indic-Islamic cultures was thus a development promoted first in the regional kingdoms and not until much later in the imperial center of north India, during the late sixteenth-century reign of Akbar.

On the eastern periphery: Bengal

Islam entered eastern India in the very early thirteenth century under Muhammad bin Bakhtiyar Khalji, who led raids on local inhabitants in the name of Muhammad Ghuri. Maintaining continual central control over this easternmost perimeter of the Delhi Sultanate was problematic, for Bengal was thick with jungle and traversed by multiple rivers, most notably the mighty Ganges and Brahmaputra, whose conjoined mouths feed into the Bay of Bengal. Almost immediately after Bakhtiyar Khalji declared victory in the name of his overlord, the governor who had been left in charge asserted his own authority until Iltutmish was able to rein him in. A similar pattern of initial imposition of Sultanate rule and its subsequent overthrow was seen until the mid fourteenth century, when Shams al-Din Ilyas Shah (r. 1342–57) established the first of several independent dynasties in Bengal at the twin cities of first Pandua and then Gaur, a site which today is literally half in India and half in Bangladesh. The first phase of the Ilyas Shah house lasted about fifty years until Raja Ganesh, a powerful Hindu, was able to wrest virtual control. In 1414 Raja Ganesh placed his convert son Jalal al-Din Muhammad (d. 1432) on the throne, thus restoring the Ilyas Shah dynasty. By the late fourteenth century the Husain Shah dynasty (1493–1538), often viewed as the initiators of Bengal's golden age, came to the fore, eventually making way for the establishment of Mughal authority.

Bengal is unusual in that its agrarian community, especially in the areas east of the Ganges, by and large adopted Islam. In contrast, both outside the subcontinent and elsewhere within the subcontinent, Muslim populations tended to congregate in urban areas. In his recent work, Richard M. Eaton has argued convincingly that Islamization occurred, not as is commonly believed through the threat of the sword or promise of social betterment, but with massive land reclamation and rice cultivation on what was formerly jungle and swamp. Muslim holy men were associated with this process of land reclamation. As respect grew for these advocates of agriculture that resulted in a new economic well-being, so too did the desire to espouse the faith of Islam. This process, while commencing in the pre-Mughal period, was not fully realized until the seventeenth and eighteenth centuries.

Basing his argument in part on the types of monuments built by the Islamic rulers of Bengal through the mid fourteenth century, Eaton proposes that the initial rulers of Sultanate Bengal and even their breakaway governors imposed an iron-clad Islamic rule, giving no voice to local non-Muslims. True, they provided a few free-standing minarets and large-scale mosques intended to indicate a new political and religious authority, but, as we saw in our discussion of the Delhi Sultanate, this was just one side of the coin. In the first capital of the new state, in Pandua, is the truly monumental Adina mosque of the second Ilyas Shah ruler, Sikandar Shah. Inscriptions on this mosque, dated 1375, proclaimed Sikandar Shah the sultan of Arabia and Persia, just as Aibak and Iltutmish had been given similar titles on Delhi's Qutb Minar (see Figure 2.2). The mosque's huge arched entrance evoked the arched screen at Aibak's Jami mosque (see Figure 2.1). At the same time, it referenced the legendary throne hall built at Ctesiphon, renowned as the symbol of Persian kingship *par excellence*, which was built by Khusrau, a pre-Islamic king of the Sassanian dynasty (sixth century CE). On the surface, this mosque and some other structures were intended to visually proclaim the early sultans of Bengal as ideal Islamic kings.

An investigation of the Adina mosque's interior reveals another interpretation of the monument, for here are visual devices that suggest Sufism (discussed in chapter 2) served as a bridge between formal Islam and the peoples of Bengal. On the mosque's qibla wall (facing Mecca, the direction toward which Muslims pray), nearly all the forty-one arched mihrabs or niches are adorned with hanging lamps, references to a verse in the Quran that likens god's presence to a "light in a niche" (Figure 4.1). The Quran is believed by all Muslims to be the words of god as given to the final prophet, Muhammad. Countless interpretations of the chapter from which this verse comes, known as The Light (al-Nur), have been written by orthodox theologians, but in particular by Sufis. The presence of the hanging lamps in the Adina mosque's prayer niches suggests that the patron's original intention may have been less strident in tone than indicated by Eaton. Bolstering this suggestion were two important dargahs, or saint's tombs, located near the mosque, one staffed by Sufis of the Chishti order and the other by the Suhrawardi order. The Chishti Sufis, whose path to finding god was through music and zikr (discussed in chapter 2), and the Suhrawardis, another important South Asian Sufi order, both commonly used light imagery to express god's inner, almost unfathomable, qualities. Given the importance Sufis had for the general Indian population, what made the greatest impression was not the inscriptions in an alien script few could read, but rather the multiple depictions of accessible hanging lamps in niches found in the mosque's interior and also on its exterior brick walls.

Figure 4.1 The hanging lamps carved on this prayer niche at the Adina mosque in Pandua are an allusion to Sufi teachings.

Contrary to Eaton's view, it was not really possible in this early period for a state to ignore a majority non-Muslim population and still maintain political authority. As M. Akhtarazzaman points out, not only was the Muslim ruling elite in Bengal a minority, but also they had to contend with an often adversarial Islamic government at the center. He provides convincing evidence that non-Muslims in eastern India, especially those with skills to serve the state, were treated with greater respect than generally assumed. By the mid to late fifteenth century some Hindus had risen to high positions in the administration. It is well recognized that during the fifteenth and early sixteenth centuries, during the time of Raja Ganesh and increasingly under his son and the subsequent Husain Shah dynasty, a rich multi-layered culture had emerged where seemingly rigid categories of Hindu and Muslim were constantly in flux. Sultans might enthrone themselves in the Islamic Persian traditions, but they also adopted local customs, such as purification with Ganges water at coronation ceremonies. Sufi saints, as elsewhere in the subcontinent, appealed to both Muslims and non-Muslims.

While many of these practices transcended regional polities, architecture of this period reveals features unique to Bengal. No secular material remains, only Hindu temples and Muslim mosques, tombs, and shrines. As one would expect in an area with few quarries, nearly all these buildings were brick-built, and they shared at least one characteristic that emulated local domestic architecture, a curved roof to deflect water from Bengal's extremely heavy rains. While these buildings have a common overall appearance, those which are Muslim and those which are Hindu are clearly identifiable by their architectural features. Domes, often multiple ones, dominate on Muslim buildings, while temples at this point tend to have spired superstructures. Relatively few dated temples prior to the seventeenth century survive; in contrast, Muslim structures in the twin cities of Pandua and Gaur, as well as in smaller cities, survive in great numbers. In addition, temples tend to be relatively small, at least in comparison with Sikandar Shah's massive fourteenth-century Adina mosque.

Just as brick-constructed architecture was common to both Hindu and Muslim structures, so too literature written by both Hindus and Muslims was composed in the common language of the region, Bengali. Muslim religious texts and secular Persian and Arabic ones, including poetry and prose, were translated into Bengali, while at the same time Bengali poets were composing a growing body of works devoted to the Hindu god Krishna, the eighth incarnation of Vishnu. Influenced by this popular trend, the Muslim poet Saiyid Sultan composed his *Nabi Vamsha* in Bengali between 1584 and 1586. This genealogy, loosely translated as the Lineage of the Prophets of Islam, includes the Hindu god Krishna, seemingly misplaced in a standard Islamic text yet acceptable in the context of Bengal. In the *Nabi Vamsha*, Saiyid Sultan reveals how all previous prophets, including Krishna, had erred so that the final prophet, Muhammad, was sent to redeem the world. In Bengal it seems a single individual might evoke the names of Hindu deities while simultaneously uttering the name of Allah and the Prophet Muhammad. As Richard M. Eaton suggests, the *Nabi Vamsha* essentially renders the Arab realm of the Prophet comprehensible to the tropical world of Bengal.

Sufis of a wide variety of types were present in Bengal, but just as a body of literature emerged that reveals active awareness of local traditions, so too some Sufi traditions reveal a similar interaction. Surviving texts indicate some Sufis, in Bengal and elsewhere in the subcontinent, were influenced by the yogic practices of a Hindu sect known as the Nathas. Breath control, assuming postures akin to those of yoga, and the retention of bodily fluids are among the practices associated with the Nathas that are found in Bengal and elsewhere within Indian Sufi orders like the Shattaris.

In spite of Bengal's peripheral location in the subcontinent, which might have encouraged some of the heterodoxy discussed above, it would be wrong to think of the independent sultans of Bengal as isolated from the larger world. Sultanate Bengal, situated on the Bay of Bengal, had numerous wealthy shipowners who were actively engaged in trade, not only with the sultans of India, but also with powers as far west as Venice and Portugal, and China to the east. Bullion from Myanmar, quickly converted into silver coins, was a highly desirable commodity resulting from overseas trade. Numerous types of textiles, especially fine cottons and silk, were coveted items that Bengal exported. Visitors from Asia and Europe alike were impressed by the Bengal sultan's capital at Gaur, the court and its ceremony, and the government's ability to generously feed the poor – clearly all reflections of economic well-being.

Maritime region to the west: Gujarat

Gujarat, the maritime region in western India, was closer to Delhi than Bengal, and thus took longer to cast off its ties to the center. Gujarat became independent of Tughluq Delhi about the turn of the fifteenth century, although the official date is 1407, when Zafar Khan assumed the title Muzzafar Khan. The dynasty, generally known as the Ahmed Shahs after Zafar Khan's grandson and successor, who founded the city of Ahmedabad in 1411, lasted until the Mughals incorporated Gujarat as part of their ever-expanding empire in 1573. There is little recent

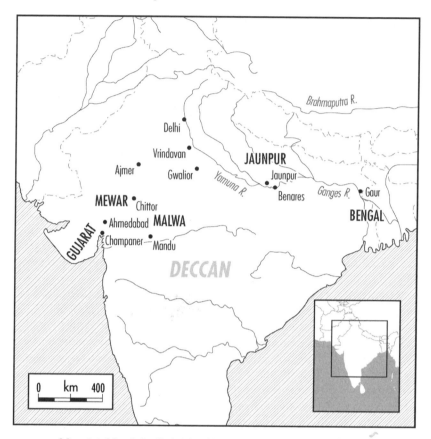

Map 4.1 North India in the fifteenth century

interpretative scholarship on Sultanate Gujarat's history and culture, but evidence, when pieced together, suggests a picture not totally dissimilar to that of Bengal. The rulers of Sultanate Gujarat were constantly engaged in warfare with their neighbors, including the Muslim rulers of the Malwa Sultanate, the Rajput *raja*s of north Gujarat and Rajasthan and, near the end of their reign, the Christian Portuguese, who were increasingly proving themselves the masters of the ocean. During the fifteenth and early sixteenth centuries, Gujarat traded teak, bamboo, spices, pearls, gold, silver, carnelian, camels, and woven cottons to Southeast Asia, Africa, the Middle East, and Europe. Just as visitors praised the capital of Bengal, so too the capitals of Gujarat, Ahmedabad and Champaner, were considered model urban centers. Usmanpur, a suburb of Ahmedabad, established by a leading Sufi of the time, was claimed by a seventeenth-century source to have had in the fifteenth and sixteenth centuries over a thousand shops, staffed by Hindu and Muslim artisans, traders, and craftsmen, among other professions.

In spite of this testimony, most histories of Sultanate Gujarat are badly in need of revision, as they tend to paint the rulers as rigidly oppressive to non-Muslims and wishing to propagate Islam at the expense of all else. Alka Patel's recent work has shown this is not true for Gujarat in the twelfth through fourteenth centuries, but work on the fifteenth and sixteenth centuries is still needed. As we have seen in the case of Sultanate Delhi and Bengal, the depiction of the Gujarat sultans as rigid and oppressive is an improbable appraisal in terms of political reality as well as actual cultural developments. The Gujarat sultans, like their contemporaries elsewhere in north India, did not make or break political agreements in terms of religion. The sultans of Malwa were no more or less a threat than the Christian Portuguese. In fact, when the Ottomans of Turkey, a powerful Muslim state to the west, wished to ally themselves with the sultan of Gujarat with the aim of ousting the Portuguese from the Arabian Sea, the Gujarat sultan saw no advantage to having the Ottomans as allies, for surely they would turn face; in the end, the Gujarat sultans scorned those advances. Gujarat's bardic traditions suggest that Hindus held high positions in Ahmed Shah's administration and that Gujarat's Muslim rulers often married Hindu Rajput women as a means of maintaining good relations with local populations.

The sultanate architecture of Gujarat is deemed by many to be the most elegant of all pre-Mughal regional styles. In basic format and plan the mosques and tombs of Gujarat sultans adhere to those of similar structures found elsewhere in north India. However, in detail and elevation these stone-carved buildings are as unique to this western region as are the contemporary brick ones to Bengal. The carvings embellishing mosques and tombs resemble motifs found on earlier local temples devoid, of course, of any anthropomorphic imagery. By and large these mosques and tombs, like their temple counterparts, avoid the use of true arches and vaults but rather employ corbelled ones. Thus, there is a tendency to underestimate the originality of these structures, for example, Ahmedabad's Jami mosque completed by Ahmed Shah in 1424, seeing them as simply rearranged temples. In fact, some scholars claim the domes and pillars come from specific older temples and go as far as to propose the temple of origin of each pillar and corbelled dome. Careful examination indicates that, as in other regions we have discussed, only the earliest Islamic structures use spolia. Architects had organized these new structures of Gujarat in such a manner that the result was an unprecedented sense of openness and space never before achieved in either Indic or Muslim traditions of western India. An excellent case in point is the Jami mosque of Champaner, where multiple open clerestories stacked one upon the other covered the prayer chamber's central bay to allow the entire interior to be illuminated. This is exactly the opposite sort of effect desired in a temple's inner sanctum (literally, womb house), where darkness is desired rather than visual clarity.

The capital cities, first Ahmedabad and later Champaner, are today dotted with numerous fourteenth- and fifteenth-century mosques, but evidence exists indicating they were carefully planned cityscapes. Today virtually nothing remains of Champaner except its mosques and fine water tanks, although excavations would surely give considerable insight into its original plan. Enough remains of Ahmed Shah's core city, Ahmedabad, though, to indicate it was planned to showcase the sultan as he proceeded from his citadel and palace, placed on an elevated hillock next to the Sabarmati river, through a triumphal triple-arched gateway to his large Jami mosque. Further underscoring the dynastic nature of this avenue leading to the state mosque were two large tomb compounds, one a domed mausoleum intended for Ahmed Shah and his male offspring and the other an open air enclosure enshrining the cenotaphs of the royal women.

Myths associated with Ahmedabad's founding stressed not only its royal nature but also its sacred aspects, as the saint Makhdum Shaikh Ahmad Khattu (1336–1445) was said to have assisted in the selection of the site and helped lay its foundation stone. Shaikh Ahmad Khattu was living in Delhi in 1398 when it was sacked by Timur and, according to later sources, he played a leading role in convincing the war lord to desist in the further killing of Delhi's citizens. The shaikh then moved to Gujarat and became Sultan Ahmed's spiritual preceptor and adviser. Sultan Ahmed's successor, Muhammad Shah, commenced a stone tomb, covered with lime to make it look like white marble, for the saint at the site of his *khanqah* (residential compound for spiritual study), transforming it into a dargah (Figure 4.2). Because of the continuing importance of the shrine, subsequent rulers then added tombs and mosques, but the most significant addition by far was a palace erected on the side of a large artificial tank. This model of juxtaposing palace and white-appearing stone shrine, emphasizing the role of the Sufi in underpinning dynastic rule, was later picked up and further manipulated in the sixteenth century by the Mughal emperor, Akbar.

A high degree of originality is seen not only in the architecture of the regional sultanates but also in the painting of this era. While it is not difficult to ascertain the dynastic patronage of most architecture, partly due to its location and often because structures bear inscriptional

Figure 4.2 Just outside of Ahmedabad is the tomb of Shaikh Ahmad Khattu where, because of its sanctity, the fifteenth-century sultans of Gujarat built their own tombs and even palace pavilions.

slabs carved with the patron's name and date of construction, the situation for illustrated manuscripts is much less clear. This is because most of these texts are no longer intact and pages for any single work are often lost, with the surviving illustrated ones dispersed among museums and private collections. Illustrated Islamic manuscripts survive, but with rare exceptions the place of origin and patron remain unknown. Some surely must have been commissioned by the sultans of Gujarat, but which ones we simply do not know. However, the subject matter of Indo-Islamic illustrated texts of this period largely parallels those found elsewhere in the contemporary Persian-speaking world. They illustrate classical Persian poetry, such as the works of the great thirteenth-century Persian poet Saadi, or epics such as the *Shahnama*, translated as The Book of Kings, a poem consisting of some 60,000 verses about the rise and fall of ancient Iranian kings. In style, the illustrations range from close replicas to contemporary work being done in Iran, with pastel colorings and round-faced Iranian type figures, to those rendered in profile or three-quarter view, closer to Indic idioms. The latter usually feature bright red or yellow grounds with angular figures wearing highly decorated clothing. The wide range of styles suggests a number of courts and artists were involved in the production of illustrated manuscripts, but to date it is rarely possible to assign any particular style to any particular region.

In contrast to Islamic illustrated texts of this period, illustrated manuscripts of the Jains survive in abundance, and many of them are fully intact. The Jains share some fundamental Indian religious doctrines with Hindus, such as the belief in the cycle of rebirth, but they reject the spiritual authority of Brahmins. Jains primarily worship the twenty-four Jinas (literally, conquerors), former kings and warriors who renounced worldly matters and achieved spiritual liberation through extreme asceticism. Although Jainism had formerly been widespread in the Gangetic area as well as in the Deccan, by the fourteenth century its adherents were mainly located in western India, as they still are today. As advocates of *ahimsa* or non-injury to living creatures, Jains are strict vegetarians and typically will not engage in agriculture because of the possibility of harming insects during cultivation. Instead, Jains have traditionally been merchants and bankers, many of them quite wealthy. Since education is highly valued in the Jain community, literacy has traditionally been high, and the commissioning of religious texts, often illustrated, was believed to not only accrue spiritual merit for the patron but also for close relatives. These manuscripts were usually kept in libraries attached to Jain temples, explaining the large number of intact ones that survive.

The illustration of Jain religious texts from Gujarat and other regions of north India has been documented since at least the twelfth century, although they surely existed prior to this time. Jain manuscripts were first written on narrow palm leaves and retained the oblong shape of these leaves even after paper was substituted for them, but surviving documents only date to the fifteenth century. Among the most popular Jain texts was the *Kalpa Sutra*, a biography that covers the lives of all twenty-four Jinas (the liberated individuals whom Jains seek to emulate), with special emphasis on the last Jina Mahavira. Appended to that text is often the *Kalakacharya Katha*, a tale about a Jain's sister who was abducted and then rescued by a foreign ruler. The narrative, when it first was composed prior to the advent of Islam, referred to some pre-Islamic Central Asian ruler, but by the height of its popularity in the fourteenth and fifteenth centuries, he was transformed into a Muslim ruler. In the illustrations, this foreign hero is depicted in the mode of a Turk, with his moon-like face in contrast to the angular ones of his Jain counterparts (Figure 4.3). These texts were written in a variety of Indic languages, including an ancient literary dialect associated specifically with sacred Jain religious texts.

Figure 4.3 In this illustrated fifteenth-century Jain text, the *Kalaka-charya Katha*, the Jain monk is depicted in an angular Indic style while the foreign king resembles a Turk.

Another text, the *Vasanta Vilasa*, meaning the Beauty of Spring, painted in the same style as the Jain *Kalakacharya Katha*, was composed in a literary version of the Gujarati language spoken by the local population of the time. Boldly celebrating the rites and joys of spring as well as the god Krishna, this text, at times erotic in nature, is rendered as an illustrated scroll, allowing it to be unrolled as it was read aloud to appreciative audiences. Commissioned by a Hindu patron in 1452, it praises Sultan Qutb al-Din Ahmed Shah II and eulogizes the thriving city of Ahmedabad.

Just as Hindu and Jain patrons had praised their sultanate rulers in manuscripts they commissioned, so too we have clear evidence that the rulers had high regard for local traditions in return. Perhaps there is no better example than the sultans' love of local music and the incorporation of it into their own court practice. Surviving musical treatises indicate that the Ahmed Shahs of Gujarat were fully cognizant of Hindu myths; songs suggested these royal courts were superior to those of the Hindu gods. One ruler even had a singer in his employ who performed as Saraswati, the goddess of music and learning, and danced and sang in a chariot fashioned as a swan, the special creature associated with Saraswati.

In the mid Gangetic plain: Jaunpur

Positioned between what remained of the Tughluq realm and the sultanate of Bengal, Jaunpur, also a former Tughluq province, officially broke ties with Delhi in 1396. Unlike the situation with the sultanates of Bengal and Gujarat, where Delhi did little or nothing to intervene once they asserted their independence, relations between Delhi and Jaunpur remained actively hostile. Jaunpur was not a state on the periphery; rather, its western border was contiguous with Delhi's, and much of its territory was former crown land, thus depriving the former Tughluq state and its Sayyid (1414–51) and Lodi (1451–1526) successors of considerable revenue. Delhi and Jaunpur alternately were the aggressors in frequent military confrontations. The Jaunpur armies were able to enter Delhi twice, but by 1494 Sikandar Lodi (r. 1489–1517) had sacked Jaunpur, rendering it well-nigh impotent by the beginning of the sixteenth century. Not only was Delhi a menace to Sharqi autonomy, but also threats from other sides, particularly Orissa to the southeast, were a major problem.

Despite the political insecurity of its ruling Sharqi dynasty, Jaunpur thrived as a cultural center, so much so that the Mughal ruler Shah Jahan later termed the capital in its heyday as the Shiraz of India, likening it to the city in Iran associated with famous poets and intellectuals.

Religious scholars, Sufis, and poets were invited to the city, many leaving Timur-ravaged Delhi and others coming from Syria, Iran, and Central Asia. As in other contemporary sultanates, architecture, the most public of all arts, particularly flourished. Under Ibrahim Shah Sharqi, the so-called Atala mosque was founded in 1408. Based in part on the Jami mosque known today as the Begumpuri mosque, founded by Muhammad bin Tughluq just before the mid fourteenth century in Delhi, with a large central portal that soars above its lower side wings, this Jaunpur mosque's central façade is considerably larger and even more prominent. Anna Sloan, in a recently completed dissertation, argues that this façade, which continued to be the hallmark of the new Sharqi style, was in fact a visual symbol of the new state's character. Functioning as a gateway, an emblem known to Iranian, Arab, and Indian cultures, it infused new meaning into a hitherto undistinguished local architecture. As this building type was reproduced throughout the Sharqi domain, it became a visual statement for the spread of Sharqi hegemony. Moreover, these Sharqi mosques are embellished in a manner unlike mosque architecture elsewhere in north India. Rather than featuring fine ornate carving only on pillars, as was common elsewhere in the subcontinent at this period, here walls, entrances, and other areas previously not used for embellishment were carved with patterns that derived from western Indian textiles, Central Asian designs, and more, thus showing the Sharqis as sophisticated and knowledgeable of both Indic and larger Islamic traditions. Once the Lodis of Delhi had sacked Jaunpur, even though their victory was not absolute, they began to see themselves as the usurpers of Jaunpur's glory and began to embellish Delhi with new buildings, drawing cautiously on Sharqi architectural motifs as a statement of their own new authority.

Histories of Jaunpur or about the Sharqis of Jaunpur are generally silent about non-Muslims and their place in the state. It is assumed that there was little interaction between Muslim and non-Muslim communities, although the pilgrimage center of Benares (Varanasi), long associated with the Hindu god Shiva, is situated only 60 kilometers to the southeast of Jaunpur city. However, a sumptuously illustrated *Kalpa Sutra*, dated to 1465, clearly indicates harmonious relations among the various religious communities in the region. Its colophon (the page at the end of a manuscript that typically contains information on its production) notes that a Jain family had this manuscript copied and then illustrated by a Hindu during the reign of Husain Shah Sharqi (r. 1457–77). In Gujarat and Bengal and now in Jaunpur in north India, the commissioning of expensive products such as buildings, manuscripts, and musical productions suggests that wealth was in the hands of multiple communities.

Figure 4.4 In this page from the *Nimatnama*, a recipe book dating to about 1500 and produced in Mandu, the sultan of Malwa looks on as young ladies prepare delicacies.

Inside central India: Malwa

The former Tughluq governor of Malwa, an area in central India to the east of Gujarat, established himself as an independent ruler by the early fifteenth century. Malwa's biggest rivals were the Bahmani sultans of the Deccan, the sultans of Gujarat, and the rulers of Mewar. The hill fort Mandu, embellished with palaces, mosques, tombs, and gardens, was the capital of Malwa. Not only was the sultanate of Malwa known for its creative architecture, largely provided by the local rulers, it was also known for its illustrated manuscripts. Of particular interest is the royally commissioned *Nimatnama*, executed about 1500 at Mandu. This is not the usual type of illustrated text, that is, classic Persian poetry or an adventure story associated with the heroes of yore. Rather, this is a heavily illustrated recipe book for making everything from kabobs to aphrodisiacs. Equally unusual is that each page features a prominent portrait of its patron, the king, easily recognizable by his large swooping moustaches (Figure 4.4).

It is harder to discuss Hindu patronage of painting at this time because most manuscript pages are dispersed and any historical information has been lost. Jain manuscripts, however, tended to be kept in libraries associated with temples and by and large remain intact. An illustrated *Kalpa Sutra* and *Kalakacharya Katha* dated to 1439 and produced at Mandu suggests a close cooperation between Jain merchant-bankers and the Muslim ruling elite for, as in the 1465 Jaunpur *Kalakacharya Katha*, here too the ruling sultan's name, Mahmud Shah Khalji, is given in the text. Jains were vital to the success of these independent sultanates, as their presence insured the state's economic vitality.

Rajput states and culture

Among the new states that arose in north India as Delhi's power waned in the fifteenth century were several headed by the Hindu warriors known as Rajputs. Rajput is a broad label used to designate a slew of martial groups once found throughout much of north India, although today the best known Rajput communities dwell in the state of Rajasthan. Because the term Rajput is derived from the Sanskrit *raja-putra* or "king's son," Rajputs have typically claimed the status of kshatriya or ruling warrior in the four-fold varna classification of traditional India. However, recent research suggests that Rajput did not originally indicate a hereditary status but rather an occupational one: that is, it was used in reference to men from diverse ethnic and geographical backgrounds who fought on horseback. In Rajasthan and its vicinity, the word Rajput came to have a more restricted and aristocratic meaning, as exclusive networks of warriors related by patrilineal descent and intermarriage became dominant in the fifteenth century. The Rajputs of Rajasthan eventually refused to acknowledge the Rajput identity of warriors who lived farther to the east and retained the fluid and inclusive nature of their communities far longer than did the warriors of Rajasthan.

Mewar kingdom of the fifteenth century

The first major Rajput kingdom of Rajasthan was established by the Sisodiyas of Mewar, not coincidentally the most pre-eminent of all Rajput lineages in prestige. Mewar, in southeastern Rajasthan, receives more rainfall and has better soil than many other localities within the region. An additional reason that state formation proceeded more rapidly in Mewar than, for example, in the arid expanses of western Rajasthan, was its strategic location on trade routes from Delhi and the Yamuna-Ganges doab (that is, the fertile land between two rivers) down to Gujarat. The

Sisodiya base, Chittor fortress, was situated on an isolated plateau rising abruptly above the surrounding plain and so was easily defensible. Under the Sisodiya king, Rana Kumbha, who ruled from 1433 to 1468, Mewar became the most powerful kingdom of Rajasthan. He fought against the royal dynasties of the two neighboring regions, Gujarat and Malwa, that had long been rivals to the kingdoms of eastern Rajasthan. In 1437, Sultan Mahmud of Malwa was taken prisoner by Rana Kumbha's forces but released unharmed in a chivalrous gesture. To commemorate his victory over Malwa on this occasion, Rana Kumbha commissioned the famous Tower of Victory, completed in 1460 (Figure 4.5).

In form and outer appearance this tower, nine stories high, is modeled on a tower that is part of a Jain temple, probably dating to the thirteenth century, also in the hill fort of Chittor. The Tower of Victory stands near a temple but is an independent monument. Both its exterior and interior are profusely covered with images of gods and goddesses and with scenes of victorious battles from the *Mahabharata* and *Ramayana* epics, paralleling the frequent references to Rana Kumbha's successful battles against the sultanates of Malwa and Gujarat in the Tower's lengthy inscription. The interior images bear carved labels, but to date no one has determined its overall iconographic program. Possibly this imagery is intended to play out the text of the inscription, which proclaims not only Kumbha's military success, but also his cultural achievements in building temples, wells, reservoirs, forts, and highways, as well as feeding Brahmins; in other words, the expected duties of a good Hindu king. Moreover, Rana Kumbha is declared to be an incarnation of the god Rama and also is likened to heroes in the *Mahabharata* epic. In the early nineteenth century James Tod, a figure who almost single-handedly is responsible for today's romantic notions of the Sisodiyas of Mewar, compared the Tower of Victory to the Qutb Minar in Delhi (see Figure 2.2). Both are notable for their height, which makes them visible for considerable distances. While both towers have religious imagery, in the form of gods and goddesses on the Tower of Victory and inscribed verses from the Quran on the Qutb Minar, each was really intended as a statement of its patron's political success.

Rana Kumbha is also responsible for constructing many massive forts, such as the one at Kumbhalgarh, about 110 kilometers west of Chittor in the Aravalli hills. He embellished Chittor, including the palace in which he resided. Residential architecture prior to the sixteenth century in north India rarely survives, so what remains of Rana Kumbha's fifteenth-century palace provides an unusual, albeit incomplete, view of domestic and administrative life under the Rajputs. This and comparable palaces were situated within the essentially impregnable

Figure 4.5 This nine-storied tower was built by Rana Kumbha in 1460 to celebrate his military victory over the sultan of Malwa in 1437.

walls of hill fortresses. Entered by a series of gates, Chittor's rubble-constructed palaces covered with a stucco veneer are composed of multi-storied galleries of rooms around an open central courtyard. In their ruined state it is not easy to determine with accuracy the function of the remaining structures; however, it is likely safe to assume that some courtyards were intended strictly for the use of women and others for men. Portions only intended for administration appear to have existed, in addition. One area, clearly rebuilt in the last two or three centuries, seems to have been the elevated platform from which the Rana presented himself to his nobles. Assuming that this restoration follows the spirit of the original building plans, textual sources suggest that Rajput Hindu kings and contemporary Muslim ones in north India had a similar notion of kingly protocol in formal situations such as presentations of both nobles and the ruler.

A slightly later Rajput palace survives in much better condition, due to the fact that it was constructed of stone atop the massive hill fortress of Gwalior, about 282 kilometers south of Delhi. Built by Raja Man Singh Tomar (r. 1486–1516), the palace is divided into two main sections, one clearly intended for women, as it features double walls with pierced stone screens so court ladies could observe court ritual but not be seen themselves. Paralleling the Muslim tradition of female seclusion, aristocratic Rajput women were also kept from the sight of any unrelated male. Although rules governing marriage eligibility were complex, Rajput kings and nobles tended to marry daughters from many important families in order to build up their base of allies or at times to cement a peaceful resolution to conflict.

Both the seclusion of high-born women and the making of multiple marriage alliances for political purposes are practices also found in contemporary south India. Domingo Paes tells us that the queens of Krishnadeva Raya in early sixteenth-century Vijayanagara lived in a separate section of the palace compound and were never glimpsed by any men other than eunuch messengers from the king. Twelve thousand female officials and servants staffed the extensive women's quarters at Vijayanagara, and some of them were delegated to represent individual queens during public festivals such as the Mahanavami. The subordinate kings and chiefs who were the fathers of the principal queens were invited to sit next to their overlord on the great platform during such public ceremonies, displaying to all the political importance of the royal marriages.

The Rajput palace at Gwalior has elevated balconies for royal presentation as at Chittor, instead of the great platform used at Vijayanagara. Unlike Chittor, where none of the original embellishment remains, the exquisite stone carved panels and brackets of the Gwalior palace's courtyards and interior rooms survive in excellent condition. The crisp carving of abstract geometric patterns is similar to that seen on the Islamic tombs and mosques of Chanderi, a city under the rule of the sultan of Malwa. When Babur, the first Mughal ruler of India, visited Gwalior, he was impressed by Man Singh's palace, a striking contrast to his opinion of most Indian buildings. It was probably the Islamicate nature of this Rajput palace that gave him pleasure.

Temple construction under the Rajputs

Territories under the control of the Rajput kings of Rajasthan feature temples, both Hindu and Jain, suggesting a continuum of temple construction from the twelfth through sixteenth centuries. This does not mean that temples were not occasionally destroyed by Muslim sultans wishing to make political statements, but generally they were rebuilt almost immediately. Biographies of important Jain figures and pilgrimage manuals reveal several aspects of contemporary attitudes toward temple and image desecration. These texts understood their own time period as the *kali yuga*, the most degenerate of the four ages, when the world was in a downward spiral and would have to be destroyed before it could be renewed. Interestingly it was not the Turks who were blamed for the destruction of temples, but rather demi-gods associated with the temples who were not providing adequate protection. Moreover, devotees were admonished against donating anything other than stone images of the gods, for these texts indicate that metal and jeweled images would only encourage looters.

The most important Hindu temples were those associated with royal houses. A notable example is the temple of Eklingji, about 20 kilometers north of the city of Udaipur (see Map 8.1). Originally established in the tenth century, it was rebuilt in the fifteenth century and today consists of 108 shrines enclosed by a high compound wall, 108 being an auspicious number in Indic tradition. Dedicated to a form of Shiva, it was transformed over time into a royal lineage temple intended to validate the Sisodiya Rajput rulers, who claimed the deity Eklingji was the state's real ruler and the king his human agent, the prime minister. While this temple was the most important one for the Sisodiya house, they built others too, especially in their hill forts of Chittor and Kumbhalgarh.

The thirteenth through fifteenth centuries were also a period of active Jain temple construction in areas ruled by Hindu kings. For instance, a number of Jain temples dating to the time of Rana Kumbha were constructed at his strongholds of Chittor and Kumbhalgarh. Mt. Abu, in southernmost Rajasthan just to the west of Mewar, has some of

India's most famous pure white marble Jain temples. Unlike contemporary Hindu temples, where the inner sanctum is surmounted by a tall spired superstructure which is generally visible from a distance thanks to a tall plinth on which the temple sits, these thirteenth-century Jain temples at Abu have relatively low domes and their plinths are surrounded by a cloistered gallery, thus making the structure appear rather unimpressive. Once inside, however, the picture changes as the interior is intricately carved with figures of gods and goddesses suspended from lace-like ceilings and on exquisitely rendered pillars. Images of the Jinas are found in the temples' inner sanctums. These temples, a translation in stone of the gods' heavenly realm, were provided by a wealthy Jain minister who served under a local Hindu king.

The reasons for this enclosed Jain temple type, which differs from contemporary Hindu architecture, has to do with patterns of use. Hindus do not fully enter temples. They are allowed to go as far as the entrance into the inner sanctum but not beyond, for that area is the domain of the god and the priest who serves him. Since the public space in these Hindu temples is small, relatively little time is spent inside. More time might be spent in circumambulating the temple and contemplating its exterior, richly covered with images of the gods. By contrast, Jains spend considerable time inside of temples, reading religious texts, in prayer, and in contemplation. Jains are often allowed to touch the Jina images; one of the highest acts of devotion is to wash and then decorate the Jina. Hence the Jain temple's interior décor is much more important to the devotee than its exterior. The most spectacular of these temples is one provided at Ranakpur in the Aravalli hills, not far from Kumbhalgarh, by a wealthy Jain merchant in about 1452, during the reign of Rana Kumbha. From the exterior it looks like a walled enclosure surmounted with multiple spires, while its pure white marble interior has a highly unusual plan based on an understanding of the Jain celestial assembly hall, that is, a hall built by the gods for a newly enlightened Jina to deliver a sermon.

Some of these temples were damaged in raids from Muslim armies. They were always quickly rebuilt, and again Jain biographies of temple builders offer insight into this process. In these stories the Jain patron always first asks permission from the Muslim king to build or repair the temple, which is never denied. In fact, in some of these biographies, the sultan realizes that he will obtain merit for helping others. As explained earlier, it is not Muslims who are blamed for temple destruction but demi-gods.

Thus, in the various regional kingdoms of north India we see attitudes toward minorities which are much more tolerant than are usually assumed. Jains were needed as advisers, bankers, and merchants. Muslims and Rajputs were viewed as having superior military skills. Hindus were simply the majority population, and their rich religious and literary traditions were happily employed by the sultans of Gujarat and Bengal, among others, in their own cultural production. The sort of interaction we see transpiring through the early sixteenth century would inform the world view of the future Mughal emperor, Akbar.

Religious trends in North India

Spread of Sufism

In the Indian subcontinent during the thirteenth through early sixteenth centuries, there were a variety of Sufi groups, but the Chishti order, first established by Muin al-Din Chishti at the inception of the Delhi Sultanate, became India's pre-eminent order during this period. Simon Digby has proposed that this was due to the fact that, by the fourteenth century, the Chishtis were based in Delhi, the center of political power. Nizam al-Din Auliya (d. 1325), first in person and after his death in his spiritual essence (*baraka*), was believed to be intimately linked to Delhi's prosperity. Moreover, unlike other Sufis of this time, Nizam al-Din had a ready-made publicist in the form of a noble, Amir Hasan, who recorded Nizam al-Din's conversations in what became a best-selling text. In addition, the famous poet Amir Khusrau, Amir Hasan's chief rival and also a member of the courtly elite, immortalized Nizam al-Din through poetry and songs still sung today by *qawwal*s (those who sing ecstatic songs in honor of Sufis) and known worldwide through popular recordings. However, after Timur's sack of Delhi in 1398, two things occurred. One was that the Chishti Sufis migrated to the new Tughluq successor states, establishing their own new khanqahs or residential centers in these far-flung locales. The other was a revitalization of the shrine of Muin al-Din Chishti in Ajmer, now posthumously gaining special status as the subcontinent's first Sufi, even though there had been Sufis in this area since the late twelfth century, if not earlier.

The sultans of Malwa appear to have played a critical role in the creation of an aura of importance around the grave of Muin al-Din Chishti. Having taken Ajmer in the mid fifteenth century, the Malwa ruler provided a mosque and large entrance gate to what was otherwise a simple shrine. By the fourteenth century the practice of visiting the tombs of deceased saints on their *urs* (death date; literally marriage with god) was well established. During these visits prayers were offered and the tomb was circumambulated in much the same manner as pilgrims to Mecca circumambulated the Kaaba, believed by Muslims to be the shrine erected by the Prophet Abraham in thanks to his monotheistic god for providing water in a time of need. Texts survive that promote the efficacy of pilgrimage to Ajmer, even indicating it was a viable alternate to the Hajj, that is, the pilgrimage to Mecca mandated for all able Muslims once in a lifetime. Pilgrimage manuals that advocate visiting the tombs of saints indicate money, flowers, and food should be offered for the benefit of all involved, including the poor residing near the shrine.

While the shrines of deceased saints even today continue to draw devout pilgrims, living Sufis were and still are also very much a vital part of society. These Sufis had a variety of challenges to meet, many of them contradictory. For example, the Sufi had to be charismatic in order to procure students but at the same time humble. Just as belief in the supernatural surrounded stories of temple builders, so too Sufis were believed to fly through the sky and perform extraordinary miracles, such as exercising powers which enabled them to convert non-Muslims. Other Sufis, for example, the Rishis of Kashmir, lived extraordinarily simple lives, remained celibate, and were strict vegetarians. While staunch in their belief in the Islamic creed and the supremacy of the Prophet Muhammad, the name Rishi derives from that of Hindu holy men, as does their restraint in food and sexual practice.

This belief in the supernatural powers of Sufis and Hindu holy men also set the stage for literature of the period. Some of the important works were Sufi in nature, including the famous *Padmavat* of Malik Muhammad Jayasi, commenced in the year 1540, which relates the fictional story of Ala al-Din Khalji's love for the queen of Chittor. An even more original work is the *Madhumalati* by Mir Sayyid Manjhan, dating to 1545. Employing the Indic vocabulary of *rasa* (connoisseurship, flavor, mood) and suggestion coupled with traditional Persian love lyrics, poets like Manjhan and Jayasi expressed Sufi messages in the north Indian language Avadhi, a literary precursor to modern Hindi in north India. Manjhan was a Sufi who belonged to the Shattari order, which practiced yoga like the Nathas in Bengal. He created a poetic narrative about two lovers who live in a world with a composite Indic and Islamic culture, where Muslim spiritual values peacefully coexisted with references to Hindu gods and Hindu names. Even though Manjhan lived in north India, his work recalls the type of Sufism practiced in Bengal. The imagery of this work, which may be read on multiple levels, is complex with Sufi and romantic overtones. *Madhumalati*, *Padmavat*, and other stories of this type were extremely popular and well known by wide sectors of the population.

Kabir and the Sant tradition

Commencing in about the fourteenth century in north India, a number of poet-saints known as Sants emerged as important religious voices in the Hindu tradition. Unlike the Sufi poets, who, despite their use of popular motifs, still came out of the courtly cultural context, many of the Sants were from the low castes, and they typically challenged the efficacy of priests and religious rituals, as well as the concept of caste. Their ideas bear some broad similarities to those of the Sufis: the Sants, for instance, worshipped a god that was without form and attributes, neither seeable nor knowable, as was also true of Allah. Moreover, the Sants, like the Sufis, were mystics of a sort, extolling devotion to god as a primary religious practice. The Sants wrote – or perhaps composed is more accurate, for some were illiterate – poems that were intended to be sung in their local languages. Their works provide a fascinating glimpse into a far less elite culture and audience than is the case with most surviving cultural productions of the medieval period.

The most influential of the Sants was Kabir, whose poetry is still widely known and cited today. Very little is known about Kabir's life with any certainty. He probably lived in the fifteenth century, in or near Benares (Varanasi), and was an uneducated weaver. Since most weavers in the Benares region are Muslims, many believe Kabir was born a Muslim, explaining the frequent references to Islam in his poetry. Recent analysis of Kabir's work shows it is actually more Hindu than Muslim in nature, leading some to suggest that his community was recently converted to Islam. In fact, Kabir had no use for either religious tradition, as this poem shows:

> Qazi, what book are you lecturing on?
> Yak, yak, yak, day and night.
> You never had an original thought.
> Feeling your power, you circumcise –
> I can't go along with that, brother
> If your God favored circumcision,
> Why didn't you come out cut?
> If circumcision makes you a Muslim,
> What do you call your women?
> Since women are called man's other half,
> You might as well be Hindus.
> If putting on the thread makes you a Brahmin,
> What does the wife put on?
> That Shudra's touching your food, pandit!
> How can you eat it?
> Hindu, Muslim – where did they come from?

Who started this road?
Look in your heart, send out scouts:
Where is heaven?
Now you get your way by force,
But when it's time for dying,
Without Ram's refuge, says Kabir,
Brother, you'll go out crying.[1]

Kabir attacks both Muslim and Hindu traditions, disparaging what he sees as rote knowledge and meaningless inconsistent custom. He lambastes the caste system, where some groups of humans are believed to be born higher than others, thus introducing what to his mind is a series of useless customs regarding food and pollution. For Kabir, god, whom he addresses as Ram, is the highest authority. Kabir's Ram is not the mainstream Hindu god who is an incarnation of Vishnu but rather an abstract deity without personal attributes who abhors the rule-oriented aspects of both Hinduism and Islam. Kabir's poetry was widely disseminated and found a place in several collections, among them the sacred book of the Sikhs, the *Adi Granth*. The Sikhs (to be discussed in chapter 9) were a new religious group whose founder Guru Nanak (1469–1539) came out of the same religious milieu as did Kabir and the Sants, and his religious views similarly drew on both Hindu and Islamic elements.

Growth of Krishna worship

Although elite Hindus in previous centuries had primarily focused on Shiva as the object of their worship (as we have seen, for instance, in the case of the Sisodiyas of Mewar and their allegiance to Eklingji), the situation changed from *c.* 1500 onward, after a wave of devotion toward Vishnu became more widespread. In the eastern Hindi-speaking area, Rama, an incarnation of Vishnu, became popular, as reflected in the famous text called the *Ramcharitmanas*, composed by Tulsidas about 1575. This text, in the same Avadhi language used by the Sufi poets Jayasi and Manjhan, drew from both the Sanskrit *Ramayana* attributed to Valmiki and retellings of the epic in regional languages, in particular the Tamil Rama story composed by Kamban. Tulsidas' *Ramcharitmanas* is far more reverential than the Sanskrit *Ramayana* toward Rama, whose human character is eclipsed in this text by his divine nature.

Elsewhere in the northern half of the subcontinent, both in eastern India and the western half of the Hindi-speaking area, it was another incarnation of Vishnu, Krishna, who emerged as the favored deity.

---

[1] *The Bijak of Kabir*, trans. Linda Hess and Shukdev Singh (San Francisco: North Point Press, 1983), pp. 69–70.

Among the most famous of the devotees of Krishna is Mira Bai, a historic figure associated with Chittor. Legends about Mira Bai's life are well
known to the Indian public, by whom she is revered as the composer of
dozens of poem-songs about her passionate attachment to Krishna. Little
is known with certainty, however, except that Mira came to Chittor as the
bride of Bhojraj, son of the Mewar king, Rana Sanga, in the early sixteenth
century. By about 1600, Mira Bai was included in a compendium of the
lives of bhakti (Hindu devotional) poets called *Bhaktamal*. Its author
Nabhadas mentions several aspects of her life story that are central to
the more elaborate hagiography of Mira in later centuries. Mira Bai is
said to have fearlessly rejected social conventions – "the fetters of family" and "the chains of shame" – in the adoration of her beloved god,
whom she worshipped through song.[2] Mira addressed her beloved as
Giridhar or "mountain-lifter," referring to an episode during Krishna's
youth when he raised a mountain with his hand in order to shelter the
cowherders from heavy rains unleashed by the wrathful god Indra (see
Figure 5.8).

Later hagiography tells us that Mira Bai was reluctant to marry the
Mewar prince because Krishna was her true lord and husband. She consistently refused to act like a proper bride upon reaching the Chittor
palace, failing to honor both her mother-in-law and the family goddess
of the Sisodiya lineage. Instead of serving her husband and his family,
Mira passed her days at a local Krishna temple immersed in worshipful
song or in the company of wandering saints. The so-called Mira Bai temple at Chittor is thought to be the site of her devotions, but is not the
product of her patronage, as is often claimed, for it is a structure from
some decades earlier. Mortified by her unseemly actions, the Mewar king
or Rana got Mira to drink a cup of poison, but it did not harm her due
to her great devotion to Krishna. Mira eventually escaped the bonds of
married life, so the story goes, and traveled to Vrindavan, the village on
the Yamuna river where the young Krishna had lived. After some years in
Vrindavan, Mira left for Dwaraka, in Gujarat, where Krishna had resided
toward the end of his life. When Brahmins sent by the Mewar king tried
to make her return, Mira was absorbed into a Krishna image and never
seen again.

A number of the Hindi and Gujarati songs attributed to Mira refer to
aspects of her personal life. In the excerpt translated below, for example,
from one of the most popular Mira songs, there is an allusion to the
poisoning episode:

---

[2] John Stratton Hawley and Mark Juergensmeyer, *Songs of the Saints of India* (New York:
Oxford University Press, 1988), p. 123.

> I'm colored with the color of dusk, oh *rana*,
>   colored with the color of my Lord.
> Drumming out the rhythm on the drums, I danced,
>   dancing in the presence of the saints,
>   colored with the color of my Lord.
> They thought me mad for the Maddening One,
>   raw for my dear dark love,
>   colored with the color of my Lord.
> The *rana* sent me a poison cup:
>   I didn't look, I drank it up,
>   colored with the color of my Lord.
> The clever Mountain Lifter is the lord of Mira.
>   Life after life he's true –
>   colored with the color of my Lord.[3]

The poem conveys Mira's utter abandon in her ardor for Krishna, couched in terms very similar to that of a human passion.

A long history of bhakti poetry that used the language of erotic desire in describing the devotee's longing for god preceded Mira Bai in the Vaishnava, or Vishnu worship, tradition. As early as in eighth-century south India, Tamil bhakti poets addressed Vishnu as if they were helpless, lovesick women yearning for an end to their separation from the male beloved. The adoption of the feminine voice was deemed fitting even for male poets because the weaker and more dependent position of women in India's patriarchal society was analogous to the subservient position of a devotee in relation to the gods. Female poets like Mira Bai were rare, however, a notable exception being the Tamil poet Andal, who lived around 800. Like Mira, Andal is said to have resisted marriage because of her total dedication to her true love Krishna, and Andal too eventually disappeared into a temple image of the god. Bhakti poets such as Mira Bai and Andal, who were both later worshipped as saints, were typically credited with an utter disregard for social proprieties. While the unconventional lifestyles of male bhakti saints often involved a disdain for caste observances, those of female saints generally involved a rejection of marriage. Because so much of the popular version of Mira Bai's life appears formulaic, its historical accuracy is suspect, as is the ascription of many of her alleged poetical compositions.

Although Mira Bai left behind only a body of poem-songs, two other Krishna devotees from around her lifetime inspired bhakti movements that became major religious sects: Chaitanya (*c.* 1486–1533) and Vallabha (*c.* 1479–1531). Chaitanya, a Brahmin from Bengal, initiated an intensely emotional form of devotionalism that relied on *kirtan*, the

---

[3] Hawley and Juergensmeyer, *Songs of the Saints*, p. 134.

group singing of poems accompanied by percussion instruments. Kirtan and the repetition of Krishna's name, another favorite practice among Chaitanya's followers, could produce ecstatic and even trancelike states of mind. Both Chaitanya and Mira Bai focused on Krishna as an adolescent, when he had frequent amorous adventures with the cowherding women (*gopis*) of Vrindavan village, near Mathura. Night after night, the gopis are said to have left their sleeping families behind and hurried to secret liaisons with Krishna. Chaitanya's main interest was in the love play between Krishna and his favorite gopi, Radha, which was understood as an allegory for the ecstasy of the mutual love between the soul and god.

Vallabha's sect similarly includes an element of erotic mysticism, along with the doctrine of Krishna's divine grace. Over time, however, Vallabha's followers focused increasingly on Krishna's childhood and viewed the motherly love of Krishna's foster-mother Yashoda as a more suitable attitude for a devotee than the erotic love of Radha. From the outset, Vallabha's movement, known today as Pushti Marg, was particularly appealing to merchants, perhaps because it rejects both asceticism and ascetics. The foremost of the Pushti Marg's temple deities is Shrinathji, housed today in the town of Nathdwara in Mewar, and the sect is widespread in western India. Earlier, from *c*. 1500 to the mid seventeenth century, Shrinathji had resided in the area around Mathura that was the scene of Krishna's early life. Disciples of Chaitanya joined Vallabha and his successors in establishing a strong institutional presence in the Mathura region soon after 1500; unlike the Vallabhites, they have maintained their presence at this foremost center of Krishna pilgrimage to the present day. The majority of adherents to Chaitanya's sect, known as Gaudiya Vaishnavism, are found in eastern India.

Episodes from Krishna's childhood are given considerable attention in the *Bhagavata Purana*, a Sanskrit text produced in tenth-century south India. A Telugu Brahmin by family background, Vallabha appears to have been familiar with this work, which also became popular in eastern India. It contains the oldest detailed biography of Krishna's life from birth to death, with special emphasis on two aspects of Krishna's childhood: the supernatural powers he exhibited that enabled him to rid the country of troublesome demons, and the childish pranks that won the hearts of the cowherding women. Briefly summarized, the *Bhagavata Purana* biography states that Vishnu was born on earth as Krishna in order to oppose the evil demon-king of Mathura, Kansa. Krishna had to grow up in disguise as a cowherder in the countryside around Mathura, so as not to arouse Kansa's suspicions. After an idyllic childhood and amorous adolescence, Krishna returned to Mathura city and successfully killed the demon-king. Some time later, Krishna led his cowherding people to Dwaraka, in

Figure 4.6 This page from a *Bhagavata Purana* shows the young god surrounded by cowherding women who adore him, and reflects the growing popularity of Krishna worship in sixteenth-century north India.

western India, where he spent much of his adult life. Eventually, he became involved in the affairs leading to the great battle of the *Mahabharata* epic and died soon thereafter.

By the first half of the sixteenth century – the era of Mira Bai, Chaitanya, and Vallabha – an illustrated manuscript of the *Bhagavata Purana* was produced somewhere in north India, many believe in the region of Mathura, Krishna's birthplace. The pages from it and another related illustrated text, the twelfth-century *Gita Govinda* on the erotic love between Krishna and his consort Radha, developed from the Indic painting idiom seen in the *Kalpa Sutra*. This page from an illustrated *Bhagavata Purana* depicts Krishna as proportionally larger than the adoring cow herdesses surrounding him (Figure 4.6). The figures are angular with their heads shown in profile. They wear highly ornate clothing and are seated against an intense red ground, symbolizing their passion for one another. The emotive intensity of the text is echoed in the brilliant coloring and patterning of each page. While much painting of this sort illustrates religious texts, perhaps the most daring illustrated manuscript

Figure 4.7 This sensuous page from an illustrated *Chaurapanchashika*
reveals the increasing refinement of painting in north India by the mid
sixteenth century.

produced during this period is a secular work known as the *Chaurapanchashika*, Fifty Stanzas of a Love Thief, which is an eleventh-century
erotic poem on the seduction of a young princess by her tutor (Figure 4.7).
In style the paintings of this manuscript are highly polished versions of
the *Bhagavata Purana*, but the illustrations are bold in their portrayal of
seductive acts, as the teacher lifts his pupil's skirt to educate her in ways
far beyond her parents' expectations.

Between the fall of the Delhi Sultanate after Timur's sacking of the capital in 1398 and the rise of Mughal power during the sixteenth century,
north India was divided into a series of independent sultanates and Rajput
states. In each of these kingdoms we witness the emergence of distinctive
regional literatures and highly individualistic architectural and painting
styles. These developments laid the groundwork for the cultural transformations that would begin in the later sixteenth century under the stimulus
of the Mughal empire, the second large polity in north India since 1000.
Society in north India was hardly monolithic for, as we have seen, each
regional power had multi-cultural, multi-religious populations who in
one capacity or another were vital components of the state. A growing

interest in bhakti, that is, an intense personal form of devotionalism that had earlier commenced in south India, was seen across north India during the fifteenth and early sixteenth centuries; bhakti, despite significant changes, remains important to this day. So too Sufism, popular since at least the thirteenth century, began to spread through the subcontinent in ever larger waves, as Delhi contracted as an important center and the various orders, including the Chishti, established their own headquarters in towns and cities north, south, east, and west.

5 Sixteenth-century north India: empire reformulated

A visitor touring South Asia in the year 1500 would have found a land divided into many different polities and a variety of elite cultures. By 1600, on the other hand, virtually all the northern half of the sub-continent had been brought under the umbrella of one state, the Mughal empire. This empire was a top-down enterprise: the many local societies it ruled were not eliminated or merged but rather kept together through the imposition of a set of administrative practices and a class of ruling nobles. Over time, however, imperial ideology and institutions were disseminated throughout its many constituent units and served as a catalyst for the growth of a new kind of elite Indian culture and society, one that was both composite and widespread. This chapter examines the stages leading to the revival of empire in north India and the main architect of the Mughal state, Emperor Akbar. We consider how Akbar's concept of state evolved over time and its impact on politics and policies regarding India's multi-cultural, multi-ethnic population. In addition, we analyze how state policies affected cultural production, both on an imperial as well as subimperial level, arguing that the use of specific languages and the production of architecture and even manuscripts were all part of a carefully planned political campaign.

Toward empire

Delhi under the Lodis

Timur's sack of Delhi in 1398 left the traditional capital of the north Indian Sultanate a mere shadow of its former self. Both the Sultanate and the city of Delhi gradually regained some of their former status under three rulers of the Afghan Lodi dynasty, most notably during the reign of Sikandar Lodi (r. 1489–1517). Although the Lodis shifted their capital to Agra in 1506, Delhi remained a symbolic center and was the site of abundant architectural patronage. Lodi patronage included the repair of the earlier Qutb Minar and tomb of Firuz Shah Tughluq,

115

revealing a desire on their part to associate themselves with figures from Delhi's heyday. In addition, an elaborate royal cemetery, today known as Lodi Gardens, was constructed around the tomb of Bahlul Lodi, the founder of the Lodi dynasty. Sikandar Lodi built, adjacent to his father's tomb, a mosque complex whose decoration derived in spirit, if not in precise detail, from the architecture of the early Sultanate, which had been rarely used in the preceding 200 years. Included are the presence of calligraphy on the façade, the large scale of the buildings, and use of stellate flanges on the mosque's turrets, a clear and specific reference to the Qutb Minar. This and the fact that the Lodis repaired earlier Sultanate structures suggests they looked to Delhi's past as a model for the city's future, and perhaps as a metaphor for larger Lodi aspirations.

Babur and Humayun: the first Mughals

However, those goals were to be short lived, for the Lodi dynasty came to an end on April 20, 1526, when the Central Asian prince Babur defeated the last Lodi sultan, Ibrahim, at the famous Battle of Panipat. Babur was descended from the mighty warlord Timur (d. 1405), who had conquered a huge swathe of territory extending from Central Asia to the shores of the Mediterranean. Although they thought of themselves as belonging to Timur's lineage, Babur and his family became known as Mughals, the Perso-Arabic term for Mongols, since they were also descended from the great Mongol conqueror Genghis Khan. By the late fifteenth century the courtly culture of Timur's successors, including the production of architecture and illustrated manuscripts, was considered the most refined and sophisticated in the entire Islamicate world. Thus, the Mughals, especially in this nascent period, wished their own achievements to equal those of the Timurids and their capital to rival the great city of Samarqand, Timur's home.

Babur compared his remarkable conquest at Panipat, about 130 kilometers north of Delhi, to the earlier conquests of Mahmud of Ghazni and the Ghurids, all of whom had taken India. Babur noted that his own victory was all the more phenomenal because his army was far smaller than that of the Lodis. One factor contributing to Mughal success was the use of light cannon and guns shielded by a barricade of carts, a tactic repeated to good effect a year later at Khanua (about 60 kilometers west of Agra), against a confederation of Rajputs and Afghans led by Rana Sanga of Mewar. Babur's fast-moving cavalry, deployed in classic Central Asian flanking maneuvers, was most probably the decisive factor, however. After the resounding Mughal triumph at the 1526 Battle of Panipat,

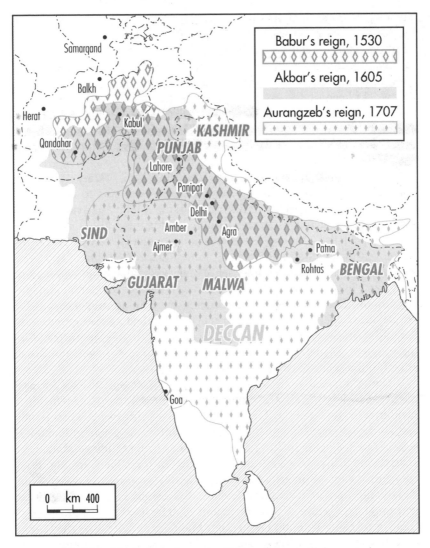

Map 5.1 Mughal empire under Babur, Akbar, and Aurangzeb

the Delhi Sultanate virtually disintegrated, and the entire territory down to the mid Gangetic plain came under Babur's sway.

Soon after his victory Babur played out his Timurid heritage by proceeding first to pay homage at the tombs, gardens, walled suburbs, and mosques of Delhi's important kings, including Aibak's Jami mosque. Babur's foremost reason for touring Delhi was a legitimizing one for, as

Ebba Koch has argued, he was retracing his ancestor Timur's steps after the conquest of Delhi in 1398. But Babur did not merely reenact the Timurid claim to Delhi, since he also visited the tombs of saints, including that of Delhi's most important saint, Nizam al-Din Auliya, something Timur had never done. In doing so, Babur added an important element that would become the essence of Mughal perception of the city by the end of the sixteenth century. Mughal interest in Delhi because of its previous Timurid connection is easy to understand, but we believe that Babur and his successors considered Delhi's value as a religious center equally important.

In spite of Babur's understanding of Delhi's symbolic role as, in his words, "the capital of Hindustan," his urgent need was to consolidate his newly won prize. Many of his high-ranking nobility had no desire to stay in India, which became increasingly intolerable as the summer heat flared, especially to those accustomed to the cooler climate of the north. Moreover, the customs and peoples of the Indian subcontinent appeared alien to Babur and his men. In order to make his military conquests more than short-lived victories, Babur needed to find ways of maintaining loyalty among his *amirs* (nobles) and reducing the seeming strangeness of the land. Babur hence continued his earlier policy of treating his supporters as comrades. In the Timurid tradition, he bonded with his supporters during frequent all-male parties where the consumption of wine and drugs added to the sense of camaraderie.

We know much about Babur's parties, habits, likes, and dislikes through his remarkable memoirs known as the *Baburnama*, written by his own hand in a form of Turkic. The text commences with events when Babur was about 10 years old and continues on, with some gaps, until about a year before his death in 1530. These writings bring to life an affable yet charismatic prince in search of a kingdom. In them we learn about an enormous range of things, including his family relationships, his passion for a young boy of the camp, detailed discussions of how battles were won and lost, his love of gardening, and what he liked and disliked about India or just simply found fascinating. Mangoes and the ways they could be eaten were among the positive. India's lack of walled gardens and running water, except large rivers, he found deplorable.

Although Babur only ruled for four years until his death in 1530, he was able to provide gardens in several important sites. The creation of gardens is not as frivolous as it might seem. Babur tells us through his memoirs that these gardens were a conscious attempt on his part to render what he considered to be an unruly India into a site of order and control. Moreover, he likened his office of kingship to that of a master gardener, making clear that these planted spaces had a political as well as a practical agenda. His gardens were modeled on Timurid ones, known as *char bagh* (that is, four-part gardens), although modifications apparently had to be made due to differences in terrain. Only one partially surviving garden, the Lotus Garden at Dholpur, about 55 kilometers south of Agra, today bears traces of Babur's patronage. Cut from the living rock, water channels link pools carved in floral forms, representing an early Mughal adaptation of Timurid aesthetics. In cities such as Agra, the gardens and their locales were named after places in Central Asia, suggesting that Babur's goal was to recreate his Timurid homeland in India.

Babur is traditionally associated with the building of three mosques in the Indian subcontinent, a form of patronage in which he never engaged in the Timurid homeland. However, once Babur had proclaimed himself emperor, he needed to legitimize this new Mughal rule. He thus used the traditional idiom of Islamic kings to cast himself as a faithful Muslim ruler over idolatrous non-Muslim subjects. The patronage of two of these three mosques was not directly Babur's, including the infamous so-called Baburi mosque at Ayodhya built by a noble, Mir Baqi, in 1528–29 and destroyed by Hindu fundamentalists in 1992. Here we will focus only on the Kabuli Bagh mosque, built by Babur at Panipat in 1527–28, which was clearly geared toward proclaiming his political aspirations. The plan of the Kabuli Bagh mosque, as well as aspects of its vaults, emulated the imperial Timurid mosque type as much as was possible in India, a land at this point lacking Timurid-trained architects and engineers. In contrast to the single-aisled, multi-bayed contemporary north Indian imperial mosque, the Kabuli Bagh mosque was much closer in plan to those royal ones in Samarqand with great vaulted entrances. While it was a religious structure, the Kabuli Bagh mosque, built over the site of Babur's defeat of the last independent sultan of Delhi, served as a political statement of new Mughal hegemony (Figure 5.1).

Although the dynasty lasted until 1858, when the British exiled the last Mughal ruler to Rangoon, shortly after Babur's death in 1530 a crisis developed which nearly snuffed out the nascent house. Babur was succeeded by his son, Humayun, who was less pragmatic than his father in matters of state. Interested in astrology, illustrated books, and in building innovative palaces, including the founding of a citadel in Delhi which he named the Din Panah ("Refuge of Religion," today known as the Purana Qila), Humayun lacked political skills. His enemies included Rajputs, the sultan of Gujarat, and the claimant to the Lodi throne among others who wished to rout the Mughals from India. His major adversary, however, turned out to be an Afghan upstart known as Sher Khan and later as Sher Shah Sur, who by 1540 was able to expel Humayun from India, forcing him eventually to take refuge in the court of the Iranian Safavid ruler, Shah Tahmasp.

Figure 5.1 The Kabuli Bagh mosque was built by Babur in celebration of Mughal victory at Panipat, the site of his momentous defeat of the Lodis in 1526.

The Sur interregnum

Sher Shah Sur (r. 1538–45) was unusual in the history of Indian sultans, for he rose from obscurity, lacking the customary high lineage, to become Delhi's most powerful ruler since the mid fourteenth century. His success can be attributed to several factors: he made his bid from the hinterlands and hence did not appear as a threat to Humayun until it was too late; through marriage, alliance, and looting he was able to amass extraordinary wealth; and his was clearly a charismatic personality, a feature of several rulers of sixteenth-century Delhi including Babur and the future Mughal, Akbar. An additional factor was Sher Shah's ability to raise a massive army composed not only of Afghans but also of groups drawn from north India's diverse communities. As Dirk Kolff has shown, he assured their loyalty through a regular salary and consistent discipline. Sher Shah's interest in India's multiple communities is also displayed in his inscriptions, some of which were written in both Indic and Persian languages.

After he became master of Delhi in 1540, Sher Shah implemented, on a larger scale, practices that he had introduced earlier while the *de facto* ruler of eastern India. These included the branding of horses, a procedure initially employed by Ala al-Din Khalji to ensure that horses required for service could not be counted multiple times; the notion of measuring land to calculate the tax rate; and the standardization of the silver-based monetary unit called the *rupiya*, the ancestor of South Asia's modern rupee currency. These measures were adopted and further refined by the Mughal ruler Akbar some years later. Even Abu al-Fazl, Akbar's pan-egyrist, grudgingly acknowledged Sher Shah's administrative abilities and innovations. Sher Shah was also renowned for his execution of justice and fairness to the common man.

Although ignored by most historians concerned only with administra-tive, agrarian, and fiscal practices, Sher Shah's architectural and public works projects tell us a great deal about his rule and public policies. Sher Shah is known for his prolific and widespread architectural patronage, providing exactly the sorts of buildings considered appropriate for royal sponsorship; these included roads, *serais* (inns for travelers), mosques, and forts. What is all the more remarkable is that Sher Shah built such structures from Bengal through the Punjab and restored the highway that linked the Indian subcontinent from east to west, although he only ruled for seven years. This is extremely unusual for, as the fourteenth-century Arab scholar Ibn Khaldun has observed, it is typically only the third ruler of any dynasty who is able to muster the energy and resources to build widely throughout his domain. Thus, Sher Shah's building program was clearly part of a carefully organized propagandistic campaign, designed to visually tout him as an ideal Islamic sultan. The utilitarian nature of these works contrasts with Humayun's largely frivolous architectural patronage and even with Babur's patronage of gardens whose access would be lim-ited to the elite.

Among Sher Shah's works that served the needs of the public are two forts he built, each known today as Rohtas (one in Pakistan and the other in eastern India). He also completed the Din Panah, Humayun's citadel in Delhi (see Map 7.1). These massive stone-constructed forts are concrete symbols of his military might. Sher Shah's interest in serving Islam is manifest by his most ornate mosque, the Qila-i Kuhna, inside the Delhi citadel (Figure 5.2). This mosque, even more than the one at the Lodi cemetery complex, makes explicit reference to the Sultanate past. This is seen in several features, such as the use of colored stones throughout the mosque and the cusped entrance arches – features specifically borrowed from Ala al-Din Khalji's Alai Darwaza (see Figure 2.3), recalling that Sher Shah modeled a number of his administrative reforms on those of Ala al-Din Khalji.

Sher Shah also built tombs for his long-deceased, low-ranking grand-father in Narnaul (in Haryana), and his father in Sasaram (in eastern India, about 110 kilometers east of Benares). His grandfather's mau-soleum was a square-plan tomb, like those usually built for high-ranking

Figure 5.2 Sher Shah provided the Qila-i Kuhna mosque inside his Delhi fort, designing it in a manner that recalls the 1311 Alai Darwaza of Ala al-Din Khalji.

nobles, but it was larger and more splendid than any previous one. The tomb Sher Shah provided for his father was an octagonal tomb, the type often associated with royalty; it too was larger than other tombs of this sort. In doing this, Sher Shah was creating a visual, albeit fictitious, genealogy to suggest that he had the requisite high birth demanded of Islamic rulers. For himself, Sher Shah built an enormous octagonal tomb, also in Sasaram, situated in an artificial lake (Figure 5.3). The largest tomb ever built in India up to that time, its setting is a visual allusion to the abundant waters of paradise described in the Quran, and this particular Quranic verse is carved on the tomb's interior prayer niche. The tomb suggests Sher Shah had qualities of both piety and high birth. The scale of all three tombs doubtless played some role in the Mughal decision to construct monumental imperial mausolea, so as not to be outdone by their enemy.

Humayun's return to India

Even before Sher Shah died in 1545, Humayun left Iran with the goal of retaking India, which he eventually accomplished in 1555. In the

Figure 5.3 Sher Shah's enormous tomb in Sasaram, dated 1545, was part of a planned campaign to elevate his lowly status.

meantime, Humayun established himself in Kabul, where his brother Kamran had been ruling essentially as an independent prince. Kamran had been able to establish a scriptorium, a workshop for copying and illustrating texts, in Kabul. Several esteemed Persian artists had joined this atelier, giving it considerable prestige. When Humayun wrested Kabul from Kamran, he also inherited Kamran's painting workshop, which produced highly Persianized paintings, bringing Humayun's court closer to Timurid cultural values. The most important is a painting on cloth known today as the Princes of the House of Timur. Its large size suggests that, unlike most painting of this period, it was intended for public consumption and was probably hung at court. Its subject matter, showing the first two Mughal rulers (now repainted and replaced with later Mughals) is a visual genealogy, for it originally depicted portraits of Mughal ancestors going back to Timur, thus making it a legitimizing document. The entire illustration is set in a garden, evoking Babur's metaphor of control.

The career of Akbar

Securing the empire

Only one year after his return to Delhi in 1555, Humayun fell from the steep steps of his library in the Din Panah, dying shortly thereafter. He was succeeded by his eldest son, the 12-year-old Jalal al-Din Muhammad Akbar, whose reign lasted for nearly fifty years, from 1556 to 1605. The achievements of Akbar were many; until his death he was continuously refining his ideology of the state, as well as the practical means through which this concept was executed. Through his reforms of administration and taxation Akbar created a sound and enduring foundation for Mughal governance, while his tolerant attitude and inclusive policies toward Hindus and Jains helped create a state that was more Indian in character. Akbar's court patronage of the arts placed Mughal art and architecture on a par with that of the contemporary Safavids and Ottomans.

Many consider Akbar the most brilliant emperor of the Mughal house, while others include him among South Asia's three greatest leaders, the other two being Ashoka, who ruled from 273–232 BCE, and Jawaharlal Nehru, who was prime minister of independent India from 1947 to 1964. Unlike his grandfather, Babur, Akbar did not write his own memoirs. Since he was unable to read, probably because he was dyslexic, his friend and confidant, Abu al-Fazl, wrote a detailed, lengthy, and eulogistic history of his reign. Others too, some admirers of Akbar and others foes, wrote their own chronicles of his reign, giving us a detailed picture of Akbar as a person and Akbar as a leader. Akbar comes out as a liberal who was the friend of South Asia's political minorities while at the same time furthering the strength of his own house. He was a hands-on ruler who was engaged in virtually every level of administration. He, moreover, cared deeply about India and its people, often not only experimenting with how his subjects might best be served but also exploring the very essence of human nature. An excellent case in point is the time he had infants moved to a special house where no person was to talk to them, so that the natural language of mankind might be revealed. The experiment failed, but it is a reflection of Akbar's desire to explore in a scientific manner the nature of humans and what he believed to be their common condition. His belief in a common condition that united all peoples was a key to his own political policy which embraced the notion of universal toleration (*sulh-i kul*).

The first several years of Akbar's reign were fraught with problems, as the young emperor had to contend both with Sur claimants attempting to win back the throne and with a powerful but unpopular regent whom he dismissed in 1560. Land too needed to be regained and authority asserted in what was then a shaky Mughal state. In the earliest phase of his career, Akbar's foremost concern was to secure the empire his father had so recently recovered. This entailed moving beyond the previous Mughal heartland, the territory extending from Lahore in the west to Jaunpur in the east, into adjacent territories. The initial target was Central India, whose kingdoms of Malwa and Gondwana were conquered in 1561 and 1564, respectively.

A widespread revolt from 1564 to 1567 among the Central Asian nobles who dominated the higher levels of Mughal administration caused a temporary halt in Akbar's expansionist drive. Rather like the near contemporary Safavid ruler, Shah Abbas (r. 1587–1629), who was eager to curtail the power of the disruptive Qizilbash tribe responsible for elevating his predecessors to power, so too Akbar, even earlier than Shah Abbas, began to see the merit in decreasing the power of the men who had assisted in Humayun's triumphant return to India. To reduce the number of Central Asian nobles, Akbar replaced them primarily with Persian amirs and secondarily with Indian-born nobles drawn from a variety of backgrounds, excluding Afghans who were still contesting Mughal sovereignty at the fringes of empire in eastern India. The Indian nobles were drawn from leading Muslim families who could be depended on to raise large kin-based contingents for the Mughal army. Central Asians continued to be the largest group at court, however, and some of them were very close to Akbar. One example is Abd al-Rahim Khan-i Khanan, whose patronage will be discussed later in this chapter.

Once the internal challenges to his power were suppressed, Akbar again went on the offensive, this time in Rajasthan, which flanked his territory to the south. His fiercest assault was on Chittor, the formidable base of the Sisodiya family, during the winter of 1567–68. Foremost among all Rajputs in prestige, the Sisodiyas steadfastly refused to acknowledge Mughal authority. The Mughal army finally captured Chittor after the near complete destruction of the massive fort in a siege lasting over two months, and the self-immolation of many of the fort's women, dying to preserve their honor. Perhaps as a message to the defiant Sisodiya king who had left Chittor before the siege, Akbar had thousands of the fort's remaining inhabitants slaughtered. The following year Akbar attacked the second great fortress in Rajasthan, Ranthambhor, which submitted to him with far less bloodshed (see Map 2.2 for locations of Chittor and Ranthambhor). In both cases, the Mughal army made good use of their expertise with cannon. The importance of these sieges as demonstrations of Mughal might is indicated by the prominence they are accorded in illustrations of the *Akbarnama*, the official history of Akbar's reign.

In his dealings with the Rajputs, Akbar made a decisive break with the previous practice of Indo-Muslim kings toward the Hindu rulers they had subjugated. Instead of merely reinstating them to power over their ancestral territories, Akbar sought to make the Rajputs active participants in the enterprise of empire. These Hindu warriors became the second segment of the Indian-born nobility that Akbar recruited into his imperial service. Like the Indian Muslim nobles, they too could raise armies for the emperor from among their own kin. Akbar had begun the process of incorporating Rajputs into the ruling elite as early as 1561, when he married a princess of the then insignificant Kachhwaha house of Amber. From this moment on, the Kachhwaha fortune rose as Amber's princesses became Mughal queens and mothers while princes, like Raja Man Singh, became leading generals in the Mughal army.

In the aftermath of the Mughal victories at Chittor and Ranthambhor, all aristocratic Rajput lineages except the Sisodiyas of Mewar submitted to Mughal authority. Thereafter, the Rajput princes performed a dual role. On the one hand, they were inducted as nobles in the Mughal military machine and represented the Mughal emperor in whatever capacity and locale they served. On the other hand, they also acted as figureheads of their own states and maintained their own customs, religious and social, in their homelands (*watan jagir*). However, not until the eighteenth century was it possible for Rajput princes to expand the size of their ancestral lands, since they remained under the direct jurisdiction of their Mughal overlord.

Creating an enduring state

By approximately 1570, Akbar had proved in highly public and indisputable ways that he was the paramount ruler of north India. He subsequently led fewer armies into battle personally. Notable campaigns that he did command included Gujarat in 1572–73, eastern India in 1574, and one against his half-brother Mirza Muhammad Hakim in 1581. The Kachhwaha prince Man Singh played an active role in the Gujarat campaign, vowing to build a temple at Vrindavan, a locality associated with the youth of the god Krishna. After his initial victory in Patna in 1574, Akbar entrusted the command of his eastern army to several officers, among whom was another Hindu, Todar Mal. For the rest of the decade, Akbar spent much time in his new capital at Fatehpur Sikri. Instead of military conquest, Akbar's focus increasingly turned to religious questions, as will be discussed in the following section.

The 1570s were a time when the various aspects of managing a large realm – such as the organization of the nobility, the surveying of land, and levying of taxes – were refined and standardized. The administrative structures and systems which matured in this decade were among Akbar's greatest legacies to his successors and even to states that followed the demise of the Mughals. We might therefore view the 1570s as a second phase in Akbar's career, a period when the security of the empire was no longer in doubt and attention could be directed instead to ensuring its stability over the long term. With all significant challenges to Mughal political authority eliminated, a primary task in this second phase was to strengthen the foundations of Mughal governance.

Reorganization of the imperial service – that is, the Mughal army and bureaucracy – had begun even earlier. All Mughal officers were given a specific numeric rank (*mansab*) ranging from 10 to 5,000, with those at the 500 or higher level being considered nobles. The higher the rank attained by an officer or *mansabdar*, the greater the number of horsemen he was supposed to maintain under his charge. The Mughal administrative system was hence based on the need to recruit a large number of armed men; the core of the imperial service consisted of several hundred high-ranking amirs or nobles, who between them commanded 100,000 to 200,000 mounted warriors. Their ability to induct influential men, who could draw on kin, household, and community networks in order to supply the needed military forces, was the key to Mughal success in warfare. As Jos Gommans has said, "in terms of cavalry warfare, there was nothing new, but there was certainly more, under the Mughal sun."[1] More Rajputs and Indian Muslims were included in the imperial service as Akbar's reign wore on; by the 1580s the number of Rajput, Indian Muslim, and Persian officers was roughly comparable. Akbar's officers remained predominantly Central Asian in origin, however, especially at the higher ranks, which included relatives of the king.

Mansabdars (rank-holders) were either assigned an agrarian landholding known as a *jagir*, the income from which would provide the noble's salary, or they were paid directly from the royal treasury. The jagir can be compared to the earlier iqta revenue assignment of the Delhi Sultanate, with two crucial differences. The jagir-holder or *jagirdar* had authority only over the revenue of the lands he was assigned, with administrative and military matters delegated to a separate authority. The holder of an iqta, in contrast, had wielded all aspects of state authority within his territory. Secondly, Akbar further enhanced the relative strength of the center in relation to its officers by frequently changing the size and location of jagirs, according to an officer's performance. The jagirdar thus had considerably less power than had the iqta-holder before him. Because the Mughal army paid its cavalrymen well, at a rate approximately three times higher than that of the Safavid army of Iran, the costs to the empire were enormous. An estimated 80 percent of all imperial revenues, during Akbar's reign, was allocated to the salaries and jagirs of the mansabdars, for their personal expenses and those of their troops.

[1] *Mughal Warfare: Indian Frontiers and High Roads to Empire, 1500–1700* (London and New York: Routledge, 2002), p. 120.

Starting in the 1560s, with further refinements made in the 1570s by Akbar's revenue minister Todar Mal, land and tax reforms initially instituted by Sher Shah Sur were reinstated in an improved form. All land was measured according to a uniform imperial standard to determine the agricultural yield rate. Then, based on data gathered from a ten-year period on the yield and price of crops in any particular locality, tax rates were established with greater accuracy than ever before. The taxes, which amounted to about half of the total yield, had to be paid in cash, hence continuing Sher Shah's emphasis on cash payment and his introduction of a standard, uniform silver coinage. The revenue was collected by middlemen known as *zamindars*. The term zamindar literally means landholders but it was also used in a second sense as a designation for local notables. These men essentially retained their traditional role as chiefs or leaders at the local level by paying tribute to the Mughal court, which led to little change in village or community life, while enhancing considerably the imperial coffers. Zamindars typically also maintained their own armed forces, totaling perhaps 300,000 horsemen by the mid seventeenth century.

In reaction to the centralization of power in Akbar's hands and to his progressively more unorthodox religious and social views, a rebellion broke out in 1580 among Central Asian nobles based in eastern India. Simultaneously, Akbar's half-brother Mirza Muhammad Hakim advanced into the Punjab from his base in Kabul. Although the immediate danger was quickly suppressed, both the northwestern and eastern portions of Akbar's empire continue to demand his attention for several years afterward. Akbar moved in the mid 1580s from the centrally located Fatehpur Sikri (not far from Agra) to the Punjabi city of Lahore, in order to better oversee the conquest of the northwest frontier territories and Kashmir. Bengal was brought under Mughal control in the same period, but that region remained problematic until the reign of the next emperor, Jahangir. Meanwhile, operations against the lower Indus valley region of Sind commenced. Akbar's last area of expansion was the Deccan, in which he took an increasing interest during the 1590s. By the time of his death in 1605, the Mughal empire extended from Bengal in the east almost to Herat in modern Afghanistan in the west and from the Godavari river in the south to the mountains of Kashmir in the north. The additional conquests of the third and final phase of Akbar's career, from the 1580s onward, set the basic geographical contours of the empire for the next fifty years. But it was in the area of religious thought and the arts that Akbar's innovative character came most clearly to the forefront in the last quarter-century of his life.

Akbar's religious policies

As a young man Akbar had several mystical experiences, one of which occurred in conjunction with hearing songs (*qawwali*) about the Chishti saint of Ajmer, Muin al-Din. Shortly after this experience in 1562, the young ruler resolved to visit Muin al-Din's tomb at Ajmer, thereby launching a seventeen-year period of devotion to this shrine in particular, and the Chishti order of Sufis in general. Akbar's high regard for the Chishti grew even greater when Shaikh Salim Chishti predicted the birth of sons to the heirless 27-year-old ruler. After the birth in 1571 of Prince Salim, the future Emperor Jahangir, Akbar commenced the building of a palace, known as Fatehpur Sikri, at the Shaikh's humble abode 38 kilometers from Agra. Akbar's interest in religion continued to be manifest at Fatehpur Sikri, and in 1575 he ordered the construction of a building, called the Ibadat Khana, to facilitate religious discussions. These discussions were initially held only among various Muslim theologians, but by the end of the decade non-Muslims, including Brahmins, Parsis (Zoroastrians), Jains, and Portuguese priests who had settled in Goa, were also invited to participate.

While a number of Akbar's policies, such as the state sponsorship of pilgrims going on the Hajj to Mecca, were supportive of orthodox Islam, the genuine interest Akbar showed in non-Muslim practice and belief systems offended highly placed devout Muslims. The orthodox also resented the steps that Akbar increasingly took to lessen the differences in the state's treatment of its subjects, especially the rescinding of the jizya and other taxes on non-Muslims. Akbar's extension of tax-free lands to Hindu and Jain temples, for instance, was thought to have occurred at the expense of Muslim institutions. Then in 1579 a decree was introduced that gave the emperor ultimate authority in religious decisions when ambiguity prevailed. By about 1580, non-Muslims were officially accorded the same rights as Muslims in a policy known as sulh-i kul, which translates freely as universal toleration. Abu al-Fazl, the mastermind of Akbar's state, saw sulh-i kul as the state's keystone. In order to effectively institute a policy of universal toleration, however, Akbar had to diminish the authority of the ulama, the orthodox Islamic scholars. Akbar's liberal religious policies caused enough dissent among the Afghan-descended population of eastern India to result in widespread rebellion there in the early 1580s; the latter part of Akbar's reign was directed toward military action in that region.

Abu al-Fazl, a young man belonging to a free-thinking intellectual family well versed in Islamic theology, had entered the court in 1575.

His influence on Akbar's thinking was such that ultimately Akbar's attitudes toward religion and the state were transformed. By the early 1580s Akbar's interests in orthodox organized Islam had waned, concurrent with his growing emphasis on the policy of sulh-i kul. For example, he stopped making pilgrimage to the tombs of saints and at the same time incorporated many practices associated with the veneration of light into his own court ritual. While many scholarly works on the Mughal period claim that Akbar invented a new religion known as the Din-i Ilahi, this is an older view based on mistranslations of Abu al-Fazl's writings about Akbar. In fact, the Din-i Ilahi was a discipleship order intended to bind the highest ranking nobles in complete loyalty to the emperor, not unlike the relationship that bonded the first Safavid ruler Ismail (r. 1501–24) and his Qizilbash supporters. Akbar was seen as a master (*pir*) in the Sufi sense and his devotees were like students (*murids*). The highest-ranking nobles answered directly to Akbar just as these nobles' officers answered to them, thus guaranteeing downward and upward flows of loyalty.

Akbar always showed a genuine interest in matters religious and, more than any other ruler of the Mughal house, understood that a liberal religious policy was the key to relative tranquility in the Mughal state. It thus comes as no surprise that Akbar's religious and political ideologies were intimately interlinked. Akbar's and Abu al-Fazl's religious dispositions informed state policy of which the adoption of sulh-i kul is a clear example. But sulh-i kul was part of a larger project in which Abu al-Fazl, trained in the illumination philosophy of the twelfth-century mystic Suhrawardi, cast Akbar as a Perfect Man. This is an Islamic theological concept whereby Akbar was presented as a semi-divine ruler illumined with god's light and hence superior to mere mortals. In Akbar's official history, the *Akbarnama*, Abu al-Fazl indicated that Akbar, ruling from his divinely bestowed office, had several unique qualities: one was his ability to receive extraordinary divine revelation; two, he was like a father to his subjects, borrowing from ancient Indian concepts of kingship; three, Akbar was dedicated to communal harmony, corresponding to Suhrawardi's belief that if a divinely enlightened ruler ruled benevolently, then his state would be an enlightened one. Together these three qualities generated the concept of sulh-i kul or peace toward all, perhaps the most significant aspect of Akbar's fifty-year reign.

The gradual changes in Akbar's governance over his long career steadily moved the state in the direction of inclusiveness. Akbar began his career with a group of supporters and a style of rulership inherited from his father which was heavily Islamic, and specifically Central Asian, in orientation. As his empire expanded into territories far beyond those controlled by the last dynasty of the Delhi Sultanate, Akbar broadened his base of support by inducting a number of indigenous warriors, both Muslim and Hindu, into the inner circles of power. That his inclination to be inclusive was not merely a pragmatic decision is revealed in Akbar's subsequent actions. He not only sought to eliminate distinctions in state policy based on religious affiliation, but he also transcended the boundaries between the Islamic and the Indic traditions in his own court ritual and imperial ideology. We will see shortly that he was similarly innovative in creating a composite culture when it came to the arts. The Mughal empire of Akbar's latter days, although certainly not representative of the population over which it presided, was well on its way to becoming a uniquely Indian state.

Akbar as patron of the arts

Like Babur and Humayun, Akbar also understood the value of patronizing the arts. Due to the length of his reign and extent of his resources, he was able to support artists, architects, literary figures, and musicians on a sustained basis, allowing them to develop distinguishable idioms associated with Akbar. While some of these arts – music played in the private quarters, for instance – were consumed purely for pleasure, others were a reflection of Akbar's office of kingship and involved consciously conceived modes of presentation, creating a unique imperial iconography meant to showcase this semi-divine ruler. The uniform aesthetic that developed under Akbar's guidance was composed of a fusion of Timurid and Indic models. It went on to set a standard for subsequent Mughal arts, both in its forms and in its embedded messages of dynastic greatness.

Architecture as visual manifestation of dynamic leadership

Akbar was an active patron of architecture, just as Sher Shah and his Sultanate predecessors had been, believing in the long-standing Islamic notion that architecture was the direct visual reflection of any dynamic ruler's authority. His first architectural project, Humayun's tomb, was begun shortly after his father's death in 1556. Situated in Delhi, it was close to Humayun's citadel at Din Panah and across from the tomb of the Chishti saint Nizam al-Din Auliya (see Map 7.1), thus signifying the dynasty's dual sources of legitimacy. By this time, Akbar had moved his capital to Agra, following the example of his grandfather Babur, who in turn had simply taken over the facilities of the previous ruling dynasty, the Lodis. But Delhi, which had been the primary base of both Humayun and Sher Shah, continued to be regarded as the traditional center of Muslim India. Designed by Muhammad-i Mirak, who belonged to a family of Timurid landscape architects, Humayun's large tomb in Delhi was completed in 1571. Its plan and elevation, as one might expect, was designed in the Timurid tradition and intended as a bold visual statement of dynastic origin. Yet the tomb's red sandstone facing trimmed with white marble belongs to the Indian tradition and remains the hallmark of much Mughal architecture. Placed in the middle of a walled four-part garden (char bagh), the tomb is intended to evoke not only Babur's concept of controlled order but also a larger Islamic one of paradise on earth.

Akbar's main architectural contribution was a series of fortified palaces which he built from Attock in modern Pakistan to Allahabad in order to protect his ever-growing domain. In 1565 he began to replace the Lodi period Agra mud fort with an awe-inspiring red sandstone one. Only a few of the original 500 interior pavilions built by Akbar in Agra survive. The most notable is the so-called Jahangiri Mahal, part of the women's quarters. Its exterior, like Humayun's tomb, is red sandstone traced with white marble. The interior combines both Indian and Central Asian elements; for example, the open central courtyards recall those of the palace built for a Hindu king in Gwalior (see chapter 4), while some of the pillared interiors are stone translations of pillar types used in Timurid buildings. Other courtyards feature elaborately carved brackets, recalling those of western India. The plan and decor of the Jahangiri Mahal are particularly rich examples of the fusion of Indian and Timurid conventions at Akbar's fortified palace in Agra, which for Abu al-Fazl was "the center of Hindustan." The blending of Central Asian and Indian cultures that Akbar brought about in the sphere of politics is thus paralleled in his architecture, just as it was in the painting and the other arts he sponsored.

Akbar's largest and perhaps most important complex is the city and palace he founded at Fatehpur Sikri, his second capital. Located within a day's ride from Agra, Akbar commenced the Fatehpur Sikri project in 1571 out of the respect he held for Shaikh Salim Chishti, the Sufi who successfully predicted the birth of his son and heir. Fatehpur Sikri remained the official capital until 1585, when troubling events in the northwest made the court shift to Lahore. Much of the main palace is extant; red sandstone pavilions linked by gardens and courtyards comprise the royal complex. There are a number of buildings still on the periphery, while excavations carried out largely in the 1980s and 1990s have revealed extensive remains of the women's quarters, shops, and a number of other structures. Although some of the extant and excavated areas can be identified with certainty, the original functions of others remain ambiguous, and scholarly opinion is divided on their purpose.

Figure 5.4 This white marble tomb was built at Fatehpur Sikri for Shaikh Salim Chishti, who had predicted the birth of Akbar's son.

One focal point of the palace whose purpose is clear is the khanqah built for Shaikh Salim. Entered on the south by an enormous arched entrance gate known as the Buland Darwaza, towering 54 meters high, it surpasses in height Timur's own palace in modern Uzbekistan. While ostensibly built to celebrate Akbar's successful acquisition of Gujarat in western India, it more immediately underscored Akbar's links with the Chishti order. In the khanqah's interior open courtyard is an enormous Jami mosque, the largest in Akbar's India, whose façade and interior exhibit a combination of Timurid and Indian elements. However, the nucleus of the courtyard is the white marble tomb of Shaikh Salim himself (Figure 5.4). At this time white marble was reserved for saints' shrines alone, although under Akbar's successors it would also be used for imperial monuments. Shaikh Salim Chishti died in 1572, but his tomb was not completed until 1580–81, ironically at a time when Akbar had begun to abandon the veneration of Sufi saints.

The main entrance to the administrative and residential portion of the palace complex at Fatehpur Sikri is the Hathiya Pol or Elephant Gate, probably intended as a grand ceremonial gate for Akbar himself. Once inside, the palace consists of numerous pillared pavilions composed of red sandstone, much of which is ornately carved. The post and lintel nature of the structures is a long-standing Indian one, but the carved motifs derive from both Indian and Timurid forms. The large quadrangular courtyard to the east of the Elephant Gate served as the Public Audience Hall (Diwan-i Amm), with Akbar's pillared throne in the west wall. Thus, when Akbar's subjects faced him they were looking in the direction of the qibla, that is, the direction of prayer, in accordance with the evolving imperial ideology that cast the king as semi-divine.

The area to the west of the Public Audience Hall appears to have had ceremonial and administrative functions. At the southernmost end was Akbar's viewing window (*jharoka-i darshan*) through which he presented himself to his subjects, thus playing out his role as a father to his people. Moving north on a direct line is Akbar's bedroom, known as the Khwab-gah, and the Anup Talao, a square pool in the center of which was a pavilion; today only the base remains. Contemporary texts indicate this area was the site of the Ibadat Khana, where religious discussions took place, but it is difficult to reconcile the remains with textual descriptions. Further north on this same axis is an unusual structure that is traditionally considered to be Akbar's Diwan-i Khass or Private Audience Hall. In the center of the room's interior is an elaborately carved pillar that extends about halfway up the room's total height. This platform is believed to have served as Akbar's throne where he projected himself as the pillar of the Mughal state (Figure 5.5).

Fatehpur Sikri is considerably more Indian in appearance than is Humayun's tomb or even the Agra fort's Jahangiri Mahal. During the period that Akbar was building at Fatehpur Sikri, the 1570s, he was concerned with retaining the favor of his Indian Muslim and Hindu subjects while correspondingly reducing the power of the dominant Central Asian and Iranian nobility. These politically motivated moves are mirrored in the architectural style used at Fatehpur Sikri. Imperially sponsored architecture under Akbar thus reflects his ideological interests, which over time increasingly came to focus on the non-Muslim aspects of the society he ruled. Just as Akbar's involvement with orthodox Islam had gradually waned by the 1580s, so too did Akbar eventually turn away from the traditional royal emphasis on monumental architecture. Handing over the responsibility of constructing monuments to the nobility, Akbar became more engrossed in the production of lavish illustrated manuscripts in his later years.

Painting the imperial image

Throughout Akbar's reign a large and active painting workshop was maintained, from which illustrated manuscripts and album pages were

Figure 5.5 The top of this pillar inside Akbar's Private Audience
Hall at Fatehpur Sikri served as the emperor's throne.

produced in prodigious numbers. While Humayun had only Iranian artists in his workshop, Akbar's painting atelier also included Indians, in parallel with the changing composition of his nobles. A third influence, that of European prints, also entered the court shortly after Akbar's accession to the throne. Artists were drawn to the figural types, the use of shading to indicate volume, and the element of naturalism in European art, as well as the presence of distant landscapes in the background. Over time, the manipulation of Persian, Indian, and European features by highly skilled artists allowed a sophisticated style to evolve where the natural and the stylized could happily reside on a single page.

The two earliest projects of the court reflect the king's changing concerns as he grew older. The first project appears to be a manuscript of the *Tutinama*, Tales of the Parrot, which was initially executed in the 1560s (Figure 5.6). Although the styles of the 218 illustrated folios vary, almost all of them suggest that Indian artists trained in the styles of the *Chaurapanchashika* and other contemporary paintings worked on this project. The *Tutinama* was composed by the fourteenth-century Indian poet, Ziya al-Din Nakhshabi, who wrote in Persian. It is a series of stories within a story about a woman whose husband is away for extended periods of time; to maintain her chastity, the parrot tells a story each night to keep her from meeting her lover. This small size book with its moralistic tales must have had some interest for the teen-aged Akbar, for he had a penchant for good stories. But more likely this book was intended for his *haram* who included female kin, wives, and their many women servants. During this period, Akbar was establishing his authority through marriage alliances to important Muslim and Hindu families; thus, the haram began to match the diversity of the nobility.

The *Tutinama*'s message, control of women, should be understood in the context of powerful older women who were dominating court affairs until the young Akbar was able to get the upper hand. In spite of the seeming invisibility of Mughal court women, they had important roles to play. Young women were vital to the on-going success of the dynasty, as they bore and reared children. Older women were not only power makers and breakers, but often important advisers, as in the case of Akbar's mother Hamida Banu Begum. Holding the prestigious position of queen mother for about fifty years until her death in 1604, in her youth she had accompanied Humayun into exile. The queen owned an illustrated copy of the *Ramayana*, a Hindu epic about the exploits of the god Rama, in Persian translation. Its narrative may have appealed to her since she, like the heroine Sita, spent many years in difficult and often dangerous conditions in exile. A royal order issued by her gifting tax-free lands to the son of Vallabha, the founder of a Krishna bhakti movement, suggests that she,

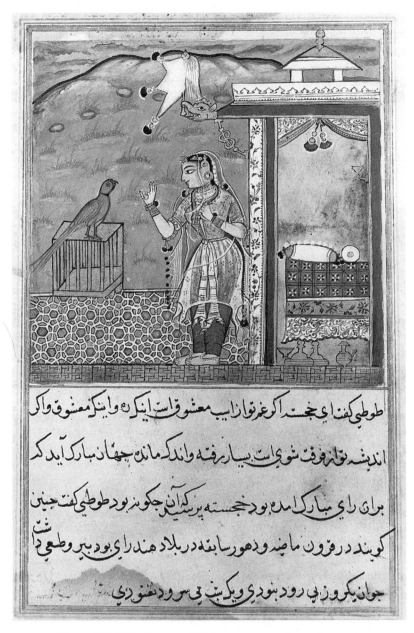

طوطی کفتای خجسته اگرغرقوار بی معشوقاست ابنکره وابنکرمعشوقوا کر

اندیشه تولهونت شویات بسیاررفته واندکرما بنجهان مبارک آیدکر

برای رای مبارک امدوبود خجسته پرسید انکوبرود طوطی کفت چنین

کویندردوزون ماصدودهورسایندهدربلاد هندرای بودیبیروطوعا

جوانی بکرویزی رودبودیویکبنی ی سرودمغنودی

Figure 5.6 This illustrated *Tutinama*, a story about the need to control women, was probably intended as a message for the ladies of Akbar's court, who until this time had been a dominating force.

like her son, was interested in religious traditions outside of Islam. During her life she played a role in major events such as the ouster of Akbar's regent and Akbar's reconciliation with Salim, the future Jahangir. She was so trusted that she served for a while as governor of the Punjab. The importance of women at the Mughal court should not be surprising, given the relatively strong status of women in Turco-Mongol society. Moreover, Timur himself claimed his right to rule on the grounds of his marriage to one of Genghis Khan's descendants.

The second illustrated manuscript project, *Dastan-i Amir Hamza,* probably executed between 1562 and 1577, was much more extensive in scope. It was the story of the fictitious adventures of Amir Hamza, an uncle of the Prophet Muhammad. The text originally contained 1,400 illustrations compiled in fourteen volumes. The entire project was initially supervised by Mir Sayyid Ali and then Abd al-Samad, two Iranian painters brought to India by Humayun, but clearly Indian artists worked on it also, as indicated by the volume of the figures, the choice of colors, and the manner of presenting the narrative. These large-scale folios were held up for Akbar to see as the adventures were read to him. Packed with dramatic battles and miraculous escapes, the theme of this manuscript would have been much closer to Akbar's own tastes during a period when his life was filled with military campaigns aimed at the consolidation of empire.

Although European prints had made an impact on Mughal painting as early as the production of the *Tutinama* and *Hamza* stories, in 1580 Portuguese Jesuit priests came from Goa to Akbar's court with gifts, among which was a multi-volume illustrated *Royal Polyglot Bible* printed between 1568 and 1573 at Antwerp. In time, many Flemish and Dutch prints entered the court as well. These illustrations were studied and adapted by Mughal artists who incorporated them, sometimes wholesale and more often with modifications, into their own creations. The themes of the prints, and especially images of the Virgin Mary, Jesus, and various saints, had special interest for the emperor, his successor Jahangir, and his artists. Mary was equated with the progenitor of the Timurid house, a princess who had been impregnated with divine light, and became a popular title for court women. So, for example, Akbar's mother Hamida Banu Begum was given the title Maryam Makhani, Mary of the (Mughal) house, after her death. Jesus, when paired with Mary, was a reference to Akbar, who was descended from the Timurid princess mentioned above. While the Jesuits presented these illustrations to the Mughal court hoping for wholesale conversion, the Mughals were only interested in using Christian images to project their own semi-divine image (Figure 5.7).

Figure 5.7 Imagery of Mary, equated with the progenitor of the Mughal house, a princess who had been impregnated with divine light, was popular with Akbar and Jahangir.

Hindu texts also caught Akbar's attention, and he had both the great Indian epics, the *Mahabharata* and the *Ramayana*, translated into Persian and illustrated, as well as the *Hari Vamsha*, or Lineage of Krishna, an appendix to the *Mahabharata*. This page from the *Hari Vamsha*, painted in a Mughal manner, shows Krishna holding up a mountain to protect villagers from a huge storm (Figure 5.8). Akbar believed that such translations would help promote harmony between the major religious and social systems of the subcontinent. The task of translating these epics from Sanskrit into Persian was entrusted to various court members including al-Badauni, an orthodox cleric who found this task reprehensible. Illustrations, Akbar believed, enhanced the didactic value of these translated texts. Akbar's personal *Ramayana*, completed in 1588, consists of 176 illustrations, each one executed by the court's finest artists. Both the quantity and quality of the illustrations suggest Akbar's personal interest in this text. Following Akbar's example, some of his highest ranking nobles also commissioned illustrated Hindu texts, as we shall see shortly. Also illustrated and translated into Persian was the *Baburnama*, the Turkic memoirs of Babur, a man whose curiosity and charisma equaled Akbar's own. At least six illustrated copies of Babur's memoirs survive, indicating the importance of this text for the Mughal house.

This interest in translated epics and newly written histories, which matured in the second half of Akbar's reign, may seem surprising, since as a prince Akbar was an undisciplined student who never learned to read. However, he was extremely intelligent as well as voraciously curious, and had many books and literary works read to him. Indeed, Akbar's patronage of Persian literature was unrivaled in India up to this time, as Muzaffar Alam has shown. Babur, his grandfather, had written in and promoted Turkic, but Humayun favored the more cosmopolitan language of Persian. Akbar's choice of Persian as the Mughal administrative language rather than Hindavi, a range of north Indian vernaculars which were finding increasing popularity outside of court circles, might seem to conflict with Akbar's predilection for things Indian. Increasingly Iranians, recent immigrants to India, were chosen as administrators, especially in low to mid level positions where secretarial and accounting skills were needed. Iranians were also the favored court poets. But as Akbar secularized schooling, traditionally the venue for religious education, Hindus also began entering schools to learn Persian and thereby become eligible for positions in the Mughal administrative system. For Muslims, Persian was one of the languages of Islam, yet for educated non-Muslims, it represented a language with minimal sectarian implications. Because Hindavi dialects changed within short distances, Persian also had the advantage of being comprehensible over a larger area. Akbar opted for Persian as

Figure 5.8 Akbar commissioned the Persian translation of a number of Hindu works and had them illustrated to enhance their didactic value. Here the god Krishna protects villagers from a storm by holding up a mountain as if it were an umbrella.

the language of administration and of literary patronage, since it allowed him to "negotiate the diversities of Indian society" and culture.[2] In time, Persian became a pan-Indian literary language comparable to the older language of Sanskrit in its wide circulation.

Commencing in the early 1580s, Akbar began to commission illustrated works on the history of Islam and his own lineage such as the *Baburnama*, intended as legitimizing documents showing he was the rightful successor to the Timurid/Mughal throne. By far the most important of these texts was Abu al-Fazl's *Akbarnama*. Many believe that the illustrated copy today in the Victoria and Albert Museum in London was the one actually presented to the emperor. As Susan Stronge has recently argued, its 116 illustrations were probably executed for one of Abu al-Fazl's earlier drafts of the text. Its style indicates that it was produced in the imperial atelier sometime between 1586 and 1590, a period when Abu al-Fazl was exercising profound influence over Akbar.

Almost half of the illustrated folios contain portraits of Akbar, who is easily and immediately recognizable. In these pages there are generally many people present, but all the same the viewer's eye is quickly drawn to the emperor. A double-page composition depicts the young emperor, mounted on a mad elephant, tearing across an unstable pontoon bridge that spans a raging river. Akbar remains calm in the face of adversity when others are clearly panicking, claiming he mounted the elephant to test god's faith in him (Figure 5.9). This event transpired just before Akbar first decided to visit the shrine of Muin al-Din Chishti, as if one incident led to another, hinting at the young king's divinely inspired status. Even in the face of adversity, Akbar is illumined with god's divine grace. Akbar saw himself as a controller of elephants, a metaphor for his ability to rule, and there are an unusual number of paintings in this *Akbarnama* where he calms or rides elephants. Akbar may have publicly enacted the role of elephant controller when he passed through the Elephant Gate into the palace at Fatehpur Sikri.

In this painting of Akbar riding the mad elephant and most others from this *Akbarnama* manuscript, Akbar wears extremely simple clothing, usually white, while most of the other people depicted wear either more elaborate or brightly colored garb. White is a color associated with purity, often used to denote the spiritual purity of saints and ascetics, and is also the color of the main Chishti tombs. The choice to depict Akbar wearing white, especially in illustrations associated with Chishti saints such as the scene where Akbar is walking on foot to the Ajmer

---

[2] Muzaffar Alam, "The Pursuit of Persian: Language in Mughal Politics," *Modern Asian Studies* 32 (1998): 348.

Figure 5.9 This illustrated page from the *Akbarnama*, done sometime between 1586 and 1590, depicts an incident when Akbar miraculously survived riding a mad elephant.

shrine to give thanks for the birth of his son, seems a conscious one. The color of his clothing links Akbar with the shrine of Muin al-Din Chishti, casting him also as a saint (Figure 5.10). During this pilgrimage to Ajmer made on foot for a distance of 365 kilometers, Akbar claimed the authority to decide who would be the tomb's caretaker. Two years earlier, in 1568, when it was learned that Akbar intended to visit the Ajmer shine, the attendant at the shrine had a vision of Muin al-Din proclaiming Akbar's spirituality to be even greater than his own, that is, greater than the famous saint's.

Music at the court

Akbar was particularly fond of music and cultivated it both for personal pleasure and to enhance his own image. The official orchestra of the Mughal court was an ensemble known as a *naqqar* or *naubat*, composed of kettle drums, various sorts of trumpets, and cymbals. It would announce the emperor's presence in the traditional Islamic manner. Paintings of historical events from Akbar's reign, most notably those of the *Akbarnama*, show that the naubat was continually present whether Akbar was actually in residence in a permanent court or on the move in the imperial camp. Akbar himself understood musical theory and even composed music of the art music variety, that is, music for enjoyment and appreciation rather than the ceremonial music of the naubat. Chronicles, both visual and written, tell us that instrumentalists from Khurasan and Central Asia as well as singers from India resided in Akbar's court and provided entertainment for semi-public and private functions. By far the most famous singer was the legendary Tansen, whom Akbar acquired from a subject prince early in his reign in 1562. Musical ensembles portrayed in paintings included instruments from both India's long musical tradition as well as those from the western Islamic world. While we do not know for sure how this music sounded, Akbar's interest in creating a composite Perso-Indian visual culture suggests the same sort of fusion transpired aurally.

The careers and patronage of two nobles

Imperial artistic patronage had considerable impact on nobles, whether they were Rajputs or Muslims from diverse backgrounds, inspiring them to emulate Mughal tastes. Two of the highest-ranking nobles of Akbar's reign were Abd al-Rahim Khan-i Khanan and Raja Man Singh of the Kachhwaha house. Although different in religious affiliation and ethnic origin, these men were contemporaries who each had an unusual

Figure 5.10 After the birth of his son, Akbar walked on pilgrimage to the shrine of Muin al-Din Chishti in Ajmer, as shown in this page from the *Akbarnama*.

familiarity with the court. An examination of their patronage of art gives us an opportunity to understand the scope and tastes of the Mughal nobility.

Abd al-Rahim (1556–1626) was the son of Akbar's first prime minister, a Muslim from Central Asia. Abd al-Rahim himself was born in India and is an example of the kind of loyal foreign-descended noble who formed the mainstream of Akbar's ruling elite. Raised at the court, Abd al-Rahim was made commander of the entire Mughal army, earning him the title of Khan-i Khanan, even before he was thirty. He, like Man Singh, had achieved the highest rank possible by the time he died.

The Khan-i Khanan's interest in and promotion of Persian literature actually surpassed that of the imperial court. He composed poetry in some of the several languages he had mastered, including Persian, Hindavi, Arabic, and Turkic. The Khan-i Khanan was famed for his large library. Like Akbar, he had a range of tastes, for after he saw Akbar's illustrated *Ramayana*, he too commissioned one of his own, and many of its paintings are similar to those in Akbar's imperial *Ramayana* (Figure 5.11). What is significant here is Khan-i Khanan's patronage of a Hindu text, a subject that reflects Akbar's promotion of the policy of universal toleration, sulh-i kul. We thus see how Mughal nobles spread imperial ideology through their own patronage. Raja Man Singh also sponsored poets, although the languages he promoted were Indic ones. Their extensive patronage of the literary arts led one poet to describe Man Singh and the Khan-i Khanan as promoters of Akbar's imperial prestige.

Despite the fact that Akbar engaged in few new building projects after he departed Fatehpur Sikri in 1585, his nobles continued to build, doing so on his behalf. Both Raja Man Singh and the Khan-i Khanan maintained active architectural projects during the period in which Akbar seems to have lost interest in providing buildings. His nobles fulfilled their obligation, one whose roots may be seen as early as the 1570s when Akbar issued orders that mosques and khanqahs should be built by his nobility in Ajmer. The expectation that nobles would build is evident at the beginning of the reign of Akbar's successor, Jahangir, for in 1605 he issued twelve accession orders, the first of which stated that it was the duty of the nobility to build in the hinterlands and thus encourage population growth and stability. In issuing this command to his nobles, Jahangir was apparently making official an already established practice.

The patronage of the Khan-i Khanan closely followed Akbar's model, adhering to standards established by the great Timurids. Aside from commissioning lavish manuscripts, he also built gardens, palaces, and tombs, none of which still survive. The degree to which the Khan-i Khanan emulated Akbar's example reflects the fact that he had no other allegiance or

Figure 5.11 This page from Abd al-Rahim Khan-i Khanan's illustrated *Ramayana* shows the Hindu god Rama stalking a demon who has assumed the form of a golden deer.

responsibility beyond that to the emperor. By contrast, Raja Man Singh Kachhwaha (1550–1614), whose patronage also followed the Timurid model, had a more complicated series of allegiances, resulting in works with more complex meanings. He was a Hindu, a minority among the Mughal elite, and the head of his own ancestral Rajput line as well as being a Mughal noble. Like the Khan-i Khanan, Raja Man Singh was a prince close to Akbar who grew up at the Mughal court. His aunt married Akbar while his sister married Akbar's successor, Jahangir. Man Singh was a major military commander and had a pivotal role in subduing territory in the hinterlands, especially in eastern India. At Akbar's death, he had the highest rank of any noble except the king's own sons.

Man Singh erected buildings in part to satisfy his own needs and in part to serve the Mughal house. He provided gardens, palaces, temples, and mosques in both his ancestral lands and in the larger Mughal territory. His first project, a garden at Wah (today in Pakistan), was commissioned when he was serving as governor of the northwestern frontier region. This is an area long associated with Hindu and Muslim lore. Set in the foothills of the Hindu Kush mountains, Wah was regarded by seventeenth-century Mughal chroniclers as ranking next only to the famed Shalimar gardens in Kashmir. Man Singh's garden consisted of a large central tank with pleasure pavilions at the tank's far end. Built over a natural spring, water in the tank is crystal clear even today. Imperial praise for the garden suggests that the Mughal emperors felt it corresponded to a "perfect" Mughal pleasure garden suitable for rulers descended from the great Timurids of Central Asia.

The garden, however, was perceived in yet another manner by its Hindu patron. Wah's surroundings – hills dense with trees and water – also match descriptions in ancient Indian texts of settings appropriate for temples and for the dwellings of the numerous Hindu deities. While the tank and setting at Wah were appreciated by the imperial Mughals as an appropriate Mughal pleasure retreat, to Man Singh personally, who knew that the gods were attracted to the waters, waterfalls, trees, and spring-fed tanks, this garden must have evoked a more personal response.

Man Singh's best known project is the massive Govinda Deva temple, located at a site that had been recently identified as Vrindavan, the place where the god Krishna spent much of his youth (Figure 5.12). The rebuilding of the temple was completed in 1590, fulfilling a vow the prince made when he was victorious in Akbar's Gujarat campaign of 1572–73. Man Singh's decision to undertake this project must have been driven by larger imperial interests, for Akbar had been endowing temples and their priests at Vrindavan as early as 1565. Thus, just as the Khan-i Khanan commissioned an illustrated Persian manuscript of the

Ramayana, knowing that doing so would please the emperor, so too did Man Singh build at a site favored by Akbar. The temple, the largest one constructed in north India since the twelfth century, was built in the red sandstone preferred by the imperial Mughals for building material. Its interior vaults and pillars were inspired by those used at Fatehpur Sikri and other imperial sites, but in fact were technologically more innovative than those of Akbar's own buildings, creating open spaces and height never before achieved in Mughal buildings.

Man Singh built several other temples that were intended both to celebrate Mughal victories and to commemorate recently deceased family members, including one for his mother, one for his father, and one for his heir apparent, Jagat Singh. The temple commemorating his heir, erected in the Kachhwaha palace compound at Amber, is highly unusual in that its exterior is covered with figural sculpture, rare in north India since even before the twelfth century. All the same, the temple's entrance and porch evoke the contemporary architecture of Akbar. This temple, like the one built for the image of Govinda Deva that had only recently been discovered in Vrindavan, has a large porch, needed for the crowds assembled for darshan (auspicious sighting) of the image which lasts from fifteen minutes to an hour, seven times a day. As the popularity of this type of veneration for Krishna associated with the bhakti movement increased, temple formats had to accommodate this change from individual to congregational worship. Man Singh's patronage was instrumental in making this change. By providing temples throughout the domain in a recognizably Mughal style, Man Singh was helping to spread Akbar's official policy of sulh-i kul, just as the Khan-i Khanan did by commissioning an illustrated *Ramayana*. To further promote the concept of sulh-i kul, Man Singh provided at least two mosques and supported the shrine of a Muslim saint.

Man Singh built several palaces, including two in his ancestral lands. But the largest and most important is the one he provided in eastern India at the hill fort Rohtas, previously associated with Sher Shah. Man Singh's Rohtas palace is the largest non-imperial palace of the entire Mughal period, and many of its features suggest that Man Singh intended to signal his role as Akbar's agent. For example, the entrance gate flanked by elephants and the public viewing window both recall their equivalents at Fatehpur Sikri, a privilege allowed only to the Kachhwaha princes because of their special ties to the Mughals.

There is reason to believe that to Man Singh the Rohtas palace was more than just a residence for the Mughal governor of eastern India. Palace inscriptions in Persian and Sanskrit show that Man Singh recognized his dual role as both Mughal governor and Hindu raja. The one

Figure 5.12 Raja Man Singh's Govinda Deva temple (1590) at Vrindavan reflects Islamicate styles used in imperial Mughal architecture.

in Persian implies that Raja Man Singh built the palace as a servant of Akbar, for it addresses the emperor extensively and makes only a brief reference to the actual patron, Man Singh. In the companion Sanskrit portion, Raja Man Singh omits Akbar's name altogether, asserting his own authority as head of the Kachhwaha house and identifying himself as king of kings. The use of his Kachhwaha title rather than his Mughal one, on a palace intended to serve both the governor's needs and those of the state, underscores the dual nature of the relationship between the raja and Mughal emperor. Under the Mughal state system, serving the emperor included defending one's own religion, honor, and even patrimony if necessary. Thus, evoking a title that symbolized Rajput ideals and aspirations did not conflict with Man Singh's role as Akbar's governor, for both were vital to the successful functioning of the Mughal empire. Raja Man Singh, like his contemporary Abd al-Rahim Khan-i Khanan, championed Mughal causes by his patronage of the arts, giving visual substance to Akbar's political and social agendas.

The basic foundations of the Mughal empire had been firmly laid by the time of Akbar's death in 1605. Akbar's policy of toleration remained largely intact through the reigns of the next two Mughal emperors, although over time the empire took on increasingly conservative attitudes toward religion. In like manner, the administrative apparatus continued to develop along the lines laid down by Akbar, and the diversity of the ruling class instituted by Akbar was maintained by subsequent Mughals. The role of the arts in promoting political agendas was well established throughout the sixteenth century and would escalate through the mid seventeenth century, both in the Mughal heartland and in the homelands of subordinate nobles. The ideology that was formulated within Akbar's court was the product of a coming together of many talented men, who disseminated it widely among their own circles of influence. Mughal culture would, in time, be transmitted to virtually every elite society within the subcontinent.

End Essay #4

6 Expanding political and economic spheres, 1550–1650

By the time of Akbar's death in 1605, a qualitative change in the scale of political and economic activities in the Indian subcontinent had occurred. The sheer size of the empire Akbar left behind is an important factor, for an estimated 110 million people resided within its borders out of a total South Asian population of slightly less than 150 million. Akbar implemented a more systematic and centralized form of rule than had prevailed earlier, which led to greater uniformity in administrative practices over a vast territory. At the same time, Akbar's economic policies stimulated the growth of commercial activity, which interconnected the various parts of South Asia in increasingly close networks. His stipulation that land taxes be paid in cash forced peasants into the market networks where they could obtain the necessary money, while the standardization of imperial currency made the exchange of goods for money easier. Above all, the long period of relative peace ushered in by Akbar's power, and maintained by his successors throughout the seventeenth century, contributed to India's economic expansion.

The greater circulation of people, goods, and practices that characterized India in the centuries after 1550 is also found in Europe and other parts of the world in this era. After direct sea links were established between Europe, Asia, and the Americas around 1500, a global economy spanning diverse regions of the world gradually emerged. This is one reason the 300 years from 1500 to 1800 are often described as the early modern period by historians. Simultaneous with the shrinking distances between various regions of the world was a general trend toward the growth in size and complexity of institutions internal to each society. Thus, we witness the rise of a series of great empires: that of the Ottomans and Safavids in the Middle East and the Ming-Qing dynasties of China, as well as the Mughals of India. The technologies of control employed by these early modern empires were much more effective than those of their predecessors and paved the way toward the efficient bureaucracies of the modern world. In this chapter, we examine developments within India in the hundred year period from 1550 to 1650, with particular attention to those representing aspects of early modernity.

Part I: The Mughal north

Careers of Jahangir and Shah Jahan

Both of Akbar's successors came to the throne only after a period of conflict with their fathers. The Timurid tradition did not recognize the right of the eldest son to automatically accede to the throne, making years of court intrigue inevitable before the succession was determined. In the case of Salim, the future Jahangir, the road to the throne included arranging in 1602 the assassination of Akbar's close advisor, Abu al-Fazl, whom he was convinced stood in the way of his father's acceptance of him as heir. Although Akbar, Raja Man Singh, and others championed the cause of Khusrau, Salim's teen-aged son and Man Singh's nephew, the diverse network of supporters Salim had built up over the years enabled him to obtain the throne upon the death of Akbar in 1605. Jahangir's third son, Khurram (later to become Shah Jahan), quickly emerged as his father's handpicked heir apparent. Like Jahangir before him, Khurram immediately began to develop a huge coterie of supporters, and was immensely successful, so much so that, even though he had lost favor with his father, he was still able to claim the throne after Jahangir's death in 1627. The competition inherent in the Timurid method of succession has often been viewed by scholars in negative terms, as disruptive and destabilizing to the empire. However, Munis Faruqi has recently convincingly argued that the system forced each aspiring heir to create diverse networks of support, leading to the integration of new groups into the empire.

Prince Khurram, a brilliant military strategist, was responsible for the main victory of Jahangir's reign. Although Akbar had ruthlessly besieged the Sisodiya fortress of Chittor (discussed in chapter 5), this proud Rajput house refused to acknowledge Mughal authority and serve as mansabdars in the Mughal system. Total defeat of the Sisodiyas had been considered all but impossible, when Khurram reversed the situation, commencing a relentless campaign against them in 1614. He forced Rana Amar Singh Sisodiya to capitulate the following year. Jahangir was ecstatic over this extraordinary victory and for the next seven years Prince Khurram was the apple of Jahangir's eye. His status as heir apparent came under question only after he had a falling out with Nur Jahan, Jahangir's powerful queen. In the power struggle following his father's death, Khurram nonetheless proved himself the strongest and ascended the throne in 1628.

Jahangir had married the woman he came to call Nur Jahan, or Light of the World, in 1611 when she was a widow in her mid thirties. Rumored to be beautiful and certainly brilliant, she eventually took over the reins of state once Jahangir became incapacitated due to poor health caused at least partially by excessive consumption of wine and opium. She was the only woman of the Mughal court ever allowed to mint coins in her own name, a royal prerogative. Her influence was so great that several members of her family, including her father and brother, were appointed to the highest official positions. While Nur Jahan remained absolutely faithful to Jahangir's causes throughout his life, by 1619 she had begun to fear that Khurram would diminish her exalted position once he ascended the throne. The queen, in an attempt to thwart this situation, married her daughter from her first marriage to Jahangir's youngest son, signaling the break between her and Khurram and this prince's fall from favor. Even after Khurram took the throne as Shah Jahan, however, members of Nur Jahan's family remained prominent at court, and Shah Jahan's beloved Queen Mumtaz Mahal was herself Nur Jahan's niece. It is incorrect, however, to assume that all these family members acted as a homogeneous block, as is commonly believed, for they differed, for example, in which prince they supported as Jahangir's successor.

Shah Jahan was a more militarily vigorous ruler than had been his father, whose indolence and passivity has often been criticized. Under Shah Jahan's rule (r. 1628–58), the Mughal empire was at the height of its power, wealth, and international glory. He pursued frequent military campaigns, particularly during the first twelve years of his reign, when he subjugated recalcitrant nobles and made some minor territorial acquisitions in eastern India, Sind, and the northwest. In 1636 a moment breakthrough was made in the ongoing Mughal campaign to take the Deccan. At that time the Mughals signed a treaty with the two major Deccan houses, the Adil Shahs of Bijapur and the Qutb Shahs of Golkonda, bringing relative peace between the Mughals and the Deccan Sultanates for the next twenty years.

Shah Jahan was militarily less successful in the second half of his reign, when he tried on several occasions to reclaim land belonging to his Central Asian ancestors. The thinly populated and barren lands of Central Asia could offer little in the way of added resources to the wealthy Mughal empire. But the dream of reconquering the Timurid homeland had persisted since the days of Babur, and no subsequent Mughal emperor was more fervent in this desire than Shah Jahan. His Timurid ancestry was critical to Shah Jahan's perceptions of himself as emperor, so much so that upon ascending the throne Shah Jahan assumed a title used by Timur, proclaiming himself to be a world conqueror. Similarly, in the opening pages of the official chronicle of his early reign, the *Padshahnama*, Shah Jahan had his own portrait face that of his illustrious ancestor, Timur. In pursuit of his ambitions, Shah Jahan twice sent Mughal armies to Balkh in northern Afghanistan, but in the end had to withdraw. Equally humiliating were Mughal efforts to regain Qandahar, in south-central Afghanistan, which had been lost to the Safavid dynasty of Iran during Jahangir's reign. Qandahar was a more valuable place than Balkh or any other Central Asian city, since it straddled the main overland trade route from South Asia to Iran, via the Bolan Pass (see Map 5.1). Once again, the Mughals expended tremendous effort to no avail, and Qandahar remained under Safavid control.

There were few radical departures in imperial policy while Jahangir and Shah Jahan ruled. Jahangir in particular followed Akbar's example closely. Even though he was responsible for the murder of Abu al-Fazl, Jahangir largely subscribed to Akbar's concept of state that Abu al-Fazl had masterminded. Jahangir perceived himself as a light-filled ruler, in much the same way as had Akbar, and encouraged artists to find innovative ways to promote this ideological concept. Shah Jahan, on the other hand, assumed a much more traditional attitude toward Islam and abandoned the royal cult of discipleship. These moves toward orthodoxy on the part of Shah Jahan may have partly been necessitated by a backlash that had grown over the years against the liberal attitudes of Akbar and Jahangir. Shaikh Ahmad Sirhindi (1564–1624) was an influential critic of the Mughal government's failure to strictly follow the *sharia* (Islamic religious law, including the teachings of the Quran and the sayings of the Prophet Muhammad, that governs all aspects of a Muslim's life). His ideas continued to spread even after his death.

Shah Jahan engaged in a revamping of the mansabdar system, necessitated by the substantial inflation in both the number of nobles and their average rank that had taken place since Akbar's day. Shah Jahan took several measures to alleviate this situation by, for example, reducing the number of horses that needed to be provided by the nobles and also by adjusting the income the nobles received. His new pay-scales and other modifications were the most significant alterations to Akbar's administrative policies in more than fifty years and were maintained by the next Mughal emperor, Aurangzeb. Yet the continual growth in the numbers of these rank-holders remained a persistent problem throughout the second half of the seventeenth century.

One notable change in the Mughal court during the reigns of Jahangir and Shah Jahan was the greater number of high-ranking nobles who were Iranian in origin. In Akbar's day, Muslims of Central Asian descent (Turanis) had dominated the top levels of the administration, followed by ethnic Persians from Iran. The situation was reversed under Jahangir and Shah Jahan, as more and more Iranis obtained prominent official posts, especially in matters relating to finance. The dominance of Iranis in high positions was partly a result of Nur Jahan's influence, for her father had migrated to India from Iran before she was born, and many of her relatives were promoted after her marriage to Jahangir. Even during Shah Jahan's reign, Iranis remained the single most powerful group at court long after Nur Jahan had lost all power, suggesting that other factors were at work as well.

The prestige of Persian language and culture had once unified a vast swathe of territory extending from northern India to Central Asia and as far west as Anatolia. Educated Persian-speakers had thus long sought employment in the Islamic courts of South Asia. Beginning in about 1400, however, the world of Persian culture began to fragment, and the Persian language increasingly came to be identified with the region of Iran alone. In Anatolia and Central Asia, forms of Turkic language came to be favored, while regional literary cultures received patronage in the India of the late fifteenth and early sixteenth centuries. Akbar resuscitated the centrality of Persian in north India when he made it the language of all levels of administration in the Mughal empire. This was in part due to the closer cultural ties with Iran that had been forged by the Mughals during the Sur interregnum, when Humayun was expelled from India and took refuge in the Safavid realm. Thus, from the late sixteenth century onward, there was increasing contact between India and Iran, both culturally and in the form of a flow of people from Iran to India.

It is not difficult to understand why some Iranians would have wished to leave their homeland, for a fairly strict form of Shia Islam had been decreed the sole official religion of the Safavid state since the early sixteenth century. Those who subscribed to other faiths or were not particularly observant of the sharia would have found the heterogeneous social and intellectual milieu of the Mughal court far more congenial and rewarding. Opportunities for advancement in India were much better than in Iran, for, as Sanjay Subrahmanyam has argued, Persian-speaking Iranis were kept out of positions of power in the Safavid state. Consequently, Iranis emigrated to both the Mughal north and the Deccan Sultanates in considerable numbers.

Despite the greater wealth of the Mughal realm, the Mughals accorded considerable deference to the Safavid emperors of Iran as retainers of a long-standing Persianate cultural tradition. A sense of cultural inferiority may have underpinned Mughal attitudes toward the Safavids, but so too did a sense of rivalry. In the expanding geographic horizons of the early modern period, the Safavids were worthy "others" with which to compare

Figure 6.1 In this allegorical painting Jahangir embraces Shah
Abbas while standing on a globe. It illustrates Jahangir's imagined
superiority over his Safavid rival through a visual play on his name,
which means World Seizer.

and contrast themselves. The competitive nature of their relationship is well illustrated by the famous painting known as Jahangir's dream, which depicts Jahangir embracing his contemporary Shah Abbas I, the most acclaimed of all Safavid rulers. The two men, who never actually met, are represented as being on intimate terms but at the same time the figure of Jahangir, who stands on a lion, looms over and metaphorically dominates Shah Abbas, standing on a passive lamb, literally pushing Abbas into the sea. A striking aspect of the painting is the globe, revealing that European advances in map-making had been rapidly transmitted to Mughal India. The Indian subcontinent and the Persian Gulf are recorded with particular accuracy in this illustration (Figure 6.1). This painting is not a fluke; two other paintings from the courts of Jahangir and Shah Jahan are discussed in the following chapter that similarly contain maps on globes. They suggest that the Mughal court was very conscious of the larger world setting within which they operated.

The world maps in Mughal paintings also reveal the aspiration of the Mughal emperors to be rulers of the world or, perhaps more accurately, to be rulers that the world would recognize as great. Their grandiose self-conceptions are indicated by the names they chose upon their accession to the throne: Salim assumed the title Nur al-Din Jahangir Badshah Ghazi, meaning Warrior Emperor World Conqueror (who is) the Light of the Faith, while Khurram called himself Shah Jahan, King of the World. In line with their elevated titles, visual images of the two emperors tended to be considerably more formal than those of Akbar: Jahangir and Shah Jahan are frequently depicted alone in portraits, for instance, whereas Akbar was often placed among crowds in action scenes. Court life also became more ceremonious in the first half of the seventeenth century, as we will see in chapter 7. Accompanying the trend toward larger-scale polities and institutions in the early modern period, then, was a resurfacing of the ideal of universal empire.

The Mughals and maritime trade

The Mughal empire was based in the interior of a large land-mass and derived the vast majority of its revenues from agriculture. Because of this, the Mughal emperors are often said to have lacked interest in the coastal territories of the subcontinent and their flourishing maritime trade. Agriculture was certainly the mainstay of the Mughal economy, and the early Mughal court was familiar only with overland or river routes to other regions. Not until the conquest of Gujarat in 1572 did the empire reach the ocean – Akbar, who led the Mughal army in this campaign, is said to have ridden to the Gujarat coast specifically in order to get his first glimpse of a sea. The Mughals never did create a navy, leaving them at a great disadvantage against the Portuguese and later the Dutch and English. And the coastlines of the subcontinent continued to be regarded as a frontier, with all the social diversity and deviance from norms that are associated with the far reaches of empire. But, over time, both the royal family and the high court nobles became involved with the trade that was taking place over the seas, first in Gujarat and later in Bengal.

Despite the presence of Portuguese enclaves along India's west coast – in Diu, Daman, Goa, and Cochin – Gujarat's maritime trade prospered during the sixteenth century. To be sure, fleets of Portuguese ships patrolled the waters off Surat and Cambay, ensuring that all local shipping had been licensed by and paid duties to them. In the long run, however, this meant that local ships going to the Persian Gulf and the Red Sea had superior Portuguese armament to protect them, and so Gujarat's westward trade kept growing. Gujarat merchants had also benefited from the Portuguese attacks on the Malabar coast in the early 1500s; as Malabar ports like Calicut declined, trade goods from Southeast Asia were rerouted to Gujarat instead. Over the course of the sixteenth century, Portuguese control over shipping lanes weakened, making them even more dependent on Gujarat as a place from which they could purchase not only spices but also goods to ship home to Europe and use for bartering in the Indian Ocean.

A valuable addition to all cargoes headed out from Gujarat were textiles, the most important export item produced in Gujarat (Figure 6.2). Gujarat had been selling cotton textiles to the Middle East, and most probably Southeast Asia, since at least the thirteenth century. The range of textiles manufactured in Gujarat was very broad: from the extremely expensive silk *patola* or double ikat fabrics (where the threads of both the warp and woof are tie-dyed prior to weaving, creating a reversible design) to the plainly woven and coarse cotton textiles printed with wood-blocks. While there was much interest in the finer varieties of cloth from Gujarat – patola pieces, for instance, were used only on ceremonial occasions in some areas of island Southeast Asia – the bulk of the demand was for the cheap, coarse varieties of cotton textiles. Soon after their arrival in the Indian Ocean, the Portuguese found themselves buying cloth from Gujarat in order to exchange it for the nutmeg, cloves, and other fine spices of Indonesia that they most wished to obtain, along with Malabar pepper. The practice of using Indian textiles as a medium of exchange was so widespread in Indonesia that the prices of spices were often given in terms of Indian cloth in the trade agreements made by the Portuguese there, rather than in any form of cash.

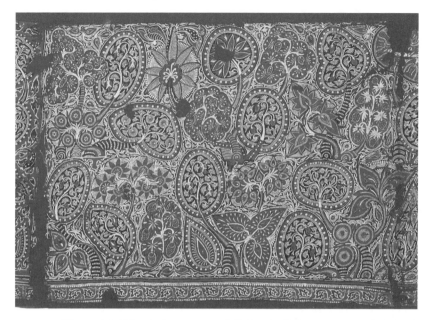

Figure 6.2 The design range of Gujarati cloth was tremendous and demand for such cloth was great. This piece intended for the eastern Indonesian market is completely hand painted in white, blues, and reds.

The initial interest of the Mughals in the Gujarat coast was in providing safe passage to Indian Muslims making the pilgrimage to Mecca by sea. Among the pilgrims who departed from Gujarat on the way to Mecca was the elderly Gulbadan Begum, Humayun's sister and Akbar's aunt, who began what turned out to be a seven-year journey in 1575, accompanied by several other noblewomen from the Mughal court including one of Akbar's wives. Once Gulbadan arrived in Arabia, after having been delayed by the Portuguese at Surat for about a year for lack of proper documentation, she remained in Arabia for another three years, performing the pilgrimage four times. While returning to India, she was shipwrecked and forced to stay for some time in Aden. In spite of the difficulties of sea travel, by the early 1600s several members of the Mughal royal family including Jahangir, his mother, and his wife Nur Jahan owned ships that participated in international trade as well as in the transport of pilgrims. The most active Mughal investor in maritime commerce was Shah Jahan, who had half a dozen large ships built after he became emperor. Due to their size and the pressure exerted by imperial officials on local merchants, Shah Jahan's ships carried the bulk of the freight being taken to the Middle Eastern ports of Bandar Abbas and Mokha for several years.

Many other high-ranking Mughal nobles followed in the imperial family's footsteps in either investing in ships or in their cargoes. The interest of the court and nobility in commercial activities persisted throughout the seventeenth century and was a major shift in their orientation from the days of the early Mughals. It may have been due to the influence of the growing Irani faction at court, who had considerable expertise in finance and experience combining trade with statecraft.

The Mughal ships were based mainly at Surat, which had become the most important maritime city of Gujarat as the waters near Cambay grew difficult to navigate. During the seventeenth century, Surat was not only the premier port of the Mughal empire but also the largest coastal city along the entire western Indian Ocean. In 1660 it probably had a population of 100,000 and may have doubled in size by 1700. Surat owed much of its prominence to the fact that it was the terminus of a major overland route from Agra and Delhi. It also had a fertile hinterland from which to secure food and other resources, as well as a wealthy banking community. Situated on the Tapti river, Surat had a mediocre harbor, but its other advantages ensured it the foremost place among Indian port cities on the west coast. When the first Europeans other than the Portuguese sought to establish trading posts in Mughal India, Surat was the site in which they were most interested (Figure 6.3).

Around 1600, both the Dutch and the English sought entry into the lucrative commerce between Europe and Asia that had provided so much wealth to the Portuguese over the past century. The Dutch and English governments did not get directly involved in efforts to corner a share of the Indian Ocean's vast trade, unlike the Portuguese whose ships and personnel were under the authority of the Portuguese crown. Instead, the Dutch and English governments each gave a private company – the Verenigde Oost-Indische Compagnie (VOC) in the case of the Dutch and the East India Company (EIC) in the case of the English – the monopoly over trade between their respective nations and Asia. Unlike the Portuguese who were motivated by the desire to spread Christianity and gain an empire, as well as by profits, the Dutch and English intrusion into the Indian Ocean was initially impelled by mercantile objectives. Since the Dutch and English trading companies had the backing of their governments, however, they did increasingly represent their nation's interests in this distant part of the globe.

When the Dutch and English first tried to conduct trade at Surat, they were violently opposed by the Portuguese. The Mughal emperor, who was reluctant to provoke Portuguese anger and thereby jeopardize the safety of Indian ships, at first turned a deaf ear to Dutch and English pleas for trading rights. Several years of conflict on the waters between the Red

Figure 6.3 This seventeenth-century Dutch depiction of Surat's busy port shows many ships in its harbor while camels and bullock carts are on the shore to transport goods for export and import.

Sea, the Persian Gulf, and India's west coast ensued. After the northern Europeans demonstrated that they could inflict substantial damage on both Indian and Portuguese vessels, the Mughal court realized it was in its own best interests to welcome these counterweights to Portuguese power. The first English "factory" (a compound including warehouses and residences) in Surat in 1613 was built with the permission of local authorities, and by 1617 they had received official permission from Emperor Jahangir himself to establish factories in several parts of the empire. The Mughals clearly understood the value of maritime commerce and wanted to keep the sea routes to and from India open; they consistently tried to maintain freedom of trade along India's coasts to the best of their ability, although hampered by the lack of a navy.

Part II: The peninsular south

Successor states to the Bahmanis

At the same time that the Mughal empire was being consolidated in north India, new states that had arisen from the disintegration of the Bahmani and Vijayanagara kingdoms were flourishing in peninsular India. Although the successor states to the Bahmani Sultanate were in place by around 1500, they reached their greatest heights only after the defeat of Vijayanagara in the 1565 Battle of Talikota. The best spoils of that victory went to the Adil Shahs of Bijapur, situated immediately north of the Vijayanagara capital, who thus acquired the rich fertile lands and mineral resources of the Raichur doab (the area near the confluence of the Krishna and Tungabhadra rivers) that had long been a bone of contention. The two other important dynasties to succeed the Bahmanis were the Nizam Shahs of Ahmadnagar, who controlled much of what is now Maharashtra, and the Qutb Shahs of Golkonda, who were based in northern Andhra Pradesh. The remnants of Vijayanagara power withdrew from Karnataka after 1565 and retrenched in southern Andhra Pradesh. Adding to the complex political landscape of peninsular India between 1550 and 1650 were several successor states to Vijayanagara that arose in southern Karnataka and the Tamil country. The Bahmani and Vijayanagara successor states resembled their predecessors in numerous respects, especially in their artistic and linguistic cultures, but the greater movement of people, goods, and ideas that was characteristic of the early modern era was to shape these new states in important ways.

The independent Deccan Sultanates were all derived from the Bahmani state and so exhibit some similarities. The most obvious one was the issue of Afaqi–Deccani balance within the nobility, a situation inherited

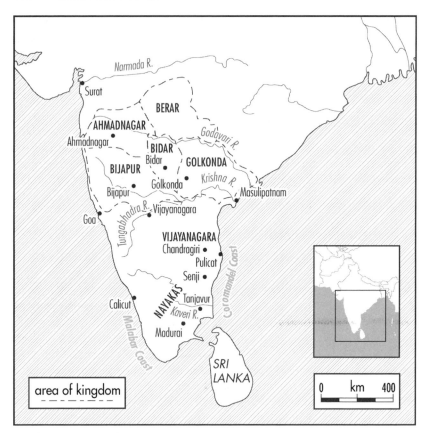

Map 6.1 South India, *c.* 1550

from the Bahmanis. The Afaqis were the foreign faction, predominantly
Persian-speaking Iranians, though Arabs and even Africans were represented among them. The Deccanis were descendants of Muslims who had
migrated from north India, along with indigenous converts. The tension
between the two factions went back to the fifteenth century, a period
in which there was extensive immigration to the Deccan from outside
the subcontinent. A Portuguese estimate from the early 1500s puts the
size of the foreign immigrant population in the Deccan at between 10,000
and 12,000 people; among them were military men, scholars, merchants,
and Sufis. Immigrants from the Middle East continued to arrive in the
Deccan during the sixteenth century, most notably in the period up to
1575. In contrast, the flow of people from Iran and the Arabic-speaking
world had sharply declined in north India during the fifteenth and early

Figure 6.4 The Char Minar was the centerpiece of the Qutb Shah's new city of Hyderabad founded in 1591.

sixteenth centuries, only to begin rising again in the last decades of the 1500s. As a result, the impact of Iranians and the Persian culture they brought with them was considerably greater in the Deccan of *c.* 1600 than in the Mughal north.

An important consequence of the Iranian presence was the spreading of the Shia faith of Iran's Safavid dynasty, which had many more adherents in the Deccan than in contemporary north India. Shia Islam received the unwavering support of the Qutb Shahs of Golkonda, where it was established as the official state religion. The Shia allegiance of the Qutb Shahs is especially evident in their new capital, Hyderabad, founded in 1591 right next to Golkonda city. Hyderabad, replete with palaces and gardens, was a planned city designed with the enormous Char Minar as its centerpiece, as Deborah Hutton has described. The Char Minar gateway, essentially a triumphal arch, was situated at the intersection of two major crossroads (Figure 6.4). The gate's top story contains a mosque, flanked on its four corners by minarets. The stucco décor on the gateway's interior is shaped in the form of *alams* – standards used by the Shia to commemorate the tragic events of Muharram when Husain, the Prophet Muhammad's grandson, was martyred by opponents in 680 CE. Shortly after the construction of the Char Minar, the royal Ashur Khana was built. It is a large building dedicated to holding huge metal alams used during the commemoration of Ashur, the tenth day of Muharram when Husain was martyred. Husain has special importance for the Shia who accept the Prophet Muhammad's family and their spiritual successors, rather than the historical caliphs of Islam, as spokespeople for Islamic authority. Not only were alams intended to be stored in the Ashur Khana, but exquisitely rendered depictions of alams in enameled tile also embellish parts of the interior walls. Small alams rendered in stucco are commonly found in the religious architecture of Hyderabad, thus underscoring a visual connection to Shia Islam.

Some rulers of Bijapur were equally ardent promoters of Shia Islam. The entrance of the surprisingly plain tomb of Ali Adil Shah (r. 1558–80), for instance, displays an overtly Shia inscription. However, there is virtually no building intended solely for Shia use in Bijapur, unlike the case in the Qutb Shah city of Hyderabad, probably because the Adil Shah state frequently switched its support between Shia and Sunni Islam. A striking aspect of Ali Adil Shah's tomb is its location near several important Sufi shrines inside the city walls. Traditionally, it is believed that Shia Islam and Sufism are antithetical to one another; however, Deborah Hutton argues that this was not the case at Bijapur, where Ali Adil Shah not only chose to be buried near Sufi shrines but had also earlier been crowned at one. Ali's tomb demonstrates that in Bijapur the choice between being

Figure 6.5 Sufis, depicted interacting with visitors in this early seventeenth-century painting from Bijapur, had an important role in the transmission of Islamic beliefs not only to the court but also to the masses in the Deccan.

Shia and being a Sufi did not have to be made, for both were embraced by the culture of the Adil Shah's court.

Sufi centers had existed in the Deccan since the early fourteenth-century conquests of the Delhi Sultanate. The first Sufi order to be transplanted to the peninsula was that of the Chishtis, the most popular group in the north. Members of other Sufi orders migrated to the Deccan from the Middle East or from other areas of the subcontinent slightly later, in the fifteenth and sixteenth centuries. By the seventeenth century, Sufis in Bijapur were varied in affiliation and diverse in their interests, as Richard M. Eaton's work has demonstrated. Some Bijapur Sufis worked closely with the court and received land grants in return; this intimate link with Sufis and their ideas is revealed in the painting, poetry, and prose produced by the court elite (Figure 6.5). Other Bijapur Sufis shunned contact with the courts and instead focused on spreading their ideas through literature. They wrote not only in Persian but also in a form of proto-Urdu unique to the Deccan known as Dakani. Dakani resembled north Indian languages in grammar and syntax, but incorporated many words from the Arabic and Persian languages and was written in the Perso-Arabic script. Because it combined elements drawn from both the Indic and Islamic traditions, Dakani was a perfect vehicle for the composite culture that flourished in the early modern Deccan Sultanates.

Sufis are often credited with the transmission of Islamic beliefs to the less educated masses of the Indian subcontinent, a process that was under way in the Deccan by the seventeenth century. One means by which the populace was acquainted with the basic doctrines of Islam was through folk poems, especially those sung by women while performing household tasks like spinning thread or grinding grain. Written versions of these folk songs were composed by Bijapur Sufis belonging to the Chishti order, but oral versions must have existed in the regional languages of the Deccan as well. Sufis also contributed to the spread of Islamic religion through the cult of the dargah, that is, worship at saints' tombs. People of all walks of life, both Hindu and Muslim, were attracted to the spiritual power (baraka) that was supposed to emanate from the sites where famous Sufis, venerated as saints, were buried and were believed to be intercessors to god. Through such influences, segments of the Deccan population gradually came to adopt increasingly Islamic lifestyles over several generations. By the early twentieth century, roughly 10–20 percent of the people in the Deccan identified themselves as Muslims.

Compared to north India, however, the Islamic segment of Deccan society was always small. This led to another characteristic feature of the Deccan Sultanates that distinguished them from the Mughal north: the incorporation of numerous indigenous people into the state system.

The heavy reliance on indigenous warriors and Brahmins was especially evident outside the capital cities, for the Deccan countryside was largely ruled through local leaders who spoke the local Marathi, Kannada, and Telugu languages. These local leaders assimilated many aspects of the Islamicate culture of the Deccan courts, and their languages also adopted numerous words from Persian, most strikingly in the area of administrative and fiscal terminology. In turn, the regional languages of the Deccan received considerable patronage from the sultanates. At the Adil Shah court at Bijapur, state documents were often issued in Marathi, one of the local languages. The Qutb Shah rulers of Golkonda issued many of their edicts in a bilingual format, with the same text repeated in Persian and in Telugu, the language of the Andhra region. More so than in any other Deccan Sultanate, the Qutb Shahs were successful in integrating local Brahmins and warriors into their state system. Just as the Bijapur Sufis utilized the composite language of Dakani, so too did their Adil Shah rulers, as well as those of Golkonda, promote Dakani literature at their courts. Persian, the official language of the Mughal court, was used in the Deccan for keeping records and writing histories like the famous chronicle (*tarikh*) by Firishta, although some of the rulers were actually much less proficient in Persian than in Dakani, Telugu, or Marathi.

The mingling of Indic and Islamicate traditions is exemplified at the courts of the two Deccan rulers most famous for their cultural patronage: Ibrahim Adil Shah II (r. 1580–1627) and Muhammad Quli Qutb Shah (r. 1580–1611). Mystically inclined and a lover of music, Ibrahim Adil Shah II authored a collection of songs and poetry in Dakani known as *Kitab-i Nauras*, that is, Book of the Nine Rasas. Meaning moods or emotions, rasas were essential components of aesthetics in the Indic poetic tradition, and Ibrahim II's composition informs the audience not only about them but also about the Indian musical modes or *raga*s by which the rasas are also expressed. *Kitab-i Nauras* opens with an invocation to the Hindu goddess of learning, Saraswati, followed by praise of the Prophet Muhammad and then the Chishti Sufi saint Gesu Daraz. Ibrahim II was sometimes known by the Indic title Jagat Guru or teacher of the world, in a well-deserved acknowledgment of his love of learning.

In keeping with his enthusiasm for the rasas, Ibrahim II founded Nauraspur, a royal palace city adjacent to Bijapur, in 1599. His new city, destroyed by a rival sultan in 1624, also reflected his eclectic tastes and interests. While little remains of this circular city about one and a half times as large as Bijapur, Deborah Hutton's recent work shows that the construction of Nauraspur was Ibrahim's statement that he was in the league of great builders such as Sher Shah Sur, Akbar, the Safavids of Iran, as well as other Deccan kings including those erstwhile ones of

Vijayanagara. In the middle of the city was a royal center consisting of a large audience hall surrounded by a nine-sided wall, a visual reference to the nine rasas. This audience hall was similar to one provided by Ali Adil Shah in Bijapur. Rather than solely celebrating the institution of kingship, as we see in Shah Jahan's palace architecture (see chapter 7), this palace at Nauraspur was meant for the celebration of all that was associated with Nauras, that is, the nine flavors or moods. Encompassed in these nine flavors were the moods evoked by hearing music and poetry and by viewing painted images and dancing, as well as wine made from nine juices. Ibrahim even invented a new holiday associated with the celebration of the culture of Nauras, which entailed day-long festivities featuring music and recitations of poetry and stories.

Portraits of Ibrahim Adil Shah II reveal a striking difference between the sensibilities of the Mughal court and those of the Bijapur court. Portraiture under Akbar's successors, Jahangir (r. 1605–27) and Shah Jahan (r. 1628–58), became increasingly rigid and formalized, presenting the Mughal emperor as a light-filled Perfect Man, an Islamic theological concept (see Figure 7.3 for an example). These Mughal portraits are often set in recognizable court settings intended to display their roles as autocratic temporal kings. By contrast, portraits of Ibrahim II reflect his intense interest in Sufism as well as in Indic culture. Depictions of him set in landscapes shrouded in mist emphasize the ruler's contemplative mood rather than his absolute authority. Perhaps the most famous shows him wearing the wooden beads of a mystic around his neck and holding castanets, reflecting his love of music (Figure 6.6). Ibrahim II's catholic tastes, combining Indic and Islamicate sensibilities, more closely resemble Mughal India under Akbar than under Jahangir and Shah Jahan, whose portraits show them bejeweled with precious stones appropriate for men of worldly power (for their names mean World Conqueror and King of the World, respectively), not the beads of a saint.

Ibrahim Adil Shah II's counterpart at Golkonda was Muhammad Quli Qutb Shah, who also composed many poems in Dakani, collected in his *Kulliyat*. Poems in this royal work display the influence of bhakti and other Indic poetic genres, for they address god in the feminine voice unlike later Indo-Islamic lyrics, as Carla Petievich has pointed out. The *Kulliyat* also contains poems praising seventeen beautiful women from different castes and religions, although it is not clear whether these were actual people or ideal types. In any case, Muhammad Quli has often been linked to a Hindu consort named Bhagmati in texts composed outside the Golkonda region, which allege that he first called his new city of Hyderabad Bhagnagar in her honor. The sultan's association with Hindu women is confirmed in a painting created at the Qutb Shah court two

Figure 6.6 Ibrahim Adil Shah II's portrait shows him in a contemplative mood, holding castanets and wearing the beads of a mystic saint that signify his love of music and his interest in Sufism.

Figure 6.7 This painting is usually identified as the wedding procession of Muhammad Quli Qutb Shah of Golkonda (r. 1580–1611) and his Hindu consort Bhagmati.

or three decades after his death, which apparently depicts the sultan on the occasion of a wedding with a woman whose forehead marking seems to identify her as a Hindu (Figure 6.7). The sultan's distinctive appearance matches portraits of him made during his life for European visitors to his court.

As the Golkonda state grew, its main port city Masulipatnam achieved a dominant position along India's southeastern or Coromandel coast (roughly equivalent to the coastline of the modern states of Andhra Pradesh and Tamil Nadu). One reason Masulipatnam became much more prosperous than any Nizam Shah or Adil Shah port on the west coast, where the Portuguese had several fortified settlements and a large fleet, was due to the notably smaller official Portuguese presence in the Bay of Bengal. With little opposition from the Portuguese, Masulipatnam became a center not only for international trade but also for the transport and redistribution of goods from other coastal areas such as Bengal. The construction of a road from the port to the capital city of Golkonda by Muhammad Quli Qutb Shah contributed to its prosperity, for goods could then be carried overland from Masulipatnam via Golkonda to the bustling commercial center at Surat in Gujarat. By about 1650, Masuli-patnam had grown to a population of 100,000, comparable both to Surat and to the combined cities of Golkonda-Hyderabad.

The initial orientation of Masulipatnam's maritime trade was toward Southeast Asia (modern Indonesia, Malaysia, Thailand, and Myanmar), a region where trade goods from the Coromandel coast had been coveted for centuries. Toward the end of the sixteenth century, a break-through occurred when a new sea link was established between Masulipatnam and the Middle East. Previously, the direct sea routes from the Mid-dle East had all been to ports along India's west coast, either in Gujarat or the Malabar coast. Masulipatnam was the first port on India's east coast to link the eastern and western sectors of Indian Ocean travel and trade. Its success in doing so had much to do with the initiative of Golkonda's rulers, who were Shia Muslims and thus sought close relations with Safavid Iran and who also, like the Mughals, wanted to provide direct passage to Mecca for pilgrims. Moreover, much of the capi-tal investment in Masulipatnam's shipbuilding and maritime trade came from Iranians who had immigrated to the Golkonda kingdom. Just as we saw in the case of the Mughal court under Jahangir and Shah Jahan, Iranian immigrants to India often combined skills in statecraft with a keen interest in international commerce. Themselves representatives of the greater mobility of people across national borders in the early mod-ern period, the Iranians in both the Mughal and Golkonda states stimu-lated a further shrinking of the distances between different regions of the world.

The most valuable item Golkonda exported was diamonds, for it had the largest alluvial diamond mines in the world at this time. Golkonda's high-caliber iron and steel were also in great demand. But the item most closely associated with Masulipatnam port's maritime trade was cotton textiles. Although the Golkonda region produced muslin (a thin fabric with open weave and finely spun yarn), it, and the rest of the Coromandel coast, was best known for its chintz. Chintz is a general term for cotton fabrics whose designs are produced after the cloth is already woven; these designs could be block printed but often were hand applied with pen and brush or a combination of both techniques. The artist's creativity was better reflected in hand-painted Coromandel chintzes than in the block-printed designs that were typical of textiles from Gujarat. Multiple stages were involved in the application of color to a Coromandel chintz, generally including the use of both mordants (substances that bind dyes to cotton, which is not naturally color absorbent) and of resists (wax or other items that prevent color from adhering to cloth). India was technically centuries ahead of the rest of the world both in the vividness of its dyes and in their

Figure 6.8 This elaborate seventeenth-century textile served as the decorative lining for a tent. Its design suggests that it was originally intended for a south Indian or Sri Lankan market.

permanence. The Golkonda region was especially fortunate because a bright red dye-producing plant grew in the Krishna river delta, not far from supplies of excellent indigo (which yielded a deep blue color) as well as raw cotton.

Golkonda's textiles were so highly regarded that they were favored by the Mughal elite of the seventeenth century. The French traveler

François Bernier reported in 1665 that the main tents where Aurangzeb held court while traveling from Delhi to Lahore were lined inside "with beautiful hand-painted chintz, manufactured for the purpose at Maslipatam." Aurangzeb's private tents, Bernier tells us, were surrounded by tall screens and some of these were "lined with Maslipatam chintz, painted over with flowers of a hundred kinds."[1] At least five large chintz textiles from Golkonda were acquired by Rajput princes of the Kachhwaha house, possibly while on campaign in the Deccan, and placed in the storehouse of their Amber palace between 1639 and 1685. Among these is a double-arched panel that most probably served as part of the decorative lining for an elaborate tent. One panel of this vibrant hanging, painted largely in shades of red, depicts a double-headed mythic bird carrying a small elephant in each of its mouths and reflects south Indian or Sri Lankan taste, indicating it was probably made for one of these markets (Figure 6.8).

The unique cultures of the Bijapur and Golkonda Sultanates, blending both Indic and Islamicate traditions with a strong Iranian overlay, continued to flourish throughout much of the seventeenth century. Their fellow Bahmani successor states farther to the north fared less well, under pressure from the Mughals. By the mid 1630s, the Mughals had annexed northern Maharashtra and forced the Adil Shahs and Qutb Shahs to sign a treaty acknowledging their overlordship. For the most part, however, these two Deccan Sultanates were left undisturbed and, with their northern borders now secure against Mughal attack, they went on the offensive against territories to their south. Bijapur acquired southern Karnataka and the fortress of Senji (also spelled Gingee) on the Tamil coast, thereby terminating several Nayaka states that had arisen in the aftermath of the Vijayanagara empire's collapse. Golkonda, for its part, annexed all of southern Andhra and put an end to the last dynasty of Vijayanagara rulers. Eventually both Bijapur and Golkonda were defeated and incorporated within the Mughal empire in the 1680s.

Vijayanagara and the Nayaka states

Soon after the fateful battle in 1565 when the Vijayanagara army was defeated by the combined forces of the Deccan Sultanates, the capital was shifted from Hampi, which was close to the Vijayanagara kingdom's former northern border, to a more distant location in southern Andhra.

---

[1] *Travels in the Mogul Empire, AD 1656–1668*, trans. A. Constable, 2nd edn. (New Delhi: Munshiram Manoharlal, 1992), pp. 361–62.

The first site chosen came under attack more than once, and the capital was moved again, to Chandragiri, even farther away from Bijapur and Golkonda cities. Chandragiri was a small town, situated in the linguistic and cultural border zone between the Tamil country and the Telugu-speaking Andhra region. It had the advantage of being close to the great temple town of Tirupati, whose wealth was so widely known that a plundering expedition from Portuguese Goa had been planned in the 1540s, though abandoned in the end. Travelers to Chandragiri often toured Tirupati town as well, as we see in the case of Jacques de Coutre, a European gem trader who visited in 1611:

> We left for the city of Chandreguiri, where the emperor had his court after the rebellion [1565]. We arrived at this place, which was very lovely and walled just like Belur [Vellore]. It had a castle atop a very high hill, and at its foot was the palace of the emperor; it was a large and sumptuous edifice . . . And the city had great suburbs, and it was teeming with people. I was there for five days; and I went alone from there to the diamond mine in a palanquin . . . I left the walls of the city and made my way more than two leagues through its suburbs till Tripiti, the city of the pagode [temple] which is so called, and it seemed that it was all one city.[2]

The palaces at Chandragiri were built by Venkatapati II (r. 1586–1614), the greatest ruler of Vijayanagara's last royal dynasty, the Aravidus. The Aravidu kings continued the early practice of building secular palace structures in a style that fused traditional Indic with Islamicate forms. The large edifice at Chandragiri mentioned by de Coutre was probably the Raja Mahal, or King's Palace, a rectangular three-storied structure with Islamicate arched openings. The center of the building's façade has a large projecting portal, bearing Indic tiered, stacked superstructures resembling temple spires.

Although the Aravidu kings attempted to replicate the greatness of their imperial predecessors and may have succeeded in the eyes of people like de Coutre, their kingdom was but a mere shadow of what Vijayanagara had once been. After 1565, the Nayaka lords of many localities, especially in the Karnataka area, asserted their independence. The borderlands between Andhra Pradesh and Tamil Nadu remained under the Aravidu dynasty's overall rule. But most of the Tamil country was in the hands of three Telugu-speaking Nayaka warrior families, all of whom had entrenched themselves in the far south around 1530, during the heyday of Vijayanagara's imperium. The largest and wealthiest of the three Nayaka kingdoms was based at Madurai, an ancient city on the Vaigai river. A

---

[2] Sanjay Subrahmanyam, *Penumbral Visions: Making Polities in Early Modern South India* (Delhi: Oxford University Press, 2001), p. 47.

second, more compact, Nayaka state controlled the fertile Kaveri river delta from Tanjavur, another Tamil city with a long history. The third, and most tenuous, of the Vijayanagara successor states was founded at Senji (Gingee), not far from the Aravidu base in Chandragiri – a geopolitical reality that hampered Senji's expansion. For the most part, the Nayaka kings continued to pay homage to the Vijayanagara throne, even under the Aravidu dynasty, and they also generally remitted a portion of their revenues to Chandragiri until the 1630s. The authority of the Aravidu and Nayaka kings was often contested by numerous small warrior chieftains, who built fortified strongholds in the countryside. The former Vijayanagara empire was thus, by 1600, highly fragmented.

Already in the early sixteenth-century heyday of Vijayanagara, the peninsula had experienced the early modern trend of increased elite migration. Telugu-speaking warriors, in particular, had moved into upland sections of the Tamil country in a form of internal colonization. A multi-linguistic milieu had been created at court by the fact that the empire encompassed several linguistic regions. This trend culminated in the post-1565 era, when the remnants of Vijayanagara power were concentrated in the Tamil south, outside the core area of the original empire. Even more than before, we witness the transposition of the culture of the southern Deccan onto that of the Tamil area and the resulting emergence of a common south Indian high culture. The urbane court of the Tanjavur Nayakas was especially active in its promotion of Sanskrit and regional literatures, most notably in the genre of dance drama known as *yakshagana*. One yakshagana composed by a Tanjavur prince about his father, Raghunatha Nayaka (r. 1612–34), includes a scene where accountants speaking in different languages – Tamil, Telugu, and Kannada – bicker amongst themselves, perhaps reflecting some tension between the diverse constituents of the kingdom.

The Nayaka kings are best known as patrons of literature, but they also made efforts to emulate their Vijayanagara predecessors by constructing buildings in the imperial idiom. The Nayaka palace in Madurai is an outstanding example of a seventeenth-century monument that combines Islamicate with Indic traditions. Its great arched audience hall, embellished with stucco sculptures of attendant figures and mythic beasts, clearly indicates awareness of the palaces at Chandragiri, yet surpasses them in terms of lavish extravagant forms. However, the most significant architectural accomplishment of the Nayakas was the renovation and expansion of the Minakshi temple in the heart of Madurai city, undertaken by the famous king Tirumala Nayaka (r. 1623–59), to be discussed in chapter 7. Tirumala of Madurai, perhaps more than any other Nayaka ruler, attempted to live up to the example of righteous kingship set by

Vijayanagara emperors such as Krishnadeva Raya, which stressed the patronage of temples as a central royal activity. Tirumala Nayaka also set great store on the displaying of royal greatness to the public. The Jesuit Baltazar da Costa provides some details on Tirumala Nayaka's public rituals in the 1640s:

Almost every day he appears on the terrace surrounded by his courtiers, while in front of them his elephants are drawn up in two rows, the space between them occupied by three or four hundred Turks, who form his bodyguard. When he comes out of the fortress to visit some pagodes [temples], as he is wont to do on days of festival, he is surrounded with great pomp. Sometimes he rides in a palanquin, at other times he mounts an enormous elephant . . . Next come the elephants in a long file, mounted by his nobles and chief captains, preceded by the arms and insignia of the Nayaka. Then the cavalry and the rest of the troops follow.[3]

Yet, in spite of the superficial similarities with the Vijayanagara past, the elite culture of the Nayaka kingdoms had significantly changed in its orientation. It had a far less militaristic ethos, for one thing, so that the kings are depicted in literature not so much as warrior-heroes or even as moral exemplars but rather as semi-divine and highly erotic individuals – the essence of kingship was now "a heroism not of the battlefield but of the bedroom," in the words of an insightful recent work on the Nayaka period by Velcheru Narayana Rao, David Shulman, and Sanjay Subrahmanyam.[4] The literary focus on sexual pleasure was but one aspect of a larger emphasis in Nayaka culture on *bhoga*, a term that is best expressed as consumption (from the root "to eat" and by extension "to enjoy"). In keeping with this transformation in Nayaka values was a corresponding shift in the forms of royal religious patronage. Instead of making grants of land or valuables to a deity enshrined in a temple, Nayaka kings preferred to engage in the lavish, and public, feeding of Brahmins and other worthy people within temple compounds. That is, the ephemeral act of feasting a host of individuals now took precedence over the making of permanent endowments to religious institutions.

The more hedonistic tone of the Nayaka courts may explain the explicit sensuality in sculptural images of these kings and their courtiers. There is no shortage of these images rendered on calicos, in ivory, and on stucco adorning local temples. A Nayaka courtier, for instance, is shown in an ivory statue embracing a voluptuous woman (Figure 6.9). This and similar images, found on everything from combs to bedsteads to temples,

---

[3] V. Narayana Rao, D. Shulman, and S. Subrahmanyam, *Symbols of Substance: Court and State in Nayaka Period Tamilnadu* (Delhi: Oxford University Press, 1992), p. 87.
[4] *Ibid.*, p. 190.

Figure 6.9 This carved seventeenth-century ivory showing a couple engaged in love play, a reflection of the hedonistic tone of the Nayaka court, is one of a number of similar carvings that were part of a royal palanquin.
Photo Courtesy of French Institute of Pondicherry / Ecole Française d'Extrême-Orient

reflect the widespread dissemination of the new Nayaka concept of plea-surable consumption not only in literary but also in visual terms. While loving couples have long featured in Indian art and are often said to rep-resent the soul's yearning for union with god, this particular ivory, and other objects like it, parallel the explicit erotic literature of the Nayaka period.

The new premium placed on consumption reflects the altered real-ity of the Nayaka world both economically and sociologically. Public consumption – whether by the provision of feasts on the part of the king or by the display of royal splendor – was a sign of command over liquid resources in an environment that was rapidly becoming monetized. The Nayaka economy was expanding quickly, partly because agriculture was being extended into the dryer zones of the Tamil countryside, but primarily because of the growing networks of trade, which brought in large quantities of cash. The social groups that had accompanied the Nayaka rulers in their rise to power, moreover, came not from the old landed aristocracy, but instead represented a class of upwardly mobile entrepreneurs who combined martial skills with commercial ones. By taking the risks of moving to a different region and engaging in new activ-ities, the warrior-merchants who backed the Nayakas of Tamil Nadu had forged a new and better life for themselves. Theirs was a more individ-ualistic and less class-conscious ethos than that of the hereditary upper castes. They operated on a more modest scale than did the high-ranking Iranian entrepreneurs of Golkonda, who have been described as "port-folio capitalists" on account of the diversification of their investments and their straddling of the spheres of commerce and politics. Nonetheless, the warrior-merchants of the Nayaka south contributed to the growing commercialization of its political economy.

Sales taxes from the market towns that were springing up through-out the territories of the far south, as domestic trade grew, benefited the Nayaka and Aravidu states. So too did the customs duties levied on exports from the numerous ports along the Coromandel coast. Imports, on the other hand, were charged only very light duties, indicating that the southern rulers wanted to encourage the flow of international trade into their realms. They, like the Vijayanagara emperors of earlier times, sought horses from overseas in order to strengthen their armies. Pre-cious metals were another import that was eagerly desired. Substantial quantities of gold entered south India in the seventeenth century, provid-ing the supplies for its ample gold-based currency. This was a contrast to the Mughal north, where silver coins were the primary unit of the monetary system. Throughout the seventeenth and eighteenth centuries, there were massive flows of bullion (i.e., gold, silver, and copper) into the subcontinent from other parts of the world. Much of the bullion came originally from the huge quantities of silver mined by the Spanish in Latin America, which circulated through European markets before coming to India via the Middle East or the direct sea routes from Europe. African and Japanese gold also entered the subcontinent, all in response to the enormous overseas demand for Indian products. Without these supplies of precious metals from abroad, the monetization of the early modern Indian economy would undoubtedly have proceeded at a much slower pace.

While indigenous merchants participated in the booming international trade of seventeenth-century south India, an increasing share went into the hands of Europeans. The Coromandel coast was studded with European enclaves: the Portuguese were at Nagapattinam in Tanjavur territory and at São Tomé-Mylapore in the Chandragiri realm by the early 1500s; the Danes were in the Tanjavur port of Tranquebar as well as Golkonda's Masulipatnam by the 1620s; and in 1640 the English finally settled in Madras (Chennai), within the Chandragiri kingdom, after first trying several other sites. By far the most dominant group among the European traders were the Dutch, who arrived on the Coromandel coast during the first decade of the seventeenth century. They soon came to an agreeable arrangement with the Qutb Shahs of Golkonda, but their trading post at Masulipatnam ranked second to their primary settlement at Pulicat, on the central Coromandel coast near Chandragiri. The Coromandel coast was the source of the overwhelming bulk of the items acquired in India by the Dutch trading company (VOC) for its intra-Asian or country trade during the entire 1600s, an era when the Dutch were in the ascendance in Indian Ocean waters.

It was the Dutch who mounted the first serious challenge to Portuguese naval supremacy in the Indian Ocean, because they were better financed and equipped than the English. Like the Portuguese, the Dutch wanted to corner the European market in fine spices. Their strategy was quite different from that of the Portuguese, who had based themselves in southwestern India and tried to monopolize the spice trade through controlling the ships that carried spices for sale. The Dutch decided instead to monopolize spices at their sources, the places where they were actually produced. This meant that their main area of interest was Indonesia rather than India. From their base at Batavia (modern Jakarta) on the island of Java, the Dutch systematically attacked all competing interests. The official Portuguese presence in Southeast Asia was well-nigh eliminated when in 1641 the Dutch captured Malacca, the renowned entrepôt that had been in Portuguese hands for a century. The Dutch then started to deprive the Portuguese of their possessions in South Asia, taking Sri Lanka in 1658 and ports on the Malabar coast in the 1660s.

Even before the 1640s, when the Dutch became the foremost of the European traders, they encountered the same problem the Portuguese had faced earlier. The islanders who grew spices were not interested in exchanging them for European goods or even necessarily for precious metals. The main item they sought in return for the sale of their spices was Indian cloth, and so the Dutch had no alternative but to set up trading posts in the subcontinent. One reason for choosing the Coromandel coast initially was its proximity to Southeast Asia. But it also appears that Southeast Asians of the seventeenth century preferred textiles from the Coromandel coast to those from Gujarat or Bengal. A wide variety of colors and designs were produced in the south, tailored specifically for different segments of the Southeast Asian markets. The Thais, for example, liked textiles painted with a fine thin finial motif in their borders which were quite different from distinctive tastes in other regions of Southeast Asia. Designs and tastes were probably transmitted from buyer to producer through the circulation of books containing textile patterns, like those that survive from nineteenth-century Java.

While the northern Coromandel region in Golkonda territory was known for its high-end cloth, central and southern Coromandel specialized in cheaper textiles that were sold in the largest quantities. The influx of Indian textiles into Southeast Asia was enormous: as many as 400,000 pieces were imported into the Spice Islands of Indonesia alone in a single year during the early 1600s, according to one estimate. They had a profound and lasting impact on textile preferences and production within Southeast Asia. Not only was the art of batik (patterning cloth with the use of wax as a resist medium) introduced to Indonesia via Indian textiles along with the patola or double ikat technique of weaving, so too were many of the designs used in indigenous textiles for centuries thereafter.

Although examples of Coromandel cloth made for the Southeast Asian market are quite plentiful, it is difficult to assign specific dates to abstract designs and to identify where exactly they were produced. The cloth hangings from Golkonda discussed a few pages previously can be pinpointed in time only because clerks in charge of the royal Kachhwaha Rajput storehouse marked the dates of their acquisition on the back. Similarly, a few wall hangings from elsewhere on the Coromandel coast can be assigned to the pre-1650 era because they depict Europeans, whose costumes can be definitively dated. For instance, a wall hanging now at the Brooklyn Museum has been dated to the decade between 1610 and 1620 on the basis of the dress worn by European-looking figures in one of its seven panels. The hanging was clearly produced somewhere south of Masulipatnam on the Coromandel coast, for it reveals numerous influences from the imperial Vijayanagara style of mural painting. It was probably commissioned by a court, since each of its panels illustrates a different community of people – European, Thai, Javanese or Malay, Persian or Turkoman, Indo-Islamic, Indic, and indigenous tribals – in the setting of a courtly audience. Nina Gwatkin has tentatively linked this wall hanging to the Chandragiri court of Vijayanagara's last, Aravidu, dynasty, partly on the basis of stylistic similarities with palace buildings there. In addition, Chandragiri controlled Pulicat port, where numerous international visitors seeking trading privileges and diplomatic recognition arrived. It was from Pulicat that much of the Dutch trade with Southeast Asia was conducted.

In one of the panels of this wall hanging courtiers are shown seated beneath engrailed Islamicate arches, surrounded by attendants (Figure 6.10). The dress worn by the females is similar to that seen in nearby wall paintings created during the height of the Vijayanagara empire. The dress of the men embraces both Indic and Islamicate styles: Indic ones are reflected in the unsewn lower garments or bare chests of some men, whereas Islamicate styles are seen in the tailored diaphanous tunics of others. The practice of switching between Indic and Islamicate types of clothing, depending on the occasion, was adopted earlier at the imperial Vijayanagara court in Hampi, Karnataka, and was continued into the seventeenth century and later by its less powerful successors. The rich and varied imagery of this hanging's panels mirrors the variety of peoples who passed through the cosmopolitan royal court at Chandragiri. It serves as a vivid testament to the ever-growing spheres of communication and exchange in the early modern Indian Ocean.

Soon after the Brooklyn Museum wall hanging was created, the importance of the Chandragiri court declined. During the long reign of Aravidu Venkatapati II (r. 1586–1614), the Vijayanagara kings had regained a portion of their former authority and luster. Much of that was lost again, this time permanently, when years of violent dispute over succession to the Vijayanagara throne weakened the Aravidu dynasty and divided the Nayaka states of Senji, Madurai, and Tanjavur. When the Deccan Sultanates of Bijapur and Golkonda turned southward after securing their northern boundaries against the Mughals in the treaty of 1636, neither Chandragiri nor the Senji Nayakas were able to oppose them effectively. Both those kingdoms were lost by 1650, while the Tanjavur Nayakas were displaced in the 1670s by a segment of the Maratha Bhonsle clan. Only the Madurai kingdom lasted into the eighteenth century, although

Figure 6.10 This panel, one of seven from a seventeenth-century wall hanging, shows elite men and women elaborately dressed in a manner similar to that of Vijayanagara's imperial heyday, while the wealth of the Chandragiri court is reflected in the abundant jewelry they wear.

the artistic creations of the Nayaka states were to have an enduring influence.

Throughout this chapter, we have repeatedly noted the increasing number of people and objects that circulated in bigger and bigger spheres of movement, both within the subcontinent and in the larger context of the Indian Ocean. This world-wide phenomenon is perhaps the most striking feature of the early modern period. To be sure, there were tremendous regional variations in our broadly painted picture of the early modern world: some regions still remained largely outside the newly emerging international global economy as did many segments of any given society's population. The growth of large empires, another trait we have associated with early modernity, is similarly applicable to only some parts of the world. Other objections to the concept of an early modern period have been lodged on the grounds that it represents an imposition of a European stage of historical development upon non-Western societies where it does not fit, or that it suggests the inevitability (and similarity) of the modernities that appear from 1800 onward. By applying the concept of early modernity to South Asia, we do not mean to imply that historical change in the diverse regions of the globe proceeded in a uniform manner or within an identical time frame. Yet, viewing South Asia within the larger early modern setting is extremely useful, for it helps us better appreciate the dynamism of the historical processes that were unfolding in the subcontinent, as in many other places during this era. It also helps us recognize South Asia's significance to other regions and other peoples, who were increasingly drawn to it in search of economic opportunities. The wealth of South Asia, and the excellence of its manufactured goods, were renowned in the early modern world; many foreign visitors were also impressed by the opulence of its royal courts. We thus turn our attention to the culture of South Asia's seventeenth-century elites in chapter 7.

7   Elite cultures in seventeenth-century South Asia

By the first half of the seventeenth century, much of the Indian sub-continent was dominated by Mughal rule, although subordinate king-doms and independent ones continued to flourish, especially in the south. In all these realms there was a strong sense of courtly ceremony and religious ritual, coupled with a strong code of appropriate behavior on the part of both men and women. As the European presence in India grew, their demand for Indian goods and trading rights increased, thus bringing even greater wealth to already flush Indian courts. The elite spent more and more money on luxury goods and sumptuous lifestyles, and the rulers built entire new capital cities at times. All of these factors resulted in greater patronage of the arts, including textiles, paintings, architecture, jewelry, and weapons to meet the ceremonial requirements of kings and princes. At the beginning of the seventeenth century, the liberal attitudes toward religion set in place by Akbar predominated in much of north India, but as the century advanced a sense of conser-vatism set in. Hand in hand with these new attitudes and increased wealth, rulers from all areas in India increasingly built elaborate and often large temples, mosques, and shrines, to proclaim their own particular religious affiliations. In this chapter, we look at the cultural production of India's seventeenth-century courts, both Muslim and Hindu, and at the religious institutions they patronized.

The Mughal court

Court culture under Jahangir and Shah Jahan

The Mughal empire was India's most powerful and prestigious polity throughout the seventeenth century. The Mughals remained superior in wealth and overall power to their closest contemporaries, the Ottomans of Turkey and the Safavids of Iran, who were also Muslim dynasties. While Jahangir did little to expand Mughal territory, under the generalship of his son Prince Khurram (the future Shah Jahan), the Mughals were able to defeat the last of the powerful independent Rajputs of west India, the Sisodiyas. Carved images of the Sisodiya king and prince were installed outside the Mughal palace, a visual reminder to all of the Mughals' ultimate authority. Some hinterland territories, including parts of the Deccan, that had been able to resist Mughal domination earlier under Jahangir were incorporated into the empire during Shah Jahan's reign. While Shah Jahan's campaigns in Central Asia and Qandahar were unsuccessful, the vast empire consisting of twenty-two provinces had untold wealth and a massive army by the middle of the seventeenth century.

The cultural policies of Jahangir and Shah Jahan became increasingly formalized and were equally important as political developments, for while the arts were aesthetically refined and pleasing to behold or hear, they also had a meaning which was rooted in dynastic image. Ultimately, Mughal attitudes toward the arts and other arenas of refinement influenced elite societies throughout the subcontinent. Not just individual acts such as the *cornish* (formal prostration before the emperor) were charged with meaning, but also entire events lasting multiple days took on lives of their own. Since the beginning of Mughal rule in India, the imperial presence was rarely fixed at a single location; rather, Mughal emperors, princes, and their mansabdar nobles frequently moved considerable distances, in part to consolidate territory and in part to serve as tangible reminders of Mughal authority. Accompanied by massive armies, fine elephants, horses, and countless vehicles, such processions made it virtually impossible to ignore the imperial presence. The Mughal emperors used these processions to their advantage, combining pilgrimage to the tombs of the Chishti saints with visits to imperial Mughal tombs and hunting, thus projecting the image of a powerful dynasty underpinned by a popular religious order.

An examination of architecture, coupled with paintings showing the emperor and court using those structures, gives us an indication of how the Mughals wished to be perceived. We saw in chapter 5 how Mughal artists depicting Akbar used pictorial devices of color and scale to suggest the emperor's light-filled status. Commencing with Jahangir, a new device, the nimbused head, was adopted to express this imperial status. A double-page portrait shows the Sufi saint Muin al-Din Chishti, handing Jahangir a globe on top of which is a Timurid crown, symbolizing the emperor's right to rule. Wearing a halo indicating his semi-divine status, Jahangir, whose name means the World Seizer, receives these tokens of the Timurid realm from Muin al-Din, by now regarded as the spiritual guardian of the Mughal house. In Jahangir's personal memoirs, the emperor recalls that early in his childhood the dying Shaikh Salim, also of the Chishti Sufi order, had placed his turban on the young prince's head,

Figure 7.1 This double page allegorical portrait shows the Sufi saint Muin al-Din Chishti, handing Jahangir (r. 1605–27) a globe on top of which is a Timurid crown, which symbolizes the emperor's right to rule.

saying that the prince would be the saint's spiritual successor. Jahangir and subsequently his son, Shah Jahan, enacted this role of spiritual successor by endowing Chishti shrines when on pilgrimage and in thanksgiving for military victory. Such patronage must be viewed as an attempt to link Mughal temporal rule to a spiritual source, specifically the one that once had guided Akbar. It was also motivated by personal piety; over time the renewed Chishti–Mughal link suggests an increased orthodoxy in official policy, especially once Shah Jahan came to power. Further underscoring the Mughal–Chishti alliance in Jahangir's portrait are the emperor's lustrous pearl earrings, which were a sign of his devotion to the saint whom he credited with curing him of an illness in 1614. Both saint and king are bound together by the wearing of white clothing, although Jahangir's elaborate jewelry and sash indicate his temporal as well as spiritual role as ruler. This portrait clearly had tremendous dynastic import, since Shah Jahan later had his father's portrait removed from the album and replaced it with that of his own (Figure 7.1).

Other portraits of Jahangir include one probably intended for an illustrated copy of Jahangir's own memoirs, the *Jahangirnama* (Figure 7.2).

Figure 7.2 In the upper right corner of Jahangir's throne is a painted image of the Virgin Mary, a reminder of the Mughal's descent from a line of illustrious kings born of a princess who was miraculously impregnated by a ray of light.

Figure 7.3 Shah Jahan, whose name means King of the World, here is depicted standing on a globe, with the lion and lamb peacefully coexisting beneath his feet symbolizing his just rule.

Here a nimbused Jahangir is enthroned in his Public Audience Hall before the nobility. In the upper right corner of his white marble throne, known as a *jharoka* (not to be confused with the jharoka-i darshan, which is a viewing window at the edge of a palace and accessible to the public), is a painted image of the Virgin Mary. Such imagery was extremely popular with Jahangir and several illustrations for Mughal histories indicate that such paintings adorned Jahangir's throne. Just as was the case in Akbar's paintings, the inclusion of the Virgin Mary was yet another reminder to those present, and one considerably easier to see than the artist's imagined halo, that the emperor Jahangir was descended from a long line of illustrious kings born of the Mongol princess Alanquwa, who was miraculously impregnated by a ray of light (see Figure 5.7).

While Shah Jahan rejected the explicit Christian imagery of the Virgin Mary in his portraiture, other devices were used to extol his semi-divine status. In the portrait of Shah Jahan Standing on a Globe, a play on his name, King of the World, he is offered the crown and sword of kingship by European-style winged cherubs who reside in the heavens (Figure 7.3). A cherub holds over Shah Jahan's nimbused head a canopy on which is inscribed his lineage back to Timur, indicating his god-chosen status as emperor. Below his feet the lion and lamb coexist peacefully, a sign of Shah Jahan's just rule. Above the animals are the scales of justice flanked by holy men, again stressing the link between dynasty and religion. Shah Jahan here, as in every portrait, is depicted in profile view, for, as Ebba Koch has argued, this view was mandatory since it involved the least distortion in appearance and was the most ideal.

While this sort of allegorical painting tells us much about how the Mughal emperors wished to be perceived, the illustrated official histories of the seventeenth century indicate how court ceremonies were enacted. A double-page composition depicting Prince Khurram's return from the Deccan in 1617 shows Jahangir on his elevated marble throne embracing his son with deep love and respect (Figure 7.4). Beneath the two royal figures on the painting's left side are the grandees of the court. Each person's name is noted on his portrait, indicating exactly who was in attendance; only those who held a rank of 500 or higher were allowed to stand in such close proximity to the king; others of lesser rank stood outside, as shown on the right side of the painting. On the right, we see the naubat (orchestra) that was sounded, here with trumpets and drums, to announce the imperial presence. On the left is an elephant so highly valued that his name was included in the text. We also are shown trays of jeweled swords, cups, and other valuables which the prince is presenting to his father. This painting highlights the formal nature of the Mughal court, where attendance was required for any noble in

Figure 7.4 In this double page composition from the *Padshahnama*, Jahangir receives Prince Khurram, the future Shah Jahan, on his victorious return from a military campaign in the Deccan.

Figure 7.4 (*cont.*)

residence; even those who were serving in the hinterland were expected to present themselves in court annually. Where a noble stood was dictated by his rank. Gift-giving was a very elaborate ritual and was a vital part of Islamicate court ceremony. Some of the valuable gifts that the prince or any other noble presented to the emperor would be accepted and the rest returned. Fine elephants were considered excellent gifts. The emperor too gave gifts, especially robes of honor and jeweled swords, to his grandees. These were always accepted, never rejected.

The court, as it moved from venue to venue, did not always perform in permanent buildings but sometimes in gardens. The Mughals since the time of Babur enjoyed gardens, and they could be large char bagh or smaller courtyard gardens that were integral parts of palaces and mansions. Gardens in the hills of Kashmir were especially appreciated. There in 1634 on the edges of Dal Lake in Srinagar, Shah Jahan further embellished the world-famous Shalimar garden that he had commenced as a prince. The entire garden is divided laterally by a broad stream that runs from the mountains behind through a series of terraces to the lake below. Shalimar was divided into two parts, one for private imperial use and the other for imperial audiences. The Kashmir Shalimar garden served as a model for another one constructed on the plains of Lahore in 1641. Here a remarkable engineering feat brought water from a considerable distance, thus enabling the construction of the garden. At the Lahore Shalimar garden, a third terrace was placed in the middle of the original two found in the Kashmir garden. Its marble throne, surrounded by cooling waters, served as a royal seat. To own a garden or even to spend time in one, where running water, fountains, and cooling plant life defied the intense heat of summer, was a luxury activity of the elite, essentially the equivalent of holidaying in Hawaii or spending time at an elegant spa.

Gardens were also part of the great imperial mausoleums built for each of the Mughal emperors throughout the mid seventeenth century. Jahangir built for Akbar a tomb, centered in a formal Mughal char bagh, just outside of Agra in the early seventeenth century. A Persian inscription on the complex's entrance gate reads: "These are the gardens of Paradise, Enter them and Live Forever," making clear that the setting is intended as an earthly replica of the gardens of paradise promised to the faithful on the Day of Judgment. The most famous of these garden tombs is the Taj Mahal in Agra, known officially as Rauza-i Munawwar or the Illumined Tomb (Figure 7.5). Largely built between 1632 and 1647 by Shah Jahan as a tomb for his favorite wife Mumtaz Mahal, who died in childbirth in 1631, it almost surely was also intended as the emperor's own tomb. Its name, Rauza-i Munawwar, an epithet shared with the Prophet Muhammad's tomb in Medina, suggests that Shah Jahan, who perceived

Figure 7.5 The world famous Taj Mahal, officially known as the Illumined Tomb, was built largely between 1632 and 1647 in Agra as a mausoleum for both Shah Jahan and his favorite wife.

himself like Muhammad as a Perfect Man, always intended the Taj to be his tomb. In any event, he was buried there after his death in 1666. While court historians give us precise clues as to the meaning of many of Shah Jahan's buildings, for example, the jharoka-i darshan (public viewing window) at the Agra fort in which the emperor's appearance is likened to that of the sun, no such textual suggestions concerning imagery exist for this tomb. Much historical information is known, but scholars disagree on the symbolism of the Taj Mahal. One scholar has argued that it is a visual representation of the Throne of God as envisioned on the Day of Judgment, while others disagree strongly with this interpretation. Whatever its larger meaning, the extensive use of white marble must have been intended to evoke a sense of divine presence, for by now white marble was utilized exclusively for the tombs of saints and for buildings meant solely for the emperor. Shah Jahan, more than any other Mughal emperor, employed architecture as a way to accentuate his own semi-divine status.

Mughal tombs were more than buildings to house the dead; they too were used performatively. Readers of the Quran were employed around the clock, thus ensuring permanent income to a large number of people. The urs (literally, wedding) of the deceased was celebrated on an annual basis, commemorating his or her union with god. Originally the urs was a ceremony associated with the death anniversary of a deceased saint, but by the seventeenth century, if not a little earlier, it had become an important part of Mughal ritual as well. These ceremonies were both elaborate and costly. Maintaining the large imperial tombs, both the multiple buildings and elaborate planted gardens, was expensive. When a tomb was built, a trust (*waqf*) was established to ensure its maintenance. In the case of the Taj Mahal, the income of thirty villages guaranteed its support.

Shahjahanabad: the new capital

The Mughal emperors had multiple palaces across the domain and moved frequently between one and the other. Most of these were fortified and had been commenced by Akbar and in some cases by even earlier Mughals. They were then remodeled by subsequent rulers. Initially, Shah Jahan's major residence was the Agra fort first constructed by Akbar. It was refurbished nearly completely by Shah Jahan, who added a number of white marble buildings intended for imperial use, among them two mosques, a private audience hall, and a pillared public audience hall. But, in spite of these additions, Shah Jahan felt that the streets of Agra were too narrow for imperial procession. He decided to build a new capital in Delhi, the traditional seat of Muslim authority in north India, which he named Shahjahanabad, that is, the Abode of Shah Jahan. Today, Shahjahanabad is the area of the capital known as Old Delhi. Located to the north of the early Mughal city of Din Panah, work began on Shah Jahan's walled city in 1639, and it was inaugurated in 1648.

In the seventeenth century, two bazaars graced the city, including the most important one that linked the palace's main west gate with the city's west gate. Known today as Chandni Chowk, this area was a tree-lined esplanade through whose center ran a canal, probably inspired by reports of Isfahan, built about forty years earlier in Safavid Iran. Here and elsewhere in Shahjahanabad, the leading ladies of the court played a significant role in the city's embellishment. Two of Shah Jahan's wives provided mosques, while his daughter Jahanara built an enormously important serai in the center of Chandni Chowk. Elsewhere in the city were the mansions of the elite, the most important of which were allotted waterfront plots. Extensive char bagh gardens were found throughout the city. The Frenchman François Bernier compared it to Paris in terms of its beauty, extent, and number of inhabitants.

Shah Jahan provided Shahjahanabad with an enormous Jami mosque close to the fortified palace (Figure 7.6). Commenced in 1650 and completed in 1656, it was the largest mosque in Mughal territory. Called the World Showing Mosque (Masjid-i Jahannuma), it stands at the city's highest point. Shah Jahan himself claimed it was modeled on Akbar's great mosque at Fatehpur Sikri; similarities include the impressive entrance gates approached by high stairs, the interior court, and the mosque's façade. This emperor was doubtless also aware of imposing, massive mosques that had been built somewhat earlier by the Ottomans and Safavids, his two major rival Muslim dynasties. His Jami mosque must be seen as a counter to their architectural expressions and an indication of Mughal greatness in the larger Islamic world. The Jami mosque's façade bears inscriptions that are written in a manner unique to scribing Quranic verses, but, in fact, they are in Persian and not in Arabic, the language of the Quran. Moreover, they are not even religious in content. Rather, they are encomiums praising Shah Jahan and his just rule.

The mosque was clearly intended to showcase the emperor as the upholder of orthodox Islam, and the city's straight spacious main avenues allowed Shah Jahan to parade through the streets in the manner he wished. The palace, accessible only to the elite, also showcased him in his role of King of the World. Unfortunately, the original walls that divided the various parts of the fort into garden courtyards were dismantled by the British after the uprising of 1857, so that the experience of visiting the fort today is a far cry from its original conception. The main gate, centrally located

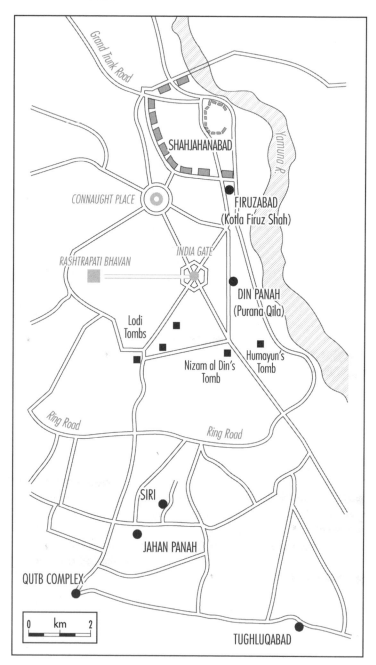

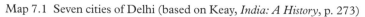

Map 7.1 Seven cities of Delhi (based on Keay, *India: A History*, p. 273)

Figure 7.6 This mosque was the public showpiece of Shah Jahan's new capital, Shahjahanabad, and at the time of its construction between 1650 and 1656 was the largest mosque in India.

on the fort's west, led immediately to a long covered bazaar, which in turn led directly to the Naubat Khana, an entrance to the palace's Public Audience Hall.

The pillared Public Audience Hall (Diwan-i Amm) was an important place of court ceremonial intended to evoke the great audience hall of Persepolis, which was believed to have been founded by Solomon, the ultimate symbol of justice. This hall faced Shah Jahan's marble throne, designed as a high platform surmounted by a curved roof (known as *bangla* after the Bengal style) supported on bulbous baluster columns, drawn from European illustrations of holy and royal settings; these architectural features at the time were exclusive to Shah Jahan (Figure 7.7). Visually they called attention to the emperor's role as a semi-divine ruler. So, too, the inlaid panels embedded in the back wall of the throne were used to signify an Islamic understanding of Solomon's throne, that is, the seat of the ideal just ruler, a notion we have seen in Shah Jahan's portraiture. These panels, mostly from Italy, depicted birds, animals, and even the figure of the Greek Orpheus taming wild animals. Orpheus was a metaphor for justice, and where justice prevailed, the lion and lamb could peacefully co-exist, as depicted in other Mughal paintings done under Shah Jahan (see Figure 7.3).

Due east of the Public Audience Halls are the royal chambers that overlook the Yamuna river. Arranged on a north–south axis, a canal bisects each room, including the royal quarters for Shah Jahan and his daughter Jahanara, the Private Audience Hall, and a bath (*hammam*). The white marble of these chambers is often inlaid with rare stones, as, for example, in the bath and the Private Audience Hall. Shah Jahan's fascination with paradisiacal imagery, as well as visual themes of just rule, is amply manifest in this portion of the palace. On a panel leading into Shah Jahan's sleeping quarters is a high relief carving in marble that is covered with the gold gilt of the scales of justice, a reference to the emperor's perception of his own rule. Close to this carving is a lengthy inscription that praises Shah Jahan and likens his creation to the mansions of paradise. In the nearby Private Audience Hall, verses from the fourteenth-century Indian poet Amir Khusrau are painted on the walls, proclaiming the structure a paradise on earth.

Shah Jahan's palace, like his painting, was artfully contrived to highlight the Mughal ruler's status. This pertained to every aspect of the dwelling, even to details such as the image of Orpheus on the throne that could hardly be visible even to the nobles standing in attendance at court. The palace at Shahjahanabad reflects an almost slavish sense of flattering the ruler and reveals the extremely hierarchical nature of the mid seventeenth-century Mughal court.

Figure 7.7 Shah Jahan's especially designed throne for the Public Audience Hall of his Shahjahanabad palace, with its curved roof, bulbous columns, and inlaid panels, was intended to showcase him as the King of the World.

Gender roles and lifestyles of the Mughal elite

The system developed by Akbar that assured the loyalty of a high-ranking officer to the Mughal emperor lasted into the late seventeenth century. Ready to appear in court, to serve on the battlefield or as an administrator of a province or city, the high-ranking noble believed his emperor was an illumined being and also knew the emperor could confiscate all his belongings and property at death, although usually these were redistributed to his male and female heirs. Officers who served in the Mughal *mansabdar* system – whether high-ranking as in the case of the great amirs (nobles) like the Khan-i Khanan (see chapter 5), or low to medium ranking, as in the case of fort keepers, bookkeepers, secretaries, and so on – all considered themselves as *khanazad*s (literally, sons), that is, as affiliates whose positions were hereditary. Their service to the emperor was a familial one and they conformed to the sophisticated etiquette of Indo-Persian culture in terms of behavior, dress, and speech, as well as by being loyal, courageous, and honorable. Rosalind O'Hanlon has pointed out that, while these qualities were fundamental to the loyal amir, so too was an understanding of how to behave in a public world that was overwhelmingly male. Akbar promoted the view that a khanazad should conform to the Indian tradition of heterosexuality and not the Persian custom which allowed bisexuality, as we saw in the case of Babur. The subject of O'Hanlon's case study, a high-ranking noble, Muhammad Baqir Najm-i Sani, appears to adhere to this heterosexual ideal, although never stating it outright in his collected sayings, written during Jahangir's reign. The initial part of Sani's memoirs upholds the notion of the khanazad's absolute loyalty to the emperor, which he argues includes giving sincere but discreet advice on the state of imperial affairs to ensure good governance. The second part of his text concerns friendship and wealth. To Sani, sincere and genuine friendship without a desire for promotion for political or economic gain is the most important personal aspect of being a man. Money, he then explains, is essential, for with it friends can be helped and poverty, the source of disaster and disgrace, averted.

Without wealth it would not have been possible to dress the part of a high-ranking noble. Paintings of the court indicate that the turbans and tunics worn by men were from a large variety of richly woven and embroidered fabrics (see Figures 7.1, 7.2, 7.3, 7.4). In the summer, diaphanous cotton tunics were worn over colorful, tight leggings, while in the cooler season heavier materials were favored. Jewels, including pearls and rubies, were part of court attire, as was a two-handled jeweled dagger that was tucked into the waist sash. This article of clothing was often the most elaborate of the entire ensemble, at times woven with pure gold threads.

The furnishings of every noble's house also needed quality carpets, gold, silver, or hard stone fittings such as *hookah* bases, wine cups, rose-water sprinklers, and other items required in order to indicate a high standard of fine living. In addition, a ready supply of similar objects, but especially jeweled daggers, turban jewels, and robes of honor, needed to be on hand to present to others as rewards and favors. The imperial court and the wealthiest nobles maintained their own artisans and factories to custom-make these materials and works.

To date we know of no text concerning gender norms for women in Mughal India similar to those that exist for Mughal men, nineteenth-century Muslim women, and even women in Nayaka south India. While Mughal women might be largely invisible to anyone outside the haram except their male relatives, due to the practice of *purdah* or seclusion, this does not mean they were powerless or necessarily lived confined lives. The female members of court, their children, attendants, and many female servants lived within the haram, a large, highly organized establishment inside any palace guarded by eunuchs and armed women. Inside the walls of the haram, women were educated, had access to friends, relatives, astrologers, midwives, artisans, poets, dancers, and so on, but they were all female. While the mention of a haram tends to evoke Orientalist notions of licentious behavior, much serious business transpired within these walls. For example, a designated woman of the haram heard the petitions of needy women, just as the emperor listened to those of men. The common notion that once a woman went inside this walled compound, she would never come out is patently untrue, for a number of sources, both Mughal and European, make it clear that women went out to hunt and travel. When the court moved from venue to venue, the haram was included.

The roles played by Mughal queens and princesses in promoting various court factions and trade, and their role in patronizing architecture, literature, painting, fashion, and religion are well known. Jahangir's mother, like his grandmother, bore a title equating her with Mary, considered one of the most virtuous models of female behavior. Jahangir's mother took an active interest in court life, and important ceremonies such as weddings frequently took place at her house. She also hosted weighing ceremonies, during which a king or prince would be weighed against gold; these events were considered auspicious since the precious metal was distributed to holy men, the poor, and the needy. Like other queens and queen mothers, most of whom were given titles evoking exemplary Muslim women, Jahangir's mother issued edicts and provided architectural patronage; in her case, a large mosque in Lahore and a step well and serai in the indigo-growing territory of Bayana. Royal woman were often the source of beneficence that was religiously meritorious for themselves and the recipients.

By far the most powerful woman in Jahangir's court was his favorite wife, Nur Jahan (Light of the World). In his memoirs, Jahangir remarks several times that Nur Jahan was an excellent marksman; tradition claims she fashioned clothing styles, created new carpet designs, and was a poet. We do know for certain that her father was Jahangir's finance minister, and after his death she assumed all his assets, thus giving her extraordinary wealth. Her brothers were also highly placed in the Mughal administrative system, but the family did not form a single faction, as is commonly believed. For example, after Nur Jahan abandoned her support of Khurram as the heir apparent, one of her brothers continued to support him. But her power cannot be denied: she had coins minted in her name, issued imperial orders, held jagirs (revenue assignments from lands, which were generally granted only to men), gave robes of honor and precious gifts to important nobles, and had drums sounded in her honor after they were sounded for Jahangir. In addition, she was a highly educated and generous sponsor of literary figures. Her patronage of architecture was exceptional and included pleasure gardens, palaces, and serais that contemporary European travelers claimed she commissioned in order to be remembered by posterity. A number of Nur Jahan's architectural projects survive, the most important of which is the tomb she completed in Agra for her parents about six years after their deaths in the early 1620s. The white marble tomb is heavily inlaid with semi-precious stones and set in a char bagh garden, continuing the earlier tomb tradition established with Humayun's and Akbar's tombs. Its exquisite inlay-designs, depicting cypress trees, fruit, wine vessels, and abstracted flowers, were probably intended as visual metaphors for paradise (Figure 7.8).

Shah Jahan's wives played a significant role in embellishing his new city Shahjahanabad by providing large red sandstone mosques. Their patronage of a uniform mosque type that echoed Shah Jahan's even larger Jami mosque can be understood as a dynastic statement. However, the most important woman in Shah Jahan's time was not a wife but rather his eldest daughter Jahanara, who after her mother's death in 1631 served as the leading lady of the court. Jahanara was deeply religious and provided several mosques in Agra and elsewhere. She wrote a biography of Muin al-Din Chishti and gave large sums to his shrine in Ajmer, adding the white marble pillared porch before the entrance of his tomb. Also a patron of gardens and serais, Jahanara supported her brother Dara Shikoh in the war of accession that broke out after Shah Jahan was believed to be dying in 1657. In its aftermath, she remained with the imprisoned Shah Jahan until his death in 1666. Her sister, who supported Aurangzeb, the

Figure 7.8 This fine tomb in Agra, completed in 1627–28, was built by
Nur Jahan for both her parents, but it is commonly known as the tomb
of Itimad al-Daula after her father.

victor in this dispute for the throne, lived in Delhi during this period; her
mansion was the refuge of poets and litterateurs.

Mughal women were expected to be pious and virtuous, but that did not
stop them from serving as power brokers and political agents. While living
behind the veil, women could travel and hunt, make potent statements of
their presence through large-scale architectural patronage, and in some
rare cases exert their authority through the use of the naubat, the minting
of coins, and the issuance of orders.

European perceptions of Mughal India, 1600–1658

India's natural resources attracted European merchants eager to gain
trading rights or simply make their fortune, as well as various Catholic
orders hoping to gather souls into their flock. Thus, Europeans from a
number of countries including Portugal, England, Holland, and parts
of modern Italy were in India during the sixteenth and seventeenth
centuries; some of these travelers had actual contact with the court,
while others, usually less educated, had to rely on the gossip and general

observation of more common folk. Diaries, letters, and even journals were kept by many Europeans, some simply wishing to record their daily transactions and others hoping to make their mark in the burgeoning body of travel literature that was quickly becoming popular in Europe. Kate Teltscher has argued convincingly that all these travelogues are steeped with a western Christian bias and tended to imagine India as the Other, that is, as strange and exotic. Thus their writings should not accepted as absolutely accurate.

Jesuit priests, as noted in chapter 5, had been invited to Akbar's court as early as 1580, and they were also at Jahangir's court, although his memoirs are completely silent about their presence, as they are also about Sir Thomas Roe, the ambassador to India from the court of James I of England. The Jesuits learned Persian and could communicate well with the Mughal ruler, often explaining the meaning of imagery or the Christian doctrine. The taste for European and European-style painting escalated at the beginning of Jahangir's reign. For example, we have already noted that a portrait of the Virgin appeared above Jahangir's jharoka (see Figure 7.2). Murals with Catholic-inspired imagery were important components of court settings during Jahangir's reign. Recently cleaned walls at the Lahore fort have revealed portraits of Christian saints interspersed with those of imperial princes. While the Jesuits misunderstood the Mughal use of Christian imagery as an interest in conversion, it was actually employed as a means of expressing the spiritual superiority of the Mughal lineage who, like Jesus, had also been miraculously conceived. The concept of Mughal spiritual superiority, elaborated in literary terms by Abu al-Fazl at Akbar's court, found a perfect visual expression through this appropriation of Christian Catholic imagery.

Another European who had considerable contact with the Mughal court was Sir Thomas Roe, the first official representative of the fledgling English East India Company. He was in India from 1614 to 1618, producing a manuscript of his observations that many consider to be the most reliable contemporary analysis of Jahangir's court. However, as several writers have pointed out, Roe, who knew no Persian and was steeped in an Oxford University humanist education, must be read with caution. Recent work by Colin Mitchell argues that Roe's tendency to interpret the imperial court and its activities as a stage presentation reflects his own cultural background, since there was an extremely close relation between plays and political events in Jacobean England. His text describing the politics of the contemporary Mughal court uses the language and themes of Jacobean theater. So too his belief that all advancement within the mansabdar system was the result of gifts and cash had a similar origin, for Roe had little grasp of merit as a reason for promotion. As much as Roe misunderstood Mughal ceremony and political developments, Jahangir too had little understanding of an elite male who was sent to make trade treaties, a preoccupation beneath an esteemed military man, the chief model comprehensible to Jahangir and his contemporaries. Thanks to Nur Jahan's brother, Roe was able to find favor in Jahangir's eyes; the small portrait of the emperor Roe was given meant that he was included in the emperor's inner circle. The common ground between Roe and Jahangir was based on an appreciation of painting. Jahangir, understanding that the European believed his culture superior to that of the Mughals, proved to Roe that Mughal artists were capable of copying European portraits so well that Roe had considerable difficulty in recognizing the original. This exercise went far beyond the ability to copy; it showed Roe that Mughal cultural achievements were on a par with European ones technically and that royal portraiture had a similar symbolic meaning in both cultures.

While it is possible to see how Mughal imperial ideology was perceived and often misunderstood by Europeans in India, how the Mughal elite and ordinary subjects perceived Mughal ideology is less clear. The writings of Bernier, Peter Mundy, Niccolao Manucci and other Europeans in India during the seventeenth century indicate that bazaar gossip about the imperial family and their elite was rampant. In the common view, Shah Jahan was perceived as lascivious, arrogant, and intolerant, certainly not characteristics he wished to project in his official image, thus suggesting that imperial propaganda may not always have hit its intended mark. While orthodoxy is the reason usually given for Aurangzeb's rejection of much of the pomp of Shah Jahan's courtly ritual, he may well have realized that the extreme formality, hierarchy, and ceremonial of the court was in fact backfiring.

Rajput courts

Rajput counterpoint: the court of Mewar

The significance of Akbar's 1568 conquest of Chittor, the seemingly impregnable fortress base of the Sisodiyas, was so great that it was illustrated in a double-page composition in the *Akbarnama*, today in the Victoria and Albert Museum. In spite of Akbar's victory, the Sisodiyas, the most important of the Rajput houses, refused to recognize Mughal sovereignty until Prince Khurram, the future Shah Jahan, was able to force Rana Amar Singh Sisodiya to submit to the Mughals in 1615. A treaty was drawn which stipulated that the Sisodiyas could not repair Chittor without Mughal permission; in return, the Sisodiya heir apparent was allowed to attend the Mughal court in his father's stead. Delighted by this turn of events, Jahangir gave a gold railing to the tomb of Muin al-Din Chishti and provided a hunting pavilion on the shores of the lake at Pushkar, one of western India's most sacred sites, presumably much to the horror of its largely vegetarian Hindu pilgrims. Shah Jahan later erected a mosque at the shrine of Muin al-Din Chishti in Ajmer in celebration of the Mughal victory over Mewar. In addition, several paintings intended for the official histories show Jahangir receiving Prince Khurram after this event, as well as Rana Amar Singh's literal submission before the prince. The most powerful gesture though was the installation of marble statues of the subjugated Rana and his son outside Jahangir's Agra palace, to serve as constant reminders of Mughal strength. In doing this, Jahangir was emulating Akbar, who also had images made of two leading Rajputs who died at the siege of Chittor.

Less than happy with his forced capitulation to Mughal authority, the next Mewar ruler, Rana Jagat Singh (r. 1628–52), commenced rebuilding Chittor's walls. His son and successor, Raj Singh, continued the project. Shah Jahan tore down the Chittor fortifications in 1654, and once again the Rana submitted to the Mughals, offering gifts. In general, the Sisodiyas acted in a predatory manner when the Mughals were distracted elsewhere and then placated them through subservient acts of gift-giving.

At the same time that he rebuilt Chittor's walls, Jagat Singh commissioned two notable works, each of which was intended as a counter to contemporary Mughal patronage. In 1652 he inaugurated his enormous Jagdish temple, located prominently and strategically near the palace in Udaipur (Figure 7.9), which had become the Sisodiya capital after Akbar's sack of Chittor, 110 kilometers to its northeast. As Jennifer Joffee has argued, the temple, built only two years after Shah Jahan's Jami mosque in Shahjahanabad was commenced, was clearly Jagat Singh's response to both Mughal authority and to Shah Jahan's World Showing mosque. Through this act, the Mewar house was suggesting, in spite of its subordinate status, that it was on a par with the Mughals. The large scale of both Jagat Singh's temple and Shah Jahan's Jami mosque, the fact that the names of these two kings are virtually identical in meaning King of the World, and the similarity of lengthy inscriptions that praised the prowess of each patron and his esteemed lineage, all point to a correspondence between the two dynasties. Beginning in the mid seventeenth century, the Sisodiyas began to show unprecedented interest in promoting their Rajput genealogical heritage, a response to long-standing Mughal interest in their Timurid heritage.

Figure 7.9 Rana Jagat Singh built the Jagdish temple (1652) in his capital Udaipur as a visual response to the Shahjahanabad Jami mosque of
his contemporary and rival, Shah Jahan.

Jagat Singh's massive seven-volume illustrated manuscript of the
Ramayana, an ancient Indian epic, was also commissioned with Mughal
cultural production in mind. The subject matter was not uncommon,
but J. Losty has argued that it may have had a special meaning for the
Sisodiyas, who claimed descent from the solar dynasty of ancient Indian
warriors which included Rama. In some folios the Sisodiya seal, a sun
with a face, is placed in the center top of the page, thereby reinforcing
the association with Rama's solar dynasty. This particular *Ramayana* is
the equivalent for the Sisodiya house of the *Akbarnama* and other official
chronicles for the Mughals (Figure 7.10).

The style of its illustrations, which consciously avoids the idiom of
Mughal painting, is a further sign that the work was intended as a foil
to Mughal production. The paintings, many of which were done by the
Muslim master artist Sahibdin, adhere to the style of earlier *Bhagavata
Purana* illustrations. Other features of the manuscript draw on Rajput
traditions, not Mughal ones, including the depiction of the same person in multiple scenes on a single page. For example, on one folio the

Figure 7.10 Rana Jagat Singh's *Ramayana* is the Sisodiya equivalent of Mughal illustrated histories such as the *Akbarnama* and *Padshahnama*.

antihero Ravana is depicted eleven times. This calls attention to the fact that style cannot be linked to the religion of any artist as is often thought, but is rather a matter of training and taste. Although the seven-volume *Ramayana* commissioned by Jagat Singh bears dates between 1649 and 1653, in fact, Losty has calculated that it must have taken about twelve years to complete, due to its massive number of folios. The quality and quantity of these illustrations is yet another indication of the personal interest the Sisodiyas took in this legitimizing project.

Rajput allies: the court of Amber

Although the Rajput Sisodiyas of Mewar and the Rajput Kachhwahas of Amber both owed allegiance to the Mughals, their relations with the Mughals were quite different. Mewar's relations with the Mughals, as we have discussed, were largely adversarial. By contrast, the Kachhwahas had close and amicable relations with the Mughals, marrying daughters to both Akbar and Jahangir. Through the reign of Shah Jahan and during the early years of Aurangzeb's reign, the Kachhwahas held very high positions in the Mughal administrative and military system. Mirza Raja Jai Singh (r. 1622–67), whose rule was roughly contemporary with that of Shah Jahan, was one of the two highest officers of the court excluding the imperial princes. He was succeeded by his son Ram Singh (r. 1667–89), who was considered less important in the Mughal pecking order under Aurangzeb, a general reflection on the lower status of Rajputs in the mansabdar system in this period. These Kachhwaha rajas spent little time in their capital of Amber (see Map 8.1), but were still able to make substantial additions to the city and ensure that culturally the Amber court mirrored the Mughal one.

An enormous map dated 1711 depicts Amber in elevation and labels all the important houses, streets, gardens, temples, and mosques, demonstrating that the city was substantial and diverse in population (Figure 7.11). Enough of the structures on the map still survive to indicate that it is accurate. Part of an addition that Mirza Raja Jai Singh made to Raja Man Singh's Amber palace is closely modeled on Shah Jahan's palace architecture. Known as the Jai Mandir, the top story of this quadrangular complex is made of white marble, like the public viewing window at Shah Jahan's Agra palace and Shah Jahan's jharoka in his Shahjahanabad palace (see Figure 7.7). The Amber pavilion has a curved bangla roof, a feature which during this time was reserved for the emperor alone. However, just as the Kachhwahas were allowed to have a public viewing window in their own palaces during Akbar's and Jahangir's reign, the use of the bangla roof was extended to Mirza Raja Jai Singh during Shah Jahan's reign, due to the Kachhwaha's favored status.

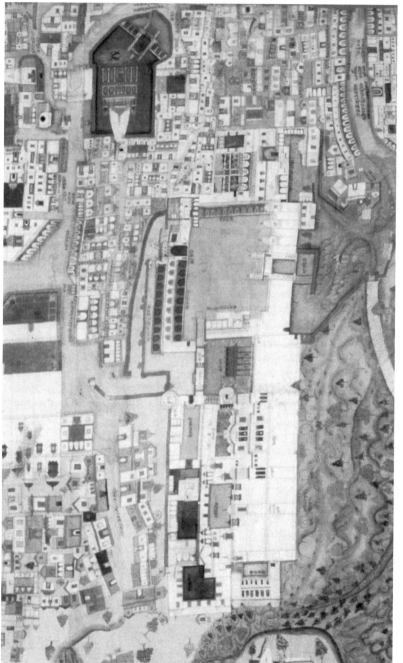

Figure 7.11 This detail of the 1711 map of Amber shows that Mirza Raja Jai Singh's palace is similar to palace architecture under Shah Jahan.

Other aspects of Jai Singh's architectural patronage were less slavish to Mughal tradition. His Amber palace's Public Audience Hall, modeled on the open porches of his ancestor Man Singh's temple architecture, is highly innovative. Pillars line the sides of the rectangular Audience Hall, leaving an open central space that is reminiscent of the mandapa of a temple. By contrast to the image of a righteous Kachhwaha ruler installed in an Audience Hall resembling part of a temple, Shah Jahan's pillared Public Audience Halls are meant to evoke the royal splendor of Persepolis.

Aside from texts that indicate the importance of the Kachhwaha kings to the Mughals, the inclusion of these rajas in attendance upon the emperor in paintings for imperial Mughal histories also visually underscores their significance. Portraiture under the Mughals had become so precise that it is possible to trace the changes in appearance of some courtiers and princes from youth to old age. It is not surprising, given their close Mughal affiliation, that the Amber court chose to establish their own workshop with painters clearly trained in the high Mughal style. Another rather different painting style was also found in Amber, one closer in idiom to the two-dimensional paintings of earlier *Bhagavata Puranas*. It was used largely to depict *ragamalas*, a series of paintings which depict moods (rasas) established by the playing of raga musical modes, or for other illustrations in the classic Hindu or Jain traditions. As we saw in chapter 5, Man Singh Kachhwaha was able concurrently to serve both Mughal and his own personal needs, a trend that continued into the seventeenth century as the Kachhwahas continued to effectively act simultaneously as rulers of their own ancestral land and as high-ranking nobles of the Mughal court.

Women in the Rajput courts

Like the Mughals, the Rajput courts practiced polygamy and sequestered their women. Polygamy may have been the result of a number of traditions, but certainly a major motive for it was the desire to gain political allies and to further territorial expansion. However, unlike the Mughals who had much freedom in marrying their sons, Rajput kinship rules limited eligibility. While each party had to belong to the same caste, the bride and groom had to come from different clans. Aristocratic women kept the name of their paternal clan after marriage, revealing its continuing importance in the alliance formed through marriage. Recently, Frances Taft has argued that the current belief among many Rajput houses that they never married their daughters to the Mughals is a nineteenth-century construction, and not a reflection of reality in the sixteenth and seventeenth centuries. The ruling houses of Rajasthan maintained detailed marriage records, in part to determine matters of succession and in part to adhere to the complex rules of matrimonial acceptability. In spite of the existence of these records and other sources, even less is known about individual women of the Rajput courts than about those of the Mughal courts.

What we do know, in general, is that Rajput queens and princesses held jagirs, provided religious structures, and had major roles in shaping court politics, just as in the case of Mughal women. Also like Mughal royalty, Rajput princesses lived in guarded harams. The women's quarters at the Udaipur palace of the Sisodiya dynasty provide an excellent example of the physical appearance of haram quarters. Essentially a replica of the men's quarters, the women's area is a multi-storied enclosure centered around an open courtyard. Each of the many queens and concubines had their own quarters and an array of attendants to go with them, not dissimilar from the Mughal system. In keeping with the principles of purdah or seclusion of women, neither the Mughal nor Rajput courts produced portraiture of women. Dancing girls, musicians, attendants, and generic princesses are shown, all sumptuously dressed, but not in the individualized manner that men are depicted in both Mughal and Rajput painting. Paintings of men indicate that styles of clothing, especially turbans, differed slightly from one Rajput court to another.

In some respects Rajput and Mughal culture remained separate. One of these was in the matter of education in the Rajput courts, which remained relatively unimportant for most males and was considered a detriment for women. Attitudes toward widowhood are another case in point. Islam allows for the remarriage of widows; in fact, Nur Jahan herself was a widow before her marriage to Jahangir. High-caste Hindus, on the other hand, opposed widow remarriage, with some believing that the wife should immolate herself on her husband's funeral pyre, a practice known as *sati*. Although it has been illegal since 1829, an instance of sati occurred as recently as 1999, and the issue is still an emotional one. The extent to which sati was practiced in the past is unclear, but it was particularly associated with aristocratic Rajput families. Wives or concubines who had no living sons would at times become satis, in part to demonstrate that to a good Hindu wife a husband is like a god without whom there is no life. Memorials might be erected for the deceased satis, sometimes in a royal enclosure. At Ahar, just outside of Udaipur, are the royal commemorative grounds for the Sisodiyas. The pavilion commemorating Rana Amar Singh (d. 1620) bears carved panels that show the ruler and his six queens, who are depicted showing their hands in gestures that express devotion to their husband (Figure 7.12). Commemorative architecture, not usually part of Hinduism, in western India adopts forms formally

Figure 7.12 This detail from the sati memorial of the Sisodiya king
Amar Singh (d. 1620) shows carvings of the wives who were immolated
in his funeral pyre.

associated with the Muslim tomb, giving it a unique meaning for the Hindu sati.

Pious constructions

While we have mentioned temples, mosques, and saints' tombs in our treatment of seventeenth-century elites, it has been usually in a political context and not as part of a discussion of religious beliefs. We are not, however, suggesting that the construction of the Jagdish temple in Udaipur and the Jami mosque in Shahjahanabad were simply political statements rather than acts of genuine piety. However, our focus thus far has been on the reasons for patronage in the political culture of the era. While political goals might not have been far from the minds of the patrons, it is equally important to realize that religious devotion is much more significant than any political message for the majority of people worshipping in these structures. In this section we will examine temples and mosques from different geographical areas: east, south, and north India.

Terracotta temples of seventeenth-century Bengal

Earlier in this book we discussed the origins of bhakti, an intensely personal devotion to a deity. Bhakti first originated in south India and played a large role in the religious life there. Nowadays, thousands of devotees may come on a daily basis to have darshan (auspicious sighting) of the deity at a site like the Madurai Minakshi temple, to be discussed below, but even if these pilgrims arrive at the temple with a large group of people, they still perform worship as individuals and not as a congregation. In sixteenth-century north India, various sects began to promote group singing and dancing before a deity's image as a way of finding union with god. Most notable is the Gaudiya Vaishnava sect founded by Chaitanya, which advocated a deeply intense personal relationship with the god Krishna, based on the complete devotion that his lover, Radha, had for him. Vrindavan, a site near Mathura associated with Krishna's youth, was the headquarters of this movement, and the temple Raja Man Singh built there was provided expressly for this type of devotion to Krishna. The temple's large porch, an innovation in sixteenth-century north Indian architecture, was for singing and dancing before the image and for devotees to have his darshan. Devotees could behold their deity seven times a day, each timing associated with a different ritual service such as the waking of the god, the offering of food, and the preparations for the deity's sleeping. The activities and the accompanying music would vary slightly for each ritual service. The worship here is congregational, for crowds sing and chant in unison.

Even though Chaitanya was from Bengal, by the seventeenth century many of his teachings were beginning to be forgotten there. Advocates were sent from Vrindavan to convert the Malla ruler of the western portion of modern West Bengal state to Gaudiya Vaishnavism. The Mallas, while theoretically tributaries of the Mughals, appear, very much like the Sisodiyas, to have vacillated between periods of aggression and submission; however, because the Mughal hold on seventeenth-century Bengal was somewhat tenuous, less is written about them in contemporary histories.

The Malla rulers created a second Vrindavan in Bengal during the seventeenth and eighteenth centuries. This was done by the development of landscape, poetry, texts and especially through the construction of a new temple type, called *ratna*, meaning a bejeweled temple. More than 400 of these brick-constructed temples are found in West Bengal and Bangladesh, most dedicated to Krishna (Figure 7.13). Pika Ghosh's recent work shows that they consist of a ground floor where the devotees together celebrate, in song and dance, the love Radha and Krishna had for one another. To accommodate the traditional role of Hindu priests and the new role of the congregation in Bengal, the ground floor of the inner sanctums of these temples had a double axis. The normative east–west axis was for the priests and their ritual activities. The second, north–south, axis was for the devotees who needed considerable space to gather *en masse* to perform their devotions. On the temple's exterior on this level are images of Krishna's life and emblems of the dance which Krishna performed as a sign of his divine love. Atop the ground floor is another story where the two deities, Radha and Krishna, are taken during festivals to preside over the community; ritually these gods are reenacting their passion for one another, as is made clear by the images of sexual intercourse on the exterior of this upper story. The devotees below could see the priests worshiping the gods through an open window, and the initiated understood the spiritual significance of the upper level.

The ground floor of these temples derives from the brick-constructed, sultanate period mosques of Bengal, discussed in chapter 4, which were congregational spaces. By echoing these plans, the Malla royal patrons suggested that they were the heirs to the Bengal Sultanate. Many of the Bengal sultans had been supportive of Hindu poets and culture, and were viewed as considerably more approachable than the current Mughal overlords. By supporting community temples and providing free daily food in them, the Malla kings were drawing support for themselves. Like

Figure 7.13 The double story Shyam Ray temple, dated 1643, is especially designed to facilitate a new form of devotion in Bengal for the
deity Krishna and his consort Radha.

the nobles and rulers of Vijayanagara, the dress mortal men wear in the terracotta panels decorating these temples is the Islamicate tunic, showing that the Malla kings wished to show they were part of that sophisticated, cosmopolitan world. By contrast, the gods are lightly clad as usual in traditional Indic clothing. Serious tensions existed between the Mughals and the Mallas, but the Malla desire to be seen as the rightful successors of the Bengal sultans illustrates that the tensions were mainly political in origin and not religious.

The Ajmer shrine

Mughal ties with the Chishti saints, maintained by Akbar until 1579, were revived by Jahangir and sustained by Shah Jahan. Jahangir, we noted earlier, showed his allegiance to Muin al-Din Chishti by wearing pearl earrings in a double-page composition showing this saint handing emblems of legitimacy to Jahangir (see Figure 7.1). There are at least four paintings that depict Jahangir visiting the Ajmer shrine. When Jahangir chose Ajmer as the headquarters for his campaign against the Sisodiya king Rana Amar Singh in 1613, he proceeded to the Chishti dargah on foot, as his father had done earlier. Jahangir's interest in the Chishti shrine of Ajmer stimulated nobles to patronize it as well, not surprisingly, considering that one of the emperor's orders upon taking the throne had been to build throughout the empire. Shah Jahan visited Ajmer throughout his life, for the city and its most important shrine had special significance for him. It was here that his victory over Rana Amar Singh of Mewar while still a prince had been celebrated. The victory inspired his construction of an imperial white marble residence on Ajmer's lovely Ana Sagar lake and of buildings at the shrine of Muin al-Din Chishti.

The dargah of Muin al-Din Chishti is a large complex with multiple structures built over time. In the seventeenth century, the dargah had two large entrance gates. The earlier one, dating to the fifteenth century, was behind a second one provided by Shah Jahan in 1654 to celebrate his success in tearing down Chittor's walls. Once inside, a number of structures and institutions are passed including the huge cauldrons for cooking vast quantities of food on a daily basis. The current cauldrons are replacements for ones donated in the sixteenth and seventeenth centuries by Akbar and Jahangir. The focal point of the shrine is the tomb of Muin al-Din which was clad in white marble probably during Akbar's reign, with an area for women donated by Jahanara, Shah Jahan's daughter (Figure 7.14). A second key area in the shrine is Shah Jahan's large white marble mosque, aligned with the tomb's qibla. A lengthy inscription on the mosque specifies that it was built in celebration of Shah Jahan's

Figure 7.14 The white marble tomb of Muin al-Din Chishti in Ajmer, dating to the Mughal period, is the most visited Sufi shrine in all India.

initial victory over the Sisodiyas. With so much Mughal artistic patronage since the time of Akbar intended to denigrate the Sisodiyas, it is easy to understand why the Mewar house would counter with its own patronage and propaganda. Whatever the intention of the initial patronage, however, any political message is far from the minds of the shrine's devotees.

What, then, would a devotee have experienced on a pilgrimage to the shrine? The current rituals at the shrine must be somewhat different than in the seventeenth century, yet they are apparently rooted in earlier Mughal practice and may provide some guidance as to what happened in the past. Today, the Ajmer dargah is a site of constant activity year round, as pilgrims come to pay homage to the saint and even stay inside the complex for as long as a week. For those who wish to ask the saint to act as an intercessor to god on their behalf, an elaborately embroidered cloth to cover the tomb known as a *chadar* is presented to the shrine. The chadar is carried in procession, led by musicians much like those depicted in paintings of Mughal processions, while devout pilgrims reach out in a frenzy to clasp the cloth that will touch the holy shrine. Seated near the tomb are qawwals, singers of ecstatic music, possibly descended from the same families that Akbar heard singing in praise of Muin al-Din. The air is perfumed by the heaping baskets of pink rose petals showered upon the saint's tomb.

There are daily ceremonies such as the cleaning of the tomb, weekly ones such as the performance of qawwali and sama (ecstatic songs in honor of Muhammad and Sufi saints), and monthly ones where the entire Quran is recited, but the most important is the annual urs, celebrating the saint's marriage or union with god upon his death. The crowds that gather over about a six-day period are enormous. Many of the ceremonies done on a daily, weekly, or monthly basis are performed during the urs but on a much more intense level. While the majority of pilgrims who pay homage at the Ajmer shrine are Muslims, Hindus and people of other faiths come on a regular basis as well.

Madurai's Minakshi temple

After the fall of the Vijayanagara capital in 1565, warrior nobles of the former empire assumed the role of kings in the far south. The most powerful of these Nayaka kings were the rulers of Madurai, in the southernmost area of the Tamil-speaking zone (see Map 8.1). The Nayaka rulers utilized different styles in their palace and temple architecture, just as had been done at the Vijayanagara imperial capital. An Islamicate style was used for palaces, as can be seen in the cusped, arched and lobed dome of the Nayaka palace in Madurai, and the traditional trabeated one for temples. The greatest of their temple complexes is the Minakshi temple in Madurai, which attracts over 20,000 devotees daily. This complex, measuring 254 by 238 meters, is located in the center of the city (Figure 7.15). It has been built over many centuries, but much of its current appearance and size dates to the seventeenth century. We noted that the custom of building large temples with enormous gopuras (gateways) commenced under the Vijayanagara kings, and this trend escalated under the Nayakas. The Jagdish temple in Udaipur is large in contrast to most other north Indian temples, but compared to a south Indian temple of the Nayaka period, especially the Minakshi temple, the Udaipur temple is dwarfed. The Minakshi temple is really two separate temples enclosed by rectangular walls, with an enormous gopura on each side, one of which is nearly 50 meters high. In addition to the two temples are a number of pillared halls and a large stepped tank used for ceremonial purposes. Virtually every exterior surface of the temples, gopuras, and halls is covered with carved and painted images of gods, goddesses, animals, mythic creatures, and even portraits of one of the major patrons, Tirumala Nayaka (r. 1623–59), and his wives. The devotee proceeds from a brilliantly bright exterior space into an increasingly darkened interior; that is, the devotees' journey for darshan of the deity is played out architecturally in terms of light and dark. Before visiting the temple in the morning and evening, the devotee bathes and dresses in appropriate garb. Women wear bright silk saris and flowers in their hair, while men wear *dhotis*, an unsewn wrapped garment, without a shirt or tunic, just as in the portrait images of Krishnadeva Raya, the great Vijayanagara king, discussed in chapter 3. Worship at the Minakshi temple is not a passive experience, rather it is one where the devotee is constantly moving amid a high level of noise from ringing bells. Color abounds on the painted pillars, on the clothes of women, and on the flowers offered to the gods. The taste of the prasada, food first offered to goddess and then returned to the devotee as a blessed substance, sweetens the mouth. Smoke from incense and from the camphor lamps waved before the deities add to the mystery and excitement. Opening the senses is a way of opening oneself to god.

The principal deity of the temple is Minakshi, a local goddess who was transformed into a consort of Shiva; according to tradition, she defeated Shiva in battle and he then married her. Shiva is the secondary deity at this temple, unusually, and a sign of his lesser status is the fact that he is worshipped after the goddess. As at all large south Indian temples, the deities are represented by more than a single image. There is the large permanent one made of stone, a four-foot green image in the case of Minakshi, and smaller bronze ones that are used for processions when

Figure 7.15 This aerial view of the massive Minakshi temple complex shows its multiple *gopuras* dominating the city of Madurai, once the capital of a Nayaka kingdom.
Photo Courtesy of French Institute of Pondicherry / Ecole Française d'Extrême-Orient

the images are paraded around the city during multi-day festivals, both symbolizing the role of the gods in ordering the universe.

Traditional Indian views on kingship state that it is the ruler's duty to protect his subjects and uphold the realm's religious institutions, a goal which is achieved by insuring that temple rituals are properly maintained. Tirumala Nayaka accomplished this by generously supporting temples and their priests with various gifts including feasts (see chapter 6). He is also credited with merging two separate festivals, the all important celebration of the marriage of Shiva and Minakshi at the Minakshi temple with another festival at Madurai's major Vishnu temple. By fusing the two festivals together into a single one, Tirumala Nayaka successfully integrated the various high-caste traditions of worship in the Tamil south. Tirumala Nayaka, like many other Telugu-speaking warriors who came to power in the Tamil land, may have been perceived as an outsider by the local population and thus have needed to validate his role as king even more than usual.

In summary, we see that in seventeenth-century South Asia, a number of religious traditions were practiced by people from all walks of life, but funded by the elite. These traditions, whether Hindu or Muslim, were sensory experiences involving the smelling of flowers, the tasting of food offerings or holy water, the hearing of music or bells, and the seeing of bright colors, while having darshan of the gods or a sight of the beloved saint's tomb.

Elaborate courtly culture touched many aspects of elite and religious life in seventeenth-century South Asia. Throughout the Indian subcontinent, as courts became increasingly aware of each other's activities, the desire to possess manuscripts, produce architecture and luxury arts, and refine ceremonies that would show one ruler as either equal or superior to another accelerated the production of visual and performative culture. The money spent on their creation is truly a testimony to India's extraordinary resources. While only the wealthy could consume the subcontinent's fine textiles and accessories, reside in its splendid buildings and gardens, listen to court music, and view exquisitely executed manuscripts, people from all walks of life could and did enjoy religious ceremonial, which became increasingly important for the elite and common people alike. All the senses – sight, smell, touch, taste, and sound – were activated as much of what transpired in court was replicated in various religious contexts.

The roughly hundred years from 1650 to 1750 were marked by a series of radical political and social changes in South Asia. Many of these changes were triggered by developments that transpired during the nearly fifty-year reign of the sixth Mughal emperor, Aurangzeb (r. 1658–1707). This Mughal emperor remains the most controversial in the popular mind and even, to some extent, in scholarly literature. Aurangzeb is often compared unfavorably with Akbar, whose reign also spanned close to half a century. In part, this is due to the work of J. N. Sarkar, the first modern historian to write extensively on Aurangzeb. Sarkar held Aurangzeb personally responsible for the reversal of the tolerant policies first fostered by Akbar, which were instrumental in unifying the vast territories of the Mughal empire in the minds of many scholars. Instead, in Sarkar's view, Aurangzeb promoted an aggressively Islamic state that discriminated against Hindus and other non-Muslims, leading to a loss of unity and the decline of empire. Other scholars have accused Aurangzeb of weakening the empire not so much by his orthodox religious stance as by his prolonged campaign to pacify and annex the Deccan.

In this chapter, we look at both these charges against Aurangzeb, as well as at the Maratha community which opposed Mughal expansion fiercely, and at political developments after Aurangzeb's death. The more pronounced Islamic cast of Aurangzeb's reign is often portrayed as a sudden and dramatic break with the past, but in fact a gradual trend in that direction had been building since the death of Akbar. And so it is with the religious policies of Aurangzeb's two immediate predecessors that we begin our discussion.

Religious and cultural trends

Religious policies of Jahangir and Shah Jahan

In both his own attitudes and in the state's practices, Jahangir for the most part continued along the lines set by Akbar. Jahangir not only maintained earlier grants given to temples, mosques, and religious leaders of all kinds, but he even increased their number considerably. Like his father, Jahangir had an eclectic interest in religion on a personal level. Jahangir also reverted to Akbar's earlier practice of revering Sufi saints of the Chishti order, partly out of political expediency and partly because he felt a genuine tie between himself and the memory of Shaikh Salim Chishti, who had predicted his birth and for whom he had been named. Akbar had turned away from his public allegiance to the Chishtis in the early 1580s, in pursuit of the more ecumenical concept of sulh-i kul or tolerance for all religions. Jahangir's devotion to the Chishti Sufis was one step in the greater Islamic orientation of the Mughal state that developed slowly over the seventeenth century.

Another group with whom Jahangir had warm relations initially was the Naqshbandis, a Sufi order that was both more politically engaged and more conservative than the Chishtis. The Naqshbandis had been befriended by Jahangir when he was still a prince hoping to become the next emperor. But Jahangir could not tolerate the criticism of Shaikh Ahmad Sirhindi, a Naqshbandi Sufi leader who was highly popular among Indo-Muslim conservatives. Sirhindi was outspoken about the government's failure to follow strict Islamic sharia law and his bluntness so offended the emperor that Sirhindi was imprisoned for about a year. Sirhindi's impact is not to be underestimated, for he wrote hundreds of letters expressing his views on how Islam was being corrupted in contemporary South Asia. He blamed Akbar's religious policies, the evils of the widespread Chishti practice of sama which incorporated music into worship, and the insidious infiltration of the Shia faith espoused by leading Iranian immigrants. His letters were widely distributed, and so Sirhindi's influence increased rather than diminished after his death.

As a means of distancing himself from his father, Shah Jahan assumed a much more traditional attitude toward Islam, even while still a prince. Prince Khurram, the future Shah Jahan, paid homage to the shrines of important saints in Bengal and Bihar while posted there, and also vowed to abstain from drinking alcohol as stipulated by the sharia. His strict adherence to fasting during the Muslim holy month of Ramadan amazed his followers; one of them declared that it was only because of his immense love of god that the prince could manage to consume no food or drink from sunrise to sunset in the extraordinary heat of Bengal. Once he assumed the throne, Shah Jahan continued his attempts to appear as a devout Muslim in his public behavior and to enact the role of a good Islamic ruler. Among his official acts was the substitution of the full prostration before the emperor, introduced by Akbar, with a lesser bow that was more acceptable to the Muslim faithful, who believed only god deserved their total submission. It is likely that such moves were nods to Sirhindi's conservative supporters.

Shah Jahan also somewhat curtailed the construction of new Hindu and Jain temples, in accordance with a strict interpretation of sharia, which limits the privileges of non-Muslims. But he maintained the sponsorship of religious institutions and people that his father and grandfather instituted; here, there was no change in policy. And the two most famous instances of temple destruction ordered by Shah Jahan were both in response to political opposition. Bir Singh Deo's Chaturburj temple at Orchha, in central India, was partially destroyed in response to difficulties that Shah Jahan was having in quelling Bir Singh's rebellious successor. Likewise, Shah Jahan's destruction of temples in Mewar in 1654 resulted from the Mewar ruler's rebuilding of the Chittor fortification without Mughal permission. All the same, Shah Jahan's progressively more conservative religious policies would be amplified by his son, Aurangzeb, in part out of genuine piety but in part to show that he was better fit for kingship than his near-apostate brother, Dara Shikoh, and his father, whose lifestyle was outwardly pious, but whose private life style was rumored to be anything but.

Aurangzeb's rule: a cultural assessment

In 1657 Shah Jahan became very ill, sparking a war of succession among the imperial princes, who believed the emperor was dying. Aurangzeb, a brilliant military tactician, emerged as victor in the armed struggle for the throne and imprisoned the now recovered Shah Jahan inside the Agra fort until his death in 1666. One reason that Aurangzeb consciously built his own public image as a devout Muslim was to whitewash the fact that imprisoning his father was against the sharia. Aurangzeb crowned himself twice, the second time in the palace of Shahjahanabad in an elaborate ceremony befitting a Mughal emperor. Before and immediately after his coronations, he dispatched his brothers and other relatives also vying for the throne, thus eliminating most familial opposition.

Aurangzeb's allegiance to orthodox Islam and his personal piety are indisputable and led to some change in court ceremony. In the late 1660s and the 1670s, Aurangzeb's court became more austere as he prohibited the use of gold in men's garments, stopped being weighed against gold on his birthdays, and ceased the practice of presenting himself to the public in his jharoka-i darshan (public viewing window) because it was not in accordance with the sharia. He also banned music at court and dismissed the literary men who compiled the official histories of the dynasty. Painting was an art whose patronage declined in the Mughal court, but because painters left that court for others, it continued to flourish in the Deccan and at Rajput courts.

While such orders reflect the orthodoxy of Aurangzeb's own religious beliefs, this emperor was not entirely consistent in his actions. Despite his prohibition against ostentatious clothing for court nobles, the emperor continued to display himself to them on Shah Jahan's gold bejeweled Peacock Throne. And while the use of luxury goods at court was ostensibly discouraged, Aurangzeb still made ceremonial gifts to worthy nobles as valued marks of honor: jeweled swords and elaborate robes often woven with gold threads and embroidered with pearls, of the sort discussed in chapter 7. Even though Aurangzeb may have desired an austere court, he knew in reality that, if he failed to present himself as an all-powerful king of kings and favor his grandees in the well-established Mughal manner, many would exchange their loyalty for that of another competing court.

Shah Jahan's prolific patronage of architecture would remain unmatched by any Indian monarch, but Aurangzeb, in keeping with his personal interests, built several mosques. Among them are the Badshahi mosque in Lahore, which remains the largest in the subcontinent, and the elegant private marble mosque inside Shah Jahan's fort in Delhi. On both these structures we see ornate decor of the sort that in earlier periods was reserved for palace architecture, now transferred to the building type Aurangzeb considered the most important. He also ordered a tomb for a deceased wife, modeled on that of the Taj Mahal. This tomb, however, marks an end to the tradition of large structural tombs. Both Aurangzeb and his sister, Jahanara, commenced a new trend in tomb construction, that is, burial in simple open-air graves at the shrines of major Sufi saints, in an expression of their piety (Figure 8.1).

Most imperial architectural and engineering activity during Aurangzeb's reign focused on enhancing fortifications, a reflection of the emperor's belief that expansion of territory was the obligation of a good ruler and the reality of his frequent military campaigning. As in earlier periods, the nobility were responsible for building in both Delhi and the provinces. However, unlike in earlier periods, the ruler no longer set the model for an ideal architectural aesthetic. Under Shah Jahan, certain architectural forms including a curved roof known as bangla (see Figure 7.7) were reserved for imperial use only and symbolized Shah Jahan's semi-divine status. Interestingly, mosques built by various nobles, constructed almost immediately after Aurangzeb's succession, began to use these features, suggesting the devaluation of this visual form even before Shah Jahan's fall from power. Aurangzeb was disinclined to commission new secular structures embellished with forms he considered unIslamic, in keeping with his personal ideology, but was willing to sit

Figure 8.1 The simple open-air grave of Princess Jahanara (d. 1681) at the Sufi shrine of Nizam al-Din Auliya in Delhi marks a new trend in tomb construction for the elite.

on his father's elaborate throne since that reinforced his image as an absolute ruler. Similarly, portraiture of this ruler throughout his entire reign continued to depict him with his head surrounded by a halo even when he was humbly positioned in prayer, suggesting a need to present himself as both regal and pious.

Aurangzeb's increased religious orthodoxy has been considered a death knell to the arts under the Mughals, but this too is an exaggeration. It is true that, due to financial constraints and his desire to appear as a ruler guided by Islamic religious law, musicians and men of literary talent were released from service to the emperor, thus ultimately encouraging the patronage of arts by Mughal nobility and in courts elsewhere in the Indian subcontinent. Ethnomusicologist Bonnie Wade has suggested that rather than condemning Aurangzeb for his marginalization of the arts, he should be credited for causing a dispersal of patronage from the imperial center to many regional centers, which in the end encouraged new musical forms – to this we might add new literary and visual ones as well. Outside his own court, Aurangzeb put no strictures on those who practiced these arts nor on the content produced. Literature thrived in the Delhi region, especially under the sponsorship of Aurangzeb's daughter, Zeb al-Nisa, who was an accomplished poet in her own right. A number of poets still revered today worked in the atmosphere of late seventeenth- and early eighteenth-century India, some of whom produced satire outwardly critical of Aurangzeb.

Perhaps the best reflection of Aurangzeb's personal beliefs is the *Fatawa-i Alamgiri,* which he commissioned between about 1667 and 1675. This multi-volume text, originally written in Arabic and then translated into Persian, is a compilation of legal decisions consistent with the Sunni Hanafi school of law, the most commonly followed one in South Asia. The legal decisions relate to matters of personal practice such as marriage, divorce, and prayer, regarding which Islamic judges in India tended to follow local custom rather than necessarily following the sharia. By providing various interpretations of law in a single text, the *Fatawa-i Alamgiri* allowed judges to see a range of ways in which the sharia could be applied, and thus encouraged greater adherence to it. Much of *Fatawa-i Alamgiri*'s text has no bearing on the majority non-Muslim population; however, sections which deal with taxes, especially those concerning agrarian taxation, were probably an attempt to reconcile Mughal land use practices with Islamic law, according to S. M. Azizuddin Husain. Under the earlier Mughals there was a uniform land tax, but this is not in conformity with the sharia. Aurangzeb reintroduced separate taxes for Muslims and Hindus; the jizya tax on non-Muslims, levied from 1679 onward, is mandated by the sharia but led to a higher tax burden on non-Muslims and thus created considerable dislike of Aurangzeb's economic policy. The complexity of the rules and the number of exceptions must have created considerable confusion, especially compared to the uniform tax code established since the time of Akbar.

Other grounds are also given by those who charge Aurangzeb with a bias against non-Muslims. The fact that he reduced the number of Hindu officers holding high rank at the beginning of his reign, for instance, is often cited as proof of Aurangzeb's disdain for non-Muslims. What is overlooked is the reality that the percentage of Hindus in his service soared in the last decades of Aurangzeb's rule, a development that we will discuss further in a few pages. Perhaps most detrimental to the popular Indian memory of Aurangzeb is the accusation of temple destruction. Although he issued orders to destroy temples throughout the realm in 1669, in fact only some were damaged. In general, these were recent temples built by Hindu mansabdars that were destroyed in retaliation for serious discord caused in Aurangzeb's administration. For example, the Kesava Deva temple in Mathura, built about fifty years earlier by the noble who had assassinated Abu al-Fazl, was destroyed in reaction to serious riots at Mathura in which the chief Mughal officer of the city was killed. In the same manner, the famous Vishvanatha temple in Benares (Varanasi) built by Todar Mal, Akbar's finance minister, was torn down to punish Hindus who were supporting Aurangzeb's arch enemy, the Maratha Shivaji.

While Jahangir basically maintained the religious policies established under Akbar, Shah Jahan began to reverse these earlier liberal ones. Aurangzeb capitalized on Shah Jahan's nascent reversal of liberal religious policies, probably in part responding to a general conservative tenor established earlier in the century by activists such as Shaikh Ahmad Sirhindi and in part out of a personal conviction. Under this emperor, temple destruction was used at times as an official weapon, the jizya was reimposed, and a genuine attempt was made to introduce sharia law. Aurangzeb was undoubtedly ruthless in pursuit of his goals, including foremost that of territorial expansion. Anyone who impeded his ambitions or showed any signs of disloyalty was punished harshly. This desire for retribution transcended religious affiliation, for Aurangzeb was equally willing to subdue and conquer Muslim sultanates as he was any non-Muslim powers.

Shivaji and the Deccan wars

The second broad line of argument that blames Aurangzeb for the decline of the Mughal empire identifies the main problem as his preoccupation with conquering the Deccan. Conflict in the Deccan persisted throughout Aurangzeb's entire reign (r. 1658–1707), entailing enormous expenditure and commitment of human resources on the part of the Mughal empire. The territories that were finally annexed at such great cost slipped out of the empire's hands within decades and could never have yielded enough in revenues to make the conquest worthwhile. In pursuing the Deccan wars, Aurangzeb alienated much of the Mughal nobility, whose sacrifices on behalf of the empire were no longer being sufficiently rewarded in their eyes. Furthermore, the many years Aurangzeb spent in the Deccan directing the military effort meant that he neglected the affairs of the north, allowing agrarian unrest to foment and state authority to diminish there. In the privileged perspective of hindsight, many historians have seen the beginning of the empire's collapse in its extended campaigns in the Deccan.

Although the Mughal empire had absorbed the Ahmadnagar Sultanate and signed a treaty with the Adil Shahs of Bijapur and Qutb Shahs of Golkonda in 1636, the Deccan was by no means pacified at the outset of Aurangzeb's reign. The Bijapur and Golkonda sultans acknowledged Mughal sovereignty by striking coins with Mughal titles, reading the emperor's name in the Friday prayers, and even remitting an annual tribute, while continuing to act as independent kings within their own territories. And neither they nor the Mughal officers in the former Ahmadnagar kingdom had firm control over the countryside and its local warrior leaders. It was this indigenous warrior community, the Marathas, who were to prove the greatest threat to the established states of the Deccan in the second half of the seventeenth century.

Maratha identity today is inextricably linked to the memory of the great Shivaji Bhonsle (1630–80). Shivaji's father had acquired rights to land in the area near modern Pune, during the course of an ambitious but checkered career that included military service for the Ahmadnagar and Bijapur Sultanates, a brief spell as a Mughal officer, and even an unsuccessful bid for autonomy. From his home base in Pune, the charismatic Shivaji was able to carve out a small realm in the frontier regions of Bijapur and Ahmadnagar. One of Shivaji's renowned exploits occurred in 1659, after the Adil Shahs dispatched the general Afzal Khan to subdue him. The predator became the prey at a meeting near Pratapgad, one of Shivaji's fortified strongholds in the hilly terrain of the Western Ghats, where Shivaji killed Afzal Khan using a pair of iron claws. By the following year, Shivaji occupied forty forts and controlled eight passes through the Western Ghats.

Having successfully eluded the armies of the Adil Shah, Shivaji next had to contend with the Mughals. At first Shivaji maintained the upper hand with acts like his daring night raid against the encampment of the Mughal commander Shaista Khan in 1663. A few months later Shivaji led a profitable attack on Surat, the main Mughal port, which garnered over 10 million rupees worth of valuables. The growing threat Shivaji posed to the empire's interests provoked Aurangzeb into dispatching a large army to the Deccan in 1665, expressly to overpower Shivaji. It was led by Mirza Raja Jai Singh Kachhwaha, a descendant of the great general Raja Man Singh of Akbar's reign, and one of Aurangzeb's most capable commanders. Jai Singh succeeded in compelling Shivaji to surrender and agree to attend the Mughal emperor in person. Things could not have gone worse when Shivaji appeared at Aurangzeb's court in Agra, however. He had clearly expected to be treated with great honor but was placed among the lower-ranking nobles instead, leading him to protest and be put under house arrest.

Historians often lament the opportunity Aurangzeb missed at this juncture, of enrolling Shivaji into Mughal service, which might have averted years of conflict ahead. Instead, Shivaji managed to escape from Agra and return to his hill fortresses. After a several year truce he was once again able to seriously harass the Mughal and Adil Shah forces, engaging in exploits like the celebrated retaking of Simhagad, whose fortified walls his troops scaled at night and secured through hand-to-hand combat in 1670. Shivaji's territory grew to encompass much of the Western Ghats southward almost to Goa, but he could also launch forays well into Mughal lands to the north. In 1674 Shivaji proclaimed himself an independent ruler, aligning his state with the Qutb Shahs of Golkonda, at that time the most stable and wealthy of the Deccan Sultanates. By Shivaji's death in 1680, Mughal administrators in the Deccan found themselves constant victims of Maratha raids.

In 1681 Aurangzeb shifted his court from Delhi to the Deccan, with Aurangabad serving as his headquarters; he remained there until his death in 1707. His goals were to incorporate into the Mughal empire the semi-independent sultanates of the Deccan, which were accused of aiding Shambuji, Shivaji's son and successor, as well as to put an end to Maratha power. By 1686 the Mughals were able to defeat the Adil Shahs of Bijapur, the following year the Qutb Shahs fell, and Shambuji was captured and executed early in 1689. This should have been a moment of great glory for the Mughals, who had finally seemingly removed all obstacles to their full assertion of authority in the Deccan. But, in fact, 1689 was to prove a high tide mark from which the fortunes of the Mughal empire quickly receded. The empire had reached the limits of its expansion (see Map 5.1), for it was never able to digest the new territories successfully into the body politic. Nor was Maratha resistance quelled by the killing

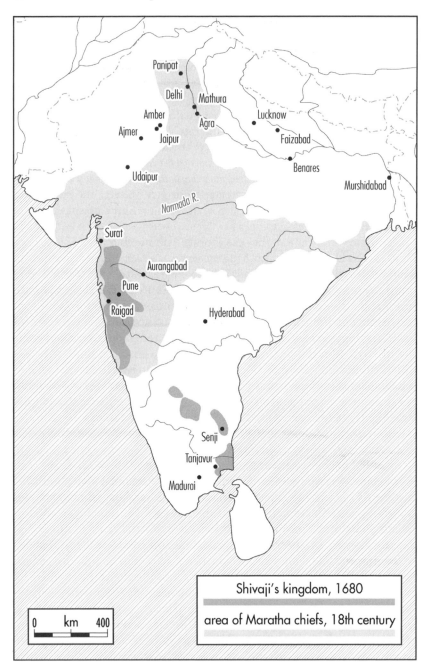

Map 8.1 Maratha expansion through the eighteenth century

of Shambuji, for the mantle of Maratha leadership was assumed next by his brother.

Aurangzeb spent the last years of his life determined to rout the Marathas, an objective that proved impossible to attain. Maratha forces working out of an extensive series of forts that dotted the hills of the Deccan harassed Mughal troops, administrators, and landholders, thus creating a sense of despair within the Mughal army about Aurangzeb's Deccan campaign. The situation was always volatile, with important Maratha families frequently switching sides, at times favoring the Mughals and at other times allying with one of the contenders to the Maratha throne. By the time Aurangzeb died in 1707, many forts had been captured, but the Marathas had already fled them, taking as much treasure as possible. They formed roving bands, often acting independently, and raided Mughal territory even across the Narmada river, the traditional boundary between the Deccan and north India.

While Aurangzeb's personal attentions were focused on the Deccan and south India, he had left his sons and grandsons to deal with the territories to the north. Problems with Jats, a peasant group involved in agricultural cultivation, arose in the area around Agra, as they engaged in wide-scale marauding and plundering, including the murder of important Mughal nobles. In eastern India problems again surfaced when irregularities in the revenue system were spotted by a young upstart, Kartalab Khan. He determined that imperial officers were keeping funds intended for the royal coffers. Upon rectifying the situation, Aurangzeb awarded him with the title Murshid Quli Khan, in reference to a noble of the same title earlier in his reign who had resolved a crisis in the revenues of the Deccan. Murshid Quli Khan in Bengal, as we shall see, became the first of the regional Mughal officers to assert his independence from the center. At the end of the seventeenth century, the Mughal hold on north India was still firm, despite the emperor's absence, but unrest was growing.

One of the most serious consequences of the prolonged military campaigning in the Deccan was its adverse effect on the empire's core element, the mansabdar nobility who constituted the principal coercive force. Even earlier, the empire had been plagued by the rising number of mansabdars, for it was natural that the sons and relatives of nobles would expect to receive official appointments themselves, and, as the empire grew, there were always talented individuals from new communities who had also to be incorporated into the ruling class. The amount of productive land was finite, however, and the mansabdars found that their jagirs – the taxes from specific tracts of land that were assigned to them instead of a salary – were less and less able to sustain an adequate standard of living and the required troop contingents.

Until the second half of Aurangzeb's reign, the situation was not yet critical. Two new developments severely impacted the workings of the system, according to many scholars: an influx of new mansabdars from the Deccan and the decision to keep much of the newly conquered Deccan territory as crown land. The Mughals tried to entice Maratha leaders to their side by offering them entry into noble circles, while high-ranking officers from Bijapur and Golkonda had to be incorporated into the empire upon the annexation of those states. The ninety-six new Maratha mansabdars and sixty-four from Bijapur and Golkonda represented over a quarter of the court nobility in the second half of Aurangzeb's reign. Their sudden ascendance was greatly resented by members of the older Mughal nobility, some of whom were facing real economic hardship in this period. Had all the conquered territory of the Deccan been available to share among the growing ranks of mansabdars, the problem of insufficient jagirs might have been alleviated, but Aurangzeb decided to keep much of it as crown land reserved for the maintenance of the imperial household. In addition, the system for assigning jagirs was becoming inefficient and corrupt, resulting in long delays between the promise of a jagir and the actual obtaining of one.

The economic problems of the Mughal nobility added to their loss of morale. With expectations for advancement thwarted and their overall position weakened, khanazads (men who served the emperor as if they were sons) were increasingly discontent. Those nobles who dwelt in north India seldom had any interaction with the emperor, whose attention was almost solely focused on the Deccan. Many officers stationed in the Deccan for years and even decades on end, far from their homes in north India, had serious doubts about the wisdom of the emperor's Deccan strategy. Their effectiveness had been undermined by financial constraints, and there was little incentive for them to fight hard in a seemingly interminable war. The increasing disenchantment of the elite class upon whom the empire depended is but one development among many that led to the waning of the Mughals. And the strains that the empire was experiencing around 1700 may have occurred even without the decades of involvement in the Deccan. Although scholars may disagree on the exact causes of Mughal decline, there is little doubt that the Deccan wars had a detrimental impact.

The Marathas

The Marathas as a warrior community

How were the Marathas able to pose such a prolonged military challenge to the powerful imperial Mughal forces? Perfecting methods of warfare first developed by troops of the Ahmadnagar Sultanate while resisting the Mughal advance, Shivaji developed a light cavalry that was highly mobile. It did not have the capacity to take forts through standard siege techniques such as sapping, mining, and artillery; nor could it withstand a charge from the Mughal heavy cavalry fighting in its traditional setting on an open plain. The Marathas avoided meeting the formidable Mughal army on the field and resorted instead to a form of guerilla warfare, relying on their superior mobility. The Maratha armies typically lived off the countryside from which their troops were drawn, something the massive and slow-moving Mughal armies could not do. The Marathas excelled at cutting off the enemy's supply lines, thus greatly curtailing their ability to function. If pursued, they would retreat into their fortified strongholds high up in the mountainous terrain of the Western Ghats.

Ultimately, the Marathas were able to thrive because of their intimate ties to the territory within which they fought. According to Stewart Gordon, the term Maratha once meant all people who spoke the Marathi language, but between 1400 and 1600 it acquired a more specialized meaning, referring only to the warrior chiefs who served the Bahmani Sultanate and its successors. That is, the Marathas were a community that arose from among the peasant masses but who gradually became differentiated from them by their martial tradition. The Maratha warriors became an elite through the rights to land revenues they acquired in return for their military service. Often they became either village headmen or *deshmukhs*, the chiefs of twenty to a hundred villages who also had the responsibility of supplying troops. Because Maharashtra was thinly populated and its climate made agriculture a risky venture, being a deshmukh could involve organizing a group of people to colonize a new agrarian settlement. The relationship between the deshmukhs and the peasant population was exceptionally close, and any central government's control of the countryside was dependent on the degree to which they could control the deshmukhs and their clients.

Most of the troops in the early days were peasants who fought part time, assembling only after the monsoons ended. Being a fighter was a relatively low-cost affair, with part of the equipment being supplied by the Maratha chief. The troops were either infantry or light cavalry, riding small locally bred horses, and wearing only light armor. The typical Maratha weapon was a lance, sometimes supplemented with a straight sword. The Mughals and their Rajput allies, on the other hand, were primarily heavy cavalry – well-armored horsemen riding larger, imported horses. They could easily crush a Maratha opponent, provided they could catch up with him in the first place.

The great differences in their equipment and mode of warfare underline the vast sociological gap that separated the Maratha warriors from those in the Mughal armies. The Marathas were a new community based in the countryside with strong peasant ties. On the other hand, the Mughal officers, regardless of their ethnic background, were part of a long-established elite culture that was oriented around the urban court and its elaborate ceremonial. The contempt that the Mughals felt for the upstart Marathas is reflected in Aurangzeb's reference to Shivaji as a "mountain rat." The formal inclusion of numerous Marathas into the administrative system made no difference to Mughal attitudes; the Marathas were never successfully incorporated into court culture and society but always remained disdained outsiders.

Shivaji's rule

Shivaji's legacy today is much greater than it was at his death in 1680. Throughout the twentieth century and increasingly into the twenty-first, Shivaji has been admired on a popular level for his role in resisting Mughal aggression. As the first non-Muslim to do so successfully on a sustained basis, he is regarded as a hero, not only for the Marathi-speaking people but for many Indians today. There is no doubt that Shivaji's desire for autonomy was deep and sincere. Nor can it be disputed that he was conscious of his own identity as a Hindu in a political universe dominated by Muslims. Shivaji is widely believed to have been personally devoted to the goddess Bhavani, and he had a traditional Indian coronation ritual performed in 1674 in order to validate his status as a true king. Where scholars, and the public, often disagree is on the extent to which Shivaji was motivated by his own religious affiliation to oppose the Mughals. Was it Hinduism that fueled Shivaji's long and arduous quest for an independent realm or were his motives more pragmatic?

Let us turn for a moment to the details of Shivaji's coronation, for this act perhaps more than any other has colored the common view of his identity as being anchored in Hinduism. The coronation was an elaborate nine-day ceremony, replete with Brahmins and Sanskrit ritual. At its core was the ancient Indian rite whereby a ruler was anointed with a variety of auspicious substances and transformed into a representative on earth of Indra, the king of gods. Following that were several public audiences, in which Shivaji received homage from his officials as well as from the large deshmukh families who had contributed to the costs of the affair. It had been centuries since a full-fledged royal coronation in the Indic mode had been conducted in the Maharashtra region, and the result was an invented tradition, a seeming revival of ancient practice that was in fact something quite new. Especially innovative were the preliminary ceremonies, in which Shivaji did penance for having lived like a

Maratha up to that point in time. The Marathas, along with many peasant cultivators throughout the subcontinent, were considered members
of the fourth or *shudra* varna in the four-fold class system of orthodox
Brahmin thought. Traditionally, however, the only legitimate kings were
those born into the kshatriya varna, ranked just below the Brahmins. The
solution to the problem of Shivaji's status was a new genealogy created
for the occasion that traced Shivaji's ancestry back to Rajput roots, for
Rajputs were widely accepted as aristocratic kshatriyas. To commemorate
his coronation, Shivaji also commissioned two poetic works, one in Sanskrit and the other in Braj Bhasa, the dominant literary idiom of north
India during the early modern era.

Shivaji clearly sought to cast himself in the mold of a traditional Indian
king, deploying many Hindu symbols in the process. And he enacted
the paradigmatic role of the Indian king as protector and benefactor
of Brahmins, whom he lavishly feted throughout the coronation ceremony. The audience for this refashioning of his self may very well have
been potential rivals within the Maratha community, for Shivaji came
from humble origins and lacked social standing in the eyes of the powerful deshmukh families whose submission he had compelled. Shivaji may
also have desired an enhanced status for his diplomatic relations with
rulers from illustrious families, like the Qutb Shahs of Golkonda, with
whom he formed an alliance soon after the coronation. In this public presentation of himself as a Hindu king, we should understand the
emphasis to lie on the "king" rather than the "Hindu" – that is, the ceremony and accompanying epic poems sought foremost to portray him
as a rightful royal figure, albeit within the Indic, rather than Islamicate,
tradition.

In practice, there was very little difference between Shivaji's emerging polity and the neighboring states. His army included Muslims, at
least two of whom rose to high command, and he employed Muslim officials as administrators. Moreover, the Maratha administrative practices
were largely continuous with those of the Deccan past. Culturally, Shivaji
resided in a larger Islamicate world, with the result that he wore Islamicate
dress and spoke a language embedded with words adopted from Persian.
And there were similarities in the Indic and Islamicate conceptions of
kingship, in which the obligation of the ruler was to promote peace and
prosperity. The many texts on kingship produced in the Islamic world
from the eleventh through eighteenth centuries reveal such sentiments.
Another trait shared by rulers in the Deccan was the expectation that
all religious traditions deserved patronage. Muslim religious institutions
continued to find patronage under the new Maratha state just as they
had under the earlier Deccan Sultanates, although at the same time the

endowment of temples and other institutions associated with Hinduism was enhanced.

Illustrations of Maratha rulers underscore a multi-faceted sense of legitimacy that draws on both Indic and Islamicate traditions. Shivaji, in a posthumous portrait, is depicted wearing the robes, sash, weapons, and regnal standards seen in Mughal and Deccan painting (Figure 8.2). In addition, the painting follows the style of the Deccan Sultanates, as one would expect given Shivaji's family background and the fact that his architecture is indebted to the Bijapur style. A portrait of Shivaji's grandson, Shahu (r. 1708–49), shows him surrounded by courtiers wearing Islamicate sewn tunics and tight trousers, but Shahu is presented as an Indic ruler, wearing a dhoti, with a bare chest. In another painting, Shahu confers with his Brahmin *peshwa* (prime minister) while his subjects are shown participating in daily activities, suggesting peace in the realm. These portraits of Shivaji and Shahu visually portray the overlapping visions of Indic and Islamicate kingship that comprise the Maratha concept of state. Today every village, town, and city in Maharashtra features a large bronze statue of Shivaji garlanded as a hero, who stands as a symbol of Hindu nationalism rather than as the representative of India's composite Maratha culture he originally was.

Marathas in the eighteenth century

In 1719, a treaty was signed between the Marathas and the Mughals which gave the Marathas considerable independence. The Mughals conceded to the Marathas the right to a *chauth* or a quarter of the government's revenues throughout the six Mughal provinces of the Deccan, acknowledging the reality that these lands were now in Maratha hands. The Maratha leader also received another 10 percent of revenues in the Deccan, in return for his role as the head of all the deshmukh families. In addition, the Mughals also gave the Marathas the right to collect chauth in Malwa and Gujarat, territories to the north and west of the Maratha homelands. This was in recognition of the conquests made by Maratha warbands which had roamed far and wide. In essence, this was the ending of direct Mughal power over most of the Deccan.

The treaty was negotiated by Balaji Vishvanath, a Chitpavan Brahmin from Maharashtra who had been appointed in 1713 by Shahu, Shivaji's grandson, to be the peshwa and chief financial officer. The position of peshwa became hereditary and its Brahmin occupants soon became the *de facto* rulers of the Maratha state based at Pune. Under the leadership of the peshwas, the state system in the Maratha homelands was made more centralized, with a new elite in the form of tax collectors, administrators,

Figure 8.2 In this posthumous portrait Shivaji is shown wearing the regalia common to the Mughals and sultans of the Deccan.

and bankers. The development of a sophisticated financial system allowed credit to be extended in any Maratha city, thus enhancing trade; it also allowed troops to be paid in cash, making it possible to increase the size of the Maratha army. Despite the peshwa's efforts at centralization, however, several Maratha chiefs belonging to the Gaikwad, Holkar, and Shinde families, among others, acted independently of Pune and set themselves up as lords in the regions outside the Maratha homelands. These chiefs extended Maratha military power into the Gangetic plain and even threatened Delhi. The Marathas finally met their match in 1761, when they were defeated by the Afghan invader Ahmad Khan Abdali at Panipat, near Delhi. Yet the Battle of Panipat was only a setback for the Marathas, who remained the dominant military power of the western part of the subcontinent until their final conquest by the British in 1818.

Cultural contributions of the Marathas

Cultural contributions under the Marathas have been little studied, with perhaps the exception of the poetry of Ramdas, who continued the bhakti tradition of Eknath and others writing in this genre. The ballad or oral tradition clearly thrived as the exploits of Shivaji and his compatriots were eulogized and romanticized, helping fuel today's image of this warrior as a Hindu devotee and nationalist. Less is known about the visual and aural arts, although it appears that the systematic patronage of the Marathas dates to the mid and late eighteenth century, when Maratha rule became more urbanized and sedentary. A particular house type called *wada* arose for the wealthy. Largely wood-constructed, these multi-storied houses were built both for defense (possessing doors with spikes to prevent forced entry and secret passages linking them to other wada) and comfort (for example, Islamicate gardens and waterways, festival halls, and multiple courtyards). The interiors were often painted with elaborate murals; unfortunately, no example pre-dating the mid eighteenth century survives.

The temple once again became a significant building type in eighteenth-century Maratha territories, as happened in much of north India during this era of declining Muslim political power and newly ascendant Hindu communities. The variations in temple types throughout the subcontinent are enormous, and little work has been done on those sponsored by the Marathas to date. Among the earliest temples built under the Marathas was one provided by Shivaji at his stronghold Pratapgad, and dedicated to the fierce goddess Bhavani, whom many claim was Shivaji's family deity. The temple is a simple domed structure modeled on the architecture of the Adil Shahs, not surprising given that Shivaji's father served in their court. Shivaji also constructed a temple in 1674 dedicated to the god

Figure 8.3 Shivaji's temple (1674) dedicated to the god Shiva at his Raigad fort is similar to the architectural traditions of the sultans of the Deccan.

Shiva at Raigad in celebration of his coronation. The overall appearance of its stone exterior and the vaulting techniques in its interior are also rooted in architectural traditions of the Deccan Sultanates, but combined in a unique manner (Figure 8.3). The square, clunky, fortress-like appearance of early Maratha temples, usually built inside forts, was transformed by the mid eighteenth century into tall, elegant temples made largely of stucco and brick. The Parvati temple in Pune, associated with a peshwa family, also has an Islamicate appearance, due to its lobed arches around the base, blind arched niches on the towering superstructure, and domes that surmount the superstructure's individual parts.

By far the most important architectural enterprise was the construction, reconstruction, and maintenance of forts. Clearly this was intimately linked to the very survival of the Marathas. Three types of forts predominate, including coastal forts, sea forts, and hill forts, of which the latter two were the most important. Sea forts, built to withstand the pounding waves, were constructed on rocky outcroppings of the shallow waters of the Arabian Sea's coast. Their function was to protect Shivaji's navy against pirates and predatory European fleets, since the small size of the Maratha ships rendered them nearly impotent. Hill forts were key to the foundation, expansion, and preservation of Maratha authority, along with the use of light cavalry. Located along major military and trade routes, these forts are situated at the top of the high peaks of the rugged Western

Figure 8.4 The massive fortifications of Pratapgad, an important Maratha hill fort, made it essentially impregnable.

Ghats range. Built according to a well-established military formula, a steep scarp was on the western side while a steep but accessible approach was on the east (Figure 8.4). Usually these forts consisted of three levels of fortified curtain walls, to prevent enemy attack. The highest level served as a citadel, where the king or family holding the fort lived. These forts were essentially impregnable; conquering one was best accomplished not through the expenditure of human lives but instead through the payment of gold to a defector within. One of the most impressive of Shivaji's forts is Raigad, about 150 kilometers southwest of Pune through the rugged mountainous Ghats. The fort's topmost level covers considerable ground and has the remains of Shivaji's palace, including the site of his coronation, temples, and water tanks. The site marking his cremation is close to the temple he dedicated to the deity Shiva (see Figure 8.3).

Disintegration of the Mughal empire

Internal response to the crisis of empire

By the end of Aurangzeb's reign the stability of the Mughal empire had been irrevocably shaken. Since the mid twentieth century, much scholarship has focused on the root cause of this malady, with scholars belonging to particular schools of thought arguing for their own particular perspective. Rather than pinpointing one cause, it would be better to recognize a variety of factors leading to imperial decline, among them a breakdown in the mansabdar system, growing factionalism at court, and the rise of regional powers like the Marathas, who were increasingly able to effectively challenge what was once undisputable Mughal superiority. Other problems, reflecting the growing reluctance of the populace to submit to imperial authority and direction, also plagued the empire in the late seventeenth and early eighteenth centuries – these will be discussed in chapter 9.

Needless to say, the factors leading ultimately to the weakening of the Mughal state also affected how the elite perceived their relation to the state. In chapter 7 we noted that the Mughal noble saw himself as a khanazad, loyal to the emperor. John F. Richards presents the case of a Rajput noble's loyal secretary, Bhimsen, who in his own writings despairs about Aurangzeb's lack of concern for his subjects' welfare, in contrast to that of the previous Mughal rulers. As a result of these new perceptions of the Mughal emperor as disinterested in them, the Mughal elite started to move away from their older self-identity as khanazads or sons who were bound to the service of the Mughal household. Rosalind O'Hanlon has argued that in the late seventeenth and eighteenth centuries Mughal nobles began to conceive of themselves instead as *mirzas*, gentlemen who adhered to a rigorous social code that insisted on a carefully regulated persona and a sense of honor equal to that of the khanazad, but simply not one linked to the Mughal emperor. The elite associated with imperial Mughal service were now individual gentlemen who experienced a new sense of disciplined self within an increasingly cosmopolitan South Asian society.

If the new norm for imperial service manifested itself as concern for one's self more than the king, let us see how this played out in the realm of the continuing cityscape of the capital. In spite of the increasing political woes in Mughal India, Delhi remained a thriving city and the ideal model to which regional rulers turned for the next 150 years. However, just as the elite gentleman had an increased sense of individual worth, so too did individual nobles begin to play an increasingly central role in the continued embellishment of Delhi, while the ruler himself took the backstage. The most important new mosques were provided by both men (often prime ministers) and women, continuing a long-standing tradition. These structures were without exception considerably smaller than those of the previous era built by the royal family, a reflection on the dwindling resources of the empire and the non-imperial nature of their patronage. Examples include the stucco-faced Sunhari mosque (1721)

Figure 8.5 In the eighteenth century small mosques such as the Fakhr
al-Masajid (1728–29), whose name means Pride of the Mosques, were
built by the elite throughout Shahjahanabad.

placed on Chandni Chowk not far from the imperial palace, and provided by the nobleman Raushan al-Daulat Zafar Khan, as well as Fakhr
al-Masajid (Pride of the Mosques) built by Kaniz-i Fatima, a widow of one
of Aurangzeb's high-ranking nobles, and unusual for this period (1728–
29) in its use of red sandstone trimmed with white marble (Figure 8.5).
    Imperial patronage tended to focus on dargahs, but access to the prem-
ier shrine at Ajmer was difficult, now that the Mughal state was essentially
reduced to the region around Delhi. The focus then shifted to another
Chishti dargah, that of Qutb al-Din Bakhtiyar Kaki, situated south of
Shahjahanabad, the newest of the Delhi cities and the current Mughal
capital. Unlike the Delhi shrine of Nizam al-Din, where considerable
Mughal construction was already apparent, the dargah of Bakhtiyar Kaki
gave eighteenth-century Mughal rulers and nobles a unique opportunity to make their imprint on a site. Bakhtiyar Kaki was a thirteenth-
century Sufi whose shrine Babur, the first Mughal, endorsed when
making his initial tour of Delhi. The saint's urs was celebrated with an
elaborate series of lights linking the dargah to the palace in Shahjahanabad, a distance of some 20 kilometers, clearly a visual link between
the Chishti and Mughal houses. Here at the dargah of Bakhtiyar Kaki

the later Mughal emperors and their nobles built their own tombs and mosques, all in white marble, the fabric long associated now with both the Chishti and Mughal royalty. These tombs, however, were not the elaborate structural mausolea of earlier Mughals such as the Taj Mahal. Now the Mughal rulers showed their piety, and hence legitimacy, with simple marble cenotaphs surrounded by screened walls left open to the air.

A major change also took place in Delhi's literary culture during the first half of the eighteenth century. Unlike other Muslim courts, such as those in the former sultanates of Jaunpur, Bijapur, and Golkonda, the Mughal court had never encouraged literary production in Indian languages, preferring to patronize Persian instead. Shortly after 1700, however, Delhi witnessed an efflorescence of writing in Urdu, an Indian language that incorporates many words from Persian and Arabic. The growing patronage of Urdu, based on the vernacular speech of the Delhi region, may in part reflect the shrinking geographical horizons of Mughal power, which now extended over no more than part of north India. But more significant in the rise of Urdu literature at Delhi was the emergence of a new class of non-noble poets and patrons. These upwardly mobile men, from a variety of backgrounds including commerce and administrative service, were not as conversant in Persian as Mughal nobles had once been, and so supported the growth of a rich literature in the more familiar language of Urdu, which gradually displaced Persian as a poetic medium in much of north India.

Emergence of independent regional states

The new norm for imperial service made rupture with the Mughal house an easier option to consider in the changed circumstances at the imperial center, beset by constant turmoil and distrust after Aurangzeb's death at the age of almost ninety. From 1707 when Aurangzeb died, to the end of 1719, there was a rapid succession of five sovereigns. Rampant factionalism at court was the main cause of this instability, exacerbated by the suspicious nature of those who did attain the throne. It was a marked change from the long era of stability that had ensued upon Akbar's ascent to the throne, with only four emperors in a period of 150 years. By the time things settled down under the relatively long rule of Muhammad Shah (r. 1719–48) it was too late; the forces of political fragmentation had already transformed the empire into a loosely bound association of states.

Within a few decades after Aurangzeb's death, a series of regional kingdoms were carved out of the former Mughal provinces, each through a somewhat different process. In essence, however, nobles throughout the provinces were seizing lands and official positions without the prior permission of the emperor. Local landholders and other groups, for their part, were proving actively recalcitrant when faced with demands from the state or its representatives for revenue. These struggles for power trickled down to all levels of society including religious grant-holders, merchants, and agricultural laborers. Conflicts were increasingly acted out on a purely local level and were not dictated from the imperial center. Former Mughal provinces were gradually transformed into independent states, but none was strong enough to exert the more centralized power that the empire had in its heyday. Therefore, for symbolic and other very real reasons, the Mughals were still regarded as the ultimate legitimizing authority, although in practical terms the Mughal state was by 1750 no more than a regional kingdom itself.

In Bengal the nobleman Kartalab Khan, later known as Murshid Quli Khan, had been appointed as the head of revenue administration in 1701 by Aurangzeb. Having rectified a financial situation disastrous to the Mughal center early in his career, he then exhibited a growing sense of independence, to the extent of even establishing a new capital, Murshidabad, named after himself. In 1717, he combined the role of governor and that of treasury head. By doing away with what had been two separate official positions, he bypassed the established system of checks and balances that had been built into the classic Mughal mansabdar system to prevent the construction of a personal power base. Murshid Quli Khan never formally severed his link to the Mughals and continued to send annual tribute to Delhi. Although he laid the foundation for a well-run and economically viable state, it was his successor who made the rupture with Delhi.

The Deccan continued to be plagued with disorder. In the face of continuing Maratha demands for revenue and tribute, Mughal officers were helpless and at times fled their posts. To counter Maratha attack, the emperor sent a seasoned general, Nizam al-Mulk (known later as Asaf Jah), to serve as viceroy of the Deccan in 1713, a post he held intermittently until 1721. During this era Nizam al-Mulk also spent a short stint at the imperial center in Delhi, where he tried to institute reform of the now wholly corrupt system by which jagirs were assigned, making himself very unpopular with those who stood to lose power and wealth in the process. Disgusted with the situation at court, Nizam al-Mulk defied the emperor's wishes and in 1724 headed toward the Deccan. There he confronted in battle a former Mughal official who had been controlling the eastern Deccan as an independent lord for some years. After his victory, Nizam al-Mulk no longer felt allegiance to the Mughals and established his own Asaf Jah dynasty, better known as the Nizams of

Hyderabad. The Asaf Jah line would head the subcontinent's wealthiest and most powerful princely state, lasting until 1948.

The rich province of Awadh, situated east of Delhi and west of Bengal, also became independent. As in Bengal, the governor was able to bypass the customary system of checks and balances by combining the offices of treasurer and governor into one. From 1722 onward, a relatively stable administrative system was created by getting rid of most jagirs assigned to nobles who served outside the state. The lack of external interference into Awadh's affairs left it virtually autonomous in action, while integration of local groups into the provincial power structure helped consolidate the state. Although the rulers of Awadh distanced themselves from Delhi, they, like Nizam al-Mulk of the eastern Deccan, came to Mughal aid in 1739 when the Iranian Nadir Shah sacked Delhi. For almost the next hundred years, the rulers of the Mughal successor states acknowledged the supremacy of the Mughals, although they failed to pay tribute.

These three increasingly independent states, all ruled by Shia Muslims of Iranian descent or affiliation, illustrate the phenomenon of regional centralization that characterized some areas of the former Mughal empire as it declined in the eighteenth century. When viewed from the perspective of the imperial center, the eighteenth century is indeed an era of decline and fragmentation. At the same time as the empire was disintegrating, some provinces that had split off from it were experiencing considerable stability and prosperity. Agricultural production grew and trade did well in certain parts of the subcontinent in spite of the commonly held belief that the eighteenth century was a period of chaos. Within the regions of Bengal, Hyderabad, and Awadh, capable rulers were consolidating power and creating more efficient administrations at the regional level. This was in part made possible by the smaller scale of the new states, which made surveillance and incorporation of local communities more feasible. For these Mughal successor states, formed through the defection of former top officials, the eighteenth century was no decline but rather an era of regional development.

A fourth area of the subcontinent where former Mughal affiliates were progressively setting up independent domains was Rajasthan. The Rajput lords of this region had ancestral lands acknowledged as their own by the imperial center; to these uncontested holdings the Rajputs gradually added more lands without imperial permission. This was done most effectively by Sawai Jai Singh (r. 1700–43), the Kachhwaha ruler of Amber, who consolidated large expanses of territory surrounding his new capital, Jaipur. Founded in 1727, the city was named after Jai Singh himself, a signal of his state's increasing distance from the Mughals. Sawai Jai Singh continued to perform loyal service as a high-ranking Mughal military officer who increasingly was consulted for his sage opinions by both the Mughals and his fellow Rajput princes. Other Rajput princes, such as the Sisodiyas of Mewar, never particularly pro-Mughal, and the Rathors of Marwar, maintained their distance from Delhi. For these Rajput states the real fear was increasingly less the Mughals than the Maratha warbands who controlled the countryside in neighboring Malwa and Gujarat.

In other parts of the Mughal empire, the transition from Mughal control to independent state was considerably more fraught than in the instances discussed above. The Punjab, for example, was devastated by internal conflict between different local groups contesting power. How peasants, zamindar landholders, merchants, and others became strong enough to present a challenge to imperial order is an issue that will be covered in chapter 9; here we remain focused on the process of disintegration happening at the highest levels of the political system, through the defection of high-ranking subordinates.

New political centers

As the political geography of the Indian subcontinent became increasingly divided into smaller coherent units, new or restored urban centers were needed to reflect the new political realities. Hyderabad had been established in 1591 by the Qutb Shahs but had fallen somewhat into disrepair when the Asaf Jahs appropriated it as their capital and renewed the city. Newly created capitals tended to look to Shahjahanabad and to Mughal architecture as the models to emulate. This is certainly true of Faizabad, the first capital established by the rulers of Awadh. While little survives of the original capital, contemporary texts claim it surpassed the beauty of Mughal Delhi, the standard by which all other cities were judged. The subsequent capital of Awadh, at Lucknow, also drew much inspiration from Mughal Delhi.

The most interesting of the new capitals were at Murshidabad in Bengal and Jaipur in what is today Rajasthan. Murshidabad was clearly a statement of Mughal affirmation within a Bengal context. Formerly a market town, its importance increased significantly in 1703 when Murshid Quli Khan shifted the capital of the Mughal province of Bengal from Dhaka to Makhsusabad, renaming the city Murshidabad. Although Murshid Quli Khan had assumed unprecedented powers for a single officer of the Mughal state, he never ceased to regard himself as a Mughal agent. Appropriately, he embellished the new capital with a Mughal-style palace and public audience hall. Perhaps the continuing, albeit tenuous, link with the Mughals is best expressed by the throne that Murshid Quli

Figure 8.6 This large Jami mosque in Murshidabad built by Murshid
Quli Khan in 1724–25, known as the Katra mosque, has several features
that link it with local Bengali traditions.

Khan used as his seat of authority. It was a large polygonal slab of polished
black stone made earlier for Prince Shah Shuja, the Mughal governor of
Bengal from 1639 to 1658. Murshid Quli Khan provided the city with a
mint, wells, and tanks.

The most significant architectural project in the new headquarters
was a Jami mosque, dated 1724–25, and called the Katra mosque today
(Figure 8.6). While the mosque's plan and overall elevation adhere to
established Mughal standards, other aspects of the mosque link it and its
patron, Murshid Quli Khan, to long-standing traditions of Bengal. The
numerous niches of the Jami mosque's façade and the weighty quality
suggested by the proportionally small entrance arches do not recall contemporary Mughal construction, but are reminiscent of the ornamentation of pre-Mughal architecture in Bengal. This break with the Mughal
ornamental style corresponds with the autonomy of its patron, despite his
nominal allegiance to the center. There is one other parallel that suggests
a link between Bengal practice and the new leader Murshid Quli Khan.
Like Sikandar Shah, the most noted ruler of fourteenth-century Bengal,
who was buried under the entrance to his Adina mosque in Pandua, Murshid Quli Khan arranged to be buried under his own mosque's entrance.

In essence, Murshid Quli Khan, increasingly free of Mughal authority, expressed a regional rather than pan-Mughal affiliation by associating himself with the independent rulers of pre-Mughal Bengal.

Surrounding the mosque on all four sides are domed cloistered chambers that served as a splendid madrasa staffed with 2,000 reciters of the Quran. Murshid Quli Khan's zeal in propagating the faith is well known from historical chronicles, not altogether surprising since he was a convert to Islam. The construction of this madrasa-cum-mosque, larger than any Mughal mosque built in Bengal, endows the city, hitherto holding little religious significance, with a dominant sacred importance – possibly an attempt to rival the traditional centers of piety in Bengal, Gaur and Pandua. Further underscoring the notion that this Jami mosque and school were attempts to secure an authoritative religious status for Murshidabad was the elaborate celebration provided by Murshid Quli Khan to honor the Prophet Muhammad's birthday. For twelve days lights arranged to depict Quranic verses, mosques, and trees (a common symbol of paradise) were illuminated for a 5 kilometer stretch that ended at the mosque. Making this display of lights all the more impressive was their simultaneous lighting at the sound of a gun. While the rulers of Murshidabad were Shia Muslims, it was Hindu and Jain moneylenders who bankrolled the state. They contributed to the city by building enormous mansions and temples, many of which survive today.

Shortly after Murshid Quli Khan shifted his capital to Murshidabad, Sawai Jai Singh Kachhwaha too founded a new Kachhwaha capital, Jaipur, replacing the older one of Amber. The names of these two new capitals, based on those of their founders, reflect a sense of independence on the part of these two nobles. While Murshidabad consisted of a few significant new structures, Jaipur by contrast was a completely planned city based, unusually for this period, on an ordered and symmetrical grid plan. Its streets were broad enough that six elephants across could easily traverse the city, thus making it an excellent place for procession, which was one of Sawai Jai Singh's objectives (Figure 8.7). This raja would often ride forth in procession to visit temples or to celebrate festivals, thus allowing his subjects to have his darshan. In order to insure the maximum impact of these royal processions, Sawai Jai Singh ordered that all the city's architecture be uniform in appearance. While today Jaipur is painted pink and is often described as the Pink City, until the late nineteenth century it was painted a cream color. Thus, the colorful carriages, elephants, and horse trappings, not to mention the bejeweled raja himself, would radiate against the uniform architectural backdrop.

Part of the uniformity of Jaipur was fashioned by a new temple type. Previously most temples in the vicinity, including those at the former

Figure 8.7 Sawai Jai Singh's new capital, Jaipur, founded in 1727, featured broad avenues and large mansions, including the Natani family's house on the street corner.

Kachhwaha capital Amber, featured high spired superstructures. Commencing with the construction of Jaipur's most important temple, the Govinda Deva, a new temple type evolved, one with a flat roof that was modeled not on any previous temple but on a Mughal Public Audience Hall. The image housed by the Govinda Deva temple was the same one for whom Raja Man Singh Kachhwaha had built his temple at Vrindavan in the late sixteenth century (see chapter 5). We noted earlier that Aurangzeb at times demolished temples built by Mughal nobles when he was annoyed by subversive action on their part. The father of Sawai Jai Singh had done just that; he had helped the Maratha Shivaji escape Mughal custody. Once that occurred, the Kachhwahas feared for the safety of the Govinda Deva image and eventually shifted it from Vrindavan to the new city of Jaipur. Sawai Jai Singh then began to regard Govinda Deva as his primary deity, considering the god to be the true ruler of Jaipur and himself, the king, only the god's human agent. He therefore created a new type of temple for Govinda Deva, based on his new role as Jaipur's ruler. This temple type became the model for all Jaipur's future temples because of its simple, non-intrusive appearance. Adding to the city's homogeneity, the adoption of a standard style for temple architecture ultimately served to enhance the king's image during procession. That is, as the city physically became seamless in appearance, it became more of a backdrop for the royal splendor that was displayed publicly in its midst.

In spite of Sawai Jai Singh's personal devotion and the fact that he was a very serious scholar of religious texts, it is not correct to see him as a ruler who espoused a Hindu state for Hindu subjects, as is often believed. Like other rulers discussed in this chapter and earlier, Sawai Jai Singh was a righteous ruler who supported Brahmins and Indic institutions; at the same time he remained loyal to the Mughal emperor, actively serving in the military and administration. He understood the value of having a multi-cultural state inhabited by various peoples whose occupations provided the highest financial support to the state's economic well-being. In this spirit, Sawai Jai Singh issued invitations to any number of communities, Hindus, Muslims, Jains, and even Sikhs among them, to move to Jaipur to practice their professions, crafts, and skills. Thus, Muslim musicians and military men came, as did scholars and businessmen who were Jains or Hindus, and also Sikhs skilled at enameling gold jewelry.

The internal process of disintegration that resulted in the formation of new states and political centers was accelerated by raids on Delhi by outsiders who sensed the empire's growing impotence. Rulers from Central Asia and farther west had long seen India as a treasure trove worthy of periodic sacking as a quick way to acquire untold wealth. We saw this in the eleventh century with Mahmud of Ghazni and in the fourteenth century with Timur. So too the Iranian king Nadir Shah, greedy for territorial gain and wealth, was able to pass through the Punjab to Delhi, which he sacked and plundered in 1739, killing possibly as many as 20,000 people. The *coup de grâce*, however, was the booty he took upon his departure, including Shah Jahan's famed Peacock Throne, along with an endless number of jewels from the Mughal personal treasury. Today many of these jewels can be seen in the vault of Tehran's National Bank (Bank-i Melli). This huge room literally dazzles and gives an idea of the Mughals' former wealth. The acquisition of this wealth also changed the Iranian concept of how kings should appear. Formerly they wore virtually no jewelry, but after Nadir Shah's return, portraits of Iranian kings show them heavily bejeweled in almost a caricature of Mughal fashion. Even though poets and writers bemoan this devastating blow to Mughal pride, in fact, the city of Delhi recovered fairly quickly from this destructive attack on it.

The Mughal emperors had virtually no army left and were dependent on the protection of the Marathas, who fought both with local Indo-Afghans and with Ahmad Khan Abdali (later Ahmad Shah Durrani), the Afghan king of Kabul from 1747 onward. Delhi was attacked by Ahmad Khan in both 1752 and 1757, inspiring a new literary poetic genre that lamented the ruin of this once brilliant city. Ahmad Khan entered India for a third and final time in 1761, defeating the Marathas and shattering their hope of dominating the former Mughal territories. In all but name, the empire of the Mughals was now a thing of the past.

9 Changing socio-economic formations, 1650–1750

The beginnings of the Mughal empire's eventual demise can be traced back to the reign of Aurangzeb in the late seventeenth century. His preoccupation with the Deccan wars and the consequent loss of morale among the nobility are two important causes of the weakening of empire, leading by the mid eighteenth century to the dismemberment of Mughal territory into numerous smaller states. In this chapter, we cover additional reasons for the political instability that engulfed the empire following Aurangzeb's death. As the empire disintegrated, local elites and communities sought, and in many cases were able to obtain, more autonomy and control over their own affairs. Each region had a different experience in the aftermath of empire, however, not only politically but also economically, with some regions faring far better than others. Events in the Bengal area were especially wrought with significance for the subsequent history of the subcontinent, for it was there that the English first obtained an extensive foothold within the internal affairs of the erstwhile empire. We therefore both begin and end this chapter with an account of the activities of the European trading companies, whose long-term effect on Indian history was so disproportionate to their numbers and even to their immediate impact on the era from 1650 to 1750.

The European trading companies

The Dutch and English trading companies, who had begun their activities in India at the outset of the 1600s, made a major contribution to the Indian economy by supplying the bullion that enabled the twin trends of monetization and commercialization to gather steam. Desire for their bullion and for revenues arising from trade led the Mughals and local rulers in the far south to permit and even encourage European traders to settle within their realms. The number and size of European trading posts went up steadily during the hundred years between 1650 and 1750; so too did the volume of trade in which they engaged.

Fueling the growth of the European trading companies was a new demand for Indian products within Europe. The large quantities of Indian textiles purchased earlier by the Dutch and English companies (the VOC and EIC, respectively) had been sent to Southeast Asia to be exchanged for spices or, alternatively, to the Middle East. Africa was another outlet for Indian cotton goods, which were used widely to purchase slaves. Very little could be sold in Europe due to lack of consumer interest. Around the middle of the seventeenth century, however, Europeans discovered a taste for chintz, the intricately patterned textiles discussed in chapter 6. Hand painted and/or printed in predominantly reds and blues on a white ground, the resist technique described earlier continued to be used for these chintz exports to Europe. The initial demand for these magnificent pieces was as household furnishings, to be displayed on walls or placed in the bedroom. Bed coverings, such as this example from the early eighteenth century (Figure 9.1), were known in English as palampores, a distorted form of the original Persian name for them.

Just as there were specific designs desired by the long-standing Southeast Asian market, so too the European market had its own particular tastes. One of the most popular patterns in Europe, shown here, is the tree of life. The designs on pieces destined for Europe were based on a combination of European, Persian, and Chinese motifs and provided rich color accents for the often dark European household interiors. The favored designs and even the thickness of the hanging or bed cover changed quite rapidly, at times leaving the exporter with outmoded goods that were difficult to sell. So, for example, palampores featuring the tree of life design continued to be popular in the late eighteenth century. But because Chinese porcelains were enjoying a vogue in Europe, the trees in later palampores were thinner, adhering more to a Chinese aesthetic than did earlier ones.

By the 1680s, Indian cotton had become hugely fashionable in Europe, not only as a covering for furniture and walls but also for clothing. Cotton was cheap and comfortable compared to linen or wool, and Indian dyes produced colors that were much brighter and longer-lasting than those of Europe. The rapidly expanding market in Europe led to a very quick rise in the volume of imports of Indian textiles. In 1682, according to K. N. Chaudhuri, the East India Company ordered 2.8 million pieces of cloth from India, a ten-fold increase over what they had ordered just two decades previously. The importance of textiles soon came to overshadow that of spices, the Asian trade item that had originally been most coveted by Europeans. The "calico craze" sweeping England became so strong that domestic linen and wool manufacturers, concerned about the state of their businesses, pressured Parliament into passing a series of laws

Figure 9.1 This hand-painted early eighteenth-century chintz bedcover is embellished with a tree of life pattern, a popular motif for the European market.

prohibiting the import or wearing of dyed and printed cloth from India. This did little to diminish the popularity of Indian textiles in England, since they could be readily smuggled in from other countries.

Most of the Indian textiles sent to Europe in the late seventeenth century were produced on the Coromandel coast of southeast India and increasingly from its southern half, where the palampore featured in Figure 9.1 was made. Prices were cheaper in the southern Coromandel, and Europeans could obtain more trading concessions there due to the competition for trade between its numerous small kingdoms. The English, for instance, had been granted a complete remission on import and export duties at Madras, the town they acquired in 1640 from a local ruler for a small fee. Madras was the biggest beneficiary of the boom in southern Coromandel trade, growing to around 100,000 in population by 1700. Another popular settlement was Pondicherry, founded by the French in 1674. Both Madras and Pondicherry allowed Indian ships to freely operate from their ports and gave each resident community the right to live by their own laws, unlike the situation at Dutch and Portuguese ports. Madras and Pondicherry both also enjoyed virtual autonomy from outside political interference, an important consideration in the early eighteenth century. There were numerous contenders for power in the far south, as the Mughal empire began to collapse in the north: former Mughal officials, the Marathas who were entrenched in Tanjavur and Senji forts, and local kings based inland from the coast.

Madras and the Coromandel trade were critical to the rise of the East India Company in the late seventeenth century, a period when it finally came to rival the strength of its Dutch equivalent, the VOC. Madras was not only the largest source of Indian textiles for the European market but also an important center for the continuing commerce with Southeast Asia. A new group of merchants involved in the Southeast Asian trade were the English private traders based at Madras, mostly employees of the EIC who used their own resources to trade on the side. Because the East India Company was the only British entity authorized to engage in international trade between Europe and Asia, private English traders could only invest in the trade within Asia that was of no interest to the Company. Many high-ranking EIC officials like Elihu Yale, governor of Madras from 1687 to 1692, amassed fortunes from their private trade. Decades later, Yale was persuaded to donate a small part of it to an institution of higher education in North America which adopted his name in gratitude. The opportunity to trade for themselves, and possibly grow fabulously rich, spurred the entrepreneurial activity of EIC employees acting as individuals. Since the Dutch trading company, unlike the East India Company, made much of its profits from trade within Asia, it prohibited its employees from engaging in any private commerce. This difference was a factor in the eventual ascendance of the English traders over the Dutch.

Although Madras was the most successful of their trading posts between 1650 and 1700, the East India Company also had settlements in other regions of India. Bombay was a Portuguese possession acquired by the British crown and given outright to the Company in 1668; like Madras, it enjoyed a good deal of autonomy. Lying off the coast of the western Deccan, Bombay consisted of a series of small islands that were drained and joined together by the English. A number of Indian merchants were quickly attracted from the main Mughal port at Surat, which was subject to Maratha attacks, to the relative safety of Bombay; within ten years its population had risen to 60,000. After its initial spurt of growth, Bombay's population increased only at a moderate rate. Political instability in the western Deccan sometimes hampered access to food supplies from the mainland, and it was difficult to obtain goods for export nearby. Its fine harbor and good defenses gave Bombay considerable military significance for the EIC, however.

In Bengal, the third coastal region in India where textiles could be obtained, the East India Company's position was weaker than in the Coromandel or western India. For the past century Bengal's premier port had been Hugli, named after the river in western Bengal where it was located. Hugli earlier had been a base for private Portuguese traders in the Bay of Bengal, some of whom were mercenaries, slave-raiders, or pirates. The Mughals, who had at long last consolidated their control over Bengal, expelled the Portuguese from Hugli in 1632 and invited other European traders there. The oil painting reproduced here shows the flourishing Dutch settlement at Hugli in 1665 with its offices, warehouses, and gardens (Figure 9.2). Just as the British used a classical European architectural style, not local Indian ones, in building their own administrative complexes, we see that so too did the Dutch. In the distance, ships sail on the Hugli river; to the right, a large tented encampment shelters a visiting Indian notable, who is being hailed by the Dutch official heading a line of men on the road. The VOC did much more business in Bengal than the EIC in this era. Although British trading activity in the region grew substantially, the value of the goods they exported from Bengal was still half that of the Dutch in the last decade of the seventeenth century.

Both Bombay and Hugli, unlike Madras, were situated within Mughal territory, and the East India Company believed local imperial officials were constantly putting obstacles in the way of its trade. In an effort to force better terms of trade, the Company sent a well-armed fleet of ten ships to India in 1686 and, in effect, declared war on the Mughal empire.

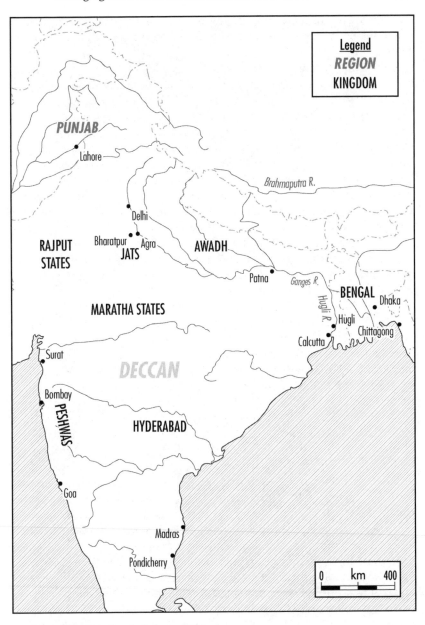

Map 9.1 South Asia, *c.* 1750

Figure 9.2 This painting of the headquarters of the Dutch trading company (VOC) at Hugli, done in 1665, shows that European style architecture was used, although the garden bears similarity to a Mughal char bagh.

Figure 9.3 This half rupee coin issued by the East India Company in 1692 resembles a Mughal coin on both sides, but bears the name of the ruling British monarchs.

They seized numerous Indian ships off the west coast and blockaded Surat port, leading to Mughal retaliation and an attack on Bombay. Things went no better for the English in the Bay of Bengal, where the objective was to capture the port of Chittagong, advance to the Mughal provincial capital at Dhaka, and negotiate a new trade agreement. The war ended instead in total failure and the peace treaty of 1690 required the EIC to pay a hefty indemnity. Continuing piracy by English freebooters off India's western shores kept tensions high, however. The Mughal emperor Aurangzeb was further irritated by a new coin issued by the East India Company at Bombay (Figure 9.3). This silver half-rupee coin was similar to Mughal coins in weight and design, but had the names of the British monarchs, William III and Mary, inscribed on it in Persian. It was seen as a direct challenge to Mughal authority, since issuing coins was the prerogative of a sovereign in the Islamic tradition. The Company was soon forced to discontinue the coin and assume responsibility for the safety of Indian ships in the western waters.

The founding of Calcutta was the direct outcome of the war with the Mughals, which forced the English to flee from Hugli. In 1690, soon after the war ended, the EIC regrouped in Bengal, this time settling downriver from the town of Hugli. By this time considerable silt had built up in the Hugli river and it was difficult for large ships to sail that far upriver; Calcutta, at a distance of 154 kilometers from the Bay of Bengal, was a more convenient location. Unfortunately, the stagnant water in the nearby marshes and swamps was a breeding ground for mosquitoes, making

Calcutta an unhealthy place to live. This did not stop the growth of the city. The EIC soon became landlords of the villages around the Calcutta settlement and built a fortified structure there known as Fort William.

By 1700, the East India Company had thus acquired the three sites of Madras, Bombay, and Calcutta that were to become the great centers of British power in the colonial era. It had also caught up to the VOC in terms of dominance in the Indian Ocean trade, although it would be several more decades before the Dutch were finally eclipsed. In the Coromandel, the English and, to a lesser extent, the French, possessed trading enclaves that were well on their way to becoming independent city-states, secure from the demands of the Indian kingdoms surrounding them. The political fragmentation of the Coromandel region, and the huge volume of its overseas trade, were the significant factors accounting for the greater European clout there. Within the Mughal empire, however, the political power of the European trading companies was still negligible. The ease with which the East India Company's attacks on Mughal ports were crushed demonstrates how English ambitions far surpassed their ability to attain them in the 1680s. Only after the final collapse of the Mughal empire did the balance of power between Indian states and the East India Company change radically.

While the English might not yet have had a major impact on India in 1700, India had become far more important to them. Their trade with India not only led to huge profits and considerable political influence for those in the East India Company, but it was also a source of national pride and concern. The nature of their export trade had also drawn the English into far more involvement with the internal economy of India by 1700. Unlike raw materials such as spices, which could be easily purchased at a port from wholesalers, textiles were a manufactured commodity that went through a complicated and lengthy production process involving spinning, weaving, washing, dying, and printing. The Europeans were entirely dependent on Indian intermediaries for the procurement of textiles from the interior; the Indian merchants in turn had to advance substantial sums of their own money in order to get weavers and others to produce the type of cloth and designs ordered by the Europeans. By 1700, the English in the Coromandel were attempting to get greater control over Indian merchants and weavers so as to obtain the quantities and quality of cloth they desired. Coromandel merchants were gradually confined to a role as broker-agents or financiers of the Europeans, rather than as their partners. The number of ships owned by Indian merchants in the Coromandel also declined as a result of the rise of English private shipping. These trends were to spread to other regions as the East India Company's dominance in local economies grew.

Peasants and zamindars

Although the cities were still firmly under the control of the Mughal state, the countryside seemed to be slipping out of its hands as peasant rebels increasingly refused to pay their taxes and took up arms during the late seventeenth and early eighteenth centuries. The large highways that joined the three great Mughal cities of Lahore, Delhi, and Agra – all with populations as large as 400,000 – were rife with bandits and outlaws, making travel and the transport of goods along this central axis of empire more and more hazardous. The uprisings in the rural areas were a different kind of threat to the empire's existence than the disaffection or even defection of some of its nobles, for they were a challenge to the entire structure of established authority. What appeared as an assault on law and order by criminal rabble from the perspective of the Mughal court can, on the other hand, be more positively interpreted as a growing wave of opposition by the rural localities to the entrenched power of the imperial elites.

The first area to be beset with lawlessness was the corridor between Delhi and Agra to its southeast. The Jat community of the Agra–Delhi countryside started to rebel as early as 1669, during Aurangzeb's reign, when villagers near the town of Mathura overcame local Mughal forces and began looting the wealthy. The rebellion spread among other Jats, peasants largely engaged in agriculture, who came together to form an army of 20,000 men, a quarter of whom had died by the time the outbreak was suppressed a year later. Renewed armed resistance to the Mughal state occurred in the late 1680s. Large bands led by Jat chiefs not only withheld the agrarian revenues that were owed to the state but also repeatedly pillaged traffic on the main roads. They even attacked Akbar's tomb near Agra and took many valuables. This was more than just the sack of a magnificent structure, it was an affront to Mughal dynastic pride, as the European traveler Niccolao Manucci observed at the time. Soon after Aurangzeb's death, the court had no choice but to appoint a Jat chief to guard the imperial highway from Agra to Delhi, in effect giving him the right to plunder at will.

Jat strength in the Agra–Delhi region reached its height in the mid eighteenth century, when one of their chiefs, Badan Singh, carved out the small state of Bharatpur south of Agra. The Jats established a fairly traditional fort at Bharatpur, but in nearby Dig built themselves an elaborate garden palace combining styles seen at Amber and Agra (Figure 9.4). Its buildings are modeled on those forms first developed under Shah Jahan; for example, curved bangla roofs on pavilions set in four-part Mughal-type gardens, with large tanks to provide cooling waters

Figure 9.4 The eighteenth-century Jat rulers of Bharatpur built a refined palace complex at Dig that shows considerable architectural innovation.

in what is otherwise land on the edge of a desert. Here the language of poetry and painting, thunder and rain evoked by the yearning of lovers, is implemented in the architecture in the form of mechanical devices allowing water to pour from the roofs as the sound of thunder is emulated. While there is a tendency to consider the Jats as unsophisticated peasants or marauders, clearly they were capable of producing sophisticated architectural creations using cutting-edge technologies.

Immediately after Aurangzeb's death, the countryside to Delhi's northwest also experienced a serious uprising. A man called Banda Bahadur took over a long belt of territory just south of the Himalayan foothills, extending from the Ravi river in the Punjab as far east as the northern Yamuna-Ganga doab (the alluvial lands between the northern Yamuna and Ganges rivers), beginning in late 1709. Described as "an army of innumerable men, like ants and locusts, belonging to the low castes . . . and ready to die," Banda's forces reportedly included as many as 70,000 to 80,000 men at times.[1] They raided wealthy towns as well as caravans traveling through the region and once even entered the outskirts of Lahore. Banda Bahadur collected revenues from the agricultural lands he

---

[1] Khafi Khan, quoted in Irfan Habib, *The Agrarian System of Mughal India, 1556–1707*, second rev. edn. (Delhi: Oxford University Press, 1999), p. 397.

captured, issued his own coins, and called himself the true emperor, in a bid to set up a separate state. For years he eluded first the local Mughal troops and later the imperial army, occasionally taking refuge in the hills where minor rajas sheltered him from capture. The threat Banda Bahadur posed to the empire was finally eliminated when he was executed in Delhi in March 1716.

Allegiance to the Sikh faith was the bond that rallied the men who fought with Banda Bahadur in this uprising, which began right after the death of Guru Gobind Singh in 1708. Gobind Singh was the tenth and last of the Sikh leaders in a direct line of spiritual transmission from the founder of Sikhism, Guru Nanak (1469–1539). Like Kabir, Guru Nanak was part of the Sant tradition, discussed in chapter 4, that rejected institutionalized forms of religion while stressing the equality of all individuals before god. Nanak's god was without form but pervaded by light, to be worshipped through meditation on and repetition of his name. From early on, special emphasis was placed on congregational activities, particularly singing hymns and eating together. Guru Nanak's poems and those of his first four successors were compiled in the *Adi Granth* text, along with poems by Sant and Sufi poets including Kabir. This holy scripture came to hold a central place in the Sikh religion after Guru Gobind Singh's death in the early eighteenth century. Without any more spiritual descendants of Guru Nanak to lead them, the Sikhs in later times turned increasingly to the *Adi Granth*, often called the *Guru Granth Sahib*, for guidance.

The belief in the continuity between Guru Nanak and the later Sikh gurus is revealed in a number of paintings that depict the first guru in an imaginary meeting with them (Figure 9.5). This example from the late eighteenth century shows Guru Nanak, dressed here in the patchwork robes of a mystic saint, indicating his piety, with his nine spiritual successors and a musician who is identified in the painting as Guru Nanak's Muslim companion, the musician Mardana. Nanak, spiritually inclined since his childhood, was educated in both Hindu and Muslim schools and had acquaintances belonging to both religions. He was influenced by Muslim teachings as well as Hindu ones, while simultaneously rejecting both religions as practiced in his day.

An accepting attitude toward Islam had long been customary among Sikhs, but during the seventeenth century they frequently came into conflict with the Mughal state. Although religious tension may have been a factor in the empire's antagonism, the main reason for its repeated attempts to suppress Sikh leaders was their growing secular power. The religion had gained considerable popularity by this time, and the Sikh gurus wielded much local influence and wealth, as well as armed support.

Figure 9.5 Paintings such as this showing imaginary meetings between Guru Nanak and the later nine gurus were popular with the Sikh devout.

On more than one occasion they supported a contender for the Mughal throne who was unsuccessful, leading to retaliation from the next emperor. For example, Jahangir executed the fifth guru Arjun Dev in 1606 for his support of Jahangir's son, Khusrau, rather than Jahangir. Violent opposition to the imperial state and hostile attitudes toward Muslims became more widespread between 1675 and 1708, the period when Gobind Singh was the Sikh guru. He was the most militant of the gurus, engaging in numerous battles himself and advocating the use of force on the part of his followers.

In 1699, Gobind Singh founded a new order, the Khalsa, which reflected the militaristic orientation the religion had taken under his leadership. Male initiates into the Khalsa order adopted the surname Singh, meaning lion, a royal symbol. They were physically differentiated from the general populace by five emblems – a dagger, bracelet, comb, soldier's undershorts, and unshorn hair on the head and face – that had strong martial nuances. The distinct Sikh identity offered by the Khalsa attracted more and more people into its fold over the course of the eighteenth century, so much so that the Khalsa is now almost synonymous with Sikhism.

Many people who considered themselves followers of Guru Nanak did not join the Khalsa, however. Notable among them was a large segment of the Khatri community to which all ten of the Sikh gurus had belonged, along with most of their fifteenth- and sixteenth-century adherents. Khatris were a high-caste group based mainly in urban centers, where they made their living as shop-keepers, traders, moneylenders, clerks, and administrators. Over time people from other backgrounds were attracted to the Sikh religion, lessening the Khatri role in it. First were the Jats, who became Sikhs in large numbers during the seventeenth century; later on, Arora merchants, various untouchable groups, and artisan-craftspeople also joined the religion in smaller numbers.

The Jats are a striking example of how new communities and new identities were arising throughout the centuries covered in this book. Jat is a broad label applied to diverse peoples who were originally pastoralists in the lower Indus region of Sind. Over time they migrated northward into the Punjab, bringing their herding lifestyle with them. Those Jats who moved into the more fertile localities of the Punjab, in its central and eastern portions, slowly took up agriculture. Facilitating the spread of agriculture in this semi-arid region was the introduction of the Persian wheel, a device powered by draught animals that drew up water from wells. By the sixteenth century, Punjabi Jats were known as peasant villagers, and some were among the land-controlling local notables of the area. In the western Punjab and other localities where settled agriculture was not productive, many Jats continued to herd animals.

The Jats also provide an important insight into how religious identities evolved during the precolonial era. Before they settled in the Punjab and other northern regions, the pastoralist Jats had had little exposure to any of the mainstream religions. Only after they became more integrated into the agrarian world did the Jats slowly adopt the dominant religion of the people in whose midst they dwelt. The affiliation of the Jats varied depending on their location: Jats living between Delhi and Agra were primarily Hindu, those in the eastern Punjab were mainly Sikh, and those of the western Punjab were Muslim. This division among Jats reflects the relative strengths of the three religions in the different regions where they settled. Similar processes of gradual incorporation into the mainstream culture were occurring elsewhere in less developed areas of the subcontinent, adding considerably to the social dynamism and religious diversity of its regional societies.

Jats were the largest component in the new Khalsa Sikh order, and many of them joined Banda Bahadur's rebellion. The disorder in the Punjab region did not subside with Banda's execution, for some of his former followers fled to the hills while others remained in the plains and continued to harass Mughal officials and travelers on the main roads. Small pockets of territory in the central and eastern Punjab gradually came into the hands of the leaders of separate Khalsa warbands. The various Khalsa chiefs became the rulers of the Punjab in the aftermath of the 1761 Battle of Panipat, in which the Afghans finally put a stop to the advance of Maratha power in north India. In the early nineteenth century, a single Sikh state was finally formed by the famous Ranjit Singh (1780–1839). Thus, the political aspirations of the Sikhs of the Punjab and the Hindu Jats of the Delhi–Agra region both eventually found expression in the formation of new states.

The bulk of the men in the Sikh and Jat armies were peasants who owned small amounts of land, and so these uprisings have often been characterized as peasant rebellions. Several noted historians, including Irfan Habib, believe that the condition of the peasantry worsened under Mughal rule. In Habib's view, the greater efficiency of the Mughal fiscal system made it possible for the state to extract agrarian revenues from cultivators at ruinously high levels. The situation was made worse by the practice of frequently transferring jagir revenue assignments, since there was no incentive for Mughal nobles to protect peasants or promote long-term agricultural development in any given locality if their association with it was to last for only a few short years. The Sikh and Jat peasant uprisings are attributed by Habib to this callous disregard of the lower classes, who could no longer endure their economic oppression. Strong support for Habib's position comes from European travelers to Mughal India, who repeatedly comment on the abject poverty of the countryside.

More recently, some scholars have suggested that Indian peasants on the whole became more prosperous during the Mughal heyday, although within the peasant ranks greater differences in income developed between those at the top and bottom. Increased expectations for future prosperity coupled with the economic means to rebel culminated, in this school of thought, in a wave of rural uprisings during the late seventeenth and early eighteenth centuries. Muzaffar Alam and others also question the characterization of these uprisings as peasant rebellions because the rebel leaders were men who occupied positions of local power. They were known as zamindars in Mughal times, a broad label that encompassed a wide range of intermediaries between the peasant cultivator and the imperial state. Zamindars typically had the right to retain a certain fraction of the revenues in the localities over which they held sway. Some of them were mighty hereditary chiefs or princes, like the Rajput lineages of Mewar or Amber, who were independent for all practical purposes within their ancestral territories. Other, much less powerful, zamindars held authority over just one or a handful of villages. They may have attained that status through descent from the original founder of the village, through conquest, or by purchasing the position from a previous holder. The zamindars who led the Sikh and Jat uprisings were of this latter, smaller, type.

The Mughals never, even at the height of their power, fully controlled the zamindar class. The foremost among them were co-opted into the mansabdar system. The Rajput chiefs, for instance Raja Man Singh discussed in chapter 5, were given watan jagirs or homeland territories in addition to the normal type of jagirs, in recognition of the power they wielded in their home regions. The imperial center was able, by this means, to secure the loyalty and military services of the Rajput chiefs as well as their kinsmen, retainers, and dependent clients. No such effort was made to incorporate the less powerful zamindars, whose writ ran only over a small locality. Instead, they were typically held responsible for the collection of tax revenues in their village or villages, which would be transmitted to provincial Mughal officials and then redistributed either to the imperial court or to those mansabdars who held jagirs in the area. Military force was sometimes needed at the provincial level to make zamindars comply with state revenue demands, but the state apparatus never penetrated individual villages or established direct ties with the peasantry. All relations with peasant-cultivators were conducted through this intermediary layer of zamindars.

Petty zamindars had intimate knowledge of local conditions and close ties with the local peasants, to whom they might even be distantly related. Because of their position, they often already had a small band of armed troops and could easily raise more; they also fortified their own dwellings when possible. Without the leadership of this class of rural gentry, it is unlikely that armed resistance by peasants could have spread as far or lasted as long as it did with the Sikhs and Jats. Zamindars may have spearheaded the campaigns of resistance against the state on some occasions, while at other times they may have joined an insurrection after it had already been initiated. In either case, it was zamindars who mainly benefited from local uprisings against state authority, rather than the peasants who fought for or with them. Thus, the primary outcome of both the Sikh and Jat rebellions was that zamindars from these communities increased the amount of territory under their control. The more successful among them even rose to the status of minor kings, as we saw with the Jat ruler Badan Singh of Bharatpur.

The Deccan also had a rural gentry similar to the zamindars of north India. In the Maratha territory, they were known by titles such as deshmukh or patil, depending on the number of villages they controlled. Shivaji, discussed in chapter 8, came from a newly ascendant deshmukh family and enjoyed the support of many of the petty gentry: the smaller deshmukh families as well as village headmen and other minor office holders. In his rise to power, Shivaji fought against the large, elite deshmukh families of the western Deccan, who had long-established privileges granted by the Bijapur or Ahmadnagar Sultanates. The Maratha movement initiated by Shivaji was therefore a struggle not only against the Deccan Sultanates and the Mughal empire, but also against the entrenched local power structure, which included a number of aristocratic Maratha clans.

Indeed, zamindars and their equivalents were rising up to oppose state demands all over the empire from the late seventeenth century onward. These men, whose power originated in local rights and authority rather than from any privileges granted by the empire, sought to cast off the mantle of the imperial state imposed on them from the top. In their bid for greater power, zamindars recruited support from among the peasantry of their localities. The Sikh, Jat, and Maratha gentry were particularly effective in mobilizing large numbers of men because of their close ties to them and to each other. Their communities were relatively new, lacked rigid class boundaries, consisted largely of upwardly mobile peasant-warriors, and possessed a strong sense of identity. When bonds between the zamindars and peasants were weaker or when the zamindars of an area had no incentive to work together, their resistance to higher authority resulted in only localized unrest. Rulers of the successful new states that splintered off from the empire were therefore able to reassert control over the unruly minor gentry in their regions. The general trend is nonetheless clear: everywhere, as the grip of empire loosened, locally based interests tried to overthrow the existing power structure for their own benefit. The disintegration of the Mughal empire was brought about not only by the disaffection of its nobility at the center but also through widespread incidents of defiance or rebellion at the local level.

Transformations of the Mughal economy

At the height of empire in the seventeenth century, the use of money, the cultivation of commercial crops, and the production of manufactured goods had all become more widespread. The intensification of monetization and commercialization meant that even peasants were now enmeshed in economic relationships that extended considerably beyond their villages. Those who held political power, from the Mughal nobility of the great cities to the petty gentry of the countryside, also became more dependent on merchants to transform the agrarian riches they controlled into the cash or credit they needed to sustain their lifestyles. Commercial activity was not only intruding deeper and deeper into local agrarian economies, it was also operating in more expansive networks across the subcontinent as the Mughal empire grew in size. Cash and credit, a wide range of goods, and even people circulated on a much larger scale during the seventeenth century than in earlier times. As a consequence, all kinds of merchants – the small village moneylender, the urban shopkeeper, the long-distance trader, and the merchant-banker – flourished.

Growing monetization and the expansion of economic networks were partly an outcome of the needs of the Mughal state. Revenues extracted from the hinterland, typically in the form of cash, had to be dispatched to the capital, while funds for military campaigns or specialized goods had to be sent out to the provinces. This process could be cumbersome, as in the early seventeenth century when Bengal's revenues were physically transported to the imperial heartland in a convoy of bullock-carts. A better means of remitting money from one place to another was soon developed, the *hundi* or bill of exchange. The hundi was a note from one banker to another, instructing him to issue a specified amount of money to the person who delivered it. Large bankers at major urban centers like Surat, in Gujarat, could readily issue hundis for large amounts to be paid out in Agra or elsewhere in the imperial heartland.

The relative ease of travel and exchange over long distances also stimulated the expansion of economic networks in the seventeenth century. Even bulky raw materials and foodstuffs were circulated from one end

Figure 9.6 The serai built by Daud Khan in the mid seventeenth century in eastern India provided housing and security for merchants and travelers.

of the empire to another. Rice, sugar, and oil from Bengal, for instance, were sent inland along the Ganges river to Agra and also down the eastern coast to the Coromandel. In its turn, Bengal imported large quantities of salt from Rajasthan. Transport costs must have been quite low, for artisans in certain areas came to depend largely on supplies from distant regions. Bengal was the source of most of the raw silk used by Gujarat's important silk textile industry, while Coromandel weavers relied heavily on raw cotton from the western Deccan. High-end luxury items like precious stones and finely worked metal ware were widely coveted and distributed.

People too had to travel to far-off places to procure goods or clinch business deals and needed safe accommodations while away from their homes. A large city like Agra had as many as sixty resthouses or serais for travelers, according to Jean Thevenot, who visited it in the mid seventeenth century. The one illustrated here was built between 1659 and 1664 by Daud Khan Quraishi while he served as the Mughal governor of Bihar (Figure 9.6). It is located in a town named Daudnagar, after Daud Khan, located not far from the city of Aurangabad on the Son river. Daud Khan had been successful in finally suppressing a local zamindar whose family had long been a thorn in Mughal authority and built this serai in celebration of the fact. Today only the arched entrance gates remain, but originally the entire complex was protected by exterior walls whose gates were locked at night. Serais were usually provided with a place of religious worship, a mosque in this instance, and cells in the perimeter walls served as the equivalent of hotel rooms. The large open courtyard could be used for animals and goods in transit. Even into the late nineteenth century many of these serais still functioned. They dotted the Indian highways and were built at a distance of a day's travel from one another.

The two linchpins of the extensive markets in finance and commodities were the cities of Agra and Surat. Goods from all over north India were transported to Agra: items like the high-quality indigo of nearby Bayana, or saffron from Kashmir far to the north, or fine muslin cloth from Bengal to the east. These commodities were distributed from Agra into the hinterland or sent westward to Lahore and southward to Surat. Surat was the main maritime outlet for goods from the imperial heartland that would be shipped out to foreign destinations or along the coasts of the subcontinent. This port also became the hub of India's financial markets because the large volume of international trade that flowed through its port brought in vast quantities of bullion.

The complex economic networks that bound the subcontinent together during the height of the Mughal empire could thrive only when there was relative security on the major arteries through which goods and people circulated. As we have seen, conditions in the imperial heartland were rapidly deteriorating in the early decades of the eighteenth century. The situation was worsened by the invading armies of Nadir Shah and Ahmad Shah Abdali, which wreaked havoc as they fought their way from Afghanistan to Delhi in the 1730s and 1750s, respectively. More and more land was lost to the effective control of the empire, either because of the defection of former nobles or through the appropriation of local power by zamindars and other rural gentry. Maratha armies based in central and western India also encroached increasingly on the empire's territory (see Map 8.1). Within the short span of a half century or so, the fabric of empire unraveled, and new, shifting configurations of power arose in many regions.

What effect did the political decentralization of the eighteenth century have on the Indian economy? For many years, historians believed that the economic benefits arising from political unification vanished along with the empire. Peaceful travel and trade became difficult, local economies were disrupted by recurrent warfare, and the misery of the common people deepened. Eighteenth-century India has been considered an era of political anarchy and economic recession, a kind of Dark Age ushered in by the collapse of the Mughal empire. The notion of an economic breakdown accompanying political disorder was promoted by the East India Company, which justified its growing involvement in internal Indian affairs during the late eighteenth century on these grounds. In the past two decades, however, several historians have challenged the assumption that imperial decline led to a weakening of the Indian economy. C. A. Bayly, for example, suggests that the devolution of imperial political and economic power to smaller domains was a largely positive phenomenon, resulting in long-term growth and stability in several regions of the subcontinent. Others believe the Mughal state's impact on local economies has been overstated and point to the encroachment of the European trading companies as a more significant development for the economy than the collapse of empire.

A closer look at the economic picture reveals considerable variation from region to region. The areas that suffered most from the decline of Mughal power were the former hubs of the diffuse, but closely intermeshed, imperial economy. The Agra–Delhi corridor was the first to be affected, due to the Jat insurrection. By 1690, large numbers of merchants and weavers had fled Agra for safer surroundings, and a Dutch trader traveling to Agra needed 300 guards for his protection. Travel between Agra and Surat became hazardous in the early eighteenth century, as internal struggles for power broke out at court after Aurangzeb's death, the Sikhs of the Punjab revolted, and Maratha power grew in western and central India. Dutch traders traveling from Agra to Surat in the entourage of the Surat governor's son reported repeated attacks by peasant-bandit armies as large as 5,000 men. As a result, Surat bankers refused to issue hundis for Agra, causing the Dutch trading company to close its trading post there in 1716. The severing of the road link to Agra and the imperial heartland led to a permanent decrease in trading activity at Surat. The number of ships based there dropped sharply and many merchants moved to other parts of India, especially Bengal.

The Punjab, one of the wealthiest provinces of Mughal India, was also badly affected by the events of the early eighteenth century. Much of the Punjab's prosperity had come from the vigorous trade with Central Asia, Afghanistan, and Iran along the grand highway that ran from the Gangetic region through Agra to Delhi. From Lahore, the Punjab's main city, one trade route went to Qandahar and on to Isfahan, the commercial center of Iran. An estimated 20,000 to 25,000 camel loads had traversed the Lahore–Isfahan corridor yearly in the early seventeenth century. Another route ran from Lahore to Kabul and then into Central Asia. Horses were the chief item imported from the west, while various textiles were the primary export. Some of these textiles were produced within the Punjab, one of the four main regions in India manufacturing cotton goods for export along with Gujarat, the Coromandel coast, and Bengal. The disintegration of Iran's Safavid empire (1501–1722) and the growing strength of Afghan tribes also had a detrimental impact on Surat, whose major export markets by 1700 were in the Middle East.

Other regions of India that had not been as central to the imperial networks of exchange had a different experience in the eighteenth century. The Maratha homeland in the western Deccan, now under the direct control of the Brahmin peshwas, witnessed an expansion of agricultural cultivation. Agriculture was extended in eastern Rajasthan as well, where the leadership of the Kachhwaha Rajput rulers led to improving economic conditions. When Sawai Jai Singh (r. 1700–43) decided to shift his capital from Amber to Jaipur, 10 kilometers to the south, he took active measures to ensure the new city's economic success. He invited prominent merchant families from various localities, both within and outside the modern state of Rajasthan, to migrate to Jaipur and gave them large plots of land upon which to build their houses. The elegant mansion of the wealthy Natani family, one of the first to migrate to Jaipur, was located close to the palace and had a temple attached to it that Sawai Jai Singh often visited. Today this enormous house, based loosely on Mughal-style mansions, is divided into a girls' school and a police station (see Figure 8.7).

The economic picture is hence quite mixed. The waning of imperial power led to an economic recession lasting well into the eighteenth century in the Delhi–Agra region, the Punjab, and Gujarat. Whether regions outside the imperial system like the far south suffered any economic repercussions is unclear; nor is there a consensus on economic conditions in the central Gangetic valley or eastern Deccan. In areas like the western Deccan or eastern Rajasthan, the efforts of the new rulers actually stimulated economic growth. Bengal, a province that was already prosperous in the second half of the seventeenth century, continued to experience a boom in the early eighteenth century, for reasons we will explore shortly.

In some respects, the various regions of the subcontinent were now developing along differing trajectories, depending on local conditions. Regional economies had become so intertwined during the seventeenth century, however, that they could not fully prosper without a certain degree of long-distance trade and exchange. Some of the old routes had diminished in importance, but other routes soon supplanted them, in a reorientation of commerce that was increasingly centered on the port cities of the East India Company rather than the old sites of Mughal power. As a series of smaller states arose in the place of the large, unified Mughal empire over the course of the eighteenth century, the big Hindu

and Jain merchant firms became even more indispensable. Regional political elites had to rely on these merchant-bankers with branches in several
parts of India, because only they had the resources to conduct major
commercial transactions across regional boundaries. Without their support, the regional states of the eighteenth century could not survive, and
hence the large merchant houses came to possess considerable political
influence in the new, post-imperial era.

Another important change contributing to the blurring of commerce
and politics was the growth of revenue farming, the selling of rights to collect revenues to the highest bidder. In the past, taxes on agricultural produce had typically been gathered and transmitted by officials appointed
by the Mughal state, which had a substantial bureaucratic apparatus pre-
cisely for that purpose. The states that arose in the aftermath of Mughal
decline instead often contracted the collection of agrarian revenues to
individuals who kept for themselves whatever surplus they could gather
over and above the amount promised to the state. The authority to collect other taxes like transit duties was also sold to such entrepreneurial
revenue-farmers, as were state monopolies in the trade of certain goods.
Meanwhile, a variety of statuses and privileges that had in the past been
obtained mainly through membership in a local community, such as the
positions of village headman or zamindar, were also becoming commod-
ified, that is, available for sale, purchase, lease, or mortgage. Wealthy
merchants sometimes purchased agrarian rights or revenue farms, but
more typically advanced money to those who did.

The weakening of the Mughal imperial state, on the one hand, and
the spreading commercialization of the economy, on the other, therefore led to the rise of people who occupied an intermediate status in
society between the peasantry and the great nobility. Zamindars appropriated lands and income that had formerly been possessed by the state,
revenue-farmers took the place of state officials and controlled the flow
of revenue from the localities to regional political centers, and the services of merchant-traders became vital to all sectors of society. All three
groups – zamindars, revenue-farmers, and merchant-traders – wished to
enlarge their own wealth and power at the expense of the imperial officials
and local kings. Their interests could sometimes clash but at other times
could coincide when confronted by regional rulers attempting to consolidate central power. The support of large merchant-banking firms proved
especially vital to the rise to power of the English East India Company,
who shared their commercial interests and perspectives. We now turn to
a detailed look at Bengal's flourishing economy and the events that led to
the dominance of the English there.

Bengal: India's agrarian and commercial frontier

Bengal's prosperity ultimately derived from its phenomenal agricultural productivity. During the seventeenth century, its rice, sugar, and oil fed the needs not only of distant regions within the empire but even of far-off lands in Southeast Asia and the Middle East. The price of commodities was so low in Bengal that virtually every foreign visitor remarked on the fact. "At Hugli may be procured beeswax, pepper, civet, rice, butter, oil and wheat; all at about half the price of other places," wrote an East India Company official in 1650.[2] With food so cheap, labor costs remained low in Bengal, and its manufactured goods were competitively priced relative to other areas. Even transportation was inexpensive within Bengal, because boats could easily haul goods along the many waterways that crisscrossed the region.

Why was Bengal so remarkably productive? Much of lower Bengal was a vast delta or floodplain formed by the many streams that flowed down out of the massive Ganges and Brahmaputra river systems. Highly fertile soil was continually deposited by these streams, which were, in effect, creating productive, new land at an astonishingly rapid rate. As layers of silt laid down by the waters built up, riverbeds would overflow and new channels were carved through which the waters would run in future years. In this dynamic manner, the delta was steadily extended as the rivers continued to shift their courses over the centuries. The older centers of settlement in Bengal had all been in the northwest, and most of the waters of the Ganges had flowed into the Bhagirathi and Hugli rivers in the western end of the delta, in what is today the West Bengal state of India. But the main flow of the Ganges gradually migrated toward the southeast, and by the late sixteenth century it was entering into the Padma river in the eastern delta, in modern Bangladesh, where the Brahmaputra also contributed its waters and its silt. The eastern delta's rich soil, abundant rainfall, and ample water supplies provided ideal conditions for the cultivation of rice and other crops.

The sixteenth and seventeenth centuries witnessed a tremendous expansion of agriculture in eastern Bengal. It was a land full of jungles and swamps whose sparse population had previously mainly been fisherfolk and hunter-gatherers. Colonists, mostly Muslims, had gradually been arriving from the long-settled regions to the west, and their numbers swelled after Bengal was incorporated into the Mughal empire. As the pioneering colonists cleared the eastern Bengal wilderness and turned it

---

[2] Quoted in Habib, *Agrarian System*, p. 78, n. 52.

into cultivated land, settlements of local people coalesced around them. These local people were introduced to agriculture at the same time that they were introduced to their first world religion, Islam. Agriculture and Islam thus came to be associated along Bengal's agrarian frontier, and a large Muslim peasant community emerged in what is now Bangladesh, as described by Richard M. Eaton. Just as in the western Punjab, in modern Pakistan, the spread of Islam among the common folk of eastern Bengal was a relatively late development. And in both cases it accompanied the incorporation of local communities who were originally not cultivators into an expanding agrarian civilization.

The integration of Bengal into the Mughal empire was a major stimulus to the growth of commerce, just as it was to the growth of agriculture. Bengal was not quickly subjugated, however, for its distance from the capital, its marshy and wet terrain unsuited for cavalry warfare, and its many entrenched local lords all slowed the advance of Mughal dominion. The Mughals began the process of conquest in 1574, with the capture of the Bengal Sultanate's capital in the northwestern corner of the region, at roughly the same time that the merging of the Ganges and Padma rivers opened up a direct internal water route from the imperial heartland to eastern Bengal. In 1610, the Mughals moved their local base to Dhaka, and soon thereafter the eastern delta was finally subdued. Bengal's richest agrarian zone was now easily accessible, and its products were carried away in increasing quantities to supply the great metropolises of the empire.

Shortly after the final pacification of Bengal, the Mughal ruling elite began to invest heavily in the trade of what was essentially their new colony. Involvement in commerce started at the very highest levels, among the imperial princes and governors posted to the province, but a range of other Mughal officials also participated. Although high-ranking Mughal nobles sometimes tried to corner the market in certain goods or claim precedence in the buying of imports, overall their interest in Bengal's trade was a positive factor. The safety of the ports and waterways was made a high official priority, leading to a crackdown on the rampant piracy of the Bay of Bengal. It also led to the infusion of substantial capital resources into local enterprises and infrastructure. As one example, when Muhammad Sayyid Ardistani, formerly Mir Jumla of the Golkonda kingdom, joined the Mughal nobility in the mid 1650s, he brought his own fleet of over ten ships with him to Bengal along with his personal fortune. The majority of the large ocean-going ships in Bengal during the seventeenth century were in fact owned by Mughal nobility and officials.

By 1690, the same year that Calcutta was founded, the Mughal elite had largely withdrawn from Bengal's commerce. Local shipping declined as a consequence, along with the largely Muslim community of merchants who had engaged in overseas trade. Mounting problems within the empire and disruptions in the internal circulation of goods did not diminish Bengal's prosperity, however. Its trade networks had already begun to orient themselves more toward the sea than toward the internal waterways, and the entrepreneurial role formerly occupied by the Mughal elite and its Muslim merchant associates was increasingly filled by the European trading companies. They worked in conjunction with the numerous Jain and Hindu mercantile families who had migrated to Bengal in the Mughal heyday, mainly from Gujarat and Rajasthan. These Indian merchants had supplied the ports with export goods, purchased imported commodities on a wholesale basis, and acted as bankers for the Mughal elite; they continued to do so for the Europeans.

The European trading companies had been active in Bengal for some decades, but earlier in the seventeenth century it was less important to them than the Gujarat and Coromandel regions. Bengal did not produce the spices that Europeans coveted nor the cheaper variety of textiles that were exported in bulk to Southeast Asia, the Middle East, and Africa. Aside from various foodstuffs and raw materials, Bengal's main export was expensive cloth, both cotton and silk, aimed at the high end of the market. Unlike the Coromandel coast where the expertise was in the dying of textiles, Bengal was known for its high-quality weaving that resulted in thin, diaphanous muslins and other fine fabrics. Only after European interest in Indian textiles was aroused, and an enormous new market created, did Bengal become critical to the commerce of the foreign trading companies. Their growing dependence on Bengal's textiles was spurred by recurrent shortages of supply in the Coromandel as well as rising costs there. The Dutch were the first to turn to Bengal as the primary source of textiles for Europe. While the VOC had purchased only slightly over a quarter of the cloth destined for Europe from Bengal in 1675, by 1700 Bengal provided three-quarters of its textile exports to Europe. The English were slower to shift their focus from the Coromandel, but almost half of the Indian cloth they sent to Europe came from Bengal by 1710 and by the mid eighteenth century most of it did.

One reason the English ultimately surpassed the Dutch in Bengal was the special concession they received from the Mughal emperor Farrukhsiyar in 1717. According to imperial decree, the EIC was exempt from all customs and transit duties in return for an annual fee of 3,000 rupees; meanwhile, the Dutch VOC was paying roughly forty times as much on customs duties. English employees of the EIC claimed the same right to exemption of duties on their private trade, and more ships belonging to them came to be based in Calcutta, rising from about ten ships in the first decade of the 1700s to at least fifty in the 1750s. Since the English private traders of Calcutta could not ship goods to Europe because that was a monopoly of the Company, they concentrated instead on commerce to the Malabar coast, Surat, and the Persian Gulf. Formerly, many of the ships sailing back and forth from Bengal to Surat, the most important destination of the Calcutta fleet, had been owned by wealthy Muslim merchants of Gujarat. The Gujarat ships dwindled rapidly, and, by the mid eighteenth century, English private traders thoroughly dominated the Bengal–Gujarat maritime route. In the process, Hugli port was eclipsed by Calcutta, which reached a population of about 120,000 in 1750.

The rise of private English shipping in the eighteenth century thus led to the waning of Indian shipping between the Bay of Bengal and the Arabian Sea, just as it did on the route from the Coromandel coast to Southeast Asia. Indian long-distance merchants were more and more dependent on the English in order to export and import goods overseas. English private traders also began intruding into the substantial internal trade in commodities, not only in other localities within Bengal like Dhaka, but as far up-country as Patna. Although the understanding was that the English should confine their activities to purchasing goods for export or disposing of imported items, in fact they also dealt in bulk commodities for domestic consumption such as salt and grain. The English further abused the terms of agreement by extending their own tax-exempt status to the goods of favored Indian merchants. By 1750, the East India Company had made considerable inroads into Bengal's economy and had extensive dealings with local merchants and bankers.

The on-going prosperity of Bengal, and the growth of European commercial activities there, was facilitated by its political stability. Under the excellent stewardship of Murshid Quli Khan in the early eighteenth century, Bengal's system of revenue collection was strengthened, and a greater degree of political centralization was instituted at the regional level. Although Murshid Quli Khan's reforms led to a sharp reduction in the overall number of zamindars, there was a corresponding growth in the size and power of several large zamindars. Fifteen zamindar families like those based at Rajshahi, Nadia, and Burdwan (all located strategically on major rivers) accounted for almost half of the region's revenues in 1727. Both Murshid Quli Khan and his successor, Shuja Khan (r. 1727–39), continued to send about 10 million rupees annually to Delhi, a massive tribute that served to mask the reality of Bengal's self-governance. Assisting the rulers of Bengal in collecting and remitting these huge sums was the Jagat Seth banking house. Jagat Seth, meaning "merchant of the world," was a title conferred on the head of the family by a Mughal emperor, indicating the favor he had curried at the imperial court. The Jagat Seth firm had a monopoly over the minting of coins in Bengal and functioned in essence as the banking arm of the regional government. Only with the cooperation of the large zamindars and banking firms could the Bengal state run smoothly.

Things remained largely stable under Alivardi Khan, who ruled from 1740 to 1756, although Maratha armies from central India made several destructive campaigns into western Bengal. The expense of fighting the Marathas caused Alivardi Khan to demand additional tribute from the major zamindars, the wealthy merchant-bankers, and the European trading companies. His successor, Siraj al-Daula, who was only nineteen when he became ruler in 1756, moved quickly to strengthen his power. He succeeded only in alienating important interests in his realm. Among them was the powerful Jagat Seth, whom Siraj al-Daula struck after being refused an exorbitant tribute of 30 million rupees. When Siraj al-Daula heard that the EIC was improving its fortifications at Fort William in Calcutta, he took that as a threat to his sovereignty and ordered the successful capture of the fort. The East India Company, the Jagat Seth and other banking families, important officials in the regional administration whom he replaced with his own men, and several leading zamindars were now among Siraj al-Daula's many enemies.

Even a decade or two earlier, the East India Company might have needed a long time to regroup and take back their critical base at Calcutta. But the English and French trading companies had been at war with each other for some years in south India, and so a British fleet with British soldiers had been sent out to Madras in order to aid the East India Company there. This British force now sailed from Madras to Bengal and soon retook Calcutta. It was commanded by Robert Clive, who had achieved distinction in the south Indian wars between the English and French traders.

The earlier conflict in south India had other significant repercussions for what was to transpire in Bengal, because it had revealed the many benefits that Europeans could gain through military intervention into internal Indian political disputes. Between 1746 and 1754, the French and English trading companies in south India not only fought each other, but they also allied themselves with competing contenders to the thrones of Hyderabad in the eastern Deccan and Arcot in the Coromandel. In return for their military assistance and political support, both European companies received large grants of revenue rights, while some of their employees profited through individual investments, loans, or the purchase of revenue farms from the rivals in these succession disputes. Small forces of several hundred European foot-soldiers, assisted by contingents of Indian artillerymen whom they had trained, easily won victory over larger indigenous armies in a series of battles during the course of this south Indian conflict. Indian armies still relied primarily on cavalry, which could not use the improved weaponry of the eighteenth century effectively, whereas European infantry forces were now extensively drilled in fighting in formation using firearms and light field artillery. The demonstration of European military superiority during the south Indian wars made powerful Indians eager to enlist their help, and the East India Company was more than willing to do so.

Back in Bengal, the East India Company therefore joined the Jagat Seth banking family and others in a plot to get rid of Siraj al-Daula. In the famous Battle of Plassey, fought in June 1757, few of Siraj al-Daula's soldiers were willing to engage the British troops, and he was killed soon afterward. One of Siraj al-Daula's generals, who was in on the plot and whose contingent had stood on the sidelines during the battle, became the new ruler of Bengal. But the English had realized that the riches of Bengal were now readily available to them and pressed hard for cash payments, trading monopolies, and zamindar rights. They put a second, even more amenable, puppet ruler in place in 1760, who also proved unsatisfactory to the East India Company. In 1764, the Company won a resounding victory against an army sent by the king of Awadh and the Mughal emperor in support of this ruler of Bengal. The East India Company had, in just a few short years, become the dominant political player within Bengal, with the backing of influential mercantile and zamindar interests operating in an environment where power was already heavily commercialized.

Individual Englishmen employed by the Company did very well for themselves in this era, quickly and rapaciously amassing princely sums that soon came to seem scandalous even to their countrymen back in England. Their luxurious lifestyles emulated that of local lords, so much so that former Company officials who returned to England with riches were dubbed nabobs, after the Indo-Islamic term *nawab* designating a deputy or provincial ruler. In this example of a Company painting, that is, a painting commissioned by a British patron from an Indian artist, we see an East India Company official relaxing with a hookah and attended by his servants, behaving very much like an Indian gentleman might at home (Figure 9.7). The man portrayed in this watercolor, made in Bengal between 1760 and 1764 by Dip Chand, is most probably William Fullerton, a surgeon in the Company's service who was mayor of Calcutta in 1757.

How was it possible for the English to attain this position of power by the mid eighteenth century, when just eighty years earlier they could so

Figure 9.7 William Fullerton joined the East India Company in 1744 and assumed a lifestyle typical of the Indian elite, including the smoking of the hookah.

easily be vanquished by the Mughals, even on the seas where they were strongest? An obvious answer lies in the disintegration of the Mughal empire, resulting in the emergence of numerous smaller states in its place. Yet that explanation does not suffice, for at least several of these new states were strong enough, had they wished, to oust the East India Company from their realms. The East India Company, and the other European traders, represented a valuable internal source of income to the rulers of regional states which they wanted to retain. The Europeans by this time also controlled almost all of the long-distance overseas shipping, which had largely superseded the overland trade routes, and so were the only significant conduit through which items like bullion or textiles could enter or leave India. Over the hundred plus years that the English in particular had been operating within India, they had formed numerous associations with Indian merchants that were intensified by the complexity of procuring textiles. The economic opportunities provided by working with European trading companies aligned Indian mercantile interests with their own and could, as we have just seen in the case of Bengal, give these Europeans a decisive advantage in any confrontation with an Indian state.

The fact that the lines between political and commercial power had become so indistinct by this time also facilitated the entry of the East India Company, essentially a business enterprise, into the Indian political arena. Moreover, the EIC could call upon its nation's resources for assistance when necessary; at several critical moments both before and after the Battle of Plassey, Britain supplied military forces and/or money that sustained the Company's rise to power. By the mid 1700s, the superior training methods and firepower of European armies also gave the English a military edge and provided another incentive for Indian political elites to welcome their presence. All these factors account for the East India Company's ability to acquire Bengal and its riches, which launched them on the path that would lead to dominion over all of India.

Epilogue

British success at the Battle of Plassey in 1757 marked a decisive upswing in the East India Company's fortunes, for less than a decade later in 1765 the Mughal emperor gave it the official right to collect Bengal's revenues. This was little more than a recognition of the Company's actual position as *de facto* ruler of Bengal; by this time the independent government of Bengal had been rendered toothless. A good deal of Bengal's resources was already entering the coffers of the EIC and its employees; now all of the state's revenues would officially belong to the Company, except for the annual tribute owed to the Mughal emperor in Delhi. The conferment of an official position on the East India Company was primarily a pragmatic means for the imperial court to ensure that it obtained some small share of Bengal's riches. Its symbolic significance was tremendous, however, since it meant that the English were now formally incorporated into the Mughal imperial system. Foreigners and merchants they might be, but now they were also sanctioned participants in the realm of Indian politics.

In practical terms, by 1765 the Mughal state was merely a small regional kingdom among a welter of others. Several Mughal successor states had made cash payments to the imperial dynasty in their first decades of existence, but by this time had ceased to express any loyalty other than in name. Yet none of the new states was strong enough to become the central power that the Mughal empire had been at its height, and so none could command the respect that the Mughals had formerly earned. Despite the dismantlement of its empire, the Mughal court continued to be regarded as the ultimate source of legitimacy in much of eighteenth-century India. The new states also adopted the ceremonial etiquette and cultural practices that were first established under the Mughals. They maintained the custom of giving gifts in the form of jeweled swords and robes of honor, for example, and they felt compelled to build elaborate cities, palaces, and gardens in order to express their strength in a tangible manner.

Following their lead, the East India Company continued to pay homage to the symbolic authority of the Mughal dynasty, even decades after 1803 when it replaced the Mughals as the real power in Delhi. Persian, the language of the Mughal court, was retained as the Company's official administrative language until 1835, while coins were struck bearing the image of the Mughal emperor, who remained a respected figurehead until the revolt of 1857–58. Meanwhile, Calcutta, Madras, Delhi, and Bombay grew to be extensive, sophisticated cities with European-style buildings that were, in some cases, more grand than their counterparts in Britain. Certainly the comforts that many of the British in India enjoyed – a life with multiple servants and large open houses with huge gardens – were much more luxurious than what they could have experienced back home.

The legacy of the Mughal empire lived on in the administrative and fiscal practices of the post-imperial age. Its successor states retained Mughal official titles and aspects of the old Mughal bureaucratic structure, military system, and revenue assessment and collection procedures. Even those who had militarily opposed the Mughal empire, such as the Marathas and Sikhs, adopted a number of their characteristic practices, especially in the fiscal sphere. Mughal influence was so pervasive that their Perso-Arabic administrative terminology eventually replaced indigenous equivalents in the far south, where the Mughal imperium had never extended. The East India Company, in the early days after its recognition by the Mughal house as Bengal's official revenue-collector, also preserved some Mughal administrative practices, although its own distinctive systems were instituted later on as the belief escalated that British rule and customs were superior. Considerable portions of the older Mughal judicial system remained in place even after one based on English custom was introduced, in part to avoid political and social repercussions with the Company's Indian subjects.

The pretense of being a Mughal servant and the preservation of Mughal forms could not mask the East India Company's catapulting wealth and power. It used a portion of the Bengal revenues to rapidly expand its military forces. By 1782 the Company had 115,000 men, 90 percent of whom were Indian, stationed in various areas of the subcontinent, and they were soon deployed against the state of Mysore in southern India and some years later against the Marathas in western India. Bengal's revenues also financed the Company's purchases of items intended for export to Europe, and for a quarter century the EIC could dispense with the bullion imports that they had for so long supplied in exchange for Indian goods. The Company even used resources from Bengal, including opium, to pay for its new thirst for Chinese commodities, among which tea reigned supreme. The burgeoning English commerce with China caused a shift in trade toward the eastern seas, after about a century during which the westward routes from India to Europe had been the most important. The dominance of English traders in the Indian Ocean was hence extended to the South China Sea in the late eighteenth century.

Indian merchants, who had originally been their partners and collaborators, were badly affected by the economic supremacy of the English in the late eighteenth century. English intrusion into the South China Sea reduced the few opportunities left for Indian merchant-traders to engage in overseas commerce, after they had already been largely driven out of ship-owning. Within Bengal and adjacent areas in eastern India, the internal trade in commodities had been opened up to the EIC and its private traders after Plassey, and the greed they displayed soon occasioned concern even in England. The Company created trade monopolies for itself in items as lucrative as salt, saltpeter, and opium, while private traders dealt in valuable commodities like raw silk, sugar, and indigo. Once the English had established clear dominance in a certain sector, such as textiles, they began to enforce harsh terms on the Indians who produced and distributed those items in both Bengal and the Coromandel. The poverty of Indian weavers is traced by some scholars to this era of plummeting wages. Some individual merchants continued to prosper from their association with the English, but the scope of activity for Indian merchants had been drastically reduced on the whole.

Both economically and politically, therefore, the Battle of Plassey ushered in a new age of English ascendancy. An increasing number of historians consider the 1820s or 1830s to be the true beginning of the colonial period, on the other hand, for it was only then that fundamental transformations in economic and political structures occurred. By the 1820s, the East India Company had demonstrated its military strength against every potential contender with the exception of the Sikhs far to the northwest; after a century of political decentralization consequent to Mughal decline, power had now been centralized in British hands. In an even more startling shift, India lost its centuries-old position as an exporter of manufactured goods to the rest of the world in the early nineteenth century, and became instead primarily a supplier of raw materials to the British empire. British traders and businesses in India were so prosperous and influential that they no longer required the finances of Indian bankers or the services of Indian agent-brokers, which left Indian capital with few outlets other than moneylending at the local level. Even intermediaries like revenue-farmers were eliminated, and the position of zamindars weakened, when the British made their revenue arrangements directly with peasants in many areas of India. The British also began intervening in non-economic spheres more consciously in the 1820s and 1830s, as they came to see themselves as the stewards of India's progress toward a higher civilizational state.

Throughout all these changes, and even after the last Mughal emperor was exiled to Rangoon and the royal house abolished following the 1857–58 revolt, the Mughal empire continued to retain a lingering hold on the English imaginary. In 1858 all powers formerly held by the East India Company were transferred to the British crown, and Queen Victoria was declared Empress of India in 1876, assuming what was essentially a Mughal title. The leaders of the British Raj, the British government in India after 1858, continually represented themselves as legitimate successors of the great Mughals.

In 1877, a huge celebration known as the Imperial Durbar was organized in recognition of Victoria's new status as Indian empress, and much of it was modeled on Mughal ceremonial, from the riding of magnificently decorated elephants to an assemblage of princes reminiscent of Mughal courtly processions and the gathering of nobles at the imperial court. The British Raj's adaptation of Mughal performative and visual culture was a compelling reminder of their claim as the heirs of Mughal greatness, a message that was further underscored by the holding of the Durbar in Delhi. Even though Calcutta was the capital of the Raj in 1877 and Delhi was no more than a city badly damaged during the events of 1857–58, the British chose the former Mughal capital for their Imperial Durbar, since only that city fully evoked the associations with the magnificent Mughal past that they desired. The British had come a long way within a century, from professing to be the servants of the Mughals to asserting equality with them, but what is most remarkable is the long-lasting shadow the Mughals cast on subsequent rulers of India.

During the second half of the nineteenth century and the early twentieth century, the British decided that an architecture designed by English architects, using elements of older Indian buildings, was appropriate for new British institutions such as museums, post offices, courthouses, and even hotels. It was also used for the schools and houses of Indian princes, who were being trained to behave as English gentlemen. Known as the Indo-Saracenic, this architectural style drew from many of the buildings we have discussed here, especially Mughal architecture and the buildings of the Adil Shahs in Bijapur. Indian painting had much less interest for Europeans, although Mughal art was valued and collected for London's new museums. However, at the turn of the twentieth century, Indian nationalist artists began to evoke older painting styles of the Mughals, and Rajput artists began to assert their own Indian identity.

Ironically, even though the British saw themselves as the legitimate successors to Mughal authority and were happy to employ a Mughal architectural vocabulary in the new Indo-Saracenic style, the general attitude toward Muslims was beginning to shift. This was in part due to the role several Muslim states, notably the Mughals and Nawabs of Awadh, played in the 1857–58 uprising, which led the British to suspect all elite Muslims of disloyalty. This is not to say that the British had earlier been uniformly positive in their view of Indian Muslims. The allegedly cruel and tyrannical character of Indo-Muslim rule, represented as a form of Oriental despotism, had long been a tenet of European writing on India. The belief that the British colonial regime was far more just and principled than those of the Mughals and various sultanate predecessors was what vindicated their wielding of power in a far-off foreign land, in British eyes. Moreover, the EIC and other European traders had for centuries preferred to work with Hindu merchant-financiers rather than Indian Muslim ones, who might have undue political clout or connections. Nonetheless, Islamic culture was familiar and comprehensible to Europeans, compared to the exotic polytheism of Hinduism, and early Company officials had learned the Persian language well before they became conversant with Sanskrit.

During the second half of the nineteenth century, simultaneously with their increasing antipathy toward Indian Muslims, the British conviction that South Asian society was fundamentally divided along religious lines grew stronger. This conviction was not only expressed in British modes of thinking about South Asia's peoples but also in their policies toward them. In the long run, the British thus intensified and solidified the sense of religious difference within the subcontinent, leading Indian nationalists and others in the early twentieth century to cast the Muslims of India's past as similar to the colonial British of their present in being alien invaders and oppressors. By about 1900 the rulers of Vijayanagara, for example, were presented not as kings who promoted a cosmopolitan culture that valued Islamicate traditions, but rather as champions of Hinduism against predatory Muslims. The situation is no better today, as Hindu nationalists refute any contributions Indian Muslims may have made, while their common South Asian heritage is often denied in Pakistan. All of this has served to obscure the rich composite culture of South Asia that we have written about in this text, which started to come into being after 1200 and fully matured during the Mughal era. We stand firm in our own conviction that South Asian society and culture cannot be properly understood without an appreciation of the many interactions and exchanges, some negative but many positive, between Muslim and non-Muslim traditions and peoples. We therefore urge our readers to think about the past in a manner that matches its contemporary attitudes and not read the present into the context of the past.

Biographical notes

ABD AL-RAHIM KHAN-I KHANAN (1556–1626) One of the most important members of the nobility under the emperors Akbar and Jahangir, he was commander of the Mughal army, earning him the title of Khan-i Khanan. An important patron of Persian literature, he owned a renowned library.

ABU AL-FAZL (1551–1602) Akbar's closest advisor, Abu al-Fazl was instrumental in the development of Akbar's concept of state. His two works, *Akbarnama* and *A'in-i Akbari*, contain much information on Akbar's political activities and imperial ideology, as well as on conditions within the empire.

AIBAK (d. 1210) Qutb al-Din Aibak was a military slave of Turkic origin who first served as a general for Muhammad Ghuri and then became governor of the newly acquired Indian territories. Upon Muhammad Ghuri's death in 1206, Aibak declared himself an independent ruler, thereby becoming the first Delhi sultan.

AKBAR (r. 1556–1605) The third and, many think, the most important Mughal emperor, who was responsible for the empire's policies of tolerance.

ALA AL-DIN KHALJI (r. 1296–1316) He was the most powerful and important Muslim ruler of South Asia in the pre-Mughal period. From his base in Delhi, Ala al-Din Khalji was able to extend the Delhi Sultanate's military presence into much of southern and western India. At the same time, he instituted substantive economic and administrative reforms that benefited his subjects and centralized power in his hands.

AURANGZEB (r. 1658–1707) The sixth Mughal emperor, who introduced more conservative policies toward non-Muslims than had previously prevailed in the Mughal state. Aurangzeb also embroiled the empire in a lengthy war in the Deccan that sowed the seeds of Mughal political decline.

BABUR (r. 1526–30) The first Mughal emperor, who was originally from Central Asia and made his successful bid for India from his capital in Afghanistan. He wrote his own memoirs known as the *Baburnama*, detailing his life and adventures.

CHAITANYA (*c.* 1486–1533) A Hindu religious leader who initiated an intensely emotional form of devotionalism to the adolescent form of the god Krishna. His sect focused on the love-play between Krishna and his favorite among the cowherding women, Radha, which was understood as an allegory for the ecstasy of the mutual love between god and the individual soul.

DEVARAYA II (r. 1432–46) Generally considered to be the most important ruler of the first of four dynasties that ruled over the kingdom of Vijayanagara in south

India. Due to the incorporation of Muslim troops and military techniques into his army, the Vijayanagara state controlled both the eastern and western coasts of the peninsula during Devaraya II's reign.

GULBADAN BEGUM (c. 1523–1603) The sister of the second Mughal emperor, Humayun, who wrote a history of her brother's reign known as the *Humayun-nama*. Through her book we gain insight into the daily lives of Mughal court women.

GURU NANAK (1469–1539) A poet-saint who was the founder of the Sikh religion, which stressed a formless god and the equality of all individuals.

IBRAHIM ADIL SHAH (r. 1580–1627) This mystically inclined ruler of the Bijapur Sultanate in the Deccan was renowned for his patronage of art, architecture, and music.

JAGAT SINGH (r. 1628–52): A king (*rana*) of the Rajput Sisodiyas of Mewar who broke his house's treaty with the Mughals by rebuilding the walls of his fort at Chittor. He was also an active patron of art and architecture.

KABIR An important figure who bridged the divide between orthodox Hindu and Muslim traditions, Kabir probably lived in the fifteenth century. His poetry is celebrated even today because it disparages the hypocrisy of organized religion and conventional society.

KRISHNADEVA RAYA (r. 1509–29) Under Krishnadeva Raya, the best-known and most important ruler of Vijayanagara, the kingdom attained its largest size and its greatest degree of centralization. He was also a great patron of temples and literature.

MAHMUD OF GHAZNI (r. 998–1030) A Turkic ruler from Afghanistan who is remembered for his many raids into India, ranging as far east as the Gangetic plain and culminating in the sacking of the Hindu Somanatha temple in 1025–26. Historians disagree as to whether the desire for wealth or religious animosity was Mahmud's main motivation and he is still the subject of much controversy.

MIRA BAI Born among the Mertiyo Rathor Rajputs, Mira Bai married into the Sisodiya royal family of Chittor in the early sixteenth century. Renowned for her devotion to Krishna, she wrote passionate poetry dedicated to this Hindu god whom she considered her true husband. Still widely sung today, the corpus of poems attributed to her has grown over the centuries.

MUHAMMAD QULI QUTB SHAH (r. 1580–1611) An important ruler of the Golkonda Sultanate who was famous for his patronage of Dakani poetry and founded a new capital city, Hyderabad, in the Deccan.

MUHAMMAD TUGHLUQ (r. 1324–51) This Delhi sultan was able to extend the kingdom to the south and even established a second capital, Daulatabad, there. Although the Sultanate reached its maximum extent early in his reign, by the end it was considerably smaller due to rebellions on the part of dissatisfied factions.

MUIN AL-DIN CHISHTI (d. 1236) A mystic-saint who is thought to have introduced the Chishti Sufi order into India from Afghanistan around 1200. His fame grew over time, and he eventually became the patron saint of the Mughal dynasty. His tomb-shrine in Ajmer is perhaps the most important Sufi site in India, and still attracts thousands of devotees annually.

NIZAM AL-DIN AULIYA (d. 1325) An important spiritual descendant of Muin al-Din Chishti. During his life many people from all spheres, royal to humble, sought his counsel; even today his shrine in Delhi is of major importance.

NUR JAHAN (1577–1645) The powerful wife of the fourth Mughal emperor, Jahangir (r. 1605–27), Nur Jahan wielded considerable political authority and essentially assumed the reins of state during Jahangir's later years. She was responsible for the rift that occurred between Jahangir and his son and successor, Shah Jahan.

RAJA MAN SINGH (1550–1614) The highest-ranking noble in the Mughal emperor Akbar's court, Raja Man Singh was a Hindu and also the head of his ancestral Rajput line, the Kachhwahas of Amber. He served as a Mughal governor, most notably of Bihar and Bengal, and was a prolific patron of architecture.

RAJARAJA CHOLA (r. 985–1014) A ruler of the south Indian Chola dynasty, based in modern Tamil Nadu state, whose successful military campaigns, along with those of his son Rajendra Chola, made his kingdom the largest and most powerful state of eleventh-century India. Under his direction and patronage, the Rajarajeshvara temple in Tanjavur, the Chola capital, became the tallest and best-endowed Hindu temple of its day.

RANA KUMBHA (r. 1433–68) Under him, the western Indian kingdom of Mewar became the most powerful in the area. In commemoration of his many victories against neighboring states, both Hindu and Muslim, he built temples and a victory tower at his capital, Chittor, which many today view as an assertion of Hinduism against Islam.

SAWAI JAI SINGH (1688–1743) Like his ancestor, Raja Man Singh, Sawai Jai Singh was both a loyal Mughal officer and the head of the Rajput Kachhwaha princely line. In 1727 he founded the city of Jaipur, based on a grid plan.

SHAIKH AHMAD SIRHINDI (1564–1624) A Sufi leader of the Naqshbandi order whose conservative views on Islam and society influenced the development of Mughal polity long after his death.

SHER SHAH SUR (r. 1538–45) An upstart sultan of Afghan descent who was able to assume authority in much of north India, temporarily ousting the Mughals from power. He is noted for his administrative reforms, many of which were adopted and improved under Akbar.

SHIVAJI BHONSLE (1630–80) A Maratha warrior who, by his use of guerilla warfare, successfully hindered Mughal plans to subdue the western Deccan. His successors and other Maratha chiefs went on to become more powerful than the Mughals in the eighteenth century. Today, many admire Shivaji as a paragon of Hindu resistance against Muslim rule, but this characterization of him is a relatively late phenomenon.

TIRUMALA NAYAKA (r. 1632–59) A ruler of the Nayaka kingdom of Madurai, a successor state to the Vijayanagara empire. Tirumala was famous for his patronage of the great Minakshi temple at Madurai, in modern Tamil Nadu.

Bibliography

Abu al-Fazl ibn Mubarak. *The Akbar Nama of Abu'l-Fazl*, trans. Henry Beveridge. Delhi: Ess Ess Publications, 1977 [1902–39].

A'in-i Akbari, trans. H. Blockmann. Osnabruck: Biblio Verlag, 1983 [1868–94].

Akhtarazzaman, A. "The Muslim Rulers and Their Non-Muslim Subjects in Thirteenth and Fourteenth Century Eastern India." In *Essays in Memory of Momtazur Rahman Tarafdar*, ed. Perween Hasan and Mufakharul Islam, pp. 132–48. Dhaka: Dhaka University, 1999.

Alam, Muzaffar. *The Crisis of Empire in Mughal North India: Awadh and the Punjab, 1707–1748.* Delhi: Oxford University Press, 1986.

"The Culture and Politics of Persian in Precolonial Hindustan." In *Literary Cultures in History: Reconstructions from South Asia*, ed. Sheldon Pollock, pp. 131–98. Berkeley: University of California Press, 2003.

The Languages of Political Islam, India 1200–1800. Chicago: University of Chicago Press, 2004.

"The Pursuit of Persian: Language in Mughal Politics." *Modern Asian Studies* 32 (1998): 317–49.

Alam, Muzaffar and Sanjay Subrahmanyam, eds. *The Mughal State, 1526–1750.* Delhi: Oxford University Press, 1998.

Aquil, Raziuddin. "Conversion in Chishti Sufi Literature (13th–14th Centuries)." *Indian Historical Review* 24.1–2 (1997–98): 70–94.

Ara, Matsuo. "The Lodhi Rulers and the Construction of Tomb-Buildings in Delhi." *Acta Asiatica* 43 (1982): 61–80.

Arasaratnam, S. *Maritime India in the Seventeenth Century.* Delhi: Oxford University Press, 1994.

Maritime Trade, Society and European Influence in Southern Asia, 1600–1800. Aldershot, Hampshire: Variorum Publishing, 1995.

Asher, Catherine. "Amber and Jaipur: Temples in a Changing State." In *Stones in the Sand: The Architecture of Rajasthan*, ed. Giles Tillotson, pp. 68–77. Mumbai: Marg Publications, 2001.

The Architecture of Mughal India. Cambridge: Cambridge University Press, 1992.

"The Architecture of Raja Man Singh: A Study of Sub-Imperial Patronage." In *The Powers of Art: Patronage in Indian Culture*, ed. Barbara Stoler Miller, pp. 183–201. New Delhi: Oxford University Press, 1992.

"Delhi Walled: Changing Boundaries." In *City Walls: The Urban Enceinte in Global Perspective*, ed. James Tracy, pp. 247–81. Cambridge: Cambridge University Press, 2000.

"Gardens of the Nobility: Raja Man Singh and the Bagh-i Wah." In *The Mughal Garden: Interpretation, Conservation, Implications*, ed. Mahmood Hussain et al., pp. 61–72. Lahore: Ferozsons, 1996.

"Legacy and Legitimacy: Sher Shah's Patronage of Imperial Mausolea." In *Shari'at and Ambiguity in South Asian Islam*, ed. Katherine Ewing, pp. 79–97. Berkeley: University of California Press, 1988.

"Mapping Hindu–Muslim Identities Through the Architecture of Shahjahan-abad and Jaipur." In *Beyond Turk and Hindu: Rethinking Religious Identities in Islamicate South Asia*, ed. David Gilmartin and Bruce B. Lawrence, pp. 121–48. Gainesville: University of Florida, 2000.

"Piety, Religion and the Old Social Order in the Architecture of the Later Mughals and Their Contemporaries." In *Rethinking Early Modern India*, ed. Richard B. Barnett, pp. 193–228. New Delhi: Manohar, 2002.

"A Ray from the Sun: Mughal Ideology and the Visual Construction of the Divine." In *The Presence of Light: Divine Radiance and Religious Experience*, ed. Matthew Kapstein, pp. 161–94. Chicago: University of Chicago Press, 2004.

Asher, Frederick, ed. *Art of India: Prehistory to the Present*. Chicago: Encyclopaedia Britannica, 2003.

Athar Ali, M. *The Mughal Nobility Under Aurangzeb*, revised edn. Delhi: Oxford University Press, 1997.

Azzizuddin Husain, S. M. *Structure of Politics Under Aurangzeb, 1658–1707*. New Delhi: Kanishka Publishers, 2002.

Babur, Zahir al-Din Muhammad. *The Baburnama: Memoirs of Babur, Prince and Emperor*, trans. and ed. Wheeler M. Thackston. Washington, DC: Freer Gallery of Art, Arthur M. Sackler Gallery and Smithsonian Institution, 1995.

Bailey, Gavin. *The Jesuits and the Grand Mogul: Renaissance Art at the Imperial Court of India, 1580–1630*. Washington, DC: Freer Gallery of Art, Arthur M. Sackler Gallery, and Smithsonian Institution, 1998.

Banerji, Naseem Ahmed. *The Architecture of the Adina Mosque in Pandua, India: Medieval Tradition and Innovation*. Lewiston, NY: Edwin Mellen Press, 2002.

Baqir Najm-i Sani, Muhammad. *Advice on the Art of Governance: Mau'izah-i Jahangiri, an Indo-Islamic Mirror for Princes*, trans. Sajida Sultana Alvi. Albany: State University of New York Press, 1989.

Barani, Zia al-Din. *The Reign of Alauddin Khilji, Translated from Zia-ud-din Barani's Tarikh-i-Firuz Shahi*, trans. A. R. Fuller and A. Khallaque. Calcutta: Pilgrim Publishers, 1967.

Barendse, R. J. *The Arabian Seas: The Indian Ocean World of the Seventeenth Century*. Armonk, NY: M.E. Sharpe, 2002.

Barnes, Ruth, Steven Cohen, and Rosemary Gill. *Trade, Temple and Court: Indian Textiles from the Tapi Collection*. Mumbai: India Book House, 2002.

Bartlett, Robert. *The Making of Europe: Conquest, Colonization and Cultural Change, 950–1350*. Princeton: Princeton University Press, 1993.

Bawa, Vasant Kumar. "The Politics of Architecture in Qutbshahi Hyderabad: A Preliminary Analysis." In *Studies in History of the Deccan: Medieval and Modern*, ed. M. A. Nayeem *et al.*, pp. 329–41. Delhi: Pragati Publications, 2002.

Bayly, C. A. *Rulers, Townsmen and Bazaars: North Indian Society in the Age of British Expansion, 1770–1870*. Cambridge: Cambridge University Press, 1983.

Beach, Milo Cleveland. *Mughal and Rajput Painting*. Cambridge: Cambridge University Press, 1992.

Beach, Milo Cleveland, Ebba Koch, and Wheeler Thackson. *King of the World: The Padshahnama, an Imperial Mughal Manuscript from the Royal Library, Windsor Castle*. London: Azimuth Editions and Sackler Gallery, 1997.

Begley, Wayne E. "The Myth of the Taj Mahal and a New Theory of its Symbolic Meaning." *The Art Bulletin* 61 (1979): 7–37.

"The Symbolic Role of Calligraphy on Three Imperial Mosques of Shah Jahan." In *Kaladarsana: American Studies in the Art of India*, ed. Joanna Williams, pp. 7–18. New Delhi: Oxford and IBH Publishing, 1981.

Begley, Wayne E., and Z. A. Desai. *Taj Mahal: The Illumined Tomb: An Anthology of Seventeenth-Century Mughal and European Documentary Sources*. Cambridge and Seattle: Aga Khan Program for Islamic Architecture and University of Washington Press, 1989.

Bernier, François. *Travels in the Mogul Empire, AD 1656–1668*, 2nd edn, trans. A. Constable. New Delhi: Munshiram Manoharlal, 1992.

Blake, Stephen P. *Shahjahanabad: The Sovereign City in Mughal India, 1639–1739*. Cambridge: Cambridge University Press, 1991.

Brand, Michael and Glenn Lowry. *Akbar's India: Art From the Mughal City of Victory*. New York: Asia Society Galleries, 1985.

Breckenridge, Carol A. "Food, Politics and Pilgrimage in South India, 1350–1650 A.D." In *Food, Society and Culture*, ed. R. S. Khare and M. S. A. Rao, pp. 21–53. Durham, NC: Carolina Academic Press, 1986.

Brennig, Joseph J. "Textile Producers and Production in Late Seventeenth Century Coromandel." In *Merchants, Markets, and the State in Early Modern India*, ed. Sanjay Subrahmanyam, pp. 66–87. Delhi: Oxford University Press, 1990.

Byrant, G. J. "Assymetric Warfare: The British Experience in Eighteenth-Century India." *Journal of Military History* 68 (2004): 431–69.

Calkins, Philip B. "The Formation of a Regionally Oriented Ruling Group in Bengal, 1700–1740." *Journal of Asian Studies* 29.4 (1970): 799–806.

Chandra, Pramod. "Notes on Mandu Kalpasutra of A.D. 1439." *Marg* 12.3 (1959): 51–54.

Chandra, Satish. *Medieval India: Society, the Jagirdari Crisis and the Village*. Delhi: Macmillan India, 1982.

Medieval India from Sultanat to the Mughals, Pt. 1: Delhi Sultanat (1206–1526). New Delhi: Har Anand, 1997.

Chattopadhyaya, Brajadulal. *Representing the Other? Sanskrit Sources and the Muslims (Eighth to Fourteenth Century)*. New Delhi: Manohar, 1998.

Chaudhuri, K. N. *The Trading World of Asia and the English East India Company, 1660–1760*. Cambridge: Cambridge University Press, 1978.

Comissariat, M. S. *A History of Gujarat Including a Survey of its Chief Architectural Monuments and Inscriptions*. Bombay: Longmans, Green and Co., 1938.

Cort, John. "The Jain Sacred Cosmos: Selections from a Medieval Pilgrimage Text." In *The Clever Adulteress & Other Stories: A Treasury of Jain Literature*, ed. Phyllis Granoff, pp. 245–90. Oakville, Ont.: Mosaic Press, 1990.

Currie, P. M. *The Shrine and Cult of Mu'in-al-din Chishti of Ajmer*. Delhi: Oxford University Press, 1989.

Dale, Stephen Frederic. *The Garden of the Eight Paradises: Babur and the Culture of Empire in Central Asia, Afghanistan and India (1483–1530)*. Leiden and Boston: Brill, 2004.

Islamic Society on the South Asian Frontier: The Mappilas of Malabar, 1498–1922. Oxford: Oxford University Press, 1980.

Das, Asok Kumar. "An Introductory Note on the Emperor Akbar's *Ramayana* and its Miniatures." In *Facets of Indian Art: A Symposium Held at the Victoria and Albert Museum*, ed. Robert Skelton *et al.*, pp. 94–104. London: Victoria and Albert Museum, 1986.

Datta, Rajat. *Society, Economy and the Market: Commercialization in Rural Bengal, c. 1760–1800*. New Delhi: Manohar, 2000.

Davis, Richard H. *Lives of Indian Images*. Princeton: Princeton University Press, 1997.

Dehejia, Vidya. "The Treatment of Narrative in Jagat Singh's *Ramayana*: A Preliminary Study." *Artibus Asiae* 56 (1996): 303–24.

Delvoye, Françoise "Nalini." "Music Patronage in the Sultanate of Gujarat." In *The Making of Indo-Persian Culture: Indian and French Studies*, ed. Muzaffar Alam *et al.*, pp. 253–80. New Delhi: Manohar, 2000.

Digby, Simon. "The Sufi Shaikh as a Source of Authority in Medieval India." *Purusartha* 9 (1986): 57–77.

War-Horse and Elephant in the Delhi Sultanate. Oxford: Oxford University Press, 1971.

Doshi, Saryu, ed. *Shivaji and Facets of Indian Culture*. Bombay: Marg Publications, 1982.

Dundas. Paul. *The Jains*. London and New York: Routledge, 1992.

Dunn, Ross E. *The Adventures of Ibn Battuta: A Muslim Traveler of the 14th Century*. London: Croom Helm, 1986.

Eaton, Richard M. "The Political and Religious Authority of the Shrine of Baba Farid." In *India's Islamic Traditions, 711–1750*, ed. R. M. Eaton, pp. 263–84. Delhi: Oxford University Press, 2003.

The Rise of Islam and the Bengal Frontier, 1204–1760. Berkeley: University of California Press, 1993.

Sufis of Bijapur: Social Roles of Sufis in Medieval India. Princeton University Press, 1978.

"Temple Desecration and Indo-Muslim States." In *Beyond Turk and Hindu: Rethinking Religious Identities in Islamicate South Asia*, ed. David Gilmartin and Bruce B. Lawrence, pp. 246–81. Gainesville, FL: University Press of Florida, 2000.

Entwistle, A. W. *Braj: Centre of Krishna Pilgrimage*. Groningen: Egbert Forsten, 1987.

"Representations of Ala'uddin Khalji." In *Studies in Early Modern Indo-Aryan Languages, Literature and Culture*, ed. A. W. Entwistle and C. Salomon, pp. 115–38. New Delhi: Manohar, 1999.

Erdman, Joan L. "Jaipur: City Planning in 18th Century India." In *Shastric Traditions in Indian Arts*, 2 vols., ed. A. L. Dallapiccola, pp. 219–33. Stuttgart: Steiner Verlag, 1989, vol. I.

Ernst, Carl. W. *Eternal Garden: Mysticism, History, and Politics at a South Asian Sufi Center*. Albany: State University of New York Press, 1992.

Ernst, Carl W. and Bruce B. Lawrence. *Sufi Martyrs of Love: The Chishti Order in South Asia and Beyond*. New York: Palgrave Macmillan, 2002.

Faruqi, Munis. *Princes and Power in the Mughal Empire, 1569–1657*. Ph.D. dissertation, Department of History, Duke University, 2002.

Faruqi, Shamsur Rahman. "A Long History of Urdu Literary Culture, Part 1: Naming and Placing a Literary Culture." In *Literary Cultures in History: Reconstructions from South Asia*, ed. Sheldon Pollock, pp. 805–63. Berkeley: University of California Press, 2003.

Flood, Finbarr B. "Pillars, Palimpsets, and Princely Practices: Translating the Past in Sultanate Delhi." *RES* 43 (2003): 95–116.

Friedman, Yohanan. *Shaikh Ahmad Sirhindi: An Outline of his Thought and a Study of his Image in the Eyes of Posterity*. Montreal: McGill University Institute of Islamic Studies; McGill-Queens University Press, 1971.

Fritz, John M. "Vijayanagara: Authority and Meaning of a South Indian Imperial Capital." *American Anthropologist* 88 (1986): 44–55.

Fritz, John M. and George Michell, eds. *New Light on Hampi*. Mumbai: Marg Publications, 2001.

Fritz, John M., George Michell, and M. S. Nagaraja Rao. *Where Kings and Gods Meet: The Royal Centre at Vijayanagara, India*. Tucson, AZ: University of Arizona Press, 1984.

Fuller, C. J. *Servants of the Goddess: The Priests of a South Indian Temple*. Cambridge University Press, 1984.

Ghosh, Pika. *Temple to Love: Architecture and Devotion in Seventeenth-Century Bengal*. Bloomington: Indiana University Press, 2005.

Gittinger, Mattiebelle. *Master Dyers to the World: Technique and Trade in Early Indian Dyed Cotton Textiles*. Washington, DC: The Textile Museum, 1982.

Glynn, Catherine. "Evidence of Royal Painting for the Amber Court." *Artibus Asiae* 56.1–2 (1996): 67–93.

"A Rajasthani Princely Album: Rajput Patronage of Mughal-Style Painting." *Artibus Asiae* 60.2 (2000): 222–64.

Glynn, Catherine and Ellen Smart. "A Mughal Icon Re-examined." *Artibus Asiae* 57.1–2 (1997): 5–15.

Gommans, Jos J. L. *Mughal Warfare: Indian Frontiers and High Roads to Empire, 1500–1700*. London and New York: Routledge, 2002.

The Rise of the Indo-Afghan Empire, c. 1710–1780. Delhi: Oxford University Press, 1999.

"The Silent Frontier of South Asia, ca. A.D. 1100–1800." *Journal of World History* 9.1 (1998): 1–23.

Gommans, Jos J. L., and Dirk H. A. Kolff, eds. *Warfare and Weaponry in South Asia, 1000–1800*. Delhi: Oxford University Press, 2001.

Gordon, Stewart. *The Marathas, 1600–1818*. Cambridge University Press, 1993.

Marathas, Marauders, and State Formation in Eighteenth-Century India. Delhi: Oxford University Press, 1994.

Granoff, Phyllis. "The Householder as Shaman: Jain Biographies of Temple Holders." *East and West* 42 (1992): 301–17.

"Tales of Broken Limbs and Bleeding Wounds: Responses to Muslim Iconoclasm in Medieval India." *East and West* 41 (1991): 189–203.

Granoff, Phyllis, ed. *The Clever Adulteress & Other Stories: A Treasury of Jain Literature*. Oakville, Ont.: Mosaic Press, 1990.

Grewal, J. S. *The Sikhs of the Punjab*. Cambridge: Cambridge University Press, 1990.

Guenther, Alan. "Hanafi Figh in Mughal India: The Fatawa-i Alamgiri." In *India's Islamic Traditions, 711–1750*, ed. Richard M. Eaton, pp. 209–30. New Delhi: Oxford University Press, 2003.

Guha, Sumit. *Environment and Ethnicity in India, 1200–1991*. Cambridge: Cambridge University Press, 1999.

Gulbadan, Begum. *The History of Humayun (Humayun-nama)*, trans. Annette S. Beveridge. London: Royal Asiatic Society, 1902.

Guy, John. *Woven Cargoes: Indian Textiles in the East*. London: Thames and Hudson, 1998.

Guy, John and Deborah Swallow, eds. *Arts of India: 1550–1900*. London: Victoria and Albert Museum, 1990.

Gwatkin, Nina. "The Brooklyn Museum Hanging." In *Master Dyers to the World*, ed. Mattiebelle Gittinger, pp. 89–92. Washington, DC: The Textile Museum, 1982.

Habib, Irfan. *The Agrarian System of Mughal India 1556–1707*, 2nd edn. Delhi: Oxford University Press, 1999.

Habib, Irfan, ed. *Akbar and His India*. Delhi: Oxford University Press, 1997.

Medieval India 1: Researches into the History of India 1200–1750. Oxford University Press, 1992.

Habib, Mohammad. *The Political Theory of the Delhi Sultanate (Including a Translation of Ziauddin Barani's Fatawa-i Jahandari, circa, 1358–9 A.D.)*. Allahabad: Kitab Mahal, 1961.

Habibullah, A. B. M. *The Foundation of Muslim Rule in India*, 2nd edn. Allahabad: Central Book Depot, 1961.

Hambly, Gavin R. G., ed. *Women in the Medieval Islamic World: Power, Patronage, and Piety*. New York: St. Martin's Press, 1998.

Hawley, John Stratton. *Songs of the Saints of India*, trans. J. S. Hawley and Mark Jurgensmeyer. New York: Oxford University Press, 1988.

Horstmann, Monika, ed. *Images of Kabir*. New Delhi: Manohar, 2002.

Hudson, Dennis. "Siva, Minaksi, Visnu – Reflections on a Popular Myth in Madurai." In *South Indian Temples*, ed. Burton Stein, pp. 107–18. New Delhi: Vikas Publishing House, 1978.

Huntington, Susan L. *Art of Ancient India: Buddhist, Hindu, Jain*. New York: Weatherhill, 1985.

Hutton, Deborah. *The Art of the Court of Bijapur*. Bloomington: Indiana University Press, forthcoming.

"Hyderabad: Monuments Related to Indo-Persian Culture." *Encyclopaedia Iranica*, ed. Ehsan Yarshater. New York: Center for Iranian Studies, Columbia University, forthcoming.

Ibn Battuta. *The Rehla of Ibn Battuta (India, Maldive Islands and Ceylon)*, trans. Mahdi Husain. Baroda: Oriental Institute, 1953.

Jackson, Peter. *The Delhi Sultanate: A Political and Military History*. Cambridge: Cambridge University Press, 1999.

Jahangir, Nur al-Din Muhammad. *The Jahangirnama: Memoirs of Jahangir, Emperor of India*, trans. and ed. Wheeler M. Thackston. Washington, DC: Freer Gallery of Art, Arthur M. Sackler Gallery; New York: Oxford University Press, 1999.

Joffee, Jennifer. *Art, Architecture and Politics in Mewar, 1628–1710*. Ph.D. dissertation, Department of Art History, University of Minnesota, 2005.

Joshi, Varsha. *Polygamy and Purdah: Women and Society among Rajputs*. Jaipur and New Delhi: Rawat Publications, 1995.

Juneja, Monica, ed. *Architecture in Medieval India: Forms, Contexts, Histories*. Delhi: Permanent Black, 2001.

Kabir. *The Bijak of Kabir*, trans. Linda Hess and Shukdev Singh. San Francisco: North Point Press, 1983.

Karashima, Noboru. *Towards a New Formation: South Indian Society under Vijayanagar Rule*. Delhi: Oxford University Press, 1992.

Keay, John. *India: A History*. New York: Grove Press, 2000.

Khafi Khan, Muhammad Hashim. *Khafi Khan's History of 'Alamgir (Being an English Translation of the Relevant Portions of Muntakhab al-Lubub)*, trans. S. Moinul Haq. Karachi: Pakistan Historical Society, 1975.

Khan, Ali Muhammad. *Mirat-i Ahmadi: A Persian History of Gujarat*, trans. M. F. Lokhandwala. Baroda: Oriental Institute, 1965.

Mirat-i Ahmadi Supplement, trans. Syed Nawab Ali and C. N. Seddon. Baroda: Oriental Institute, 1928.

Khan, Iqtidar Alam, ed. *Akbar and His Age*. New Delhi: Indian Council of Historical Research and Northern Book Centre, 1999.

Khandalavala, Karl and Moti Chandra. "An Illustrated Kalpasutra Painted at Jaunpur in A.D. 1465." *Lalit Kala* 12 (1962): 9–15.

Khusrau, Amir. *The Campaigns of Alauddin Khalji Being the English Translation of "The Khaza'inul Futuh" of Amir Khusrau*, trans. Mohammad Habib. Bombay: D. B. Taraporewala Sons, 1931.

Koch, Ebba. *Mughal Architecture: An Outline of Its History and Development (1526–1858)*. Munich: Prestel, 1991.

"The Architectural Forms." In *Fatehpur-Sikri*, ed. Michael Brand and Glenn Lowry, pp. 121–48. Bombay: Marg Publications, 1987.

Mughal Art and Imperial Ideology: Collected Essays. Delhi: Oxford University Press, 2001.

Kolff, Dirk. *Naukar, Rajput and Sepoy: The Ethnohistory of the Military Labour Market in Hindustan, 1450–1850*. Cambridge: Cambridge University Press, 1990.

Kulke, Hermann. "Maharajas, Mahants and Historians: Reflections on the Historiography of Early Vijayanagara and Sringeri." In *Vijayanagara – City and Empire: New Currents of Research*, ed. A. L. Dallapiccola and S. Z. Lallemant, pp. 120–43. Stuttgart: Steiner Verlag, 1985.

Kumar, Sunil. "Assertions of Authority: A Study of the Discursive Statements of Two Sultans of Delhi." In *The Making of Indo Persian Culture*, ed. Muzaffar Alam *et al.*, pp. 37–65. Delhi: Manohar, 2000.

     "Qutb and Modern Memory." In *The Partitions of Memory: The Afterlife of the Division of India*, ed. Suvir Kaul, pp. 140–82. New Delhi: Permanent Black, 2001.

Laine, James. *Shivaji: Hindu King in Islamic India*. New York: Oxford University Press, 2003.

Lawson, Philip. *The East India Company: A History*. London and New York: Longman, 1993.

Leach, Linda. *Mughal and Other Indian Paintings from the Chester Beatty Library*, 2 vols. London: Scorpopom Cavendish, 1995.

     Paintings from India. London: Nour Foundation in association with Azimuth Editions and Oxford University Press, 1998.

Leslie, Julia. *The Perfect Wife: The Orthodox Hindu Women According to the Stridharmapaddhati of Tryambakayajvan*. Delhi: Oxford University Press, 1989.

Levi, Scott C. "Hindus Beyond the Hindu Kush: Indians in the Central Asian Slave Trade." *Journal of the Royal Asiatic Society* 12.3 (2002): 277–88.

Lewis, Martin W. and Karen E. Wigen. *The Myth of Continents: A Critique of Metageography*. Berkeley: University of California Press, 1997.

Losty, J. P. "Sahib Din's Book of Battles: Rana Jagat Singh's *Yuddhakanda*." In *The Legend of Rama: Artistic Visions*, ed. Vidya Dehejia, pp. 101–16. Bombay: Marg Publications, 1994.

Ma Huan. *Ying-yai Sheng-lan, "The Overall Survey of the Ocean's Shores" (1433)*, trans. and ed. J. V. G. Mills. Cambridge: Hakluyt Society, 1970.

Manjhan Rajgiri, Mir Sayyid. *Madhumalati: An Indian Sufi Romance*, trans. Aditya Behl and Simon Weightman. Oxford: Oxford University Press, 2000.

Marshall, P. J. *Bengal: The British Bridgehead, Eastern India 1740–1828*. Cambridge University Press, 1987.

     East Indian Fortunes: The British in Bengal in the Eighteenth Century. Oxford: Clarendon Press, 1976.

Marshall, P. J., ed. *The Eighteenth Century in Indian History*. Delhi: Oxford University Press, 2003.

McLeod, W. H. *The Evolution of the Sikh Community*. Oxford: Clarendon Press, 1976.

Metcalf, Thomas R. *Ideologies of the Raj*. Cambridge: Cambridge University Press, 1994.

     An Imperial Vision: Indian Architecture and Britain's Raj. Berkeley: University of California Press, 1989.

Michell, George. *Architecture and Art of Southern India: Vijayanagara and the Successor States*. Cambridge: Cambridge University Press, 1995.

     "Revivalism as the Imperial Mode: Religious Architecture during the Vijayanagara Period." In *Perceptions of South Asia's Visual Past*, ed. Catherine

B. Asher and Thomas R. Metcalf, pp. 187–97. New Delhi: Oxford and IBH; American Institute of Indian Studies, 1994.

Michell, George and Mark Zebrowski. *Architecture and Art of the Deccan Sultanates*. Cambridge: Cambridge University Press, 1999.

Mirza Nathan. *Baharistan-i Ghaybi: A History of the Mughal Wars in Assam, Cooch Behar, Behar, Bengal*, 2 vols., trans. M. I. Borah. Gauhati: The Government of Assam, Dept. of Historical and Antiquarian Studies, Narayani Handiqui Historical Institute, 1936.

Misra, S. C. *The Rise of Muslim Power in Gujarat: A History of Gujarat from 1298 to 1442*. Bombay: Asia Publishing House, 1963.

Mitchell, Colin Paul. *Sir Thomas Roe and the Mughal Empire*. Karachi: Area Study Centre for Europe, 2000.

Mittal, Sushil, ed. *Surprising Bedfellows: Hindus and Muslims in Medieval and Early Modern India*. Lanham, MO: Lexington Books, 2003.

Morgan, David. *The Mongols*. Oxford: Basil Blackwell, 1986.

Moynihan, Elizabeth B., ed. *The Moonlight Garden: New Discoveries at the Taj Mahal*. Washington, DC and Seattle: Arthur M. Sackler Gallery and University of Washington Press, 2000.

Nakhshabi, Ziya al-Din. *Tales of the Parrot: The Cleveland Museum of Art's Tutinama*, trans. Muhammad A. Simsar. Cleveland: Cleveland Museum of Art, 1978.

Narayana Rao, Velcheru, David Shulman, and Sanjay Subrahmanyam. *Symbols of Substance: Court and State in Nayaka Period Tamil Nadu*. Delhi: Oxford University Press, 1992.

Nath, R. *Antiquities of Chittorgadh*. Jaipur: Historical Research Documentation Programme, 1984.

Nilakantha Sastri, A. *A History of South India from Prehistoric Times to the Fall of Vijayanagar*, 4th edn. Madras: Oxford University Press, 1976.

Nizam al-Din. *Nizam ad-din Awliya: Morals for the Heart: Conversations of Shaykh Nizam ad-din Awliya Recorded by Amir Hasan Sijzi*, trans. Bruce B. Lawrence. New York: Paulist Press, 1992.

Noble, William A. and Ad Ram Sankhyan. "Signs of the Divine: Sati Memorials and Sati Worship in Rajasthan." In *Idea of Rajasthan, Vol. 1: Constructions*, ed. K. Schomer *et al.*, pp. 343–89. New Delhi: Manohar Publishers and American Institute of Indian Studies, 1994.

O'Hanlon, Rosalind. "Manliness and Imperial Service in Mughal North India." *Journal of the Economic and Social History of the Orient* 42 (1999): 47–93.

Orr, Leslie C. "Gods and Worshippers on South Indian Sacred Ground." In *The World in the Year 1000*, ed. James Heitzman and Wolfgang Schenkluhn, pp. 225–54. Lanham, MD: University Press of America, 2004.

Paes, Domingo. "Narrative of Domingo Paes." In *A Forgotten Empire*, trans. and ed. Robert Sewell, pp. 236–90. Delhi: Asian Educational Services, 1982 [1900].

Paramananda, Kavindra. *The Epic of Shivaji*, trans. James W. Laine and S. S. Bahulkar. Hyderabad: Orient Longman, 2001.

Patel, Alka. *Building Communities in Gujarat: Architecture and Society during the Twelfth through Fourteenth Centuries*. Leiden: Brill, 2004.

Pearson, Michael. *The Indian Ocean*. London: Routledge, 2003.
    The Portuguese in India. Cambridge: Cambridge University Press, 1987.
Petievich, Carla. "Dakani's Radha-Krishna Imagery and Canon Formation in
    Urdu." In *The Banyan Tree: Essays on Early Literature in New Indo-Aryan
    Languages*, vol. I, ed. Mariola Offredi, pp. 113–28. Delhi: Manohar, 2000.
    When Men Speak as Women: Vocal Masquerades in Indo-Muslim Poetry. Delhi:
    Oxford University Press, forthcoming.
Pinch, William R. "Same Difference in India and Europe." *History and Theory*
    38.3 (1999): 389–407.
Pollock, Sheldon. "The Sanskrit Cosmopolis, 300–1300: Transculturation,
    Vernacularization, and the Question of Ideology." In *Ideology and Status of
    Sanskrit*, ed. Jan E. M. Houben, pp. 197–247. Leiden: E. J. Brill, 1996.
Prakash, Om. *European Commercial Enterprise in Pre-colonial India*. Cambridge:
    Cambridge University Press, 1998.
    "From Hostility to Collaboration: European Corporate Enterprise and Private
    Trade in the Bay of Bengal, 1500–1800." In *Commerce and Culture in the Bay
    of Bengal, 1500–1800*, ed. Om Prakash and Denys Lombard, pp. 233–59.
    Delhi: Manohar and Indian Council of Historical Research, 1999.
Prasad, Pushpa. *Sanskrit Inscriptions of the Delhi Sultanate, 1191–1526*. Delhi:
    Oxford University Press, 1990.
Ramaswamy, Vijaya. *Textiles and Weavers in Medieval South India*. Delhi: Oxford
    University Press, 1985.
Rangaswami Saraswati, A. "Political Maxims of the Emperor Poet, Krishnadeva
    Raya." *Journal of Indian History* 6 (1925): 61–88.
Raychaudhuri, Tapan and Irfan Habib, eds. *The Cambridge Economic History
    of India, Vol. 1 c. 1200–c. 1750*. Cambridge: Cambridge University Press,
    1982.
Razzaq Samarqandi, Kamal al-Din. "Kamaluddin Abdul Razzaq Samarqandi:
    Mission to Calicut and Vijayanagar." In *A Century of Princes: Sources
    on Timurid History and Art*, trans. Wheeler M. Thackston, pp. 299–321.
    Cambridge, MA: The Aga Khan Program for Islamic Architecture, 1989.
Richards, John F. "Early Modern India and World History." *Journal of World
    History* 8.2 (1997): 197–209.
    "The Formulation of Imperial Authority Under Akbar and Jahangir." In
    Authority and Kingship in South Asia., ed. J. F. Richards, pp. 285–326. New
    Delhi: Oxford University Press, 1998 [1978].
    Mughal Administration in Golconda. Oxford: Clarendon Press, 1975.
    The Mughal Empire. Cambridge: Cambridge University Press, 1993.
    "Norms of Comportment among Imperial Mughal Officers." In *Moral Conduct
    and Authority: The Place of Adab in South Asian Islam*, ed. Barbara Metcalf,
    pp. 255–89. Berkeley: University of California Press, 1984.
Richards, John F., ed. *The Imperial Monetary System of Mughal India*. Delhi:
    Oxford University Press, 1987.
Rubies, Joan Pau. *Travel and Ethnology in the Renaissance: South India Through
    European Eyes, 1250–1625*. Cambridge: Cambridge University Press, 2000.
Saran, Richard D. and Norman P. Ziegler, trans. and annotated. *The Mertiyo
    Rathors of Merto, Rajasthan: Select Translations Bearing on the History of a*

Rajput Family, 1462–1660, 2 vols. Ann Arbor, MI: University of Michigan Centers for South and Southeast Asian Studies, 2001.

Sarkar, J. N. *The History of Aurangzib Based on Original Sources*, 5 vols. Calcutta: M.C. Sarkar, 1924–30.

Schomer, Karine and W. H. McLeod, eds. *The Sants: Studies in a Devotional Tradition of India*. Berkeley: Berkeley Religious Studies Series; Delhi: Motilal Banarsidass, 1987.

Seyller, John. *The Adventures of Hamza: Painting and Storytelling in Mughal India*. Washington, DC and London: Freer Gallery of Art, Arthur M. Sackler Gallery, Smithsonian Institution and Azimuth Editions, 2002.

Workshop and Patron in Mughal India: The Freer Ramayana and Other Illustrated Manuscripts of 'Abd al-Rahim. Zurich and Washington DC: Artibus Asiae Publishers in association with the Freer Gallery of Art, Smithsonian Institution, 1999.

Sherwani, H. K. and P. M. Joshi, eds. *History of Medieval Deccan*, 2 vols. Hyderabad: Government of Andhra Pradesh, 1973, 1974.

Shokoohy, M. and N. H. Shokoohy. "Tughlaqabad: The Earliest Surviving Town of the Delhi Sultanate." *Bulletin of the School for Oriental and African Studies* 57.3 (1994): 516–50.

Sloan, Anna. *The Atala Mosque: Between Polity and Culture in Medieval Jaunpur*. Ph.D. dissertation, Department of Art History, University of Pennsylvania, 2001.

Smith, Edmund W. *Akbar's Tomb, Sikandarah*. Archaeological Survey of India, New Imperial Series Vol. 25. Allahabad: Superintendent Government Press, 1909.

Stein, Burton. "Economic Function of a Medieval South Indian Temple." *Journal of Asian Studies* 14 (1960): 163–76.

"Mahanavami: Medieval and Modern Kingly Ritual in South India." In *All The King's Mana*, pp. 302–26. Madras: New Era, 1984.

Vijayanagara. Cambridge: Cambridge University Press, 1989.

Stronge, Susan. *Painting for the Mughal Emperor: The Art of the Book, 1560–1660*. London: V & A Publications, 2002.

Subrahmanyam, Sanjay. "Iranians Abroad: Intra-Asian Elite Migration and Early Modern State Formation." *Journal of Asian Studies* 51.2 (1992): 340–63.

Penumbral Visions: Making Polities in Early Modern South India. Delhi: Oxford University Press, 2001.

The Political Economy of Commerce: Southern India, 1500–1650. Cambridge: Cambridge University Press, 1990.

Subrahmanyam, Sanjay and C. A. Bayly. "Portfolio Capitalists and the Political Economy of Early Modern India." In *Merchants, Markets, and the State in Early Modern India*, ed. S. Subrahmanyam, pp. 242–65. Delhi: Oxford University Press, 1990.

Taft, Frances. "Honor and Alliance: Reconsidering Mughal–Rajput Marriages." In *Idea of Rajasthan, Vol. 2: Institutions*, ed. K. Schomer *et al.*, pp. 217–41. New Delhi: Manohar Publishers and American Institute of Indian Studies, 1994.

Talbot, Cynthia. "Inscribing the Other, Inscribing the Self: Hindu–Muslim Identities in Pre-colonial India." *Comparative Studies in Society and History* 37.4 (1995): 692–722.

"The Nayakas of Vijayanagara Andhra: A Preliminary Prosopography." In *Structure and Society in Early South India: Essays in Honour of Noboru Karashima*, ed. Kenneth R. Hall, pp. 251–75. Delhi: Oxford University Press, 2001.

Precolonial India in Practice: Society, Region, and Identity in Medieval India. New York: Oxford University Press, 2001.

"Rudrama-devi, the Female King: Gender and Political Authority in Medieval India." In *Syllables of Sky: Studies in South Indian Civilization*, ed. David Shulman, pp. 391–430. Delhi: Oxford University Press, 1995.

"The Story of Prataparudra: Hindu Historiography on the Deccan Frontier." In *Beyond Turk and Hindu: Rethinking Religious Identities in Islamicate South Asia*, ed. David Gilmartin and Bruce B. Lawrence, pp. 282–99. Gainesville: University Press of Florida, 2000.

Tavernier, Jean-Baptiste. *Travels in India*, 2nd edn., trans. V. Ball. London: Oxford University Press, 1925.

Teltscher, Kate. *India Inscribed: European and British Writing on India 1600–1800.* Delhi: Oxford University Press, 1995.

Thapar, Romilla. *Somanatha, the Many Voices of a History.* New Delhi: Penguin, 2004.

Tillotson, G. H. R. *The Rajput Palaces: The Development of an Architectural Style, 1450–1750.* New Haven and London: Yale University Press, 1987.

Tirmizi, S. A. I. *Edicts from the Mughal Haram.* Delhi: Idarah-i Adabiyat-i Delli, 1979.

Topsfield, Andrew. *Court Painting at Udaipur: Art Under the Patronage of the Maharanas of Mewar.* Zurich: Artibus Asiae and Museum Rietberg, 2001.

Vaudeville, Charlotte. *A Weaver Named Kabir.* Delhi: Oxford University Press, 1993.

Venkataramanayya, N. *The Early Muslim Expansion in South India.* Madras: University of Madras Press, 1942.

Verghese, Anila. *Archaeology, Art and Religion: New Perspectives on Vijayanagara.* Delhi: Oxford University Press, 2000.

Wade, Bonnie. *Imaging Sound: An Ethnomusical Study of Music, Art and Culture in Mughal India.* Chicago: University of Chicago Press, 1998.

"Music and Dance." In *The Magnificent Mughals*, ed. Zeenut Ziad, pp. 229–68. Karachi: Oxford University Press, 2002.

Wagoner, Phillip B. "Harihara, Bukka, and the Sultan: The Delhi Sultanate in the Political Imagination of Vijayanagara." In *Beyond Turk and Hindu: Rethinking Religious Identities in Islamicate South Asia*, ed. David Gilmartin and Bruce B. Lawrence, pp. 300–26. Gainesville: University Press of Florida, 2000.

"'Sultan among Hindu Kings': Dress, Titles, and the Islamicization of Hindu Culture at Vijayanagara." *Journal of Asian Studies* 55 (1996): 851–80.

Tidings of the King: A Translation and Ethnohistorical Analysis of the Rayavacakamu. Honolulu: University of Hawaii Press, 1993.

Welch, Anthony and Howard Crane. "The Tughluqs: Master Builders of the Delhi Sultanate." *Muqarnas* 1 (1983): 123–66.

Wink, André. *Land and Sovereignty in India: Agrarian Society and Politics under the Eighteenth-century Maratha Svarajya.* Cambridge: Cambridge University Press, 1986.

The *Slave Kings and the Islamic Conquest 11th–13th Centuries*, vol. II of *Al-Hind: The Making of the Indo-Islamic World.* Leiden: Brill, 1997.

Wright, H. Nelson. *The Coinage and Metrology of the Sultans of Delhi.* Delhi: Manager of Publications, 1936.

Ziad, Zeenut, ed. *The Magnificent Mughals.* Karachi: Oxford University Press, 2002.

Ziegler, Norman P. "Some Notes on Rajput Loyalties During the Mughal Period." In *Kingship and Authority in South Asia*, ed. John F. Richards, pp. 242–84. New Delhi: Oxford University Press, 1998 [1978].

Index

Abd al-Rahim Khan-i Khanan 125, 144–6,
      147, 148, 149, 202, 292
Abu al-Fazl 121, 124, 129–30, 132, 142,
      155, 206, 231, 292
Adil Shahs 154, 163, 166, 169, 232, 233,
      242
Afaqi xvi, 57, 58, 75–6, 163–4
Agra 131, 161, 233, 235, 265, 273, 275,
      276, 277
    fort/palace 132, 196, 208, 211, 227,
      265
    Taj Mahal *195*, 194–6, 228, 247
    tomb of Nur Jahan's parents (tomb of
      Itimad al-Daula) 204, *205*
Ahmad Khattu 92, *93*
Ahmedabad 89, 91, 92, *93*, 96
Ahmed Shahs 90, 92, 96
Aibak, Qutb al-Din 25, 26, 27, 292
Ajmer 20, 29, 32, 44, 105, 106, 129,
      142–4, 208, 246, 293
    shrine (dargah) of Muin al-Din Chishti
      142, *145*, *220*, 219–21
Akbar 105, 115, 120, 121, 123–6, *133*,
      135, *137*, *139*, *145*, *147*, 144–51,
      152, 153, 155, 156, 158, 169, 202,
      206, 211, 225, 226, 292, 294
    administrative/economic reforms 124,
      126–8, 152, 155
    early career 124–5
    military campaigns 125, 126, 128, 129,
      153, 207–8
    patronage of the arts 124, 128, 131;
      architecture 131–4; music 144;
      painting *139*, 134–44, 155, 158,
      187, 191
    personality 124
    religious policies 128, 129–31, 219,
      225–6, 231
    state ideology 129–31, *139*, 155
    translations *141*, 140–2
    (*see also Akbarnama*, Delhi, Fatehpur
      Sikri)

Akbarnama 125, 130, 142, *143*, 144, *145*,
      207, 209, 210, 292
Ala al-Din Khalji 35–41, 106, 120,
      292
    campaigns 35–7, 39–40
    economic policies 39
    patronage in Delhi *38*, 37–8, 122
    reputation 38–41
Al-Biruni 22
Alexander the Great 7, 35, 38, 44
Amber 149, 175, 211–13, 249, 252, 254,
      271, 277, 294
    Amber palace *212*, 211–13, 265
Amir Khusrau 40, 105, 200
armies 17, 18, 19, 27–8, 30, 55–6, 59–60,
      116–17, 120, 122, 125, 126, 235,
      237–8, 242, 284
Asaf Jahs (*see* Nizams of Hyderabad)
Aurangzeb 155, 175, 204, 207, 211, 225,
      227–32, 233–5, 244, 245, 248, 254,
      256, 263, 265, 292
    attitude towards the arts 227–30
    court ceremony 227–8, 290
    death 247, 256, 265, 266, 276
    Deccan conflict 232, 233
    Fatawa-i Alamgiri 230–1
    nobility 231, 233, 235–6, 245
    religious views 227
    temple destruction 231
    war of succession 227
Awadh 249, 250, 291

Babur 103, 116–19, 120, 123, 131, 132,
      140, 154, 202, 246, 292
    patronage of gardens 118–19, 121
    patronage of mosques 119, *120*
Bahmanis 53, 54–7, 60, 64, 67, 75–7, 84,
      98, 163, 237
Balban 34
Banda Bahadur, uprising of 266–7,
      270
Benares (Varanasi) 97, 107, 231

Bengal 84, 85, 128, 248, 249, 250–2, 256,
        260, 263, 277, 280–3, 287, 288,
        289, 294
    agriculture 279–80
    architecture 86, 87, 88, 216–19, 251,
        251–2
        temples 218
    Islamization of 85, 86–8
    literature 88–9
    shipping 280, 281–2
    (see also Ilyas Shahs, Murshidabad,
        Pandua, Siraj al-Daula)
Bengali xvi, 88–9
Bhagavata Purana 111, 112, 112, 113,
        209, 213
bhakti xvi, 82, 110, 114, 149, 216
Bharatpur 265, 266, 272
Bijapur 154, 163, 166–8, 169–70, 175,
        183, 232, 233, 236, 247, 272,
        293
    Sufi/ism in 166, 167, 168
Bombay 260–3, 264, 288
Brahmi xvi, 7, 14, 29, 44
Brahmins xvi, 13, 28, 30, 46–7, 64, 84,
        94, 109, 129, 169, 238, 239, 242,
        254
bullion 256, 275, 288 (see also gold, silver)

Calcutta 263–4, 280, 281–2, 283, 284,
        288, 290
Chaitanya 110–11, 112, 216–17, 292
Chandelas 15
Chandragiri 176, 177, 181, 183, 184
Chaurapanchashika 112, 113, 113, 136
China 8, 9, 51–2, 79, 89, 152, 288
chintz xvi, 173–5, 257, 258
Chishti xvi, 32, 86–8, 105, 114, 129, 131,
        133, 142, 168, 169, 187, 219, 226,
        246–7, 293 (see also Muin al-Din
        Chishti, Nizam al-Din Auliya,
        Shaikh Salim Chishti)
Chittor 35, 41, 100–2, 101, 103, 106, 109,
        125–6, 153, 207–8, 219, 227, 293,
        294
    Tower of Victory 100, 101
Cholas 14–15, 17–18, 24, 65, 74, 294
coins 29, 42, 49–50, 82, 89, 204, 205,
        263, 267, 283, 288
Coromandel 80, 172, 173, 181, 183, 259,
        264, 277, 281, 289

Dakani xvii, 77, 168, 169, 293
dargah xvii, 29, 32, 86, 92, 168, 219–21,
        246
Daudnagar 274, 274

Daulatabad 42, 43
Deccan 35, 43, 53, 75, 84, 98, 128, 154,
        156, 164–6, 168–9, 187, 191, 225,
        239, 248–9, 272, 293, 294
    Deccan wars 231–8, 292
Deccani xvii, 57, 58, 75–6, 163
Delhi 7, 8, 26, 35, 37–8, 63, 115–16,
        117–18, 121, 161, 233, 242, 245,
        265, 276, 277, 288, 290, 294
    architecture
        Firuzabad (Kotla Firuz Shah) 44,
            43–4
        Humayun's tomb 131–2
        Jahan Panah 41, 42
        Qila-i Kuhna mosque 121, 122
        Qutb complex, sultanate 29, 29–30,
            31, 33–4, 38, 37–8, 45–6, 86, 100,
            102, 115–16, 117, 121
        Shahjahanabad 196, 197, 199, 200,
            201, 208, 211, 216, 227, 228, 246,
            250
        Siri 37, 42
        tomb of Jahanara 228, 229
        Tughluqabad 41, 42
    described by Ibn Battuta 44–5
    literature 247
    Mongol attack 37
    patronage, under later Mughals 246,
        245–7
Delhi Sultanate 25, 96, 113, 117
    conquest state 45–50
    early sultans 32, 33–5
    expansionist phase 35–41
    Iltutmish 33–4
    impact on subjects 46–7
    lasting impact on Deccan 53
    under the Tughluqs 41–5
    urbanization and economy 49–50, 52
deshmukh xvii, 237, 238, 239, 272
Devaraya II 54, 56, 65, 292–3
Dig 266, 265–6
Din-i Ilahi xvii, 130, 155
dress xvii, 2, 72, 182–3, 187–8, 202, 214,
        219–21, 222, 240, 241, 257
Dutch 159, 161, 182, 183, 260, 264, 276,
        281

East India Company (EIC) 161, 256, 259,
        263, 260–4, 277, 279, 281, 283,
        284, 285–6, 287–90, 291
    William Fullerton 284, 285
economy, eighteenth-century 275–8
Eklingji, temple 103, 108
elephants 28, 56, 77, 133–4, 142, 143,
        149, 178, 187, 191–4, 252, 290

English 159, 161, 181, 260 (*see also* East India Company)

Fatehpur Sikri 126, 128, 129, 132–4, 146, 149, 197
    Private Audience Hall 134, *135*
    tomb of Shaikh Salim Chishti 133, *133*
Firuz Shah Tughluq *44*, 43–5
food 1–2, 82, 216, 219

Gajapatis 56–7, 58, 64, 75
Ghiyas al-Din Tughluq 41–2
Ghurids 25–8
goddess 13, 54, 61, 62, 222, 238, 242
gold 180–1
Golkonda 57, 59, 75, 154, 163, 166, 169, *172*, 170–2, 173–5, 181, 183, 232, 233, 236, 239, 247, 293
Gopura xvii, 14, 222
Gujarat 20, 35, 43, 80, 84, 91–6, 98, 100, 119, 126, 133, 148, 158–60, 161, 173, 240, 250, 277
    architecture 91–2, *93*
    music 96
    painting 92–6
    rulers of 91
    (*see also* Surat)
Gulbadan Begum 160, 293
Guru Nanak 108, 267, *268*, 269, 293
Gwalior 100, 102–3, 132

Hamida Banu Begum 136–8
Hampi, *see* Vijayanagara
haram xvii, 136–8, 203–5, 213, 214
Hari Vamsha 140, *141*
Hindavi xvii, 140, 146
horses 28, 49, 50, 56–9, 67, 77, 78, 120, 127, 155, 180, 187, 237, 252, 276
Hugli 260, *262*, 263, 278, 279
Humayun 116, 119, 120, 121, 122–3, 136, 140, 156, 293
Hyderabad 166, 173, 249, 250, 293
    Char Minar *165*, 166, 168

Ibn Battuta 44, 45, 51–2, 79
Ibrahim Adil Shah II 169, 293
    patronage of 169–70, *171*
Iltutmish 32–4 (*see also* Delhi Sultanate)
Ilyas Shahs 85
iqta xvii, 39, 70, 127
Isfahan 197, 276
    Great Mosque 22, *23*
Islam as binding factor 20–1, 46

jagir xvii, 127, 236, 248, 270, 271
jagirdar xviii, 127
Jahangir 129, *137*, 138, *139*, 146, 148, 155, 156, 158, 160, 163, 173, 186–91, 203–4, 206, 207, 208, 211, 214, 219, 269, 292, 294
    career 153–4
    concept of state 155, 231
    portraiture *157*, 170, 187, 188, *188*, *189*, 191, 207
    (*see also* Mughal: religious policies under Jahangir and Shah Jahan)
Jahangirnama 188, *189*
Jain/s xviii, 15, 47, 94, *95*, 99–103, 105, 124, 129, 254, 281
Jaipur 249–50, *253*, 252–4, 277, 294
Jats 235, *266*, 265–6, 269–70, 271, 272, 276
Jaunpur 84, 96–7, 124
    architecture 97
jihad 19
jizya xviii, 47, 129, 230, 231

Kabir 107–8, 267, 293
Kachhwahas 126, 144, 148, 149, 151, 175, 182, 211, 233, 249, 252, 254, 277, 294 (*see also* Amber, Jaipur, Raja Man Singh, Rajput, Sawai Jai Singh)
Kalakacharya Katha 95, 94–6, 99
Kalpa Sutra 94, 97, 99, 112, 113
Kannada xviii, 70, 74, 169, 177
Khajuraho, Kandariya Mahadeva temple *16*, 15–17
Khalsa 269, 270
khanazad xviii, 202, 236, 245
khanqah xviii, 92
Khurram 153–4, 158, 186, 187, 191, *192*, 204, 207–8, 226
kingship, Turkic concept of 22
Krishna xviii, 88–9, 96, *112*, 108–12, 126, 136, 140, *141*, 148, 216, 217, *218*, 292, 293
Krishnadeva Raya 56–8, *66*, *69*, 68–70, 74–5, 77, 102, 178, 222, 293
kshatriya xviii, 99, 239

language 2, 70
Lodis 45, 96, 97, 115–16, 119, 120, 131
    architectural patronage of 115–16, 121

Madhumalati 106
Madras 181, 259–60, 264, 288
madrasa xviii, 45, 76, 252

Madurai 176, 183, 294
  Minakshi temple *223*, 221–4, 294
Mahabharata xviii, 100, 112, 140
Mahmud Gawan 76
Mahmud of Ghazni 18–20, 22, 24, 25, 30,
    35, 255, 293
Malabar 78–80, 159, 173, 182, 282
Malwa 84, 90, 91, *98*, 98–9, 100, *101*, 105,
    125, 240, 250
  architecture 98
  painting 98
Mapillas 78
Maratha 232, 233–5, 236–8, 239, 240–4,
    245, 250, 254, 255, 259, 260, 272,
    276, 277, 283, 288, 294
  arts 242–4
  forts 243–4; Pratapgad 232, *244*; Raigad
    243, 244
  temples 242, 244
  trends of the eighteenth century 240–2
  (*see also* Shivaji Bhonsle)
Marathi xviii, 11, 70, 169, 237
Mecca 17, 21, 86, 106, 129, 160,
    173
Mewar 98, 99–102, 109, 116, 207–11,
    219, 221, 250, 271, 293,
    294
Mira Bai 109, 293
Mongols 34–5, 37, 40, 50–1, 116
Mughal 116, 202
  campaigns 187
  ceremonies, court 191, 200, 207, 287
  Chishti alliance 187–8
  cultural policies, Jahangir and Shah
    Jahan 187
  Deccan policy 240
  disintegration 244–8, 249, 254–5, 256,
    265, 285, 287
  economy 273–4, 275
  European perceptions 205–7
  gardens 118–19, 123, 132, 194, 262
  gender role and lifestyle 202–5
  legacy 288, 290
  maritime trade 158–63
  peasants, conditions of 270–1
  religious policies, Jahangir and Shah
    Jahan 225–7
  succession 153
  tombs 194–6 (*see also* Taj Mahal)
  (*see also* Akbar, Aurangzeb, Babur,
    Humayun, Jahangir, Shah Jahan)
Muhammad Baqir Najm al-Sani 202
Muhammad Quli Qutb Shah 169, *172*,
    170–2, 293
Muhammad Tughluq 41–3, 51, 52, 293

Muin al-Din Chishti 32, 105, 129, 142,
    144, 188, *188*, 204, 208, 219, *220*,
    293, 294
Murshidabad 248, 251, 250–2
Murshid Quli Khan (Kartalab Khan) 235,
    248, 251, 250–2, 282

Naqshbandi 226, 294
Nayaka xix, 57–8, 61
Nayaka states 175, 176–7, 178–80, 183,
    221–2, 294
  concept of kingship 178
  economy 180–1
  patrons of architecture *223*, 177–223
  patrons of literature 177, 178
  sculpture *179*, 178–80
  (*see also* Tirumala Nayaka)
Nayamkara xix, 57, 58, 70
Nimatnama 98, *98*
Nizam al-Din Auliya 32, 33, 39, 105, 118,
    131, 246, 294
Nizams of Hyderabad 248–9
Nur Jahan 153–4, 156, 160, 204, *205*, 214,
    294

Ottomans 91, 124, 152, 186, 197

Padmavat 41, 106
Padshahnama 155, *192*, 210
Pandua 85
  Adina mosque 86, *87*
Panipat 116
  Babur's mosque *120*
patola xix, 159
peasants 43, 265, 266, 269, 280, 289
  (*see also* Jats, Sikhs)
Persian xix, 22, 24, 27, 28, 30, 52, 77, 88,
    106, 120, 136, 140, 141, 146,
    149–51, 156, 166–8, 169, 197, 206,
    230, 239, 247, 263, 288, 291
pilgrimage, Muslim 106, 130, 160, 187,
    221
Portuguese 79–80, 91, 129, 138, 159, 160,
    161–3, 164, 172, 176, 181–2, 260
prayer, Muslim 17, 21, 28–9
Prithviraj Chauhan 26, 27
Punjab 250, 269–70, 276–7, 280

Qandahar 155, 186, 187
qawwali xix, 129, 221
qawwals 105, 221
qibla xix, 21
Quran 21, 30, 86, 122, 196, 197, 221, 252
Qutb Shahs 75, 154, 163, *165*, 166, 168,
    169, *172*, 181, 232, 233, 239, 250

Rajaraja Chola 14, 18, 24, 294
Raja Man Singh (Kachhwaha) 125, 126,
    144, 153, 254, 271
  architectural patronage 148, *150*, 211,
    213, 214, 233, 254, 294
Rajput/s 99–103, 105, 116, 119, 125–6,
    127, 148, 151, 175, 182, 187,
    207–13, 237, 239, 245, 249–50,
    271, 277, 293, 294
  courts 207–16
Ram(a) xix, 67, 100, 108, 136–8, *147*,
    209, *210*
Ramayana xix, 67, 100, 108, 136, 140,
    146, *147*, 149
  Rana Jagat Singh, *Ramayana, 210*,
    208–11
Rana Jagat Singh (Sisodiya) 208, 293
  Jagdish temple 208, *209*
  painting *210*, 208–11
Rana Kumbha 100, 101, 103, 294
Ranakpur 104
rasa xix, 106, 169–70
ritual, temple 13–14, 17, 82, 104, 216–17,
    222
rupee xix, 120, 263, *263* (*see also* East
    India Company)

Safavids 124, 125, 130, 152, 155, 156,
    157, 169, 173, 186, 197, 277
sama xix, 32, 33–5, 221, 226
Sanskrit xix, 9, 13, 17, 74–5, 83, 108,
    140–2, 149–51, 238, 239, 291
Sant xx, 107, 108, 267
Sasaram 121–2
  Sher Shah Sur's tomb *123*
sati *215*, 214–16
Sawai Jai Singh 249, 252, *253*, 254, 277,
    294
serai xx, *274*, 274–5
Shah Jahan xvi, xx, 96, 158, 173, 186, 187,
    188, 191, *192*, 194, *195*, 196–200,
    207–8, 219, 227, 228, 231, 255,
    265, 294
  administration 155–6
  career of 153, 154–6, 196–200, 204,
    207–8, 211–13
  portraiture 170, *190*, 191, *192*
  (*see also* Delhi, Mughal: religious policies
    under Jahangir and Shah Jahan;
    Shahjahanabad)
Shahnama 22, 93
Shaikh Ahmad Sirhindi 155, 226, 227,
    231, 294
Shaikh Salim Chishti 129, 132, 133, *133*,
    187, *188*, 226

Sharia 155, 156, 226, 227, 230, 231
Sharqis 96, 97
Sher Shah Sur 119, 120, *122*, 122, *123*,
    128, 131, 149, 169, 294
Shia xx, 13, 20–1, 64, 76, 97, 103, 108,
    156, 158, 166–8, 173, 226, 249, 252
Shiva xx, 13, 64, 97, 103, 108, 222–4,
    231–8, 244
Shivaji Bhonsle 231, 232–3, 237, 238–40,
    242–3, 254, 272, 294
  arts under 240, *241, 243*
  concept of state 239–40
  coronation 238–9, 243, 244
  legacy 232, 238, 242
  (*see also* Maratha)
Shri Vaishnava 82–3
shudra xx, 239
Sikandar Lodi 96, 115
Sikh/s xx, 108, 254, *268*, 269, 270, 271,
    272, 276, 288, 289, 293
  militarism 267–9
  religion 267
silver 42, 49, 50, 89, 121, 128, 180–1
Siraj al-Daula 283–4
Sisodiyas 86, 98, 103, 108, 109, 125–6,
    153, 187, 207–11, 214, *215*, 217,
    219–21, 250, 293 (*see also* Mewar,
    Rajput, Rana Jagat Singh, Rana
    Kumbha, Udaipur)
slaves (mamluks) 19, 25, 27, 48–9
Somanatha, temple 20, 35, 293
Sufi/ism xx, 32, 39, *73*, 76, 86, *87*, 88, 89,
    92, 105–6, 107, 114, 129, 132, 133,
    164, 166, 168, 170, *171*, 187, 226,
    228, 246, 267, 293, 294 (*see also*
    Chishti, Naqshbandi, Suhrawardi)
Suhrawardi 86–8, 130
sulh-i kul xx, 124, 129–30, 146, 149, 226
Sunni xx, 20–1, 76, 166, 230
Surat 159, *162*, 161–3, 173, 233, 260,
    263, 273, 275, 276, 277, 282

Tamil xx, 75, 83, 108, 176, 177, 221, 224
Tanjavur, Rajarajeshvara Temple *15*,
    14–16, 18, 294
taxes 39, 42, 48, 180, 230–1, 265, 266,
    271, 278, 282, 288 (*see also* Jizya)
Telugu xx, 70, 74–5, 169, 176, 177, 224
temple desecration 47–8, 103, 227 (*see also*
    Aurangzeb)
temples *15, 16*, 13–16, 17, 18, 20, 35, 62,
    64–7, *68*, 68, 69, *69*, 70, 71, 82–3,
    91–2, 103–4, 108, 129, 148–51,
    208, 216, 221–4, 227, 242, 244,
    252–4, 277, 293, 294

textiles 78, 79, 80, 89, 90, 159, *174*,
173–5, 182–3, *184*, 202–3, 257–9,
260, 264, 276, 281
for Southeast Asian market *160*, 182,
183, 257 (*see also* chintz)
Timur 45, 92, 97, 105, 113, 115, 116,
118, 123, 133, 154–5, 191,
255
Tirumala Nayaka 177–8, 222, 224, 294
Tirupati 176
Shri Venkateshvara temple 68, *69*, 82–3
trade 5–7, 51, 52, 77–80, 81–2, 89, 90,
99, 152, 183, 185, 207, 242, 249,
275
maritime, Deccan 172–3
(*see also* East India Company, English,
Mughal: maritime trade, trading
companies: European, Verenigde
Oost-Indische Compagnie)
trading companies, European 256–64,
281, 283–4
transport 12, 265, 273–4, 279
Tutinama 136, *137*, 138

Udaipur 208, 214, 216, 222
ulama xx, 21, 84
Urdu xxi, 247
urs xxi, 105, 196, 221, 246

Vallabha 110–11, 112
Varna xxi, 99, 239
Verenigde Oost-Indische Compagnie
(VOC) 161, 181, 256, 259, 260,
262, 264, 281
Vijayanagara *66*, *68*, 53–75, 163, 170,
176–7, 183, 221–2, 291, 292–3, 294
after 175–6, *184*, 183–5
capital city *61*, *62*, 60–3, 81
concept of kingship 63–4, 67

domestic economy 80–3
dress 72, *73*, *87*, 187–8, 202, 219
elephant stables 71, *71*
European observation of 57, 58, 61–2,
63
Islamicate influence at 70–2, *73*
Mahanavami festival and platform *62*,
61–3, 67, 74
maritime trade 77–80
militarism in 59–63
mosque/dharmasale 71, *72*
Muslims in army 56, 70
origins of kingdom 53–4
queens 63, 68, 102
Ramachandra temple 62, 65–7, *68*
temples, consumers of goods 82–3
temples (Jain, Shiva, Vishnu) 71
Virupaksha deity, temple and gopura
64–5, *66*
Vishnu xxi, 13, 65, 108, 110
Vrindavan 109, 126, 148–9, 217
Govinda Deva temple *150*, 148–51, 254

women 41, 63, 68, *69*, 92, 94, 102, 106,
126, 132, *137*, 138, *139*, 148, 170,
172, 197, 203–5, 219, 222, 225–7,
228, *229*
marriage 91, 102, 172, 211, 213–14
Rajput courts 213–16
seclusion of women 102, 203
(*see also* Gulbadan Begum, Hamida
Banu Begum, haram, Mira Bai, Nur
Jahan, Sati)

zamindar xxi, 128, 265, 271–3, 276, 278,
282, 283, 289
Zamorins 78
zikr xxi, 32–4
zimmi xxi, 47